Hotel
Human Resource Management

饭店人力资源管理

主编 / 吕勤 副主编 / 郭颂 徐施

北京·旅游教育出版社

前　言

"人力资源"一词是由著名管理学家彼得·德鲁克(Peter F. Drucker)于1954年在《管理的实践》一书中提出的,德鲁克认为"企业唯一真正的资源是人"。当代社会"人力资源"将取代企业所拥有的其他资源(如土地、房屋、设备、原材料等),成为最重要的战略性资源。

改革开放以来,我国饭店业取得了长足的进步。随着饭店业的发展,对这一行业中的各种研究也勃然兴起。饭店业是一个劳动密集型的行业,人的因素尤为重要,人力资源管理在现代饭店管理中的地位与作用也日益增强。所以关于饭店业人力资源管理方面的探索和研究也得到了饭店企业的高度重视。饭店企业如何进行工作分析与工作设计、如何招聘到所需要的优秀员工、如何开展培训、如何进行绩效评估和薪酬管理、如何实行纪律和降低流失率、如何通过EAP帮助员工缓解压力、如何帮助员工规划职业发展、如何建设高效的团队和优秀的企业文化等人力资源管理中的各个环节,已经成为探讨饭店企业核心竞争力的关键点。

饭店人力资源管理是饭店管理专业的一门专业核心课程,本教材是一本双语教材,其特色及创新在于一方面借鉴了AH&LA教材建立的一个比较完整的饭店人力资源管理的理论建构,让学生对国外的理论概念(原汁原味的,不是翻译或改编过的)和实践发展有直观的了解和认识,同时反映了国内外新的研究成果,引用一些国外学者的最新成果和图表等,尽量使新的研究成果应用于教学实践中;另一方面,本教材也兼顾了中文教材较好的逻辑性和体系完整的特征,还将结合我国饭店人力资源管理的实践,具有中国特色。该教材不是简单的中英文对照教材,不是所有地方都需要中英文一一对应。其中英文的主要内容包括:(1)对相关概念的原始描述;(2)理论在实践中应用的一些工具和方法;(3)国外报刊中的新闻报道和案例。

本教材由吕勤教授提出思路和构建框架,具体内容由吕勤、郭颂、徐施、叶琴、尹晶莹、陈少华、纪冉、黄敏、连子编撰,最后由吕勤和郭颂统稿。本书中没有标注资料来源的图表等为编者自己归纳整理或者在课堂教学中使用多年的。此外,本书受到北京市财政专项"专业建设—新专业建设—酒店管理"(编号:354016)资助,在此深表谢意。

由于编者水平有限,书中难免有疏漏和错误,希望使用这本教材的老师和同学们对教材中的不完善、不妥当之处提出批评和改进的意见。

目 录

第1章 21世纪的管理理念
   (the Concept of Management in 21st Century) ………… 1
   本章概要(Summary of This Chapter) ………… 1
   开篇引例(Beginning Story) ………… 1
   第一节 管理思想的演进(The Revolution of Management Theory) ………… 2
   第二节 以人为本的管理理念
       (The Management Theory of People-oriented) ………… 13
   案例分析(Practice Case Analysis) ………… 25
   名词解释(Key Terms) ………… 26
   复习思考题(Questions for Review) ………… 27
   研究前沿(Research Front) ………… 27

第2章 工作分析与工作设计(Job Analysis and Job Design) ………… 31
   本章概要(Summary of This Chapter) ………… 31
   开篇引例(Beginning Story) ………… 32
   第一节 工作分析(Job Analysis) ………… 32
   第二节 工作设计(Job Design) ………… 42
   案例分析(Practice Case Analysis) ………… 46
   名词解释(Key Terms) ………… 48
   复习思考题(Questions for Review) ………… 49
   研究前沿(Research Front) ………… 49

第3章 沟通与团队合作(Communication and Teamwork) ………… 54
   本章概要(Summary of This Chapter) ………… 54
   开篇引例(Beginning Story) ………… 55
   第一节 沟通(Communication) ………… 55
   第二节 团队合作(Teamwork) ………… 69
   案例分析(Practice Case Analysis) ………… 81

名词解释(Key Terms) ·· 82
　　复习思考题(Questions for Review) ································ 84
　　研究前沿(Research Front) ·· 84

第4章　招聘(Recruitment) ·· 88
　　本章概要(Summary of This Chapter) ······························ 88
　　开篇引例(Beginning Story) ·· 88
　　第一节　招聘概述(Recruitment Overview) ······················ 89
　　第二节　招聘的渠道和方法(Recruitment Channels and Methods) ········ 92
　　第三节　人员甄选(Personnel Selection) ·························· 102
　　第四节　人员录用(Personnel Employment) ······················ 107
　　第五节　人员招聘评估(Personnel Recruitment Assessment) ········ 109
　　案例分析(Practice Case Analysis) ·································· 111
　　名词解释(Key Terms) ·· 112
　　复习思考题(Questions for Review) ································ 114
　　研究前沿(Research Front) ·· 114

第5章　培训(Training) ··· 123
　　本章概要(Summary of This Chapter) ······························ 123
　　开篇引例(Beginning Story) ·· 123
　　第一节　饭店培训概述(Training Overview) ····················· 124
　　第二节　培训程序(Training Process) ······························· 130
　　案例分析(Practice Case Analysis) ·································· 139
　　名词解释(Key Terms) ·· 140
　　复习思考题(Questions for Review) ································ 142
　　研究前沿(Research Front) ·· 142

第6章　评估和辅导(Evaluation and Coaching) ················ 146
　　本章概要(Summary of This Chapter) ······························ 146
　　开篇引例(Beginning Story) ·· 146
　　第一节　绩效评估的益处(Benefits of Performance Evaluation) ······ 147
　　第二节　有效评估的障碍及常见问题
　　　　　　(Effective Evaluation Barriers and Common Problem) ······ 151
　　第三节　评估过程和方法(The Appraisal Process and Methods) ······ 154

第四节　绩效评估的主体（Who performs the Evaluation）·········· 167
第五节　辅导（Coaching）·········· 169
案例分析（Practice Case Analysis）·········· 172
名词解释（Key Terms）·········· 174
复习思考题（Questions for Review）·········· 176
研究前沿（Research Front）·········· 177

第7章　饭店薪酬与福利管理
（Compensation Management and Welfare Management）·········· 185

本章概要（Summary of This Chapter）·········· 185
开篇引例（Beginning Story）·········· 186
第一节　饭店员工激励理论（Hotel Staff Incentive Theory）·········· 187
第二节　饭店薪酬管理概述（Hotel Salary Management）·········· 194
第三节　饭店薪酬体系设计（Hotel Salary System Design）·········· 202
第四节　饭店福利管理（Hotel Welfare Management）·········· 210
案例分析（Practice Case Analysis）·········· 214
名词解释（Key Terms）·········· 216
复习思考题（Questions for Review）·········· 220
研究前沿（Research Front）·········· 220

第8章　纪律和人员流动（Discipline and Turnover）·········· 227

本章概要（Summary of This Chapter）·········· 227
开篇引例（Beginning Story）·········· 227
第一节　饭店人员流动（Turnover of Hospitality）·········· 228
第二节　纪律管理（Discipline）·········· 236
案例分析（Practice Case Analysis）·········· 244
名词解释（Key Terms）·········· 246
复习思考题（Questions for Review）·········· 247
研究前沿（Research Front）·········· 247

第9章　压力、健康、EAP与职业发展
（Pressure, Health, EAP and Career Development）·········· 255

本章概要（Summary of This Chapter）·········· 255
开篇引例（Beginning Story）·········· 255

第一节 工作压力与健康(Working Pressure and Health) ………… 256
第二节 员工帮助计划与职业发展(EAP and Career Development) … 268
案例分析(Practice Case Analysis) ……………………………… 289
名词解释(Key Terms) …………………………………………… 292
复习思考题(Questions for Review) …………………………… 293
研究前沿(Research Front) ……………………………………… 293

第10章 饭店企业文化和社会责任(Corporate Culture and Social Responsibility In Hospitality Industry) ………… 296

本章概要(Summary of This Chapter) ………………………… 296
开篇引例(Beginning Story) …………………………………… 297
第一节 饭店企业文化(Hotel Corporate Culture) ……………… 298
第二节 饭店企业社会责任
(Social Responsibility of Hotel Corporate) ………… 307
案例分析(Practice Case Analysis) ……………………………… 315
名词解释(Key Terms) …………………………………………… 318
复习思考题(Questions for Review) …………………………… 319
研究前沿(Research Front) ……………………………………… 319

参考文献(Reference) ……………………………………………… 331

第1章　21世纪的管理理念
(the Concept of Management in 21st Century)

本章概要(Summary of This Chapter)

管理思想是沿着从经验管理到科学管理再到现代管理(文化管理)的路径发展的。

21世纪是人才战略的时代,以人为本的管理理念已经成为人力资源管理的核心理念。"以人为本"的管理,就是把人看作管理中最基本的要素,以人的全面发展为核心。在管理过程中以人为出发点和中心,围绕着激发和调动人的主动性、积极性、创造性展开的,以实现人与饭店共同发展的一系列管理活动。

Management theory is developing along the path from experience management to scientific management to modern management (cultural management).

The 21st century is the era of talent strategy, and people-oriented management concept has become the core concept of human resources management. "People-oriented" management theory is an idea to make human be the basic element of management with man's all-round development as the core. During the process of management, people-oriented theory considers human both as starting point and the center, and applies around inspiring and mobilizing the initiative, enthusiasm and creativity of people so as to realize a series of management activities and common development of both people and hotel.

☞ **开篇引例(Beginning Story)**

Interview with Hervé Fournier, Vice President, César Ritz Hotel School

Q: In the time that you've been involved in the hotel industry, which has been most of your life, let's specifically say in the last 20 years and 10 years and 5 years, what would you say the major changes have been to the industry from your standpoint?

A: I think there have been a lot of changes in human resources. We're more now into appraisal, into establishing a career plan, into helping your staff. These are things that you don't think of as personnel management. It's hiring, paying salaries and firing. Those were the things. And now there's the whole aspect of developing, appraisal, helping—all this is quite new. Also in our industry, there are tracks that we establish and try to bring people through.

Q: What changes do you see coming up?

A: If we look at what's happening now, where are the best hotels in the world, they are in Asia. Why are the best hotels the ones in Asia? They are able to provide better service. However, is it really true that the product is better service? You see that they have a lot of people who are able to work, much more than here; here we had to cut personnel, cut on labor cost, and so we have people who are more efficient at what they do and systems that are more efficient. In Asia I'm amazed to see when you order coffee, you have 5 people in back, they have a lot of personnel there, sometimes because they lack the proper training and education and they don't have the systems which are in place. There are a lot of personnel to take care of you but then you realize that the service they provide is not that efficient. You could get better and faster service with one person who knows what he's doing as opposed to having 5 who have not been trained. So for the future, definitely it's always going to be the same—to use technology so that the technology helps us simplify the systems, so that we can have fewer staff members doing the job and providing the same type of service. And so it means that those people have to be properly trained and be efficient in what they do. [1]

第一节 管理思想的演进
(The Revolution of Management Theory)

管理思想是沿着从经验管理到科学管理再到现代管理(文化管理)的路径发展的。

---

[1] Adler H. Interview with Hervé Fournier, Vice President, César Ritz Hotel School. Journal of Human Resources in Hospitality & Tourism, 2005,4(2):119-127.

一、科学管理理论的诞生和发展(The Birth and Development of Scientific Management Theory)

(一)古典管理理论(Classical Management Theory)

古典管理理论产生于19世纪末20世纪初,主要是系统地研究企业生产过程和行政组织管理。科学管理之父——弗雷德里克·温斯洛·泰勒于1911年出版了其代表作《科学管理原理》,他认为科学管理的根本目的是谋求最高劳动生产率,最高的工作效率是雇主和雇员达到共同富裕的基础,要达到最高的工作效率的重要手段是用科学化的、标准化的管理方法代替经验管理。泰勒理论使人们认识到管理是一门建立在明确的法规和原则之上的科学,使管理从经验走向了科学。另两位古典管理理论的代表人物法约尔、韦伯着重探讨了大企业整体的经营管理,突出了行政级别组织体系理论。韦伯的行政组织理论,实际上是把管理非人格化,依靠单纯的责任感和无个性的工作原则,客观合理地处理各项事务。法约尔认为,无论是高层领导还是普通员工,都必须受纪律的约束,任何一个企业,没有纪律的约束都不可能兴旺繁荣。

表1-1 泰勒、法约尔、韦伯的主要理论对照比较表

姓名	泰勒	法约尔	韦伯
代表作	《科学管理原理》	《工业管理和一般管理》	《社会和经济组织理论》
尊称	科学管理之父	经营管理理论之父	组织理论之父
生卒	1856~1915	1841~1925	1864~1920
贡献	1.使管理走向科学 2.劳资双方的精神革命	1.从经营职能中独立出管理活动 2.强调教育的必要性 3.提出管理活动所需的五大职能和十四条管理原则	提出了所谓的"理想的行政组织理论"
国别	美国	法国	德国
研究重点	1.提高效率:解决"磨洋工"问题 2.盈余分配与生产率提高:劳动双方应关心的重点是什么	以企业整体作为研究对象,从"办公桌前的总经理"出发	强调组织活动要通过职务或职位而不是个人或世袭地位来设计和运作

资料来源:http://blog.163.com/jianping_069/blog/static/13097339520109745229830.

(二)行为科学管理理论(Behavioral Science Management Theory)

行为科学作为一种管理理论,始于20世纪20年代末至30年代初的霍桑实验,以后发展成为一种人际关系学派。

1. 霍桑实验

霍桑实验是1927至1932年间由哈佛大学心理学教授梅奥主持的在美国芝加哥西部电器公司所属的霍桑工厂进行的为期五年的一系列心理学实验研究。

霍桑实验共分四阶段:

(1) 照明实验

当时关于生产效率的理论占统治地位的是劳动医学的观点,认为影响工人生产效率的是疲劳和单调感等,于是当时的实验假设便是"提高照明度有助于减少疲劳,使生产效率提高"。可是经过两年多实验发现,照明度的改变对生产效率并无影响。具体结果是:当实验组照明度增大时,实验组和控制组都增产;当实验组照明度减弱时,两组依然都增产,甚至实验组的照明度减至0.06烛光时,其产量亦无明显下降;直至照明减至如月光一般、实在看不清时,产量才急剧降下来。研究人员面对此结果感到茫然,失去了信心。从1927年起,以梅奥教授为首的一批哈佛大学心理学工作者将实验工作接管下来,继续进行。

(2) 福利实验

实验目的是查明福利待遇的变换与生产效率的关系。但经过两年多的实验发现,不管福利待遇如何改变(包括工资支付办法的改变、优惠措施的增减、休息时间的增减等),都不影响产量的持续上升,甚至工人自己对生产效率提高的原因也说不清楚。

后经进一步的分析发现,导致生产效率上升的主要原因如下:①参加实验的光荣感。实验开始时6名参加实验的女工曾被召进部长办公室谈话,她们认为这是莫大的荣誉。这说明被重视的自豪感对人的积极性有明显的促进作用。②成员间良好的相互关系。

(3) 访谈实验

研究者在工厂中开始了访谈计划。此计划的最初想法是要工人就管理当局的规划和政策、工头的态度和工作条件等问题作出回答,但这种规定好的访谈计划在进行过程中却大出意料之外,得到意想不到的效果。工人想就工作提纲以外的事情进行交谈,工人认为重要的事情并不是公司或调查者认为意义重大的那些事。访谈者了解到这一点,及时把访谈计划改为事先不规定内容,每次访谈的平均时间从三十分钟延长到1~1.5个小时,多听少说,详细记录工人的不满和意见。访谈计划持续了两年多,工人的产量大幅提高。

工人们长期以来对工厂的各项管理制度和方法存在许多不满,无处发泄,访谈计划的实行恰恰为他们提供了发泄机会。发泄过后心情舒畅,士气提高,使产量得到提高。

(4) 群体实验

梅奥等人在这个实验中是选择14名男工人在单独的房间里从事绕线、焊接和检验工作。对这个班组实行特殊的工人计件工资制度。实验者原来设想,实行这套奖励办法会使工人更加努力工作,以便得到更多的报酬。但观察的结果发现,产量只保持在中等水平上,每个工人的日产量平均都差不多,而且工人并不如实地报告产量。深入的调查发现,这个班组为了维护他们群体的利益,自发地形成了一些规范。他们约定,谁也不能干得太多,突出自己;谁也不能干得太少,影响全组的产量,并且约法三章,不准向管理当局告密,如有人违反这些规定,轻则挖苦谩骂,重则拳打脚踢。进一步调查发现,工人们之所以维持中等水平的产量,是担心产量提高,管理当局会改变现行奖励制度,或裁减人员,使部分工人失业,或者会使干得慢的伙伴受到惩罚。这一实验表明,为了维护班组内部的团结,可以放弃物质利益的引诱。由此提出"非正式群体"的概念,认为在正式的组织中存在着自发形成的非正式群体,这种群体有自己的特殊的行为规范,对人的行为起着调节和控制作用。同时,加强了内部的协作关系。

2. 人际关系学派

梅奥在霍桑实验的基础上,于1933年出版了《工业文明中人的问题》一书,提出了人际关系学说,建立了人际关系学派。

人际关系学说的主要观点如下:

(1) 工人是社会人,不是经济人,即工人除了物质需要外,还有社会心理方面的需求,因此不能忽视社会和心理因素对工人工作积极性的影响,否定了当时科学管理学派认为金钱是刺激工人积极性的唯一动力的说法。

(2) 企业中存在非正式的组织。企业成员在共同工作的过程中,相互间必然产生共同的感情、态度和倾向,形成共同的行为准则和惯例,非正式组织独特的感情、规范和倾向,左右着成员的行为。非正式组织不仅存在而且与正式组织相互依存,对生产率有重大影响。

(3) 生产率主要取决于工人的工作态度以及他和周围人的关系。梅奥认为提高生产率的主要途径是提高工人的满足度,即工人对社会因素、人际关系的满足程度。如果满足度高,工作的积极性、主动性和协作精神就高,生产率就高。

表1-2 古典管理理论与行为科学管理理论对照比较表

观点序号	代表人物	泰 勒	梅 奥
1		由管理当局研究、计划、组织消除提高工作成绩的障碍	监工提高社会技能
2		注意中心为个别工人	注意中心为团体成员中的工人
3		不注意人际关系	注意人际关系
4		物质与工作环境是影响生产率提高的一个主要因素	社会环境是主要的
5		只要有机会人们会追求最大的经济报酬	强调团体成员地位,金钱诱惑处次要地位

二、现代管理理论的形成和发展(The Formation and Development of Modern Management Theory)

现代管理理论是继科学管理理论、行为科学理论之后,西方管理理论和思想发展的第三阶段,主要指第二次世界大战以后出现的一系列学派。

美国著名管理学家哈罗德·孔茨认为当时林林总总共有十一个学派:经验主义管理学派、人际关系学派、组织行为学派、社会系统学派、管理科学学派、权变理论学派、决策理论学派、系统管理理论学派、经验主义学派、经理角色学派、经营管理学派。

(一)现代管理理论形成的原因(The Causes of the Formation of Modern Management Theory)

1. 社会化大生产的客观要求

在20世纪40年代,由于工业生产的机械化、自动化水平不断提高以及电子计算机进入工业领域,在工业生产集中化、大型化、标准化的基础上,也出现了工业生产多样化、小型化、精密化的趋势。另一方面,工业生产的专业化、联合化不断发展,工业生产对连续性、均衡性的要求提高,市场竞争日趋激烈、变化莫测,即社会化大生产要求管理改变孤立的、单因素的、片面的研究方式,而形成全过程、全因素、全方位、全员式的系统化管理。

2. 解决社会矛盾是现代管理理论孕育的前提

第二次世界大战期间,交战双方提出了许多亟待解决的问题,如运输问题、机场和港口的调度问题、如何对大量的军火进行迅速检查的问题,等等,都涉及管理的方法。

3. 资本主义生产关系出现了一些新变化

由于工人运动的发展,赤裸裸的剥削方式逐渐被新的、更隐蔽和更巧妙的剥削方式所掩盖。新的剥削方式着重从人的心理需要、感情方面等着手,形成处理人际关系和人的行为问题的管理。

4. 管理理论的发展越来越借助于多学科交叉作用

经济学、数学、统计学、社会学、人类学、心理学、法学、计算机科学等各学科的研究成果越来越多地应用于企业管理。

(二) 现代管理理论的发展(The Development of Modern Management Theory)

20世纪80年代以后,随着社会、经济、文化的迅速发展,特别是信息技术的发展与知识经济的出现,管理理论呈现了新的发展趋势。

新的时期管理理论发展的特点:

1. 非理性主义倾向与企业文化

非理性主义倾向产生的背景。20世纪70年代末、80年代初,由于经营风险增大,竞争激烈,管理日趋复杂,在西方管理理论界出现了一种非理性主义倾向和重视企业文化的思潮。

2. 战略管理理论

战略管理理论产生的背景。20世纪70年代前后,世界进入到科技、信息、经济全面飞速发展时期,同时竞争加剧,风险日增。为了谋求企业的长期生存发展,开始注重构建竞争优势。这样,在经历了长期规划、战略规划等阶段之后,形成了较为系统的战略管理理论。

战略管理理论的产生与发展。安索夫(Ansoff)的《公司战略》(1965)一书的问世,开创了战略规划的先河。到1976年,安索夫的《从战略规则到战略管理》一书出版,标志着现代战略管理理论体系的形成。

3. 企业再造理论

企业再造理论产生的背景。进入20世纪七八十年代,市场竞争日趋激烈。美国企业为应对来自日本、欧洲的威胁而展开探索。1993年,原美国麻省理工学院教授迈克尔·哈默(M. Hammer)博士与詹姆斯·钱皮(J. Champy)提出了企业再造理论。

企业再造的基本含义。是指"为了飞越地改善成本、质量、服务、速度等重大的现代企业的运营基准,对工作流程作根本的重新思考与彻底翻新"。

4."学习型组织"理论

"学习型组织"理论产生的背景。20世纪90年代以来,知识经济的到来,使信息与知识成为重要的战略资源,相应诞生了学习型组织理论。"学习型组织"理论是美国麻省理工学院教授彼得·圣吉在其著作《第五项修炼》中提出来的。

"学习型组织"的基本思想认为:"未来真正出色的企业,将是能够设法使各阶层人员全心投入,并有能力不断学习的组织。"组织成员的五项修炼是在学习组织中,有五项新的技能正在逐渐汇集起来,这五项技能被他称为"五项修炼"。

(三)人性假设理论(Human Nature Hypothesis)

1. X理论与Y理论

1960年,管理学专家麦格雷戈出版了《管理理论X或Y的抉择——企业的人性面》。

麦格雷戈认为,管理者之所以会用不同的方式去管理员工,从根本上说是因为他们对"人性"有不同的看法。麦格雷戈把对"人性"的两种典型的不同看法称为"X理论"和"Y理论"(请注意,并不是麦格雷戈自己提出了两种管理理论,一种叫"X理论",另一种叫"Y理论"。实际上,所谓"X理论"和"Y理论"也并不是两种"理论"。它们只是麦格雷戈为人们对"人性"的两种不同看法所起的两个名字而已)。

"X理论"的要点是:

(1)一般人的天性都是不喜欢工作,尽可能地逃避工作;

(2)对于这些不喜欢工作的人,只有用强迫的办法,用惩罚去威胁他们,才能使他们为实现组织的目标而努力;

(3)一般人都宁愿被别人指挥,而不愿意承担责任;很少有雄心壮志,而只想得到安全。

"Y理论"的要点是:

(1)人们喜欢工作,正像人们需要娱乐和休息一样,这些都是人的天性;

(2)外力的控制和惩罚的威胁并不是促使人们去为实现组织的目标而努力的唯一的办法。人们可以通过自我引导、自我控制来实现自己的承诺;

(3)人们对目标的承诺与他们在达到这一目标之后所能得到的报偿有直接的关系;

(4)在有激励的情况下,人们不仅愿意工作,而且希望承担责任;

(5)大部分人都很聪明,都有相当丰富的想象力和创造力,可以用来解决组织中的问题;

(6)在现代工业社会中,一般人的聪明才智都只是部分地得到发挥。

总的说来,所谓"X理论"是对"人性"的一种比较"悲观"的看法,而所谓"Y理论"则是对"人性"的一种比较"乐观"的看法。作为企业的管理者，如果持"X理论"，就会认为最好的管理只能是"专制式管理"。如果持"Y理论"，即使不把"专制式管理"当作最坏的管理，也绝不会把它当作最好的管理。

如果说，人人都不喜欢工作，人人都不愿意承担责任，人人都缺乏雄心壮志，那显然是以偏概全。但是在现实生活中，这些现象又确实都是存在的。应该说，"X理论"和"Y理论"的区别，只在于"X理论"更多地列举了"人性的弱点"，而"Y理论"更多地列举了"人性的优点"。"专制式管理"当然不是最好的管理，但是不实行"专制式管理"，并不等于就可以实行"放任式管理"。

我们倾向于对"人性"抱乐观的态度。我们相信人们是会喜欢工作的，是会愿意承担责任的，是能够进行自我引导和自我控制的。我们也相信大部分人都很聪明，都有相当丰富的想象力和创造力。但是必须指出，要让人们喜欢工作，要让人们愿意承担责任，并能进行自我引导和自我控制，要让人们把尚未发挥的聪明才智充分地发挥出来——所有这些都不是无条件的，而是有条件的。对"人性"抱乐观态度的"Y理论"也认为只有在"能得到报偿"和"有激励"的条件下，人们才会充分地表现出"人性的优点"。

麦格雷戈关于人性假设的理论，概括起来有三方面的要点：

（1）管理的理论与管理者的观念是第一位的，而管理的政策与具体措施是第二位的，不能本末倒置，也不能简单混同、不加区别。

麦格雷戈在书中写道，非常显然的，经理人的养成，其由于管理当局对管理发展的正规作业而获得者，成分实属甚低；而主要乃是由于管理当局的观念所促成，包括对其所负任务本质的观念，及其为实行该项观念而制定的各项政策与实际的性质。

（2）强调在管理中要着重开发人力资源，发掘人的"潜在力量"。

麦格雷戈认为，一个事业的管理方式，往往决定管理阶层对所属人员的"潜在力量"的认知，以及对如何开发这份"潜在力量"的认知。倘使我们对管理发展的研究，系自各项管理发展计划的形式上的制度着手，我们便将走错了路。

（3）管理人员采取哪种理论假定要看具体情况，但是所持理论的观点要旗帜鲜明。

麦格雷戈认为，管理者对控制人力资源所持的各项理论假定，实为企业的整体特性的决定因素，而且还是今后若干代管理人的素质的决定因素。他的目的并不在于劝说管理人选择"X理论"或选择"Y理论"，而只是阐明理论的重要性，只是促使管理界检讨他们所持的假定，将他们的假定明确化。"唯其如此，才能开启走向未来的大门。"

2. Z 理论

日本学者威廉·大内在比较了日本企业和美国企业的不同的管理特点之后，参照"X 理论"和"Y 理论"，提出了"Z 理论"，对日本的企业文化管理加以归纳。"Z 理论"强调管理中的文化特性，主要由信任、微妙性和亲密性所组成。根据这种理论，管理者要对员工表示信任，而信任可以激励员工以真诚的态度对待企业、对待同事，为企业而忠心耿耿地工作。微妙性是指企业对员工的不同个性的了解，以便根据各自的个性和特长组成最佳搭档或团队，增强劳动率。而亲密性强调个人感情的作用，提倡在员工之间应建立一种亲密和谐的伙伴关系，为了企业的目标而共同努力。"Z 理论"将东方国度中的人文感情糅进了管理理论。是对"X 理论"和"Y 理论"的一种补充和完善，在员工管理中根据企业的实际状况灵活掌握制度与人性、管制与自觉之间的关系，因地制宜地实施最符合企业利益和员工利益的管理方法。

3. 超 Y 理论

1970 年美国管理心理学家约翰·莫尔斯（J. J. Morse）和杰伊·洛希（J. W. Lorscn）提出了一种新的管理理论。该理论从权变理论的观点出发，指出没有什么一成不变的、普遍适用的最佳的管理方式，"X 理论"并非一无是处，"Y 理论"也不是普遍适用，应该针对不同情况，将任务、组织、人员作最佳的组合，以激励工作人员取得有效的工作成绩。"超 Y 理论"在对"X 理论"和"Y 理论"进行实验分析比较后，提出一种既结合"X 理论"和"Y 理论"，又不同于"X 理论"和"Y 理论"，一种主张权宜应变的经营管理理论。

"超 Y 理论"对人性的假设如下：

（1）人们带着各式各样的需要和动机来到工作单位中的需要是取得胜任感。胜任感是指一个工作组织的成员，成功地掌握了周围的世界，其中包括所面对的任务而积累起来的满意感。

（2）取得胜任感的动机尽管人人都有，但不同的人可以用不同的方式来实现，这取决于这种需要同一个人的其他需要，诸如权利、独立、结构、成就和交往等的力量的相互作用。

（3）如果任务和组织相适合，胜任感的动机极可能得到实现。

（4）即使胜任感达到了目的，它仍继续起激励作用；达到一个目标后，一个新的、更高的目标就树立起来了。

所有的人都需要感到能胜任，但由于人的个体差异，用什么方式取得胜任感是不同的。

综上所述，"超 Y 理论"的权变观中的一个重要含义，就是我们不仅要使组织适合任务，也要使任务适合工作人员，以及使工作人员适合组织。

作为管理人员,可能采取的最佳的组织管理方法,就是整顿组织使之适合任务性质与人员。如果取得了这种最佳适合,工作单位的有效工作表现和人员的较大胜任感的动力皆可由此而生。

4. 另一种人性假设——理性经济人、社会人、自我实现人、复杂人

美国行为科学家埃德加·沙因于1965年出版了《组织心理学》,提出了人性假设的另一种分类,归纳了关于理性经济人、社会人、自我实现人、复杂人的4种人性假设。

(1) 理性经济人假设的主要内容是:

①人是由经济诱因来引发工作的动机,其目的在于获得最大的经济利益。

②经济诱因在组织的控制下,因此,人被动地在组织的操纵、激励和控制下从事工作。

③人以一种合乎理性的、精打细算的方式行事。

④人的感情是非理性的,会干预人对经济利益的合理追求,组织必须设法控制人的感情。

理性经济人的假设类似于"X理论"。

(2) 社会人假设的主要内容是:

①人的主要工作动机是社会需要,人们通过与同事之间的工作关系可以获得基本的认同感。

②分工原则和工作合理化原则使得工作变得单调而毫无意义。因此,必须从工作的社会关系中去寻求工作的意义。

③非正式组织的社会影响比正式组织的经济诱因对人有更大的影响力。

④人们最期望获得领导者对他们成绩的承认并满足他们的社会需要。

社会人假设是从梅奥等学者倡导的人际关系学派中归纳出来的。

(3) 自我实现人的假设的主要内容是:

①人的需要有低级和高级的区别,其目的是为达到自我实现的需要而寻求工作上的意义。

②人们力求在工作上有所成就,实现自治和独立,发展自己的能力和技术,以便富于弹性,能适应环境。

③人们能够自我刺激和自我控制,外来的激励和控制会对人产生一种威胁,造成不良的后果。

④个人自我实现同组织目标并不冲突,而且是一致的。在适当的条件下,个人应调整自己的目标,使之与组织目标配合。

自我实现人的假设相当于"Y理论"。

（4）复杂人的假设的主要内容是：

①每个人都有不同的需要和不同的能力，工作的动机不但是复杂的，而且变动性很大。人的许多动机安排在各种重要的需求层次之上，这种动机阶层的构造不但因人而异，同一个人也因时、因地而异，各种动机之间交互作用而形成复杂的动机模式。

②一个人在组织中可以学到新的需求和动机，因此一个人在组织中表现的动机模式是他原来的动机模式与组织经验交互的结果。

③人在不同的组织和不同的部门中可能有不同的动机模式，在正式组织中与别人不能合群，可能在非正式组织中能满足其社会需要和自我实现的需要。

④一个人是否感到心满意足，肯为组织出力，决定他本身的动机构造和他同组织之间的相互关系，工作的性质、本人的工作能力和技术水平，动机的强弱以及与同事相处的状况都可能产生影响。

⑤人可以依自己的动机、能力及工作性质对不同的管理方式做出不同的反应。

所以西方学者对这一问题的认识是经历了一个过程的。西方管理学理论中，先后出现的"经济人""社会人""自我实现人"和"复杂人"的"人性假设"，就是这一认识过程的反映。

最初，许多人都认为，人们最重视的是自己的经济利益。老板为什么要办工厂，为的是钱。工人为什么要来做工，为的也是钱。钱最能调动人的积极性，所以，人是"经济人"。后来，人们发现，企业的员工所需要的并不仅仅是钱。在不增加工资的情况下，改善人与人之间的关系，创造更好的社会心理环境，同样能提高员工的工作积极性。于是有人说，人不是"经济人"，而是"社会人"。后来，人们又发现，有了良好的人际关系，还是不能最大限度地调动员工的工作积极性；只有当工作能满足员工"自我实现"的需要时，员工才会表现出最大的积极性、主动性和创造性。于是，又有人说，人不是"经济人"，也不是"社会人"，而是"自我实现人"。那么，人到底是"经济人"，还是"社会人"，还是"自我实现人"呢？一个最新的概念是"复杂人"。"复杂人"的意思是：人是复杂的，实际上每一个人都既是"经济人"，又是"社会人"和"自我实现人"。

目前，国内一些饭店管理者在考虑如何"留住人才"时，提出要"用待遇留人，用感情留人，用事业留人"。按西方的"人性假设"来说，"待遇"留的是"经济人"，"感情"留的是"社会人"，"事业"留的是"自我实现人"。"待遇""感情""事业"三者并用，才能留住"复杂人"。

第二节 以人为本的管理理念
(The Management Theory of People-oriented)

一、以人为本(People-oriented)

21世纪是人才战略的时代,以人为本的管理理念已经成为人力资源管理的核心理念。"以人为本"的管理,就是把人看作管理中最基本的要素,以人的全面发展为核心,在管理过程中以人为出发点和中心,围绕着激发和调动人的主动性、积极性、创造性展开的,以实现人与饭店共同发展的一系列管理活动。

(一)"以人为本"的管理模式的特点(The Characteristics of the People-oriented Management Mode)

"以人为本"的管理模式是一种文化管理,其本质是以人为本,以人的全面发展为目标,通过共同价值观的培育,在系统内部营造一种健康和谐的文化氛围,使全体成员的身心能够融入到系统中来,变被动管理为自我约束,在实现社会价值最大化的同时,实现个人价值的最大化。

"以人为本"管理模式的特点如下:

1. 把企业看成有机的"人的组织",是培养人性的学校

传统上把企业看成生产产品的地方,充满机床设备、物化的东西;而从文化的角度看,企业家在市场经济中面临两种使命——赚取利润和培养人性,更重要的使命是培养员工的文化素质,增加其对企业价值观的认同。

2. 人性是管理的重要手段

从人性假设来看,企业把员工看成是有血有肉、有着自我价值实现的"文化人",每一个人的人生经历都是不可替代的,企业家是这样,每个员工也是这样。

3. "外圆内方"式管理

外圆指通过文化来实行好的管理,内方指制度的内化,慢慢把制度演变为一种习俗。文化管理很好地诠释了制度与文化的关系。文化管理寻找的是一种中性的智慧,寻找的是一种中性的管理理念。文化是制度的润滑剂,再好的制度如果没有文化的润滑则难以成为自觉的人格行为,难以内化成为习俗。制度和文化之间是相互塑造的关系。应该借鉴中国古代老子的智慧:无为而治、自我管理。

4. 重视感情和价值在管理中的运用

以前强调要什么,不要什么,感到人是一种很被动的存在;文化管理通过感情、价值观的渗透,变人的被动为主动。

(二)理想的管理者(The Ideal Manager)

理想的管理者应该是在任何时候都能使其工作团队尽显其能的人。管理者要达到的最基本的目标有：第一，使企业赢利；第二，维持员工的高昂士气。要达到这两个目标，管理者必须精通以下几方面的工作，如图1-1所示：

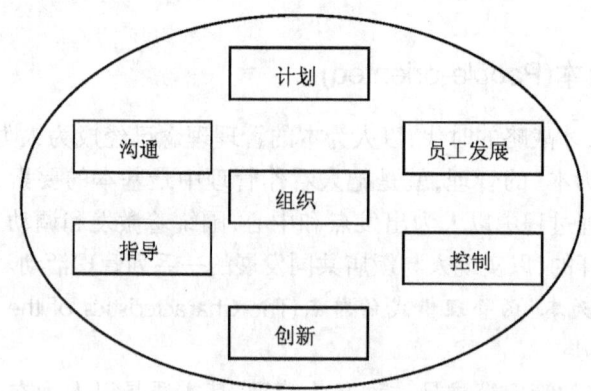

图1-1 管理者应该精通的7项工作

(1)计划。必须确定个人及部门目标，并为达到目标制定具体的策略。

(2)沟通。不仅要及时向员工通报情况，而且要多多接触、了解他们的想法，并要善于用口头和笔头两种形式向员工传达信息。

(3)组织。要有能力安排好自己的工作和部门的工作。

(4)员工发展。管理者知道如何选拔、引导、培训和激励员工。

(5)指导。今天的工作环境要求管理者授权给员工，让他们承担起更多的责任。但这不是向他们发号施令，而是鼓励和指导他们承担起责任，帮助团队的每个成员发挥出最高水平并不断进步。

(6)创新。要不断探索新途径来完善部门的工作。员工参与的创新才是最有效的创新。因此，管理者的角色不只局限于自己提出有创意的方案，还要带领员工共同寻求新的途径，更好地满足顾客的需求。

(7)控制。这包括为自己和所管理的工作团队设定标准和目标。要进行业绩评估，实施奖励措施，采取正确的行动。

(三)有效的管理手段(Effective Management Means)

1. 行为模仿

行为模仿是塑造员工行为的有力工具。

无论儿童时还是成年以后，我们通过效仿所尊敬的人的行为举止学到了很多东西。我们观察身边的重要人物，模仿他们的一言一行。服务业的管理者可以有效地利用人的这一特点,通过员工对管理者的模仿,塑造他们的工作作风。如果管理者对服务工作表现出极大的热情,员工也会热情高涨。员工看到管理者巧妙地运用沟通技巧,对付挑剔的顾客,下次他们遇到类似的情况,也会"模仿"或是照搬管理者的做法。相反,如果管理者认为顾客只会带来麻烦,扰乱工作,员工会很快受这种态度的感染,对顾客表现出同样的漠不关心。因此,管理者要对自己的态度和行为多加注意。一个对自己的工作和所在企业的发展不抱希望的管理者会将他的消极态度像病毒一样在公司内迅速传播。

管理者特别需要注意的行为:

(1) 良好的沟通技巧。展示出色的倾听技巧,无论是与员工交谈还是与顾客谈话,都要极为专注。

(2) 尊重他人。尊重每一个员工,甚至对那些不太尽责的员工,也不要当众批评或背后议论他们的缺点。

(3) 关心顾客。要让员工看到为了顾客管理者可以不辞辛苦,向他们展示如何预测客人的需求并尽一切努力来达到客人的要求。

(4) 对公司忠诚。对员工谈论起公司时,管理者要表现出乐观、积极的态度。即使对公司有所失望,也不要表露出来,否则会把这种消极的情绪传染给员工。

榜样绝非完美。错误未必不是良师——它教会我们如何对待失败和挫折,如何从困境中崛起。然而,榜样需要知识来武装。作为员工的榜样,管理者必须对管理原则、人力资源战略及管理技能有深入的了解。

2. 开门办公政策

管理者必须留出时间接待员工。

很多管理者都采用开门办公政策,即欢迎员工来反映问题,提出意见和看法,或者仅仅是聊天。管理人员最理想的做法是既不耽误日常的行政工作,又专门留出办公时间接待员工,在这段时间里,管理者要把精力全部放在接待员工上。而不能是这样的情况:管理者不是太忙就是在开会,员工经常被拒之门外。就算员工真的见到了管理者,他们的谈话也会时常被打断。

3. 走动式管理

走动式管理建议管理者要多花时间和员工在一起;不只是监督他们工作,还要多和他们交谈、了解情况。与员工进行非正式接触可能是您保持对部门情况信息灵通的最佳途径。与其他行业相比,饭店业的管理者和一线员工待在一起的时间已经很多了,但随着职位的提升,管理者会越来越把自己关在办公室里。

例如,比尔·马里奥特(Bill Marriott)因走动式管理而闻名。他很注重尽可能多地走访他的饭店的每个部门。巡视饭店时,他常常把自己介绍给普通员工而不仅仅是管理人员。对于一名餐厅侍者或客房服务人员来说,能和集团总经理握手确实让他们惊叹不已。走动式管理是和员工保持联系的有效方法。

4. 鼓励思想交流

鼓励员工进行思想交流有很多好办法，性格外向的员工可能会直率地向管理者说出他们的想法，而内向性格的员工是不会轻易开口的。如何让每个人都开诚布公地发表意见呢？设意见箱是一个简便易行的办法，很多饭店企业采纳这种方法。具体做法如下：

(1) 随便在桌上放个木盒子，上面用手随意写着"意见箱"几个字。这样做是不可能期望有人献上锦囊妙计的。明智的做法是：先搞一些宣传活动，通过海报和宣传品让员工事先对某项活动有所了解。这样，当一个引人注目的大意见箱摆放在显要的位置上时，员工们已经有了思想准备，也就会将意见和建议塞进意见箱了。

(2) 设一个专门的小组负责处理搜集到的建议并尽快作出回应。小组可采用打分的方法，按一定的标准给每条建议打分。分数高的要拿到部门会议上讨论并给予提出建议的员工表扬和一定的奖励。

(3) 在公司的业务通讯上刊出有价值的建议。这样员工和管理者都会觉得脸上有光——员工提出了建议；管理者开展了"意见箱"活动。

(4) 对于那些付诸实施并为公司节省了大量资金的建议，要考虑大力奖励建议者。

另一种让员工投身到改进服务的工作中的方法是让他们做"情报侦察员"，派他们到其他公司、企业去看看别人是如何为顾客服务的。不仅派前台的员工到别的饭店去了解他们的服务标准，还可以派他们去百货商店，看看那些人人皆知的优质服务到底是怎么一回事。

鼓励思想交流的意义是：不仅能够使企业把握最新信息，还能使员工成为企业利益的共享者。员工感到自己不再是雇员，而是企业的主人。他们会因此士气高涨。他们高涨的士气自然会对顾客服务产生积极的影响，会有益于员工做好自己的工作。

5. 使工作充满乐趣

员工为什么选择饭店这个行业？很大程度上是因为他们想象在饭店、餐厅工作会充满乐趣。但事实上饭店行业的工作又有一些固有的弊端，比如工作时间长，员工压力大等。

美国饭店协会(the National Restaurant Association)和可口可乐公司共同资助的一项择业调查表明，工作乏味是员工跳槽的一大原因。饭店行业的管理者非常重视这条信息，他们精心组织各种活动——从大型会餐到部门郊游——来激励员工，培养团队精神，建设活跃的、有生命力的、人际关系融洽的企业文化。饭店的一线员工与二线员工在工作中可能没有多少接触,但集体活动可打破部门间的界线,增进不同部门员工的相互了解,转而形成更融洽的工作关系。饭店若想留住人才,不妨尝试给平淡的工作日增加一点儿乐趣,用这种方式来抵消饭店工作固有的那些弊端。

很多饭店都在尝试将工作与娱乐结合起来。以下是这方面的一些成功的做法。

例如奇力餐厅(Chili's Restaurant)分店在每次的季会期间都要用一天的时间让管理人员对小组竞赛活动进行评选。小组竞赛活动的形式多种多样、别出心裁,比如"捕捉美好瞬间"的活动,由公司出资,让员工组成小组,带着照相机在市区内各处浏览,但返回后一定要交上"游后感"和抓拍的精彩照片。优胜的小组将获得奖品,活动总是以欢乐的晚会结束。季会结束后,公司鼓励管理人员设计出更多更有趣的活动。

某一家高档餐厅,在每天晚上开张之前都要先为自己的厨师和服务员准备一顿"家庭晚餐",让他们品尝最新的特色菜和各种酒,让厨房和餐厅服务两个部门有机会相互了解。席间还会探讨服务和操作程序方面的问题。因为太忙而不能参加晚餐的员工尽可在休息日享受免费就餐。这家餐厅,厨房的员工(厨师)亲自前往当地的农场,为餐厅的特色菜选取原料。

某一家麦当劳分店每月组织员工出游一次:野炊、划船、打保龄、漂流等。

二、以人为本的管理研究涉及的几个新概念(Some New Concepts Related to People-oriented Management)

(一)情绪劳动(Emotional Labor)

情绪劳动是伴随着西方国家从制造型经济向服务型经济转变的过程中提出来的。最先提出这个概念的学者是社会学家 Hochschild。

她于 1979 年发表了第一篇有关情绪劳动的文章——《情绪劳动、情感规则及社会结构》。在文章中,她并没有提出情绪劳动这个概念,而是先提出了另外两个重要概念:一是感受规则,指的是在具体情境中,情绪感受的范畴、强度、持久性,以及实施对象等方面的合适性,例如,在婚礼上应该感到高兴;二是表达规则,指在给定情境中表现出来的可以观察到的情绪的合适性,例如,收到礼物应该表示感谢。这两种规则的不同之处在于,前者是强调个人在生活中体验到的情绪,如悲伤、高兴、激动、失望,等等;后者主要是侧重于人们表现在外面的可以观察到的情绪,而且这种表露在外面的情绪会受到各种社会规则的制约,内心感受到的情绪并不一定会如实地表达出来。她通过对 Delta 航空公司空服人员与乘客交往的调查发现,在服务过程中,为了有效完成工作,除了需要脑力和体力方面的付出外,员工还需要调控他们的感受及表达。Hochschild把需要通过情绪方面的努力才能完成工作这一现象称为情绪劳动。

在《情绪管理的探索》一书中，Hochschild(1983)正式提出"情绪劳动"一词，并对情绪劳动做出了明确的界定，情绪劳动是"管理好情绪以创造公众可以观察到的面部和肢体表现"，而且"其表现是为了获得工资，因此具有交换价值"，使得情绪劳动与"体力劳动"和"脑力劳动"有所区别。为了更好地理解情绪劳动，Hochschild指出情绪劳动的发生需要具备三个条件：(1)必须是与公众进行面对面或者声音对声音的接触。如老师与学生、护士与病人的交流都是这种相互的直接的交流；(2)情绪劳动的目的是使顾客或者客户产生某种情绪状态或者情绪反应；(3)雇主能够对员工的情绪活动实施控制。通过制定规章制度等来约束雇员必须表现出某种情绪等。

她还列举了六类最需要运用情绪劳动的职业类型：专业性、技术型的职业；经营管理者；销售人员；办事员；服务性工作；私人家庭工作者。

在Hochschild提出这个概念之后，并没有马上引起学者们的广泛关注。直到20世纪90年代，情绪劳动才逐渐成为了组织与管理领域的一个热门话题。学者们从组织与管理的角度对情绪劳动这一现象进行探讨，纷纷提出了关于情绪劳动定义的不同观点，对Hochschild提出的情绪劳动定义进行了批评与完善。

首先是Ashforth等人(1993)的观点，他们从强调情绪劳动的外在表现为切入口，他们认为情绪劳动为"表现出合适的情绪行为"。此定义重点是在强调表现在外面的可以观察的行为，而不是内心情绪感受的管理。因为Ashforth等人认为：表现规则强调组织一方的要求，主要用于调节公共场所表现出来的外部情绪行为，感受规则强调个体一方的感受，主要用于调节个体内心实际感受到的情绪；外部表现的情绪行为是客户可以看到的，而且会直接影响客户，组织关心的是员工能否表现出所需要的情绪行为，而非个体的内部情绪感受，情绪工作应该重视组织要求的情绪行为而不是个体的情绪感受。

其次，Morris与Feldman(1996)将情绪劳动定义为"在人际互动的过程中，表达组织要求的情绪所需的心力、计划与控制"。并将情绪表达频率、对表现规则的重视程度、情绪表现的多样性和情绪失调四个维度纳入情绪劳动的内涵。他们的定义是建立在下面四个假设的基础上：情绪劳动的定义是基于情绪互动模式；当个体所感受的情绪与组织要求的情绪一致时，个体仍需要花费某种程度的心力，展现组织所要求的情绪；与Hochschild对情绪劳动的观点一致，过去由私人决定的情绪表达，现在变成市场上的商品；组织中存在着引领情绪表达的标准或规则。与Ashforth不同的一点是，他们更加强调情绪劳动者内在的心理的加工过程。

Jones(1998)在Morris等人(1996)定义的基础上，认为服务人员在工作中的交往不仅包括外部顾客,而且包括内部顾客,因此把情绪劳动定义为"在与外部或者内部利益相关者进行交往时,努力调控情绪使之与组织需要表现的情绪相一致"。可见,Jones 扩展了情绪劳动的研究对象,增加了内部利益相关者。

Grandey(2000)整理上述几位学者的看法,认为这些定义皆包含一个相同的概念:工作时,个体可以调整他们的情绪表达。所以 Grandey 将情绪劳动定义为"为表现组织期望的情绪,进行的必要的心理调节加工",即为调节情绪行为而进行的目标确认、计划、监控和信息反馈等内在心理活动。

另外,Diefendorff 等从控制论的角度出发,将情绪劳动定义为"员工持续监控自己的情绪表现与表现规则之间是否存在差异,并努力采用一定的情绪调节策略降低差异的心理控制过程"。Glomb 等人(2004)在 Ashforth 等人(1993)定义的基础上,首先考虑了情绪劳动的两个维度:一是表现维度,包括情绪表现恰当和情绪表现不恰当;二是感受维度,包括表现与内部感受相一致的情绪和不表现与内部感受相一致的情绪,并且以表现维度为横轴,以感受维度为纵轴,把坐标平面分为 4 个部分;然后引入情绪状态维度,包括积极情绪状态和消极情绪状态,并假设消极情绪表现是禁止的,积极情绪表现是允许的。这样,4 个象限分:既感受到也表现出积极情绪(真实表现);没有感受到积极情绪,但需要表现(假装表现);虽然感受到消极情绪却不把它表现出来(情绪压抑);既没有感受到也无须表现出消极情绪。在剔除"没有感受到也无须表现出消极情绪"状态之后,Glomb 等人把情绪劳动操作化定义为包括三个组成部分:真实情绪表现、假装情绪表现和情绪压抑。Zapf(2002)指出情绪劳动本质上是个人根据企业制定的情绪行为管理目标所进行的情绪调节行为。也就是说,情绪劳动的核心是对在企业中员工的情绪进行调节的过程。

(二) 主观幸福感(Subjective Well-being)

"幸福感"是研究人类良好存在的科学。现代幸福感的研究主要经历了四个重要阶段:第一阶段(1980 年以前)主要是简单描述与主观幸福感相关的人口统计学变量;第二个阶段(1980~1990 年)主要是建构有关的幸福感理论框架,探讨如何获得幸福的各种途径和跨文化研究;第三个阶段(1990~2000 年)主要是将研究方法、途径和主观幸福感测量的理论进行整合;第四个阶段(2000 年至今)的研究重心转移到幸福感概念模型的整合、幸福感理论模型的应用以及积极心理学系的构建(高红英,苗元江,2006)。

自 1967 年 Wilson 撰写《Correlates of Avowed Happiness》以来,源自心理学的情绪幸福感模型与源自社会学的认知幸福感模型,综合成主观幸福感(Subjective Well-being,SWB)的理论模型,占据了幸福感研究的主流地位,成了幸福感的代名词。

早期的主观幸福感研究主要着眼于探索主观幸福感与年龄、性别、婚姻、收入水平以及受教育程度之间的关系。本世纪以来,主观幸福感研究的重点开始发生了变化,从关注个体的工作心理体验和相关的影响因素转变为关注主观幸福感的产出变量,包括个人行为、工作效能、经济社会发展进步等。

主观幸福感是指人对自己生活的认知评价和情感体验。Diener等人(1999)在总结了三十多年来对主观幸福感的研究的基础上,提出主观幸福感的四维结构:(1)对过去、现在和未来生活的满意度;(2)积极的情感体验:如快乐、成就感、自豪等;(3)消极的情感体验:如羞耻、焦虑、压抑等;(4)对生活各方面的满意度:工作、家庭、健康、经济状况及自我。

尽管对主观幸福感概念的理解及测量方法多种多样,研究者基本上认同主观幸福感包含一个三维结构:认知因素(总体生活满意度和对生活各方面的满意度)、体验积极情感和缺乏消极情感(Diener et al., 1999)。具有较高主观幸福感的人对生活比较满意,经常体验到积极的情感,很少有消极的情感。而主观幸福感低的人则对生活不满意,经常体验到消极的情感而非积极情感。Bradbum(1969)的研究发现,积极情感和消极情感并不是同一维度相对的两端,而是两个相对独立的纬度。他认为,积极情感低并不一定意味着消极情感高;要提高幸福感,既要增加积极情感,又要减少消极情感。

Diener(1984)认为主观幸福感有三个特点:(1)主观性。主观幸福感的评定主要依赖个体本人设定的标准,而不是他人或外界的标准,一个人幸福与否只有他自己体验的感觉最真实准确,因此幸福感具有很强的主观性。(2)相对稳定性。主观幸福感是个体对其生活的整体评价。虽然在评定主观幸福感时会受到情境和情绪状态的影响,其情绪水平会变化,但长期的主观幸福感还是会相对趋于稳定。(3)整体性。指主观幸福感是一种综合评价,它包括对情感反应的评估和认知判断,即包括正向情感、负向情感和生活满意度三个维度,反映的是个体整体的主观评价,是一种综合性的心理指标,所以具有综合性、整体性的特点。

早期对于幸福感研究大部分集中在对消极心理的研究,即针对心理问题、心理疾病进行诊断与治疗,如压力和过度劳累导致的心理和生理的不健康。在幸福感研究的前期阶段,消极取向的心理学是幸福感研究的主导性模式(Huhtala & Parzefall, 2007)。随后学者们逐渐意识到幸福并非简单的对消极情绪的克服,还要综合考虑影响人们积极情感的因素时,积极心理学开始了对幸福感积极心理状态的研究(Seligman & Csikszentmihalyi, 2000)。

在对工作层面的主观幸福感的研究方面,Cotton 和 Hart(2003)提出主观幸福感包括两个维度:情感因素和认知因素。情感因素包括两个维度:积极情感和消极情感,分别用 morale 和 distress 表示。认知因素被定义为工作满意度,反映员工对他们工作满意状况的认知。他们认为,认知因素(工作满意度)能反映与判断力、辨别力相关的变量,如离职;而情感因素(积极情感和消极情感)更能与情绪方面的变量相联系,比如焦虑、生气、烦恼和冲动的行为。研究证明,积极情感和消极情感是互相独立的变量。

我国国内对于主观幸福感的研究兴起于80年代,大多是综述性的研究,主要对国外研究进行介绍、整合,实证研究还处于逐步开展的阶段。

从理论建构上看,我国的学者多数都认同Diener等学者提出的主观幸福感的概念,或者是根据该概念进行修改、完善,并在此基础上进行实证研究。

幸福感测量方面,我国学者现有的研究主要使用引进的测量幸福感的量表,现今比较流行的测量量表有生活满意度量表、费城老年中心信心量表、总体幸福感量表、纽芬兰纪念大学幸福度量表以及情感量表等。这些量表在我国都得到了广泛的应用,为我国主观幸福感的研究做出了很大的贡献。

在对主观幸福感的研究中,我国的早期研究主要集中于研究老年人的心理健康。俞正炎、马永兴、王赞舜以及胡君辰(1987)采用自编的《生活满意感心理测试问卷》对老年人的生活满意感进行了跨文化的研究;郭晋武(1992)采用生活满意感指数量表对我国城市的老年人生活满意感进行了研究;许淑莲(1993)等采用了安德鲁斯等人编制的生活质量量表、布莱德博情感平衡量表以及纽芬兰纪念大学幸福度量表研究了离退休老干部的生活质量;刘仁刚、龚耀先(2000)对老年人的幸福感进行了系列研究。20世纪90年代开始,对于其他人群的幸福感研究也逐渐展开。如王极盛及其同事(1998)对中学生主观幸福感构成的研究,并自编了初中生主观幸福感量表,把影响主观幸福感的因素分为了正性情感、学业满意感、家庭满意感、同伴交往满意感、教师满意感、自我满意感以及生活条件满意感等七个维度。邢占军(2002)提出了体验论幸福的观点,并编制了《中国城市居民主观幸福感量表的编制》;另外,还有对于青年人的研究,如黄立清(2004)的《我国城市青年主观幸福感初步研究》。国内刚刚开始关注不同地域人们幸福感是否存在差别的问题,例如2005年社会上对农民是否比城里人更幸福展开大辩论;奚恺元等对中国六个大城市居民的幸福指数进行测量;北京市社会科学项目资助"和谐指数"的研究。国内对主观幸福感的研究近年来渐渐走热,在企业管理领域,对主观幸福感如何影响人力资源的管理的研究尚处于起步阶段。

(三)组织承诺(Organizational Commitment)

组织承诺是当代组织行为学领域中一个重要的概念。组织承诺的概念从20世纪60年代起开始提出,70年代以来受到了持续的关注(Mathieu,1991)。组织承诺的研究已经得到了很大的发展,成为了一个非常热门和成熟的研究领域。在20世纪90年代,组织承诺更成为组织行为学、工业心理学领域研究的中心之一,大量的研究证明,组织承诺在预测一些重要的个体结果和组织结果变量比如工作绩效、满意度、组织公民行为、离职倾向以及离职行为等是非常重要和有效的(Meyer & Allen,1997)。

从1960年提出组织承诺的概念以来,伴随着各种研究,相应地也产生了多种定义、维度与测量方法。组织承诺的界定有两种基本观点:一种是行为说,即员工为不失去已有的位置和多年的投入所换来的福利待遇而不得不继续留在该企业的一种承诺;另外一种是态度说,即个人对组织的一种态度或肯定性的内心倾向,是个人对某一特定组织感情上的依附及参与该组织的相对程度(陈霞,段兴民,2003)。按照态度说的观点可以解释员工为什么要留在其所在的饭店,因而也是检验员工对企业忠诚程度的一种指标(余志远,朱玉华,张希,2009)。目前大部分的研究是从态度说这个角度来进行阐述的。

国内的定义如凌文栓、张治灿和方俐洛(2000)认为,组织承诺是员工对其所在组织的一种态度,组织承诺可以解释员工为什么要留在其所在的企业,因而也是检验员工对其企业忠诚程度的一种指标。它除了受契约法规的制约和工资福利等经济因素的影响外,还受到道德规范、价值观念、理想追求、感情因素及个人兴趣、能力和人格特点的影响,而且这些文化心理因素对职工的承诺行为起着决定作用。

Meyer和Allen(1997)对以前的研究进行了全面的分析和回顾,提出了组织承诺的三维度模型。即组织承诺包括情感承诺、持续承诺和规范承诺三个维度。这个组织承诺三维度模型,是目前被学术界最为广泛接受的组织承诺模型。

情感承诺指组织成员在情感上对组织认同和卷入的总强度。它是个体对一个实体的情感,是一种肯定性的心理倾向。它包含价值目标认同、员工自豪感以及为了组织的利益自愿为组织做出牺牲和贡献等成分。员工对组织所表现的忠诚并努力地工作,主要是由于员工对组织有深厚的感情,而不仅仅是物质利益。

持续承诺是指员工由于害怕离开组织带来的既得利益的损失而不得不继续留在该组织内的一种承诺。它是建立在经济原则基础上的,具有浓厚交易色彩的承诺。

规范承诺是指员工由于长期受社会的影响形成的社会责任而继续留在组织内的承诺。个体在社会化的过程中,不断地被灌输和强调这样一种观念或规范:忠诚于组织是会得到赞赏和鼓励的一种恰当的行为,以至于在个体内心中产生了顺从这种规范的倾向。同时从组织那里接受利益或好处也会使员工内心中产生一种要回报组织的义务感。

人力资源管理的活动确定了组织与员工之间不同的关系,传达对员工不同的期望,展示组织对员工不同的承诺,从而影响员工的生产率以及组织的绩效,同时也会影响员工的态度,这些态度就包含了员工的组织承诺。在1999年,Dessler在总结以往相关研究的基础上,提出了培养员工组织承诺的五种人力资源实践的重要途径:(1)遵循以人为本的价值取向;(2)组织使命的正确表述和沟通:正确表述组织使命和经营管理理念,让组织使命具有激励效应,建立相应的规章制度;(3)保证组织的公平性:建立系统性的申诉程序、提供多种沟通渠道;(4)创建一系列共同体:建立价值共同体和价值共享平台,强调交叉职能和团队协作;(5)支持员工的发展:向员工提供挑战性的工作,工作丰富化和分权,内部晋升,提供发展机会和安全保障。

国内的企业管理者和学者逐渐地开始关注和研究人力资源管理活动在培养提升员工组织承诺方面的策略及方法。如徐国华、杨东涛(2004)根据不同职业生涯阶段的员工比较研究指出:企业的人力资源管理部门应洞察处在不同职业生涯阶段的问题,关注员工的情感承诺的变化趋势,从而制定有针对性的人力资源制度和激励政策,提高员工企业价值观的认同感,强化员工的向心力。卜华白、李录生(2006)立足当前组织承诺理论研究的成果,提出了企业核心员工管理九方格模型。作为一种应用性人力资源管理模型,它为企业对核心员工管理提供了理论上的决策依据和操作上的实证途径。

(四)组织公民行为(Organizational Citizenship Behavior)

Katz 和 Kahn(1966)认为有效的组织应该有三种基本功能:(1)必须吸引并留住员工;(2)确保员工以可信赖的方式符合组织特定角色的要求;(3)员工必须有创造性与自发性行为,其行为表现超越角色规范。Berteman 等人在 1988 年将第三种行为称之为"组织公民行为",并把它定义为职务外行为,主要指对帮助同事和对组织的责任感。Organ 在 1988 年正式将 OCB 定义为在组织正式的薪酬体系中尚未得到明确或直接的确认,但就整体而言有益于组织运作成效的行为总和。

自组织公民行为提出以来,其对组织的重要性已经得到了很多研究的支持,并且这些成果被运用到企业组织甚至社会群体的组织绩效、人事管理决策、组织规范等多个方面,对组织的有效运转起到了积极的影响作用。组织公民行为是一种资源合作行为,能自觉维护整个组织的运转,减少矛盾和冲突。组织公民行为对员工的工作满意度、公平感、组织承诺和领导支持感等产生重要影响并潜在地影响整个组织的绩效。

综观组织公民行为的研究文献,发现已被确认的 OCB 种类有三十多种,而且它们中有不少概念相互重叠。通过归纳和总结可以认为,OCB 至少可以由七个维度构成:助人行为(helping behavior)、运动家道德(sportsmanship)、组织忠诚(organizational loyalty)、组织遵从(organizational compliance)、个人首创性(individual initiative)、公民道德(civic virture)和自我发展(self development)。

1. 助人行为

助人行为是 OCB 中最重要的一个维度,是指自发地帮助同事,预防和解决与工作相关问题的行为。它包括利他主义行为、保持和谐、善意调解、鼓舞团队士气、礼貌维度;人际互助;帮助同事、人际促进等。研究表明,这些内容都属于同一个维度。

2. 运动家道德

运动家道德由 Organ 在 1990 年首次提出,指个体对别人造成的不方便不仅不抱怨,而且仍然保持积极的态度,为了团体的利益甘愿牺牲一些个人的兴趣和喜好,不轻易否决别人的意见等。

3. 组织忠诚

组织忠诚包括忠诚于组织;保护组织和对组织的发展有良好意愿;支持和维护组织的发展目标;敬业精神等。组织忠诚有利于促进组织发展,保护和维护组织免于受到外来的威胁和损害,而且在组织处于逆境时个体对组织仍然保持着高度承诺。

4. 组织遵从

早在 1983 年,Smith 等人就对组织遵从进行了研究,并且将它称为一般化的遵从。它包括对组织的服从;OCB-O(organizational obedience);服从组织的规章制度和程序等。组织遵从是指个体不仅接受组织的规章制度和程序并加以内化,而且在行为中严格认真地遵守,即使在没有他人在场的情况下也是如此。

5. 个人首创性

个人首创性是由 Graham 在 1989 年提出来的一种职务外行为,它包括自愿并创造性地从事与工作相关且超出了组织要求的行为。个体愿意承担额外的工作责任,以极大热情和努力持续工作,同时也积极激励组织中的其他人。这种行为最大的特点就在于其自愿的创造性,也有人将它称为责任心,提出建设性意见,自愿承担工作任务、工作奉献等。

6. 公民道德

公民道德最初是由 Graham 在 1991 年提出来的,也被称为组织参与、保护组织等。它指员工作为组织中一个公民应有的道德行为,包括对组织的工作感兴趣,节约组织资源,保护组织财产,愿意参加组织的各项活动,参与组织战略计划制订,监控来自环境的威胁和机会等。

7. 自我发展

自我发展这个概念最初是由 Katz 在 1964 年提出来的,由 George 等人将其发展成为 OCB 中的一个重要维度。自我发展即员工主动利用业余时间,通过各种形式来开发自己的潜能,自愿接受组织提供的培训机会,来学习相关工作知识和技能,以求对组织的发展做出更大贡献。

尽管不同研究者对 OCB 的维度与命名不同,但归结起来都可以用以上七个维度加以概括。可以看到,几乎 OCB 所有的维度都与 Katz 在 1964 年提出的"革新和自发性行为"观点有着千丝万缕的关系。

 案例分析(Practice Case Analysis)

KURT LEWIN: THE PRACTICAL THEORIST

Kurt Lewin was born in 1890 in the village of Mogilno, which was then part of the Prussian province of Posen (now part of Poland). Lewin's father owned a general store, as well as a small farm, so the family was prosperous although not wealthy. In 1905, Lewin's family moved to Berlin, largely to gain better educational opportunities than were available in Mogilno. Lewin entered the University of Frieberg in 1909, initially with the goal of studying medicine. His distaste for anatomy courses contributed to Lewin's abandoning the goal of becoming a physician. He switched his interest to biology. This led to a transfer first to the University of Munich and ultimately to the University of Berlin, where he eventually earned his doctorate in 1916. After returning from military service during World War I, he began his academic career.

The years at Berlin were very productive, and Lewin's work became quite influential. At this time, Lewin began to develop an interest in the application of psychology to applied problems such as agricultural labor, production efficiency, and the design of jobs. Lewin became quite interested in scientific management, particularly the impact of this system on workers. Lewin and his family left Germany in 1933 due to the rise of the Nazi Party. He initially received a temporary appointment at Cornell University, and ultimately moved to the University of Iowa Child Welfare Research Station. While at Iowa, Lewin conducted influential studies on a variety of topics, including child development, the impact of social climates, and leadership. Following his years at Iowa, Lewin became deeply involved in the Commission on Community Relations, which was established by the American Jewish Congress. During his involvement, Lewin initiated a number of "action research" projects aimed at enhancing understanding of community problems such as racial prejudice, gang violence, and integrated housing. Remarkably, during this same time, Lewin also founded the Research Center for Group Dynamics at MIT. Lewin's work at the Center continued until his death in 1947, at the age of 56.

In retrospect, it is hard to imagine anyone having a greater impact on the field of organizational psychology and human resources than Kurt Lewin. His ideas continue to influence the study of a number of areas such as employee motivation, leadership, group dynamics, and organizational development. However, perhaps Lewin's most enduring legacy was his innovative blending of science and practice.

Source: Marrow A J. The practical theorist: The life and work of Kurt Lewin. New York: Basic Books, 1969.

Questions for Discussion:
1. Please list the contribution of Kurt Lewin in scientific management.
2. How can Lewin combine science and practice in his study?

名词解释(Key Terms)

1. 人力资源：企业中专注于员工活动的部门。这些活动包括招聘和雇用新员工、培训现有员工、员工福利与人员保留。

Human Resource: The division of a company that is focused on activities relating to employees. These activities normally include recruiting and hiring of new employees, orientation and training of current employees, employee benefits, and retention.

2. 人力资源管理：雇用和发展员工的管理原则，使他们对组织更具有价值。

Human Resource Management: The administrative discipline of hiring and developing employees so that they become more valuable to the organization.

3. 情绪劳动：对情感的操控会产生可供观察的面部和身体展现。服务工作由于具有"情绪"，以及这项工作所必需的体力劳动和脑力劳动而使得服务工作与其他类型的工作与众不同。从事服务工作的员工因技术技能和情绪劳动而获得工作报酬。

Emotional Labor: Manipulations of feeling to create a publicly observable facial and bodily display. Service work is much different from many other kinds of work because of the "emotional" as well as the physical and mental labor which this work entails. The service employees are paid not only for the technical skills but also for the emotional labor.

4. 主观幸福感：主观幸福感是一个包容性的术语，可以概念化为具有认知评价成分（即生活满意度）和两个情感成分，这是正面和负面的影响。因此，它代表生活的认知评价和个人的正面与负面的情绪两个方面。

Subjective Well-being: Subjective well-being is an inclusive term that can be conceptualized as having a cognitive appraisal component (i. e., life satisfaction) and two emotional components, which are positive and negative affects. Therefore, it represents both cognitive evaluation of life and positive and negative emotions of an individual.

5. 组织承诺:一项在员工与其组织之间建立的心理纽带,使得员工不愿离开组织。

Organizational Commitment: A psychological link between the employee and his or her organization that makes it less likely that the employee will voluntarily leave the organization.

6. 组织公民行为:任意的、不是由正式的奖励系统直接或明确认可的个人行为,能够促进组织的有效运作。

Organizational Citizenship Behavior: Individual behaviors that are discretionary, not directly or explicitly recognized by the formal reward system, and that in the aggregate promote the effective functioning of the organization.

复习思考题(Questions for Review)

1. 简述霍桑实验的内容和意义。

Describe the content and influence of The Hawthorne Experiments.

2. 请阐述"以人为本"的管理的特点。

Please describe the characteristic of "People-oriented" management.

3. 要做到"以人为本",具体可以采取哪些举措?

What measures can be taken to match the theme "People Orientation"?

4. 要成为一名有效的管理者,应该掌握哪些管理手段?

What management methods should be grasped in order to be an effective manager?

5. 请解释情绪劳动、主观幸福感、组织承诺、组织公民行为的定义。

Please make definitions for emotional labor, subjective well-being, organizational commitment, and organizational citizenship behavior.

研究前沿(Research Front)

W. Wilson's (1967) review of the area of subjective well-being (SWB) advanced several conclusions regarding those who report high levels of "happiness". A number of his conclusions have been overturned: youth and modest aspirations no longer are seen as prerequisites of SWB. E. Diener's (1984) review placed greater emphasis on theories that stressed psychological factors. In the current article, the authors review current evidence for Wilson's conclusions and discuss modern theories of SWB that stress dispositional influences, adaptation, goals, and coping strategies. The next steps in the evolution of the field are to comprehend the interaction of psychological factors with life circumstances in producing SWB, to understand the causal pathways leading to happiness, understand the processes underlying adaptation to events, and develop theories that explain why certain variables differentially influence the different components of SWB (life satisfaction, pleasant affect, and unpleasant affect).

The Components of Subjective Well-being

Moods and emotions, which together are labeled affect, represent people's on-line evaluations of the events that occur in their lives. Bradburn and Caplovitz (1965) suggested that pleasant affect and unpleasant affect form two independent factors and should be measured separately. Although the degree of independence between momentary pleasant and unpleasant affect is still debated, the separability of long-term affective dimensions is less controversial. Diener & Emmons (1984) found that pleasant and unpleasant affect became increasingly separate as the time-frame increased. Diener, Smith, and Fujita (1995) used structural equation modeling and multimethod assessment to control measurement error in affect measures. They found that the two constructs are moderately inversely correlated but clearly separable. Because SWB researchers are primarily interested in long-term moods rather than momentary emotions, they should include measures of both pleasant and unpleasant affect in their research. Kozma, Stone, and Stones (in press) discovered that various measures of SWB reflect short and long-term influences to differing degrees. In addition, in certain contexts discrete emotions such as anger, anxiety, and sadness should be assessed.

In addition to studying affective reactions, SWB researchers are interested in cognitive evaluations of life satisfaction. Andrews and Withey (1976) found that life satisfaction formed a separate factor from the two major types of affect. Lucas, Diener, and Suh (1996) used multitrait-multimethod analyses to show that pleasant affect, unpleasant affect, and life satisfaction were separable constructs. Even over 2 years and across multiple methods of assessment (e. g., self-versus informant reports), validity coefficients foreach of the three constructs were stronger than the intercorrelations among different constructs. The Satisfaction with Life Scale (see Pavot & Diener, 1993) is a valid and reliable scale for measuring life satisfaction.

Theory

It is fortunate that numerous theories have now been proposedand tested. Perhaps the most important theoretical advance of the past 30 years is the shift in emphasis from the first of Wilson's postulates (identifying which needs must be met for happiness to ensue) to the second (identifying the comparative factors that influence whether or not resources will influence well-being). Whereas the former approach attempts to identify external, situational, or bottom-up factors that consistently affect happiness, the latter approach focuses on the top-down processes within the individual.

The fact that researchers have not yet identified resources that strongly affect SWB, although once considered a failure of SWB research, now motivates many of the studies about the processes underlying happiness. Researchers have begun to examine the context provided by people's experiences, values, and goals when assessing the influence of external events on happiness. In the following section, we introduce several major conceptual models pertaining to SWB and review the evidence relevant to these models.

Early research on SWB was limited to cataloging the various resources and demographic factors that are correlated with subjective well-being. Although the most recent 30 years of research have increased our knowledge in this area, the most important contribution is in the understanding that these external, bottom-up factors often are responsible for only a small part of the variance in SWB. One's temperament and cognitions, goals, culture, and adaptation coping efforts moderate the influence of life circumstances and events on SWB. Theoretical models have been developed in each of these areas to explain how internal factors within the person moderate and mediate the impact of the environment on people's SWB. A major goal for the future is to clarify the interrelations among these factors. For example, how does personality affect one's tendency to adapt to negative events? Does adaptation exist primarily because of changes in goals?

The Causes of SWB

There is not a simple answer to what causes SWB. Studies of religion, coping, rumination, and attributions suggest that cognitive factors play an important role. Studies of people with disabilities show that objective factors can matter, but people often adapt their goals to what is possible for them. Studies of heritability demonstrate that personality plays an important role. Cross cultural studies reveal that different factors correlate with SWB indifferent societies. Different variables lead to SWB for people with different values and different goals. Researchers should be open to the possibility that different strategies work better in different environments and for different people. Thus, it is pointless to search for a single cause of happiness. Instead, they need to understand the complex interplay of culture, personality, cognitions, goals and resources, and the objective environment.

Conclusion

Our prediction is that when a review of SWB is conducted 30 years from now, progress will have been even more rapid than it has been in the past three decades. Hopefully, in 2028 nobody can possibly claim that we know nothing more than the ancient Greeks about subjective well-being. Indeed, since Wilson's review, considerable progress has been made. Wilson believed the happy person to be well-paid, young, educated, religious, and married. We would emphasize that the happy person is blessed with a positive temperament, tends to look on the bright side of things, and does not ruminate excessively about bad events, and is living in an economically developed society, has social confidants, and possesses adequate resources for making progress toward valued goals. Because research in the area is progressing rapidly, however, we know that this description will be rewritten in the decades ahead.

Source: Diener E, Suh E M, Lucas R E & Smith H L. Subjective well-being: three decades of progress. Psychological Bulletin, 1999, 125(2): 276-302.

第2章 工作分析与工作设计
（Job Analysis and Job Design）

本章概要（Summary of This Chapter）

饭店是以"人"为主体的服务组织，每个宾客的需求各不相同，饭店员工在为宾客规范服务的同时，面临着时时刻刻处理宾客投诉、羞辱、领导批评、员工不和、工作强度与薪资待遇的不符等多重压力。一线部门员工面临普遍的问题是工作强度大、时间长，薪酬待遇不尽如人意，饭店缺乏和谐的充满人情味的工作环境，缺乏对基层员工的职业生涯设计，导致员工队伍不稳定，士气低落。国内相关机构统计表明，高星级饭店普遍存在员工流失率较高的现象，其中，员工流失率在5%以下的仅为1%，流失率在5%至10%的占33%，流失率在10%至15%的占21%，流失率在15%以上的占45%。因此，饭店管理人员改善工作的环境，改进员工的工作方式，对员工的工作进行合理的分析和设计，变得十分重要。

Hotels are service organizations based on human being. Every guest has different need. When serving the guest, the hotel employees are facing problems such as dealing with guests' complaints, humiliation, managers' criticism, disagreement between employees, high workload and low pay and so on, which would make the high turnover rate and low morale of employees. According to a report, turnover rate are generally high in star-rated hotels. The rate lower than 5% is merely 1%, 5%~10% takes up 33% of the hotels, 10%~15% takes up 21% of the hotels, and higher than 15% takes up 45% of the hotels. Therefore, to improve the working environment and work mode of the employees, properly analyze and design the job for the employees are critically important.

☞ 开篇引例(Beginning Story)

Hotel and motel managers run room rental businesses. Duties vary with the size and type of the business. In large hotels, general managers are in charge of the entire hotel. They set room rates, monitor income and expenses, and supervise other staff. Large hotels have restaurants and meeting rooms. These hotels hire assistant managers to supervise the various areas of the hotel. Often, the job title of the assistant manager describes their duties. Executive housekeepers make sure that all areas of the hotel are clean. Front office managers are in charge of reservations and room assignments. Food and beverage managers oversee restaurants and banquets. They plan menus, set prices, and order supplies. Convention services managers coordinate all hotel activities related to meetings. They meet with clients and plan a schedule. Then they work with the food service and front office managers to serve and lodge the visitors. Assistant managers hire, train, and supervise the members of their staff. They use computers to write reports about their area or to order food or supplies. They may meet and talk with the general manager several times a week. Some assistant managers are in charge of accounting, sales, and maintenance. Managers of small hotels and motels perform different duties than managers of larger businesses. This is because there are fewer employees in smaller hotels and motels. Many times these managers are more likely to fill in for absent workers. Thus a manager may clean rooms, take reservations, or make general repairs. Managers in small hotels and motels have many administrative tasks. For example, they interview and hire new staff. They also keep track of the money they take in each day. Managers may schedule pick-up and delivery for the laundry service. Resident managers live in hotels and motels. They are on-call 24 hours a day. They usually work an 8-hour day, while overseeing the hotel. In their off hours, resident managers are called for emergencies or problems. In some hotels, the general manager also serves as the resident manager.①

第一节 工作分析(Job Analysis)

在饭店服务工作中,客房服务员缺乏必要的服务常识、餐厅服务员缺乏服务技

---

① http://www.hospitalityguild.com/Careers/04_Hotel_duties.htm.

能、酒吧服务员缺乏必要的训练等,都会导致经营问题的出现。同时,员工在工作中不清楚什么是饭店的期望以及怎样做好工作等问题都会直接影响到工作的效果。因此,为了真正实现以"工作"为中心,因事设岗、以岗定编,达到人与事的最佳结合,工作分析就必须从人与事两方面开展研究和分析。

工作分析是指根据饭店工作的实际情况,对饭店各项工作的内容、特征、规范、要求、流程以及完成此工作所需员工的素质、知识、技能要求进行描述的过程,它是饭店人力资源开发与管理的最基础性工作。工作分析的主要目的有两个:第一,研究饭店中每个职位都在做什么工作,包括工作性质、工作内容、工作责任、完成该项工作所需要的知识水平和技术能力以及工作条件和环境;第二,明确这些职位对员工有什么具体的从业要求,包括对员工的自身素质、员工的技术水平、独立完成工作的能力和员工在工作中的自主权等方面的说明。

一、工作分析七要素(Seven Elements of Job Analysis)

为了能够全面、准确、真实地掌握饭店各项工作的具体含义,帮助饭店确定各工作岗位所需要的工作技能,工作分析必须从以下7个方面入手收集信息。

1. 什么职位

工作分析首先需要确定的是工作名称和职位。这方面的信息可以通过工作分类来获得。所谓工作分类就是以每一位饭店员工所承担的工作责任为依据,进行实际调查,并根据工作性质、繁简难易程度、责任轻重以及任职资格等四个方面,确定工作名称并进行分类。

2. 员工完成什么样的体力和脑力劳动

现代饭店的各类工作岗位都需要员工既付出体力劳动,又要付出脑力劳动,但是由于工作性质和内容的不同,体力劳动和脑力劳动在各项工作中所占的比重不尽相同。因此,工作分析应该从脑力劳动和体力劳动两方面进行分析。

3. 工作将在什么时候完成

为了确保工作质量和工作效率,工作分析需要对完成工作的具体时间进行调查和计算;同时,这也是执行国家法定工时和保证员工身体健康的需要。具体地讲,就是要详细掌握工时和工作排班情况。

4. 工作将在哪里完成

这是指了解工作地点和物理环境方面的信息,例如,筵席服务的"整鱼除骨"工作是在餐桌上进行还是在顾客确认菜品后拿到备餐台进行;厨房的某项工作是否属于高温作业,需要什么样的照明条件等。

5. 员工如何完成此项工作

通过研究工作内容和性质,确定员工在完成一项工作时必须应该掌握的方法,以及具体的操作步骤。这方面的信息是决定工作完成效果的关键,也是工作分析的最重要的一部分。

6. 为什么要完成此项工作

这是为了了解某项工作的重要性及其如何衔接的问题,也就是要掌握该项工作与上一个环节是如何联系的,对下一步工作有什么意义,为下一步工作如何开展提供依据,并明确该项工作的隶属关系。

7. 完成工作需要哪些条件

从工作分析角度讲,完成工作所需要的条件主要包括两个方面的内容:一是承担工作的员工应该具备怎样的素质和技能;二是完成工作所需要的设备和工具,以及其他辅助性工作。

二、工作描述(Job Description)

工作描述是工作分析结果的文字表达形式。工作描述是根据工作分析的结果编制而成的,它是有关工作的范围、目的、任务与责任的广泛说明,也是工作评估、员工招聘、人力资源开发以及工作行为鉴定的基础。一套高质量的工作描述,不仅有助于员工清楚地了解饭店对其工作的预期是什么,提高员工对工作任务的明确程度,而且有利于饭店管理者准确地掌握各项工作的完成进度,及时调整、改善与下属员工的工作关系。

工作描述的基本内容包括:

1. 工作标识信息

工作描述中的工作标识信息部分包括工作名称、部门、汇报关系和工作编号。准确的工作名称应该是真实地反映工作内容的性质,并把一项工作与其他工作区别出来。但是在实践中,工作名称常使人产生误解。例如,"行政秘书"可能只是饭店公关部一位工资水平比较高的内勤人员,而具有同样工作名称的人在饭店总经理办公室则可能是参与饭店具体经营的人。为了避免工作名称混乱,可以将部门名称放在工作名称的最前面,以限定工作名称的有效范围;另一种更为有效的方法是,对工作职责不同但工作名称相同的职位,进行工作编号,详细区分。

2. 工作分析日期

工作分析日期通常放在工作描述里,这样便于及时发现是否存在由于工作发生变化而工作描述却没有及时修订的情况。有的饭店还会在工作描述中注明有效期,从而确保对工作内容定期检查,有效地减少了工作描述与实际工作脱节的现象。

3. 工作概要

工作概要是对工作的简要描述，它通常用一段简短的文字陈述工作内容，主要内容包括：工作摘要、工作范围、工作条件和物理环境，等等。

4. 履行职责

履行职责是员工完成"工作概要"所应该表现出的具体行为，主要包括简单的动作描述、行动结果、是独立承担还是与他人合作以及工作汇报关系。如餐厅经理助理的职责是：

——把脏的碗碟拿到洗碗区；

——协助服务员为客人服务；

——为客人送水及饮料；

——开业前摆台，开业期间换台；

——保证各服务区的调味品供应。

5. 工作环境

对员工工作环境的描述。

6. 工作要求指标

这个因素一般是一个独立的文件，工作要求指标写明从事一项工作要求的资格。员工的资格从培训、教育、技能、经验，以及智力、体力、个性特征中反映出来。例如行李员的工作要求指标可以包括：能够在当班的 8 小时内反复提起重 20 公斤的行李，能够与其他行李员配合工作，了解客房的位置。人力资源助理经理的工作指标包括：了解人事制度、熟悉考核方法和公平就业机会原则。

工作描述的作用除了对工作内容的描述之外，还包括：

（1）招聘：工作描述可以作为饭店招聘广告的素材。

（2）人才选拔：工作描述可以帮助饭店经理确定雇员选拔条件和面试问题。

（3）新员工熟悉工作：工作描述是让新员工熟悉工作的理想指南。

（4）培训：根据工作描述，经理可以对比员工的工作技能高下，需要什么样的培训以及如何进行培训。

（5）员工评估：业绩考评一般都直接由工作描述发展而来，工作描述是业绩考评的基础。

（6）晋升与调动：工作描述是确定某名员工是否胜任新的工作任务的依据。

Tips: Using the Internet for Writing Job Descriptions

Most employers probably still write their own job descriptions, but more are turning to the Internet. One site, www.jobdescription.com, illustrates why. The process is simple. Search by alphabetical title, keyword, category, or industry to find the desired job title. This leads you to a generic job description for that title—say, "Computers & EDP systems sales representative". You can then use the wizard to customize the generic description for this position. For example, you can add specific information about your organization, such as job title, job codes, department, and preparation date. And you can indicate whether the job has supervisory abilities, and choose from a number of possible desirable competencies and experience levels.

The U.S. Department of Labor's occupational information network, called O*NET, is another useful web tool (you will find it at www.doleta.gov/programs/onet). It allows users to see the most important characteristics of occupations, as well as the experience, education, and knowledge required to do each job well. Both the Standard Occupational Classification and O*NET include the specific tasks associated with many occupations. O*NET also provides skills, including basic skills such as reading and writing, process skills such as critical thinking, and transferable skills such as persuasion and negotiation. An O*NET listing also includes information on worker requirements (required knowledge, for instance), occupation requirements (based on work activities such as compiling, coding, and categorizing data), and experience requirements (including education and job training). You can also check the job's labor market characteristics (such as employment projections and earnings data).

编写工作描述的注意事项包括：

（1）工作描述描述的是具体工作,而不是描述工作中的人。

（2）描述要具体,尽可能少使用模糊或抽象的术语。例如,对酒吧收银工作做出的工作描述,不可以要求为"有扎实的计算机知识,头脑清楚,反应灵敏",而应该叙述为"能够熟练使用 POS 机,能够在光线较暗的情况下借助验钞器准确鉴别伪钞"。

（3）技术性的术语要附加解释,如"POS"要备注为"Point Of Sells","电子收款机系统"。

(4)语句要简明扼要,避免将工作的每一个动作都进行过于详细的描述。

(5)工作描述作为一种人力资源管理的工具,目的是激励员工更好地致力于饭店工作,而不是作为惩罚的武器来约束员工的行为,因此,其内容中不应该有任何处罚措施。

为了便于深入理解工作描述书的含义和编写饭店各项工作的说明书,下面介绍三份比较标准的工作描述书。

Table 2-1　Job Discription 1

Food & Beverage Manager	
Job Title	Food and Beverage Manager
Place of Work	A hotel
Scope and General Purpose	To supervise and control all catering outlets in a hotel to the required standards, within agreed budgetary limits and parameters of the law, particularly liquor law.
Responsible to	General Manager
Responsible for	All restaurant, room service, banqueting, stores and back of the house staff (In some cases the Head Chef will also report to the Food and Beverage Manager).
Liaises with	Head Chef Housekeeper Front of House Manager Security Manager Personnel Manager Maintenance Manager Accountant
Limits of Authority	According to each establishment

Main Duties
- To ensure the prompt and efficient service of all meals, snacks, functions and beverages to the required standards.
- To ensure that profit margins are maintained, agreed costs are not exceeded through effective control systems, including issuing against dockets, sales analysis, menu costs and cash checks.
- To ensure that restaurants and cloakrooms are clean and well maintained, that table appointments, including flower arrangements are impeccable.
- To ensure that waiters are always correctly and smartly dressed, that they offer professional and courteous service to their customers.
- To ensure that bars and cloakrooms are clean and stocked with the stipulated requirements.

- To ensure that barmen are well trained, correctly and smartly dressed and serve their customers in a professional and friendly manner.
- To ensure that room service orders are executed promptly and that they comply with the required standards.
- To ensure that room service staffs are correctly and smartly dressed and serve their customers in a professional and friendly manner.
- To ensure the efficient running of the banqueting department and that all banqueting rooms, including cloakrooms, are clean and tidy.
- To act as Duty Manager as required.
- To ensure that consumable and non-consumable goods are ordered, correctly stored and issued to the various departments.
- To ensure maximum security in all areas under your control and that staff are fully aware of the importance of key security.
- To ensure that staffing levels are correct and to agreed standards and are not exceeded without prior consultation.
- To ensure that company and statutory hygiene standards are maintained in all areas.
- To attend timely to customer complaints.
- To take the necessary steps in the event of theft, burglary or fire.
- To ensure that reports and administration requirements are timely submitted.
- To ensure that the Back of the House Department operates effectively and efficiently.
- To hold regular performance appraisals with all management staff, identifying areas for development and training needs, and ensuring that this training is effected.
- To ensure that fair discipline is effected.
- To ensure that the causes of staff grievances are investigated and the appropriate actiontaken.
- To ensure that fire and evacuation drills are held regularly.
- To ensure that bands and musicians are available when required.
- To be fully conversant with all statutory requirements regarding a food and beverage operation, that all licenses, including special licences, are timely applied for and that the conditions affecting the issues of a liquor licence are not jeopardised.
- To ensure that regular stock takes are conducted.
- To prepare and submit on the required format all information necessary for budgeting purposes, timely and accurately.
- To ensure that an effective table reservation system is in operation.
- To circulate throughout all restaurants, bars and banqueting departments, maintaining a high profile with customers and staff.
- To hold regular staff meetings.
- To be fully aware of trends in the industry and make suggestions for improvement of the catering operation.
- To attend meetings as required.
- To carry out or ensure that regular On-the-Job Training is taking place to agreed standards.
- To ensure that the most suitably qualified person is appointed in the event of a vacancy—wherever possible this should be an internal promotion.

Table 2-2 Job Discription 2

_	Personnel & Training Manager
Job Title	Personnel and Training Manager
Place of Work	Regional or area office
Scope and General Purpose	To manage the Personnel and Training function within agreed budgetary limits so that the company and the individual can benefit through the employee's ability to attain optimum performance and growth.
Responsible to	General Manager
Responsible for	Assistant Personnel Manager (In some cases also salaries administration)
Liaises with	Senior Management Department Heads
Limits of Authority	Advice and service responsibilities, not usually line authority

Main Duties
- To ensure that Job Descriptions are up-to-date and accurately describe each position.
- To ensure that Job Evaluation categories are correct.
- To ensure cost effective recruitment through the use of the appropriate source.
- To ensure that the recruitment and selection of people is done objectively and based on Job Descriptions and Man Specifications.
- To ensure that managers are trained and have the ability to conduct effective interviews.
- To ensure that the company's succession plan is meaningful and effective.
- To ensure that meaningful appraisals for all staff are carried out on a regular basis.
- To ensure that the action and developmental plans agreed at the appraisals are acted and followed up.
- To ensure the Individual Career Plans are meaningful and agree with succession plan and are the result of an appraisal.
- To ensure that new or transferred employees have an effective induction programme with is adhered to.
- To ensure that the Training Programme provides for the training needs identified at appraisals.
- To ensure that the correct people are nominated or sent on the appropriate training courses.
- To ensure follow up of all training.
- To ensure that training is cost effective and is effected for real need and not for cosmetic reasons.
- To ensure that the company's objective for labour turnover is maintained or bettered.
- To analyze labour turnover statistics so that problem areas are highlighted and the appropriate action is taken.

- To ensure that the company's personnel procedures are strictly adhered to.
- To ensure that personnel files are properly maintained and kept under lock and key.
- To ensure that the company's grievance and disciplinary procedures are observed and that all relevant documentation is completed.
- To ensure that all statutory acts and proclamations are displayed in conspicuous places.
- To ensure that legislated remuneration packages are adhered to.
- To ensure that managers are acquainted with and are applying all latest industrial relations legislation.
- To ensure effective communication relating to any industrial or strike action, so that future or contingency planning can be effected.
- To ensure that line managers are fully aware of and responding to all statutory legislation affecting the catering industry.
- To be aware of the welfare needs of employees and be available for counselling.

表 2-3 工作描述 3

酒店销售部经理工作描述书
职位:销售部经理
部门:销售部
隶属:饭店总经理
1. 了解和掌握同行的业务状况,收集业务信息。向总经理提供报告,在建立可靠的商品销售的基础上,进行经济决策。充分了解和掌握市场信息,进行市场分析和预测。 2. 组织完成宾馆酒店的业务拓展和商品的销售活动,树立和提高酒店的声誉,使宾馆饭店商品有一个好的市场。 3. 负责业务洽谈及协议,合同的制定与草签;受理个人及单位的订房、订宴会、租会议场地等业务。 4. 组织和参与 VIP 客人的接待,并将他们的信息及时地转告给有关部门,向客人详细介绍宾馆饭店的情况,了解他们的实际需求,尽量给予满足。 5. 凡大型的活动,要向有关业务的单位和个人、客户、常客发贺电、贺年卡,或者可以邀请他们参加宾馆饭店组织的庆典或纪念活动。 6. 经常对长住客、机关团体、旅行社、宣传部门等进行拜访,密切保持与他们的联系,希望在业务上得到他们的支持。 7. 对待客人要热情友好,向他们介绍宾馆的情况时要认真细致,给客人最好的印象。 8. 抓住机会进行公关活动:如在酒会、宴会、茶话会、洽谈会、庆祝会等社交活动进行宣传。 9. 建立销售业务档案,以便进行查阅。 10. 负责对部门下属进行思想的沟通、交流和定期进行业务培训。

三、工作分析的用途(The Application of Job Analysis)

工作分析可以应用于以下几个方面：

1. 人力资源计划

在饭店经营活动中，新的工作不断产生，旧的工作需要重新设计。作为饭店管理者仅仅认识到一个饭店将需要 300 名员工来提供服务才能满足顾客的需求是绝对不够的，因为饭店的每一项工作都需要不同的知识、技术和能力，有效的人力资源计划必须考虑到承担这些工作的具体要求。

2. 招聘和选择

如果招聘者不知道胜任某项工作所必须的资格条件，那么员工的招聘工作将是漫无目的的。工作分析一方面为应聘者提供了真实、可靠的需求职位的工作职责、工作内容、工作要求和人员的资格要求；另一方面，也为招聘者提供了可观的选择依据，提高了选择的透明度和有效程度，降低了人力资源选择成本。

3. 人力资源开发

工作规范书所包括的信息在确定饭店人力资源开发需求方面常常是很有价值的。如果工作规范书指出某项服务工作需要特殊的知识、技术或能力，而在该职位上的员工又不具备所要求的条件，那么就意味着必须要对其进行培训，并且帮助他们为升迁到更高的工作职位做好准备。

4. 绩效考评

工作描述书使员工能够清楚地了解饭店对其工作的要求目标，同时也为绩效考评标准的简历和考评工作的实施提供了依据，从而减少了因绩效考评引起的员工不满。

5. 薪酬管理

工作分析明确了工作的价值，为工资的发放提供了可参考的标准，保证了薪酬的内部公平，减少了员工间的不公平感。在薪酬管理方面，用货币体现某项工作的价值之前，必须了解其对饭店的相对价值。一般来讲，工作的职责越大，工作就越有价值；要求有更多的知识、技术和能力的工作对饭店来说应该更具有价值。

6. 工作安全与员工健康

在考虑工作安全与员工健康问题时，来自工作分析的有关信息也很有价值。例如，饭店应该说明厨师在厨房工作时是存在着一定危险性的，这种危险性是可能会发生火灾，或者切割烹饪原料时可能会伤及自己，等等，在厨房工作岗位的说明书和工作规范书中应该反映出这一点。

7. 管理关系

通过对饭店工作的全面分析，可以清楚地了解各工作岗位是如何衔接，以及在工作中上级与下级之间的隶属关系是如何确立的。这可以为建立组织严谨、信息流畅的管理链提供保障；同时，还有利于提高工作效率。

8. 员工发展

员工通过学习、使用工作描述书和工作规范书可以清楚地了解自己工作的发展方向，便于根据自身的工作特长和兴趣制订自己的职业发展计划；同时，饭店也有责任知道员工尽可能地将自己的职业发展计划与饭店的经营战略规划自觉地结合起来，使员工能够真正地与饭店共同发展。

四、工作分析的时机(The Timing of the Job Analysis)

1. 新成立的饭店

对于新成立的饭店一定要进行工作分析，这样可以为后续的人力资源管理工作打下基础。饭店新成立时，工作分析最主要的用途是在员工招聘方面。

由于很多职位还是空缺，所以新饭店的工作分析应该结合饭店的组织结构、经营计划等信息来进行。首先完成一个粗略的工作分析，在这一阶段，工作分析的结果只要能够为招聘员工提供必要的"工作职责"和"任职资格"即可，更为详细的工作分析可以在饭店稳定运营一段时间之后进行。

2. 当新的工作产生时

随着饭店经营业务和服务项目的变化，饭店会不断出现新的工作岗位。例如，饭店成立了自己的出租车队，娱乐部增加了保龄球项目。这就意味着需要对新增加的"出租汽车司机"和"保龄球馆服务员"等岗位进行工作分析，以保证饭店工作分析的完整性和准确性。

3. 当工作由于新技术、新工艺或新系统的引入而发生重要变化时

新技术、新工艺或新系统的应用可能对工作内容产生重大影响，同样也会对承担工作的员工提出更高的要求。只有及时进行工作分析才能重新规范工作职责，确定新的任职资格和条件。

第二节 工作设计(Job Design)

经济学家亚当·斯密在其《国民财富的性质和原因的研究》一书中详细论述了专业化的重要性，并以制作扣针为例来说明其好处。他指出，通过分工相同数量的劳动者就能完成比过去更多的工作量，原因在于：第一，劳动者的技巧因专业而增进；第二，节省由一种工作到另一种工作所损失的时间；第三，许多简化和缩短劳动的机械的发明。这种专业化分工思想为科学管理运动做了铺垫。20世纪初，随

着科学管理的兴起,工作设计成为管理研究中关注的重点。

工作设计是为了有效地实现企业目标,合理地处理人与事的关系而采取的以满足个人需要为主的工作内容、工作职责和人际关系的设计。

工作设计与工作分析关系十分密切。工作分析的主要目的是对各项工作的任务、责任、性质及工作人员的条件予以分析研究。工作设计的主要目的是在全面权衡经济原则与社会原则的基础上,找到一个企业效率和个人行为的最佳结合点,工作设计可以明确说明此时工作如何做,如何使工作者在工作中得到满足,从而既有助于发挥个人的能力、提高工作效率,又能保住每个人心情舒畅地工作,进而顺利完成企业的总任务。

为了使工作能充分满足饭店企业的各种需要,可以从以下几方面入手进行改造。

一、工作轮换与工作扩大化(Job Rotation and Job Enlargement)

由于高度的工作专业化,使每位员工所担负的工作简单枯燥,从而极易产生厌烦和不满情绪,以及缺勤和离职等消极对抗的行为,在20世纪40~60年代,企业管理当局为了解决员工对高度专业化的不满情绪,采用了工作轮换和工作扩大化的方法。

工作轮换一般用于减少员工长期重复一种工作的枯燥感。如厨师在做了一段切生菜、胡萝卜、西红柿的工作后,可以调到另一个厨房做些其他工作。这种制度要求雇员在几个不同工种之间交叉培训。

工作扩大化是扩大工作的界定,把各种任务加到一起,一般是把要求相同技能的任务合并起来,这种方法有时也被称为"横向工作扩张"。例如切胡萝卜和西红柿的工作可以和切生菜做沙拉的工作合起来。工作扩大化可以激励员工把新增的任务当成职业晋升的前兆。

二、工作丰富化(Job Enrichment)

工作丰富化的理论基础是赫茨伯格的双因素理论。这一理论认为,在工作中缺乏保健因素时,员工就会对工作产生不满情绪,当保健因素增强时,员工的不满情绪虽然会消除,但并不会产生对员工的激励,当涉及工作内容本身的激励因素(包括工作的挑战性、自主性、责任、成就等)增强时,就会提高对员工的激励水平,获得较高的工作绩效。

工作丰富化是指对工作内容作纵向扩展。强调通过提高工作的挑战性、自主性和责任来发展工作的深度,增加员工对工作计划、执行和评估的控制程度,是一种以员工为中心的设计方法。

工作丰富化是指在工作中赋予员工更多的责任、自主权和控制权。工作丰富化与工作扩大化、工作轮调都不同，它不是水平地增加员工工作的内容，而是垂直地增加工作内容。这样，员工会承担更多重的任务、更大的责任，员工将有更大的自主权和更高程度的自我管理，还有对工作绩效的反馈。工作特征模型是工作丰富化的核心。工作特征模型是由哈佛大学教授理查德·哈克曼(Richard Hackman)和伊利诺伊大学教授格里格·奥尔德汉姆(Greg Oldham)提出的。工作特征模型提供了职务设计的一种理论框架。它确定了五种主要的职务特征，分析了它们之间的关系以及对员工生产率、工作动力和满足感的影响。根据工作特征模型，工作可以从五个核心维度进行描述，它们分别是：

（1）技能的多样性：也就是完成一项工作涉及的范围，包括各种技能和能力。

（2）任务的一致性：即在多大程度上工作需要作为一个整体来完成——从工作的开始到完成并取得明显的成果。

（3）任务的重要性：即自己的工作在多大程度上影响其他人的工作或生活——不论是在组织内还是在工作环境外。

（4）自主性：即工作在多大程度上允许自由、独立，以及在具体工作中个人制订计划和执行计划时的自主范围。

（5）反馈性：即员工能及时明确地知道他(她)所从事的工作的绩效及其效率。

在这五个维度中，技能多样性、任务一致性、任务重要性表示工作的意义，自主性表示员工个人对任务结果担负的责任，反馈性表示员工能够知道工作结果。研究指出，如果工作丰富化的程序实用性强、有教育意义，便能够为员工和组织带来有意义的改变，增强员工对组织的承诺。

工作特征模型表明，核心工作的特性会导致三种关键心理状态(体验到工作意义、体验到对工作成果的责任、对工作活动实际成果的了解)，进而这些心理状态引起许多积极的成果。员工体会到了对工作的积极感受，从而了解到了他们已经很好地完成了他们非常关心的工作任务。如果这三种心理状态都存在，就激发了以自我激励为基础的激励循环。工作如果没有意义，或是责任感反馈不完，就不能充分激发人的积极性。

哈克曼和奥尔德汉姆设计出一种测定工具，称之为工作诊断调查。这种方法可以用来测定每一种工作的特性，也可以用来测定每一种心理状态，还可以用来测定员工是如何受工作结构影响的，以及员工对工作的反应程度。工作诊断调查的结果有两种用途：一是对现有的工作进行诊断，决定是否需要重新设计工作，怎样设计；二是评价工作变化对员工的影响。

为了增强核心工作特性对三种心理状态的影响效果，哈克曼和奥尔德汉姆制订了五个"实施方案"：第一，形成自然工作单位——划分基本的工作项目并将其自然组合,使其具有工作的整体性和重要性;第二,归并任务——组成较大的工作单位,使工作具有技能多样性和整体性;第三,与用户建立联系——确定谁是用户,与其建立最直接的联系,并明确用户鉴定产品或服务质量的标准,使工作具有技能多样性、自主性和反馈性;第四,纵向分配工作——缩短计划、实施和控制工作三个过程之间的距离,使工作具有自主性;第五,开通反馈渠道——通过与用户建立联系,对员工工作进行质量控制并对员工的工作情况进行总结,使工作具有反馈性。

工作特性模型及其实施方案充分考虑到了饭店员工个人之间的差异,有针对性地采取了工作多样性、自主性、同一性和反馈性等特征的再设计,集中于改革工作本身的内容,改变了工作中操作性内容和控制性内容的比例,使员工有了更大的工作自主权和控制权,同时也使饭店管理层的控制权垂直地向下转移给操作层,大大减轻了饭店管理层的工作负担,从而使饭店员工获得了强大的内激力,使得员工获得了精神上的满足,在饭店精神的建设中起到了积极的推动作用。同时,在饭店管理研究中,工作丰富化和工作再设计计划能有效增强饭店员工满意度,并能减少员工的旷工和离职。因此,有必要研究饭店员工的工作特征,这些特征如何与工作态度和组织承诺相联系,以及如何改进工作的设计。

三、工作简化(Job Simplification)

当工作人员的素质或精力难以适应复杂的工作时,就应通过提高专业化、标准化、通俗化来使职务简化。其具体做法是:详细分解工作内容,排除不必要的作业程序,重新设计人人懂得、人人安心的工作程序,以制订可行的作业计划。

饭店工作简化的目的在于采用最为经济或较为经济的工作方法。工作简化主要强调取消既不增加产值又无利于工作开展的多余的工作步骤或环节,从而达到提高工作效率的目的。

饭店工作简化可能会引起操作程序和设备的改变,必然会给员工带来一定的不适应,会要求员工改变原来的工作习惯,可能会使员工产生抵制情绪,但饭店管理人员必须采取解释、疏导等方法加以解决。因为工作简化有许多优点,可以缓解员工的疲劳、改善工作环境、提高服务质量、减少饭店餐厅无规律就餐和客房入住低谷时的人力浪费。此外,由于劳动生产率提高了,员工还可以得到更高的报酬。

工作简化过程是极其复杂的,一般要进行工作程序研究、人机配合研究等工作。这些研究对于规模较大的饭店极有价值,但饭店业对这些研究的应用却是有限的。只有对饭店服务过程中的这些细节做好分析,才能分辨出哪个部分的工作对整个服务过程是真正有用的,哪个部分是徒劳的,在重新设计服务工作程序时,就会有的放矢,对症下药。一般来说,工作简化可以按照如下步骤实施:

(1)确定将要改进的部门和工作。

(2)分析目前所采用的工作方法,包括工作所需时间、所用设备、移动距离、操作规程以及员工服务技能等。

(3)对现有工作提出问题,并采用"五点计划清单"(何时、何地、何人、为何、如何)进行分析,查找问题的原因。

(4)设计多种改进方案。

(5)选择"最佳"改进方案。

(6)优化已选定的方案。

(7)解释和实施新方案。

饭店工作简化除了服务程序的简化之外,服务动作的简化也至关重要,它不仅可以提高效率,还可以减少疲劳。一般说来,动作简化要坚持以下规则:

(1)双手同时开始、同时完成某个动作。

(2)双手反方向对称运动。

(3)曲线动作而不作直线动作。

(4)使用人体最小肢体进行工作。

(5)可用脚操作的就不用手,手可进行别的工作。

(6)物件能够随手可取。

(7)利用地心引力。

(8)工具和用品应固定存放处。

(9)使用两用工具。

(10)货架面向员工30°角时取物最为方便快捷。

案例分析(Practice Case Analysis)

As an experienced HR director, the Hotel Paris's Lisa Cruz knew that recruitment and selection processes invariably influenced employee competencies and behavior and, through them, the company's bottom line. Everything about the workforce—its collective skills, morale, experience, and motivation—depended on attracting and then selecting the right employees. In reviewing the Hotel Paris's employment systems, she was therefore concerned to find that virtually all the company's job descriptions were out of date, and that many jobs had no descriptions at all. She knew that without accurate job descriptions, all her HR improvement efforts would be in vain. After all, if you don't know a job's duties, responsibilities, and human requirements, how can you decide whom to hire or how to train them? To create HR policies and practices that would produce employee competencies and behaviors needed to achieve the hotel's strategic aims, Lisa's team first had to produce a set of usable job descriptions.

The Hotel Paris's competitive strategy is "To use superior guest service to differentiate the Hotel Paris properties, and to thereby increase the length of stay and return rate of guests, and thus boost revenues and profitability". HR manager Lisa Cruz must now formulate functional policies and activities that support this competitive strategy, by eliciting the required employee behaviors and competencies.

A preliminary analysis, performed jointly by Lisa and the Hotel Paris's chief financial officer, left the optimistic that HR could contribute measurably to achieving the hotel's strategic aims. Several employee competencies and behaviors including employee morale, employee commitment, and the percent of arriving guests receiving the hotel's required greeting had significant effects on customer and organizational outcomes such as guest satisfaction and frequency of guest returns. In turn, outcomes like these contributed measurably to the Hotel Paris's strategic goals, including profit margins, market share, and scores on industry satisfaction surveys. Lisa and her team now turn to creating a job analysis process that will help to produce the required employee competencies and behaviors.

A brief analysis, conducted with her company's CEO, reinforced that observation. They chose departments across the hotel chain that did and did not have updated job descriptions. While they understood that many other factors might be influencing the results, they believed that the statistical relationships they observed did suggest that having job descriptions had a positive influence on various employee behaviors and competencies. Perhaps having the descriptions facilitated the employee selection process, or perhaps the departments with the descriptions just had better managers. In any case, Lisa received the go-ahead to design new job descriptions for the chain.

While the resulting job descriptions included numerous traditional duties and responsibilities, most also included several competencies unique to each job. For example, job descriptions for the front-desk clerks included competencies such as "able to check a guest in or out in five minutes or less". Most service employees' descriptions included the competency, "able to exhibit patience and guest supportiveness even when busy with other activities". Lisa knew that including these competencies would make it easier for her team to devise useful employee selection, training, and evaluation processes.

来源：加里·德斯勒. Human Resource Management (Tenth Edition). 北京：清华大学出版社.

Questions for Discussion:

1. How important is job description according to Lisa Cruz?
2. What progress did Lisa made in her property?

名词解释 (Key Terms)

1. 工作分析：指确定工作的职责以及对该职位的被聘用者的能力要求。

Job Analysis: The procedure for determining the duties and skill requirements of a job and the kind of person who should be hired for it.

2. 工作描述：一个工作的职责、责任、报告关系、工作条件，并监督责任的清单——工作分析的一个产品。

Job Description: A list of a job's duties, responsibilities, reporting relationships, working conditions, and supervisory responsibilities, one product of a job analysis.

3. 工作规范：包含在工作操作中所需要的技巧与个人特质的个人规范，以及该项工作所需涉及的特殊工作环境。

Job Specification: The person specifications that list the skills and personality traits needed to perform a job and outline particular working conditions that will be encountered on the job.

4. 工作扩大化：分配额外的工人同级别的活动，从而提高他们执行活动的数量。

Job Enlargement: Assigning workers additional same level activities, thus increasing the number of activities they perform.

5. 工作轮换：系统地将工作人员从一个工作移动到另一个工作，提升团队绩效和/或扩大他或她的经验，找出长处和短处，使人在公司发挥更大的作用。

Job Rotation: Systematically moving workers from one job to another to enhance work team performance and/or to broaden his or her experience and identify strong and weak points to prepare the person for an enhanced role with the company.

6. 工作丰富化：重新设计工作的方式，增加工人体验责任、成就、成长和认同感的机会。

Job Enrichment: Redesigning jobs in a way that increases the opportunities for the worker to experience feelings of responsibility, achievement, growth, and recognition.

复习思考题(Questions for Review)

1. 工作分析包含什么要素？

What aspects are included in job analysis?

2. 工作描述的具体内容包含什么？

What are the components of job description?

3. 工作分析在饭店人力资源管理中的用途有哪些？

What are the applications of job analysis in hotel human resource management?

4. 简述工作设计包含的内容。

Describe the contents of job design.

5. 饭店应如何应用工作特性模型对员工进行工作丰富化？

How can hotel managers use job characteristic model to design job enrichment program?

研究前沿(Research Front)

Not what it was and not what it will be:
The future of job design research

This summary commentary explores the likely future directions of research and theory on the design of organizational work. The researchers give special attention to the social aspects of contemporary work, the process by which job holders craft their own jobs, the changing contexts within which work is performed, and the increasing prominence of work that is performed by teams rather than individuals.

Our approach built upon the pioneering research on job characteristics carried out by Turner and Lawrence (1965). We eventually settled on five "core" job characteristics: Skill variety (i.e., the degree to which the job requires a variety of different activities in carrying out the work, involving the use of a number of different skills and talents of the person), task identity (i.e., the degree to which the job requires doing a whole and identifiable piece of work from beginning to end), task significance (i.e., the degree to which the job has a substantial impact on the lives of other people, whether those people are in the immediate organization or the world at large), autonomy (i. e., the degree to which the job provides substantial freedom, independence, and discretion to the individual in scheduling the work and in determining the procedures to be used in carrying it out), and job-based feedback (i. e., the degree to which carrying out the work activities required by the job provides the individual with direct and clear information about the effectiveness of his or her performance).

At the time, it made sense to focus on the job itself, since jobs were what people did at work and therefore surely also should be the core concept in research on work motivation, satisfaction, and productivity. But there have been some interesting developments in organizational life over the last few decades. As is seen in the papers in this issue, and as will be discussed in the remainder of this commentary, the world of work is now different than it was then, perhaps fundamentally so. Because it is different in ways that neither we nor others who were involved in work design research anticipated, it offers opportunities for some new directions in research and theory on work design—directions that may generate enriched understanding of human and organizational behavior and, perhaps, suggest some nontraditional strategies for the design and leadership of work organizations.

The Phenomenon Has Changed...

It is not a matter of theories coming and going, or of newly developed methodologies supplanting old ones. It is, instead, that the very thing job design researchers study is being transformed. And what has happened thus far, we believe, is but a harbinger of even more profound changes that are likely to be seen in the years to come. A number of papers in this specialissue highlight some of the changes presently unfolding in the world of work, which gives us hope that the field of job design may be on the cusp of a new paradigm for research on the relationship between people and the work they do.

...But the Issues Have Not

We have come a long way since the 1970s when both researchers and practitioners were concerned mainly with identifying ways to assess and improve the properties of fixed jobs performed by individual workers. The issues that will be addressed in the future are just as challenging. But they will focus lesson rank-and-file work and more on that done by managers and professionals. They will be less concerned with the properties of specific jobs and more with ways of exploiting technological advances to help self-managing individuals and teams efficiently coordinate what they do in pursuit of collective purposes. And, as will be discussed next, they will give special attention to the interpersonal aspects of the work.

Social Sources of Motivation

As several of the commentaries in this issue suggest, there are good reasons to expect the social dimensions of the work to contribute to the motivation, performance and well-being of jobholders. These dimensions, therefore, deserve greater attention from scholars than they have received heretofore. Yet a number of questions still exist about their role. What are the social dimensions of jobs that are most likely to enhance work motivation? What theoretical frameworks are most useful in guiding research on the social aspects of work? And what individual differences, if any, moderate the relationship between the social characteristics of jobs and the responses of job holders? We offer some thoughts about these matters next.

Social attributes of jobs

Recent work by Morgeson and Humphrey (2006) suggests additional social dimensions that may contribute to employee motivation and well-being—specifically, interaction outside the organization, social support, initiated interdependence and received interdependence. These dimensions, as well as other socially relevant aspects of the work still to be identified, clearly are worthy of empirical investigation.

Conceptual issues

If future work on job design focuses on outcomes such as altruism or the acquisition of knowledge and skill, the social dimensions of work are likely to take on the status of core characteristics and, perhaps, give rise to an entirely new theoretical perspective that is distinct from that offered by JCT and other existing frameworks (e. g. , Campion&Thayer, 1985; Parker, Wall&Cordery, 2001). Once such frameworks have been developed, job design researchers with have a chance to explore systematically how the social dimensions of work contribute to personal and work outcomes, and to contrast these effects with those from studies that have focused mainly on the motivational properties of jobs.

Individual differences

Research is needed to further specify the interactions between the social aspects of jobs and jobholder personality for other kinds of responses, such as altruistic behavior, as well as studies that explore the moderating effects of individual differences other than those specified in the Big Five model. One inviting possibility is social need strength (i. e. , the degree to which an individual values opportunities for social interaction and for developing personal relationships at work), which was examined in an unpublished study by Milton Blood many years ago. Although that study did not find social need strength to moderate responses to those social dimensions of work assessed by the JDS, research that addresses other social aspects of jobs and, perhaps, that relies on alternative measures of social need strength, might well generate findings that would be of considerable conceptual and practical interest.

Work Design for Teams

"Surgical" teams

In these teams, responsibility and accountability for outcomes lies primarily with one person (the "surgeon"), but accomplishing that work requires coordinated interaction among all members in real time. Members of surgical-type teams provide the lead member, the person mainly responsible for teamproduct, all the information and assistance that they can provide. This kind of team is appropriate for work that requires a high level of individual insight, expertise, and/or creativity but that is too large or complex to be handled by any one member working alone.

Coacting groups

Individual members also are primarily responsible for outcomes in this type of team. Each member's work does not depend upon what the others do, and the output of the group is simply the aggregation of members' individual contributions. Because members work independently there is no particular reason for them to coordinate their activities in real time. A great deal of organizational work is performed by sets of people who are called "teams" but that really are coacting groups—formed, perhaps, by managers who hope that the benefits of teamwork can be obtained even as they continue to directly supervise the work of individual members. Coacting groups are appropriate only when there is little need for interdependent work by group members.

Face-to-face teams

In these teams, members are co-located and work together interdependently in real time to generate a product for which they are collectively accountable. Most existing research on team behavior and performance is about this type of team. They are appropriate for a wide variety of tasks for which creating a high-quality product requires coordinated contributions in real time from a diversity of members who have complementary expertise, experience, and perspectives.

Conclusion

The next decade, we believe, will be an exciting time for research about people doing work in organizational settings. What comes next certainly will be informed by all the research that has been done over the last few decades. But its specific features will have little in common with the studies we and others carried out back in the early days of research on the attributes of specific jobs. The reason, as is seen in this issue (and especially in the commentaries), is that the design of work is now inextricably bound up with the structures and processes of organizational systems more generally. That is, rather than specific jobs it is the often-fluid relationships among people and their various work activities that are most in need of empirical research and conceptual attention. Work design is everywhere in organizations, which attests to the importance of the topic—but which also requires fresh thinking about the phenomenon and about the most productive ways to continue to learn about it.

Source: Oldham G & Hackham J. Not what it was and not what it will be: The future of job design research. Journal of Organizational Behavior, 2010, 31: 463 – 479.

第3章 沟通与团队合作
(Communication and Teamwork)

本章概要(Summary of This Chapter)

沟通的行为和过程在饭店团队建设中相当重要。有效沟通是一种技能,是一个人对其知识能力、表达能力、行为能力的发挥,是饭店各项工作顺利进行的前提。无论是饭店管理者还是普通的员工,都是饭店竞争力的核心要素。世界上所有的管理工作都是借助于沟通才得以顺利进行,沟通是实施各项管理职能的主要方式、方法、手段和途径。沟通不仅存在于横向的饭店管理活动的全部过程,而且更存在于纵向的饭店管理活动的各个层次。本章首先介绍了沟通的定义与过程、沟通方式的分类以及在饭店经营管理中如何有效进行沟通。其次,强调了组建有效型饭店团队的重要意义,饭店团队建设中面临的困难和高效团队的形成方式。

Communication behavior and team building process is fairly important in hospitality. Effective communication is a skill. It is an application of one's knowledge, expression ability and behavior ability, and it is also the preconditon of running each work smoothly in hotel. Both managers and ordinary employees are key elements to the hotel's competitiveness. Running smoothly of corperations all over the world are by means of communication. Communication is the primarily forms, methods, means and ways in the implementation of various management functions. Communication exists not only in the horizontal management activities of the whole process, but also exists in the vertical management activities at all levels. This chapter first describes the definition and process of communication, the classification of communication and how to effectively communicate during hotel operation process. In addition to this, we emphasizes importance of building an effective hotel team, hotel team building difficulties and ways to form an effective team.

开篇引例(Beginning Story)

Training in communication skills that are specific to careers in the hotel industry is available throughout the United States from a variety of colleges, universities and online courses. Education in hotel communication skills is often part of broader hospitality, hotel management, or travel and tourism degree programs. These programs teach students the nature of the hotel industry in regard to industry business models, financing, operations, marketing strategies and customer service skills. Hospitality degrees often include many study aboard opportunities at locations where the tourism industry thrives.[①]

Readmore: How to Train in Communications for Hotels | eHow.com

第一节 沟通(Communication)

沟通是饭店管理的重要职能之一，良好的管理沟通不仅能提高管理者决策效率，还能有效增强员工满意度和责任感，促进饭店良好企业文化氛围的形成，提高饭店市场竞争力。

一、沟通的基本性质(The Basic Character of Communication)

(一)沟通的含义和过程(The Meaning and Process of Communication)

1. 沟通的含义

所谓沟通，是发送者与接收者之间的信息交换，以及双方对意义的推断和感知。著名组织管理学家巴纳德认为："沟通是把一个组织中的成员联系在一起，以实现共同目标的手段。"

2. 沟通的过程

许多饭店管理者认为沟通只是"讲清事实"，其实没有意识到这一简单问题中的复杂内容。当沟通不起作用时则会常常引起抱怨，而不是共同努力找出究竟出了什么问题。为了真正理解饭店管理者在沟通中扮演的角色，应该首先明白沟通的基本过程。沟通在发生之前，必须存在一个"要被传递的信息"，在信息发送者和信息接收者之间传送。信息先被编码转化为信号形式，然后通过信息通道传送给接收者，由接收者将收到的信号解码。这样就完成了一次信息传递。

---

① http://www.ehow.com/how_7820571_train-communications-hotels.html#ixzz1xlzcxOEM

沟通过程包括七个部分：

(1) 信息源

信息源是信息发送者，可以是希望或试图与特定接收者沟通的个人、群体或组织。

(2) 编码

沟通始于信息源编码信息、想法或思想，编码是把内心想法转换成为他人能理解的语言或代码。通常使用文字、数字、非语言信号等进行编码。而被编码的信息受到4个条件的影响：技能、态度、知识和社会一体化系统。

(3) 信息

事实上是经过信息源编码的产物。信息受到3个因素的影响：用于传递意义的编码或信号群、信息本身的内容以及我们对编码和内容的选择与安排。

(4) 信息通道

指传送信息的媒介物。管理者可以通过多种媒介进行沟通。例如：面对面沟通、会议、电话、视频会议、电子邮件、语音信箱、备忘录、照片或图片以及图表等。很多因素影响信息通道的选择，包括信息特性、受众类型、信息意图、传播时区、个人偏好。在沟通中，信息源需要确定哪种信息通道是正式的。正式信息通道由组织建立，它传递的是与工作相关的活动信息，并遵循着组织的权力网络；而个人或社会信息，在组织中通过非正式通道传递。

(5) 解码

解码是信息接收者对编码信息的翻译，将信息的文字、口头或视觉方面的内容翻译成能被理解的形式。接收者解码同样受到自己的技能、态度、知识和社会一体化系统的限制。在跨种族和跨文化的沟通中，解码是产生误解的主要因素。

(6) 接收者

信息接收者可以是个人、群体或组织。饭店管理者每天都扮演着信息发送人和接收人的双重角色。

(7) 信息反馈

一旦信息被解码，这个过程会延续，新的信息会传回给原发送者。这个过程称为反馈，即关于信息对接收者的影响的知识。反馈是对信息的传送是否成功以及传送的信息是否符合原本意图进行核实，它可以确定信息是否被理解了。

(二) 沟通的功能(The Function of Communication)

沟通不仅仅是分享信息，还具有以下七种功能：

1. 指导行动

饭店管理者通过沟通促使下属按照其所希望的方式行动。与下属沟通的过程中，指导他们应该怎么做，并对他们的工作表现作出反馈。

2. 建立关系

建立友谊、促进信任需要进行谨慎沟通,这对人际关系的发展极为重要,并且也有助于在饭店内部建立一种和谐的氛围。

3. 解释组织文化

通过与饭店管理者和其他员工的沟通,员工可以认识饭店是如何运作的,饭店的发展目标是什么,整个饭店的愿景和企业文化是什么。

4. 建立组织间的联系

员工不仅在饭店内部进行沟通,而且要与其他饭店的代表进行沟通。这使得饭店间携手合作,为实现共同目标而协调工作。

5. 展示组织的形象

饭店把关于自己的信息发送给广泛的人群,向外界宣传饭店的整体形象。

6. 产生创意

沟通可以用来激发灵感并在必要时与他人分享。

7. 提升理想和价值观

饭店方要表明自己的立场和目的,就要向他人传递并沟通。

二、沟通的基本原理(The Fundamental Tenets of Communication)

(一)饭店内的沟通方式(Ways of Communication in Hotel)

1. 正式沟通

饭店内的沟通以正式沟通为主,正式沟通按信息的流向可以分为上行沟通、下行沟通和平行沟通。

(1)上行沟通

是指在饭店内部,信息从较低层次流向较高层级,从下级流向上级。员工利用它对上级管理层提供反馈,汇报工作进度,并告知当前存在的问题。上行沟通中涉及的信息包括改进建议、进度报告、对工作问题的看法,以及新点子,例如将饭店组织目标、计划、方针、措施等传达到基层,发布任免事项,对一些具体问题提出处理意见。

上行沟通有两种表现形式,一是层层传递,即依据一定的饭店组织原则和组织程序逐级向上反映,例如基层的情况通报就是从基层部门开始,逐级反映到上级部门;二是越级反映,即减少中间层次,让决策者和基层员工直接对话。

上行沟通并不仅仅是下行沟通的反向,沟通双方地位的差别使上行沟通与下行沟通存在一定的差异。上行沟通不如下行沟通频繁,上行沟通通常也不准确。注意到类似的问题是很重要的,为了避免有限的上行沟通出现问题,很多饭店采用了一些大规模的沟通程序,根据这些程序,员工可以通过完成工作调查来将信息传递给饭店的高层领导。

(2) 下行沟通

在饭店内部,将信息从一个水平向另一个更低水平进行的沟通称为自上而下的沟通,包含指令、指导和要求——告知下属应该做什么。

在进行下行沟通的过程中,除了管理者给下属分配目标,告知政策,还应该适当考虑对下属工作的反馈,以及他们在接受沟通时渴望听取什么。员工感兴趣的六个关键领域是:

①我的工作到底能带来什么?
②我现在做得怎么样?
③有人关注我吗?
④我工作的部门做得怎么样?
⑤饭店正在朝哪个方向发展?
⑥我怎么做才能帮助饭店实现目标?

(3) 平行沟通

是指信息在饭店同一层级的不同人员之间传播,多以协调为特征。在饭店管理中,平行沟通又可具体地划分三种类型:一是高层管理员之间的信息沟通;二是饭店内各部门之间的信息沟通与中层管理人员之间的信息沟通;三是一般员工在工作和思想上的信息沟通。平行沟通既可采取正式沟通的形式,例如饭店内部的调度会、联席会议等;也可以采取非正式沟通的形式。通常是后一种方式居多,尤其是在正式的或事先拟订的信息沟通计划难以实现时,非正式沟通往往是一种极为有效的补救方式。

在存在垂直沟通体系的情况下,平行沟通有着自己独特的优势。因为平行沟通涉及的都是处于饭店同一层级的人,与处于不同层次的上行沟通或下行沟通相比,沟通更加友好。同级之间的沟通通常更加随意,进行得也更迅速。但当饭店不同部门之间为了饭店有价值的资源而竞争时,友好、合作的氛围会变为充满敌对而竞争的氛围。

2. 非正式沟通

在群体内部和群体之间,正式沟通并不是唯一的沟通系统。人与人之间的密切而复杂的联系构成了非正式沟通网络,这种沟通形式在饭店内部也很普遍。

(1) 熟人网络

人们倾向于与自己在年龄、性别、工作时间等主要可变因素上相似的人进行沟通。这是因为跟与自己不相似的人沟通相比,同相似的人进行沟通让我们感觉更加自在,相对的沟通成本比较小。这种沟通形式的局限性体现在在某种程度上将员工与他们权利不一样的其他人隔离开来,使整体沟通受到了严重的限制。

(2) 雪球效应

饭店员工的离职率是与人与人之间的非正式沟通模式息息相关的,这是一种雪球效应。雪球不是随意积累雪花的,而是聚集所经过的路途上的雪花。同样,自愿离职模式不是独立地分布在一个工作组中,而是人们相互间影响的结果。员工离职后在另一个饭店找到了一份更好的工作,那么这位员工很有可能知道谁之前离职后也在这家饭店找到了一份更好的工作。

(3) 小道消息

当员工之间相互传递某件非正式的事情时,消息就会以人们通常说的小道消息的形式——沿着非官方、非正式消息的传播途径——迅速流传。小道消息的术语为"葡萄藤",最初得名于美国南北战争时期在战区的树上挂军用电报线,如今表示的是非正式组织的非官方沟通体系。小道消息具有 3 个特点。首先,它不受管理层控制;其次,大多数员工认为它比高级管理层通过正式沟通渠道解决问题更可信、更可靠、更迅速;再次,它在很大程度上有利于人们的自身利益。

沿非正式途径传播的信息往往传播得更快,通常只需要几个小时,一方面是因为非正式沟通能够跨越正式的组织界限,另一方面非正式消息通常采用口头沟通的形式。对于口头消息来说,它比书面消息传播得更快,但是在人们口口相传的过程中,信息的准确性在不断降低。虽然非正式的传播途径可能会引起混乱,但是不能忽视非正式沟通的优点,即员工之间的非正式的交往有利于增强团队的凝聚力,也可提供良好的与他人接触的机会,进而创建和谐的工作氛围。

3. 言语沟通

在沟通中使用文字传送和接受信息,称为言语沟通。如今使用的不同沟通媒介,员工之间面对面聊天,接听顾客打来的电话,查询自己的电子邮件和备忘录等,都是在使用言语的沟通,这可以是口头形式或书面形式。

饭店一般的管理人员同别人交谈或听取别人意见的时间,大概占其工作时间的 50%~70%。这一数据显示,管理人员在工作交流时比较喜欢用言语沟通的方式来收集和传递信息。言语沟通的应用范围十分广泛,交谈、演讲、劝说、服务都离不开这个基本的语言符号系统。为了增强信息传递的效果,提高工作效率,需要掌握有效的口头沟通的技巧。

在言语沟通中,存在多种沟通媒介:传单、公报、电邮、信函、电话、视频会议、面对面交谈。在沟通中,为了达到沟通有效性的目的,需要应用多渠道的沟通。口头沟通相对于书面沟通更能引起员工的注意,但是在保存的时间长度上没有很大的优势;口头沟通能够提供多方即时的双向沟通,而书面沟通只是单向的,缺乏信息接收方的回应。

表 3-1 沟通媒介使用指南

媒介	最佳用途	使用规则
电子邮件	发送关键性信息,确认并记录事实和职务安排。	信息简明扼要。 文字永远会保留,因此不要使用讽刺或侮辱性言辞。 不要忽视常规性语法规则。
传真	所有需要签字的文件、需要批准的草案或简札可传真给无法接收电子邮件的沟通对象。	提前打电话告知对方即将发传真。 跟进传真结果,向收件人打电话或发送电子邮件确认是否收到。 避免向对方发送个人的私密信息。
信件	长篇和复杂的材料或简短的感谢信可采用邮寄形式。	检查拼写和语法。 开头总结关键点。
电话	如果无法面对面讨论,但需要在沟通信息时传达自己的情感,可打电话。	突出重点,避免出现错误。 重要的电话要预约,确定具体日期。 在说话前听对方把话说完。
面对面交谈	在沟通高度敏感的话题和信息时采用。	简明扼要,重点突出。 确保私人谈话未被他人窃听。 为会议做好计划并准备讨论相关话题。

资料来源:[美]格林伯格,[美]巴伦著.组织行为学.北京:中国人民大学出版社,2011.06.

4. 非言语沟通

是通过行为来编码意义的过程,这些行为包括面部表情、肢体动作和身体姿态,等等。沟通专家估计:每次沟通中约有 65%~90% 的内容是由非言语沟通阐释的。因此,在沟通过程中,确保非言语信号与要表达的语言讯息相一致非常重要。

(1)面部表情

面部表情表达了一种普遍性的情感认知,能传递丰富的信息。微笑代表友善、快乐和温暖,皱眉则表示不满与生气。相关研究的总结显示:面部表情和情感的关系因文化不同而变化。例如,微笑在不同国家传递的情感也不同。因此,管理者在多元化的员工群体中诠释面部表情的意义时要小心。

(2)肢体动作

肢体的移动和姿势提供了促进或损害沟通过程的额外非语言信息。适当使用手势能够增进听众对信息的实际理解。开放的身体姿态如前倾等传达了沟通的直接性,直接性表示开通、热情、亲密和愿意沟通。双臂交叉、双手交叉或者双腿交叉等姿势传达了防御性。在诠释肢体移动和姿势时,管理者要注意,肢体语言的分析会很主观,容易被错误理解,并且高度依赖于所处的情境和跨文化差异。因此,在解释肢体动作时,管理者一定要谨慎,防止不准确的理解给沟通带来额外的障碍。

(3) 身体接触

身体接触是另一个强大的非言语信号。人们愿意触摸他们喜欢的人。世界各地对身体接触的规范不同,管理者应该对这一非言语沟通差异有适当的了解。

(4) 目光交流

目光交流在沟通中的功能有四种:第一,目光交流通过传递会话的开始和结束的信号来控制会话流程。当人们开始讲话时往往环顾四周,而讲完话时会看着听众。第二,注视能促进并控制反馈,因为它反映出兴趣和关注。第三,目光交流能表达感情。人们在讨论负面消息或提供负面反馈时,会避免目光交流。第四,注视与沟通者之间关系的类型有关。

(二)饭店内的沟通渠道(Communication Channels in Hotel)

1. 链式

它是指信息在几个层次中逐级传递,只有上行沟通和下行沟通,居于两端的成员只能与其相邻的一个成员联系,而居中的成员则可以分别与两端的成员沟通信息。

现在多数饭店组织采取的是链式的沟通渠道。根据饭店的等级制度和指挥链原则,要求饭店管理者在发布指令时,不论要通过多少层次,都应该是发布命令者向直属的下级层次发布指令,一级扣一级而不能越级指挥。同时下级也不能越级上行沟通,使管理者不能及时迅速地获得基层真实情报信息,失去信息沟通的及时性和有效性。而信息经过的层次越多,失真的可能性越大。

2. 星式(轮式)

这种沟通渠道的形式是一个管理者与多个饭店员工进行沟通,但多个下级之间不相互沟通。它的优点是集中化程度高,解决问题的速度快,中心人员的预测程度高。缺点是沟通的渠道少,组织成员的满意度低,员工士气低。

3. 圆圈式

它是多人之间的沟通,管理者对几个下级进行沟通,而这几个下级再分别与各自的下级进行沟通,基层再相互进行沟通。其中,每个成员都同时与两侧的成员沟通。在这种方式中,组织的集中化和预测程度都较低,畅通渠道不多,组织中成员具有较为满意的情绪,员工士气比较高。

4. Y式

这是在多个层次的逐级沟通过程中,两位领导通过一个人或一个部门进行沟通,这个人成为沟通的中心。这种形式集中化程度高,解决问题的速度快。但成员的平均满意程度较低,也容易造成信息失真。

5. 全通道式

全通道的沟通形式是饭店企业内部沟通的未来发展趋势,这种沟通渠道使得每位成员都与其他多个成员自由地相互沟通,且无明显的中心人物。这是一种开放的网络系统,其中每个成员之间都有一定的联系,彼此了解,成员满意程度高,合作的气氛浓厚。

Table 3-2 Factors A Firm Should Consider in the Formulation of A Managerial Communications Plan

Factors (Not rank specific)
1. Good communication skills and proper etiquette by managers are essential
2. The value of learning about culture
3. Effectively practicing Managerial Communication
4. Must have a communication plan in place
5. Define the scope and the goal of the plan
6. Deciding on the critical components of the communication plan
7. Who should be in charge of disseminating information
8. Who should receive the information
9. What should the content of the information include
10. The criticality of the timing on when information should be released
11. What methodology should be used to relay the information
12. Determine how to store, track, retrieve, and, if necessary, delete the disseminated information
13. Plan for unintended consequences and how to deal with them
14. Implement an effective control mechanism that can monitor all company information to avoid distortion, tempering, and manipulation of the original information by intruders
15. Clear the Managerial Communication's initiative with legal department before implementing the final plan

Source: Camillo A, Di Pietro L. The Importance of Managerial Communication for Hospitality Organizational Settings in the Era of High-Tech Evolution[J]. Available at SSRN 1978418, 2012.

三、影响饭店内部沟通的障碍(Communication Barriers in Hotel)

在饭店的实际工作中,其内部实施的是一种层层汇报的形式,在信息沟通过程中,除了种种的错误概念外,还有一些其他障碍妨碍着个人或群体有效沟通的能力,影响有效沟通的因素主要包括以下几个方面:

(一)文化背景(Culture Background)

不同的社会环境具有不同的文化价值观,各种不同文化价值观影响下的沟通行为有很大的不同。比如在美国的社会文化背景下,饭店中的上下级沟通显得较为民主,下级可以直接向上级或者上级的上级提出自己的意见。而在日本饭店企业中则是等级森严,沟通一般都是逐层进行,因此在日本饭店中,员工之间的正式交往显得非常慎重。在我国的饭店中,人们的沟通行为更多地受到社会关系的影响。这些不同的文化背景,都在沟通的过程中形成特定障碍。

(二)外围环境(External Environment)

饭店外围环境可能导致员工分心的原因包括:噪音过高、气温过高或过低、被打扰或身体不适。为了沟通的有效进行,应尽可能选择对讲话人和听众都不会造成注意力分散的地点。例如,饭店某位优秀员工之一小王来到上级领导办公室,同上级领导讲述她与同事之间的个人事情。由于上级领导常告诫员工——办公室大门每天永远向他们敞开,小王便觉得随时可来找领导会谈。然而,领导的办公室门敞开着,外面的噪音传了进来。此外,领导若再接了两个电话,或一两个同事敲门进来与领导简谈几句。在这种情况下,便干扰了下级同领导进行有效沟通。

(三)观念、态度(Attitude)

观念是指由一定的经验和知识沉淀而成,在一定社会条件下人们接受、信奉并用以指导自己行动的理论和观点,并形成对某些事物的特定看法。相同的观念有助于沟通双方的深度交流,不同的观念则容易导致沟通的障碍。

一般来说饭店管理者在员工的心目中具有一种"心理巨大性",这势必会造成员工在上级面前战战兢兢,不敢畅所欲言;员工在饭店管理者心目中具有"心理微小性",员工认为自己人微言轻,提出的建议上级不会重视也不会采纳。所以员工没信心也不愿意向管理者提建议,造成员工有话不敢说、有事不敢问的局面。

(四)个人偏见(Personal Bias)

1. 首因效应

"第一印象"是人们初次见面时,通过对对方的仪容仪表、言谈举止的表面层次的认知而形成的人际印象。首因效应是指"第一印象"能给人留下深刻印象,产生心理定式作用,会影响着人们继续交往的意愿。

在理解首因效应时需要强调的有两点:

（1）对某人的"第一印象"，只是通过对此人的仪容仪表、言谈举止的表面层次的认知而形成的。这就是说，对某人的"第一印象"并不是通过你对他的一些内在品质的认知而形成的。因此，如果仅仅根据"第一印象"来判断此人"是一个什么样的人"，这样的判断往往是不准确的，至少是不全面的。

（2）尽管"第一印象"只是根据表面层次的认知而形成的，但是人们在初次见面以后，是否还愿意继续交往，以及按什么样的"人际距离"来进行交往，这在很大程度上要受"第一印象"的影响。因此，饭店员工要时刻保持良好的个人形象，为宾客留下优质服务的印象。

2. 刻板印象

"刻板印象"也叫"定型化效应"，是指个人受社会影响而对某些人或事持稳定不变的看法。它既有积极的一面，也有消极的一面。积极的一面表现为：在对于具有许多共同之处的某类人在一定范围内进行判断，不用探索信息，直接按照已形成的固定看法即可得出结论，这就简化了认知过程，节省了大量时间、精力。消极的一面表现为：在被给予有限材料的基础上做出带普遍性的结论，会使人在认知别人时忽视个体差异，从而导致知觉上的错误，妨碍对他人做出正确的评价。

3. 光环效应

人们往往用一些明显的品质和特点，去掩盖其他品质和特征，以致影响对知觉对象本质的全面了解和正确评价，从而产生偏见性。

人们在认知他人时，认知对象所具有的特别突出的品质总是最先被认知的。这个特别突出的品质会像太阳的光芒一样，遮住他身上其他或优或劣的品质。这就好像白天看星星，星星依然在天上，可你就是看不见。这是为什么呢？这就是因为星星被太阳的光芒所"遮掩"了。

4. 近因效应

近因效应与首因效应相反，是指对自己所熟悉的人，最近或者说最后所得到的印象最为深刻难忘，往往会改变人的看法。受近因效应的影响，管理者往往改变原有看法，做出错误判断。

5. 对比效应

也称作"感觉对比"，是同一刺激因背景不同而产生的感觉差异的现象。在实际中，人们往往受到参照物的影响，产生失真现象，从而产生怜悯或严惩效应。

（五）知觉的选择性(Selective Perception)

在沟通中，信息接收者会根据自己的需要、动机、经验、背景及其他个人特点有选择地把某些刺激信息的某些方面作为知觉对象来处理信息。在解码的过程中，信息接收者还会把自己的兴趣和期望带入信息中。

(六) 过滤(Filter)

过滤是指信息发送者有意操纵信息,以使信息显得对接受者更为有利。比如,如果一名管理者告诉上级的信息都是上级想听到的,这名管理者就是在过滤信息。

过滤发生的主要决定因素是饭店组织结构中的层级数目。饭店组织的纵向层级水平越多,过滤的机会就越多。只要存在地位上的差异,过滤活动就会存在。诸如害怕传递坏消息、希望取悦自己上级这些因素,会导致员工只告诉上司那些他们觉得上司想听到的内容,这也导致了信息的失真。

(七) 信息超载(Information Overload)

当饭店沟通网络的任何部分被超出它能有效处理的信息所困住时,信息超载就会出现。常见的信息超载表现为以下几点:

(1) 无法理解特定信息的含义;
(2) 信息容量过大;
(3) 不知道自身所需要的信息是否存在;
(4) 不知道从何种渠道获取信息;
(5) 知道从何种渠道获取信息,但不知道以何种方式获取。

(八) 语义障碍(Semantic Barriers)

同样的词汇对于不同的员工来说含义是不一样的。词汇的意义不仅仅存在于词汇中,还存在于使用者中。使用者的年龄、教育和文化背景是这方面的3个主要因素,它影响着一个人的语言风格和对词义的界定。在一个饭店企业中,员工常常来自于不同的背景,有着不同的说话风格。此外,部门的分化使得专业人员发展了各自的行业用语,使得沟通存在障碍。

四、饭店沟通管理(Communication Management in Hotel)

(一) 概念和意义(Concept and Significance)

1. 饭店沟通管理的概念

沟通管理是为了实现饭店的目标,而在饭店内各层级之间、各员工之间的进行的事实、思想、意见的传递与交流过程。

2. 饭店沟通管理的意义

饭店沟通管理是创造和提升饭店精神和饭店文化,完成饭店管理根本目标的主要方式和工具。而饭店精神与饭店文化的培育与塑造,其实质是一种思想、观点、情感和灵魂的沟通,是管理沟通的最高形式和内容。没有沟通,就没有对其精神和文化的理解与共识,更不可能认同饭店共同使命。

饭店沟通管理更是管理创新的必要途径和肥沃土壤。许多新的管理理念、方法技巧的出台,无不是经过数次沟通、碰撞的结果,以提高饭店管理沟通效率与绩效为目的,其根本目的是提高管理效能和效率。

(二)饭店内的沟通机制(Communication System in Hotel)

知道管理沟通的重要性后,不能仅仅停止在理念层面,而应落实到执行层面,必须通过内、外部沟通机制来协助执行,以执行到位,效果更好。管理沟通分为外部沟通和内部沟通。

1. 外部沟通

(1)饭店方通过公共关系手段,利用大众传媒、内部刊物等途径,与客户、政府职能部门、周边社区、金融机构等,建立良好关系,争取社会各界支持,创造好的发展氛围。

(2)饭店企业导入 CIS 企业形象识别系统,把理念系统、行为系统、视觉系统进行有效整合,进行科学合理的传播,树立良好饭店形象,提高饭店的知名度、美誉度、资信度,为饭店腾飞和持续发展提供好的环境。

2. 内部沟通

(1)建立健全规范饭店内部会议系统,使各种指令、计划信息能上传下达,相互协调,围绕饭店各项指标的完成统筹执行。通过月会、周例会、调度会、座谈会、班前班后会等形式,快速地将信息进行有效的传递,使饭店员工按计划有条不紊进行,步调一致,方向目标明确,提高工作效率和效能,使目标完成得到保障。

(2)针对饭店全体员工展开"合理化建议"活动,设立合理化建议箱和合理化建议奖。无论是技术改造、成本控制、行政管理等各领域,全面展开。从为饭店发展到献计献策,树立主人翁精神,获得好的效果,从经济各个角度收获很大。

(3)建立饭店内部刊物,每月一期,发至饭店各个层面,把饭店生产经营动态进行有效汇总,整合信息,统一全体员工思想。

(4)把某日定为饭店"沟通日"。饭店各部门总经理的门是敞开着的,欢迎各级层员工进来沟通谈话。无论是意见还是建议一并笑纳,快速做出改进,了解各级层员工的需求动态,尽可能满足他们,真正实现"以人为本",提高员工满意度,把员工当作绩效伙伴而非"打工者"雇员,形成命运共同体,而非单纯利益共同体。

(5)每月集中给该月生日的饭店员工过"生日餐会",管理层给每位生日员工发生日蛋糕,聚餐的同时,送上总经理签名的生日卡,使很多员工感到饭店大家庭的温暖,更是一心一意做贡献,提升对饭店的忠诚度和凝聚力。还有定期举办的联欢会、运动会、表彰会、优秀员工干部旅游活动等,使大家干得起劲、玩得开心,觉得自己与饭店已密不可分,人店合一,共同成长。

Table 3-3 Critical Components and Logistics of a Communication Plan

Factors	Drafting policy and creating the plan	Disseminating information	Communication tracking and storage
Who	Management	Management appointed spokes person	A trustworthy person appointed by the management
What	Policy and plan	Type of communication: internal-external; how much and level of confidentiality	All types of communication
When	At inception or by timely adoption	Timing, frequency	On going
How	Self developed, hiring experts, adoption from parentcompany, research	-Directly: memo, email, presentation -Indirectly: accessible onintranet, website -Personal: Relayed to others in person	In writing, electronically, voice and video recording, or by other means such as witness observation and taking notes
Where	Corporate office or at property level	At specified location, either with public access or private	At all designated physical locations and on cyber space
Stakeholder	All: management, employees and customers	Individuals or groups of stakeholders	All persons as appointed by the Management

Source: Camillo A, Di Pietro L. The Importance of Managerial Communication for Hospitality Organizational Settings in the Era of High-Tech Evolution[J]. Available at SSRN 1978418, 2012.

（三）饭店内的沟通技巧(Communication Skills in Hotel)

1. 赞美对方

这几乎是一个屡试不爽的特效沟通润滑剂。这个世界上的人，没有不渴望受到表扬的，学会赞美，将在任何沟通中一帆风顺。即使给领导提意见，也要先表扬后批评。不要怕人说拍马屁，把拍马屁当作对领导的激励，只要表扬的内容属实就没问题。领导与员工一样都是人，员工需要激励，领导同样需要激励。

2. 移情入境

即设计一个对现实有借鉴意义的场景，进行情境教育。在饭店项目管理培训中设计的很多游戏,用意都在于用一个显而易见的事实去启发员工的思路。

3. 轻松幽默

既是通向和谐对话的台阶和跳板,又是化解冲突、窘境、恶意挑衅的灵丹妙药。在饭店人力资源的管理中,在恰当的场合合理运用幽默可以化解矛盾,创造奇迹,使不可能的事情成为可能。

4. 袒胸露怀

又被称为不设防战术,意在向人们明确表示放弃一切防备,胸襟坦荡,诚恳待人。这是一种非语言信号,饭店管理者在同员工进行交流时,采取此种沟通策略会让员工在一定程度上放下防备,同管理者对问题进行实质性交流。

5. 求同存异

又被称为最大公约数战术。人们只有找到共同之处,才能解决冲突。饭店员工之间的争执不休,用最后一句话"都是为了工作"而握手言和。无论人们的想法相距多么遥远,总是能够找到共同性。有了共性,就有了建立沟通桥梁的支点。

6. 深入浅出

这是提高沟通效率的捷径。能够用很通俗的语言阐明一个很复杂深奥的道理是一种本事,是真正的高手。

7. 善于倾听

倾听与一般的被动的听是截然不同的。倾听是对信息进行积极主动的搜索,而单纯的听是被动的。在倾听时,接收者和发送者双方都在思考。要想听好,就必须置身于交流之中。

(1)倾听的重要性

人们确信饭店的员工每天中的一半时间是要接收他人的信息。例如,在餐厅工作的员工须在整个工作中听懂客人的点菜和指令。员工如果常与客人接触,他们就要多听客人的要求并与客人交流。由于客人的满意程度是十分重要的,因而饭店的工作人员都应学会倾听。

倾听是沟通技巧的基础,倾听的有效性与顾客的满意度正相关,与员工的离职倾向负相关。员工与管理层沟通不良也被列为员工不满的主要原因。

(2)倾听的四个阶段

①注意阶段:首先,减少阻碍倾听的因素;其次,关注说话;再次,先听完再提问;最后,听与说顺利地转换。

②释义阶段:在释义阶段,有两点需要注意:其一,确认信息的组织;其二,注意非语言信息。

③评价阶段:要善于区分事实与推论,还要评估推论。事实是现象客观的描述,能直接观察而证明其正确性;推论是根据观察的结果所做的推断与归纳。在评

估推论时,要注意:是否有事实在支持推论,支持的证据是否恰当,是否有其他信息使得原来的支持证据失去效力。

④反馈阶段:听话人可以在说话人讲话的过程中或结束后对说话人发出的信息做出反馈。

(3) 积极倾听的反馈技巧

有效倾听是需要努力和激励的习得技巧。倾听看似没有回报,但如果我们不倾听,负面结果会随之而来。对方会认为不被尊重、不受重视或者被冒犯,这些都将损害人际关系、产生工作不满、降低生产效率和降低顾客满意度。促进积极倾听的反馈技巧主要有模仿、意释、归纳总结和自我揭示、提问或澄清以及鼓励讲话人陈述。

第二节 团队合作(Teamwork)

一、工作团队的基本概念(The Concept of Work Team)

(一) 团队的定义(The Defination of Team)

在英语中 team(团队)一词的原意是:共同来拉一辆车的几匹马或几头别的牲口。而对于团队的解释是具有不同技巧的人员的组合,他们致力于共同的目的、(共同的)工作目标和(共同的)相互负责的处事方法。

(二) 有效团队的特征(The Characteristic of an Effective Team)

对于一个由人组成的团队来说,"全部都使劲"就是要有很强的进取精神,"往同一个方向使劲"就是要有很强的凝聚力。

1. 进取精神

团队的进取精神指团队成员的学习和创新,包括团队成员所创造的团队文化、团队伦理、团队形象以及团队愿景。它不是每个成员的简单相加,它所呈现的整体威力远大于部分总和。

2. 凝聚力

团队的凝聚力指团队成员之间互相吸引的程度、团队对其成员的吸引程度,是一个团队赖以生存的整体感,包括忠诚、投入、志趣相投以及为团队作出牺牲的意愿。

有凝聚力的群体的成员团结在一起是由于以下两个原因:

(1) 喜欢相互陪伴

产生于这种原因的凝聚力被称为社会情感凝聚力,它是当饭店员工个人参与到饭店群体中获得情感满足时而形成的集体感。大多数的关于群体凝聚力的讨论局限于此种类型。

（2）需要相互帮助来完成共同的目标

产生于这种原因的凝聚力被称为工具性凝聚力，是当饭店团队成员相互依赖而且他们相信如果单独工作就无法完成目标时所产生的集体感。

（三）工作团队与工作群体（Work Team &Work Group）

1. 定义

在很多饭店企业中，员工并没有真正地组成团队，饭店各个部门和其他形式组成的员工只是一种工作群体的形式。工作团队与工作群体不是一回事。在工作群体（work group）中，只有领导人才需要对"整体"负责，每一个成员并不关心自己的工作对其他员工会造成什么影响，而只是满足于完成自己的一份工作。他们不追寻完成一个总的目标，也从不对他人负责。他们的想法是："我的工作已经完成了，该看你和别人的了。"

群体是指两个或者两个以上相互作用和相互依赖的个体，为了实现特定的目标而进行的结合；相对应的工作群体是指团队成员通过相互作用，来共享信息，作出决策，帮助各个成员更好地承担各自的责任。而工作团队是指通过其成员的共同努力能够产生积极的协同作用，使其团队的绩效水平大于个体成员发挥的绩效之和。

2. 区别

工作团队与工作群体的区别在于：工作团队中的每一个成员都要对"整体"目标实现所发挥的技能、负责的责任感，以及所发挥的协同作用。

（1）目标：工作团队的团队目标是集体绩效，而工作群体的团队目标是信息共享。

（2）协同：在工作团队中，协同作用的发挥是积极的，而工作群体中不存在一种积极的协同作用。

（3）责任：工作团队在重视个体责任的同时，也注重共同责任，工作群体只注重个体化的责任。

（4）技能：在工作团队中，各个成员技能的发挥是相互补充的，在工作群体中，技能是随机的或不同的。

3. 两者的关系

明确以上的定义有助于澄清为什么现在许多饭店围绕工作团队重新组织工作过程。管理人员这样做的目的，是发挥工作团队的积极协同作用，提高团队的工作绩效。团队的广泛采用为饭店创造了一种潜力，使得饭店在不增加投入成本的情况下，提高产出水平。良好的沟通、相互的信任和明确的目的，能够使 work group

转变为 work team。

二、饭店工作团队的分类(The Catalogue of Hotel Work Team)

(一) 简单型(Simple Type)

简单型工作团队是把有相似技巧的员工组织在一起,以在规定时间内完成所有工作。通常是根据饭店的不同部门进行分类,分为前厅团队、客房团队、餐饮团队以及工程团队,等等。

团队成员往往掌握同样的技巧,从事同样的工作任务。一般都来自于统一工作地点或部门。当每位成员都训练有素时,团队的工作效率会有很大的提高。例如餐饮员工、厨房厨师、客房部员工等,他们需要按照职责完成各自的工作量。

(二) 接力型(Relay Type)

接力型工作团队指的是一部分团队成员完成任务后把接力棒递给下一名成员,由后者继续完成任务。比如迎宾员安排客人就座;餐饮服务员准确为客人点菜、记录客人的要求及特殊要求,并把这些信息传送给厨师;厨师根据信息进行食品加工并及时出菜就是一个接力型工作团队的例子。迎宾员、服务员和厨师组成的小接力团队在根据客人的要求而工作,确保达到或超过客人的期望。

在大规模的饭店中,这种接力关系更加复杂,客人是由一个部门送到另一个部门的。例如客人从停车场(如果是自己驾车到店)被传送到前台,再被传送到行李员——这是登记入住的最后环节。客人住饭店期间,接力还在继续,从餐厅门口的迎宾员到餐厅服务员,再到客房的服务员和健身房的工作人员……每个员工都是一个或多个接力团队的一员,像接力赛一样对全队有重要影响。

(三) 一体化型(Integration Type)

在一体化型工作团队中,具有不同专业技能的成员组合在一起来完成工作任务。

例如饭店中为客人安排会议的全体员工组成团队,团队中有销售部经理、餐饮部总监、客房部经理和工程部经理。他们汇集在一起计划并协调各个部门和员工的行动,确保会议取得圆满成功。在这种一体化操作中,团队成员不仅要熟悉自己工作范围的技巧,而且要有良好的沟通能力。

(四) 解决问题型(Problem-solving Type)

因为问题已经非常严重,超出个人解决的能力范围,问题的起因是以上三种工作团队在行业运营中产生了难题,所以组建解决问题型工作团队。

大约15年前,团队刚刚盛行,团队的形式彼此之间很相似,这些团队一般由来自同一个部门的5个至10个钟点工人组成,他们每周用几个小时的时间来碰头,讨论怎样提高产品的质量、生产效率和改善工作环境。这就形成了解决问题型团队。在这个团队里,成员就如何改进工作程序和工作方法相互交换彼此的看法或者主动提供建议。但是,这些团队几乎没有权力根据这些建议单方面采取行动。20世纪80年代,应用最广的一种问题解决型团队是质量圈。其由职责范围部分重叠的员工及主管人员组成,一般是8人至10人。成员定期相聚,讨论他们面对的质量问题,确定问题的起因,采取的方式包括集思广益、列举所有面对的困难、发现问题的共性或问题的起因,并采取有效的行动。

有些饭店有自己固定的问题解决团队,有些是出现了问题再组建团队设法解决问题。比如到达前台办理入住的大量客人的预订出现问题,饭店将招集前台人员、预订部人员和信息系统专家来共同查找出问题的起因,然后解决问题。

通常,解决问题型团队的工作过程如下:
(1)识别问题;
(2)制定战略分析问题;
(3)收集并分析情况;
(4)找出多种选择;
(5)评估选择,确定最佳方案;
(6)制订计划,执行最佳方案;
(7)建立负责机制和衡量系统。

Tips: The Technical Teamwork Dimension in Hotel

The breakfast shifts in the restaurant commences at 6:00 am. However, some members of the team start an hour later. At 6:00 am the main duty is to finish the "set-up" of the restaurant—which, for the most part was undertaken by the shift from the previous evening. This process, for the waiting staff, includes the laying out the cold buffets, juices, cereals, breads, jams, butter, milk, glasses, serving spoons and plates. This is completed in accordance with a check sheet held by the supervisor or team leader. The hot food was prepared by the chefs.

The kitchen staff are divided into three groups—chefs, kitchen porters and hygienists. These three groups have different uniforms. Kitchen porters perform relatively low skilled work—basic preparation tasks such as creating butter curls, making toast and producing coffee and fruit juices from concentrate. The hygienists are responsible for cleaning and tidying up the kitchen.

When the rest of the serving shift arrives for work at 7:00 am, the work progresses to the polishing of glasses and cutlery for lunch and dinner. In the meantime the team leader and host check the restaurant and make a rough plan for guest seating. At 7:30 am, there is a team briefing session where the supervisor allocates waiters to sections for serving or re-setting. It is only, however, by 8:30 am that the majority of staff can be found in the restaurant both serving and clearing up or re-setting.

In theory at least, waiting staff adhere to Trading Norms for serving. Once seated by the host the waiting staff approach guests and ask for an order of tea or coffee and toast. Other small requests can be made by customers such as fish dishes, poached eggs etc. This system normally works. When there is a "rush" of guests, however, Trading Norms are abandoned. This results in guests being seated by waiting staff or in the worse cases scenario, they end up seating themselves.

When all guests have left the restaurant waiting staff start to clear up the waste and plates. Re-usable materials are returned to storage or the kitchen where perishable, but reusable foods were dated and placed back into refrigeration. Once all the areas are cleared table cloths are taken off and sent to the laundry. Typically at this point—between 10:15 am and 10:45 am, staff will take a break. The break lasts about twenty minutes. This is followed by another team briefing where employees are allocated their next tasks.

Tables are then set according to the information provided at the team briefing. All co-ordination comes from the supervisor or team leader. Employees are afforded no autonomy. Tables are set for lunch or dinner depending if lunch is being offered on that particular day. If this process is completed quickly staff are allowed another break. However, this is rare. Compared to serving breakfasts, there tends to be a surplus number of staff which allows work to be undertaken at a leisurely pace. As a result even full-time members of staff are not guaranteed 39 hours of work per week. When there is less work available the company shares the work around rather than allowing some staff to have no work at all.

Source: Richards J, Chillas S, Marks A. "Every man for himself": Teamwork and customer service in the hospitality industry[J]. Employee Relations, 2012, 34(3): 235-254.

三、饭店工作团队形成的途径(The Pathways of Hotel Work Team Formation)

饭店内的工作团队的形成一般有四种途径：人际关系途径、角色界定途径、任务导向途径和价值观途径。

(一)人际关系途径(Interpersonal Approach)

良好的人际关系是工作团队形成的有效前提条件。它不仅包括团队成员之间情感上的亲近感，有彼此合作和沟通的愿望，并且他们相互信任、相互尊重，希望了解对方。饭店内部良好的人际关系有助于形成和谐的工作氛围，大大降低了人际沟通和协作的成本，如果饭店员工有着共同的兴趣和追求，愿意相互倾听并了解其他成员的想法，都乐于从事目前的工作，那么在工作中就会更主动地参与其中，更加乐意与他人合作，在遇到困难时，也会积极地承担责任，想办法解决问题。如果饭店员工之间不能进行有效的沟通和交流，并且不能解决彼此间的问题以及冲突，整个饭店团队就不能够顺利运作。

(二)角色界定途径(Roles Defination Approach)

工作团队是一种特殊的工作群体，它的一个突出特点是每个成员都要在团队中扮演特定的角色。常见的九种团队角色有：

(1)创造者——革新者：产生创新的思想；

(2)探索者——倡导者：倡导和拥护所产生的新思想；

(3)评价者——开发者：分析决策方案；

(4)推动者——组织者：提供结构；

(5)总结者——生产者：提供指导并坚持到底；

(6)控制者——核查者：检查具体的细节；

(7)支持者——维护者：处理外部冲突与矛盾；

(8)汇报者——建议者：寻求全面的信息；

(9)联络者：合作与综合。

饭店团队成员需要根据任务精心配备，每个人在技能上是互补的，都与其他人负责不同的事务，每个员工都清楚自己在整个饭店团队中的位置、责任以及团队其他人对他的期望。这使得团队成员能够充分发挥每个人的特长，进而产生协同作用，使得饭店团队的绩效大于员工个体绩效之和。

(三)任务导向途径(Mission-lead Approach)

任务导向是工作团队形成的常见形式。在此途径中，关注的重点不是关于人们是什么样子的，而是关于人们拥有的技能以及这些技能如何为整体做出贡献。通过任务导向途径建立团队的一个重要前提是工作团队所执行的任务和希望达成的目标对于团队来说是至高无上的。饭店员工的个人感情以及其他因素都不能是饭店团队活动中的有效部分,达到工作目标是唯一重要的事情。任务为饭店团队成员提出了聚集在一起的理由,提供了所需的资源和环境,界定了每一个员工在其中扮演的角色,也提出了相互交流信息的需要和场所。在一些不容易形成团队的饭店组织中,任务导向是建立团队的主要动因。

(四)价值观途径(Values Approach)

价值观表明一个人的基本信念,共同的价值观是团队成员联合起来的重要原因,其重点是团队成员对其正在做的事情的整体立场,以及他们所采取的价值观,而不是组成团队的个人性格或者他们所担当的角色。这里所说的团队精神或者团队文化的核心,是团队全体成员应该就其价值观和目标形成的共识。在这种模式中,团队管理最基本的特征是形成明确的任务说明,由所有希望参加团队的人进行协商。通过确保团队中的每一个成员都能够有效地工作,并且能够感知每个成员的行为是如何为团队的共同目标做出贡献的。

四、饭店工作团队形成的阶段(Stages of Hotel Work Team Formation)

(一)形成阶段(Formation Stage)

这个阶段是饭店团队发展阶段中人员的首次聚集阶段,是指团队成员明确其目标任务,并被成员广泛接受的过程。这是团队组建的初期,确定企业内部的职能部门与团队的关系是十分重要的,团队成员需要考虑如何能适应饭店团队的工作要求及自己在团队中所处的位置。期间,团队成员之间相互打量与熟悉,彼此隐藏感情和弱点,工作缺乏主动性,遵循各职位的现行规则。管理者可以通过营造多样化的场合和活动使得团队成员相互了解,得到乐趣,并邀请成员互通意见,通过具体事例制定工作标准。

(二)动荡阶段(Turbulent Stage)

此阶段,饭店员工开始熟悉饭店团队工作的方式,并确定各自的存在价值。但与此同时,矛盾也会层出不穷,主要包括员工之间的矛盾、管理者的矛盾还有团队规则与饭店整体规则之间的矛盾。这时管理者要将各种冲突公开化,学会倾听,增强沟通能力与方式,促进理解和调整。

(三)规范阶段(Specification Stage)

在"规范化"的过程中,经过动荡期的饭店团队成员逐渐开始以团队整体形象出现。在这一阶段,饭店团队建立起自己的规范准则、经营方式、沟通渠道及行为规范。团队成员之间开始有了感情发展,也出现了关怀的态度,个人需求处于次要的地位,能够意识到他人的贡献,积极投身于集体工作与集体交流中。合作成为了团队工作的基本规范,管理者应该让成员不断充实自我,努力让自己的团队成为学习型团队。

(四)运作阶段(Operational Stage)

在这一阶段,饭店团队开始能够有效地解决工作中出现的问题,工作效率极大地提高。此时,团队成员们开始忠实于自己的团队,努力、主动地为目标奋斗,自觉矫正自己的行为,并且减少了对上级领导的依赖。成员们相互鼓励,积极提出自己的意见和建议,也对别人提出的意见和建议给出积极评价和迅速反馈,促进了团队的良好沟通。

(五)满足阶段(Satisfaction Stage)

此阶段是饭店团队形成的最终阶段,团队成员认识到彼此间都是相互联系的,信任感和忠诚感的重塑有利于建立饭店团队的新目标,提高整体的行动绩效。

五、饭店内的团队建设(Team Building in Hotel)

Tips:How do techniques groups or teams enhance their effectiveness

1. The Manager's Diagnostic Team Meetings

Simply stated, the Diagnostic Team helps the top manager check the health of an organization. The team checks to see if the organization is proceeding toward its goals and entertains possibilities for change. It usually meets once or twice a year for several sessions and allows the manager to get feedback from a collective group of key individuals. Team members usually consist of department heads, staff assistants, outside consultants, and respected members of outside organizations. The team has no executive powers but functions merely to evaluate and advise. Four steps are usually involved in the process of a Diagnostic Team's functioning.

a. A meeting is held in which information is pooled and general observations shared.

b. The team picks target areas in which specific information is sought and selects methods for collecting information, e.g. interviews, questionnaires, group discussions.

c. A period of data collection.

d. Team meeting to review data, reevaluate goals, and make future recommendations.

2. The Family Group Diagnostic Meeting

This group diagnostic meeting gives the individual manager an opportunity to critique the performance in specific work areas with the people working directly under him. These meetings are held periodically with groups of up to thirty employees for periods of two to four hours. They try to focus on understanding and problem solving rather than on criticizing and defending. They are most effective with some structuring of topics, e. g., planning, future goals, what do we do best, what do we do worst, problem areas. Often data feedback is provided on the basis of studies made prior to the meeting. The Family Group Diagnostic Meeting is a quick way to establish a group rapport, but it is only a beginning. Such a meeting implies that some action will be taken by management, so that a manager must be ready to follow up in providing feedback to the group.

3. Family Group Team-Building Meeting

The team-building process involves a more elaborate sequence of procedures than does the diagnostic meeting. During a period of approximately three days, the team-building groups meet with the expectation of:

a. Capitalizing on group talents in identifying problems and opportunities.

b. Establish group commitment to change and new actions.

c. Improving working relationships.

d. Building tight team identifications.

The procedure for a team-building meeting generally adheres to the following format:

a. Setting the Objectives of the Meeting—Team-building meetings are usually conducted by a third party from outside of the company, such as a consultant. The task of setting objectives for the meeting is performed by the third party in collaboration with key management figures. General areas for consideration are chosen.

b. Collecting Information for the Meeting—This is accomplished prior to the meeting.

c. The Meeting Itself—Starting with the agenda, the group has latitude to conduct its meeting in accord with its own set of priorities. The group ultimately produces a list of action items to be implemented and determines who is responsible for each one, then sets a deadline for completion of each.

d. Follow-through—Follow-up sessions are scheduled with the whole group to see that agreed-upon actions are taken and to review problems arising in action implementations.

4. The Confrontation Meeting

The Confrontation Meeting developed by Richard Beckhard is a direct and immediate technique that enables organizations to identify problems, establish priorities, increase total management participation, and gain increased employee input in goal setting. It is designed as an intensive one-day meeting in which all management personnel are called together.

A number of variations are possible in conducting Confrontation Meetings, but generally an attempt is made to get peer managers together, both interdepartmentally and intradepartmentally, in order to evaluate the existing status of the organization and to recommend planned action changes. Once the problems and recommendations are formulated, the peer managers as a group meet in "confrontation" with the highest-level management personnel in the organization. In this meeting, these high-level managers make commitments openly regarding the recommendations they will or will not accept. When recommendations are not accepted, the reasons for their nonacceptance are discussed. At the end of the confrontation session, follow up plans are made to insure the implementation of the actions, and a follow-up review meeting is scheduled for a later date.

Source: Lundberg D E, Armatas J P. The Management of People in Hotels, Restaurants, and Clubs(Fourth edition). Dubuque Wm. C. Brown Company Publishers, 1980.

(一)饭店团队建设中所面临的问题(Problems Faced by Hotel Team Building)

1. 团队懒散性

指饭店员工在团队中的工作远不及单独工作时的展现及投入。常见的懒散性行为的解决方式主要包括：针锋相对、出示证据、使其认可、查寻原因、共同找出解决方案、辅导、鼓励和奖励。

综合来说，就是充分发挥个人的特点，使员工在饭店团队中人尽其才，并建立衡量员工在团队中的工作表现的具体量化措施。

2. 团队一盘散沙

一盘散沙是指整个饭店团队没有形成凝聚力，不能完成共同的使命和目标。

(1) 简单型

对于饭店内简单型工作团队，可以加强培训，制定"天气预报"，监控员工的日常工作或向员工提出有关行为改进方面的问题，促使员工考虑回顾所学的培训内容。

(2) 接力型

对于饭店内接力型工作团队，应使员工了解，他们本职工作的质量影响着行业中其他员工的工作。最佳方式之一是召集团队会议，邀请前台、餐饮和客房部的员工，解释团队工作对饭店中各个部门的影响。

(3) 一体化型

对于一体化型工作团队，可以使用团队建设技巧。针对成员之间缺乏信任感，则培养信任感成为头等大事；针对成员缺乏系统性的培训，进行系统的培训；沟通不畅是一体化型工作团队的通病，应被列为强调的重点。

(4) 解决问题型

在解决问题型工作团队中，必须确保饭店所制定的各种问题解决措施应贯彻于简单、接力和一体型团队的工作过程。如果饭店缺乏这些成文的措施或操作技巧，应首先对团队进行培训；还必须深入探讨各种人际冲突，适时清除团队工作中的隐患。

(二) 饭店团队建设的注意事项 (Precautions for Hotel Team Building)

1. 认识到人才是饭店团队最宝贵的资源

热忱投入、出色完成本职工作的员工，是饭店团队最宝贵的资源和资本。尊重员工，为优秀的员工创造一个和谐、富有激情的工作环境，是上至总经理下至普通员工的核心和重点。

2. 尊重每一个饭店员工的个性

尊重员工的个人意愿，尊重员工的选择权力，所有的员工在人格上人人平等，在发展机会面前人人平等。必须努力为员工提供公正平等的工作环境，营造和谐的工作氛围，倡导简单真诚的人际关系。

3. 打造、培养自己的管理团队

饭店培养属于自己的管理团队，是饭店人才理念的具体体现，持续培养专业的富有激情和创造力的队伍，让每一个员工都成长为全面发展，能独当一面的综合性人才，是饭店的一项重要使命。

4. 在饭店团队中倡导学习的良好风尚

因为学习是一种生活方式，每一位员工都应该以空杯的心态，培养自己的学习能力，迅速提升自己各方面的工作技能和综合素质。

(三)创建成功的饭店团队(Create a Successful Hotel Team)

1. 明确饭店团队目标

饭店团队目标能给饭店组织带来强大的内驱力、凝聚力,并激发人们的创造力,事实上,如果一个饭店团队不能确定明确的具体工作指标,或是具体的工作指标与整体目标毫无关系,那么饭店团队成员会因此变得困惑、涣散、表现平庸、凝聚力差。饭店团队管理者善于捕捉成员间不同的心态,理解他们的需求,帮助他们树立共同的奋斗目标。并且,在制定目标时,也要遵循目标的 SMART 原则,即具体的(specific)、可衡量的(measurable)、可实现的(attainable)、结果导向的(result-focused)和有时限的(time-bound)。

2. 组建饭店各团队人员

饭店团队的规模要适度,团队规模一般都不是很大,如果团队成员多于 12 人,他们就很难顺利开展工作。选聘也要合理,选聘时,除了考虑个人的能力、阅历和知识外,还要考虑整个饭店团队成员的优化组合效率。还应该设立灵敏的淘汰体制,饭店团队目标的实现需要全体成员相互分工协作,任一成员对具体目标完成得不好,整体目标就会受挫,饭店团队就可能会被其他团队取代,所以对待不称职的成员,我们应该让其离开,使团队真正成为精英的组合。

3. 培训饭店团队成员

团队成员不一定在一开始就完全具备团队所需的各项技能,因此对他们实施培训是重要的。这可以为团队带来很多益处:提升个人能力和团队整体素质、改进服务质量和企业绩效。在培训的过程中,也建立了学习型组织,让每一位成员都认识到学习的重要性,尽力为他们创造学习机会。在进行饭店团队学习时,饭店团队成员要学会运用深度汇谈和讨论这两种交谈方式。

4. 做好饭店团队激励

培养高绩效的饭店团队精神包括培养饭店员工对团队的高度忠诚,员工之间以及员工和领导之间相互高度信任,团队成员相互尊重,团队充满活力与热忱且不断进取。要真正形成良好的氛围,关键在于彼此的信任。没有信任就没有尊重,也就没有相互关怀和支持。管理者需要通过一定手段使团队成员的需要和愿望得到满足,以调动他们的积极性,使其主动自发地把个人的潜力发挥出来,从而确保团队目标的实现。常见的激励方式多种多样:提升薪资、改善福利、树立榜样、当众表扬,等等。

5. 保持饭店团队氛围

良好的团队氛围包括饭店员工之间的相互信任和团队开放与创新的状态。个体之间只有相互信任,才能关心共同的利益与目标;团队的开放状态,就是要不断接受新的信息和经验,与团队周围的环境进行信息交流,从而不断产生新的观念和想法。

 案例分析(Practice Case Analysis)

Sidney West recently was hired as president of one of the "grand" hotels in the world, located in a major east coast city. His selection was unusual, as West had no previous experience in the hospitality field beyond that of a professional guest. He had been a successful advertising executive.

The hotel, The Court Arms, was a landmark, known for excellent service, tradition, and a certain ambiance. When West became president, employee performance relative to this image was poor, as shown by increasing numbers of guest complaints and a decreasing percentage of return reservations. Guest were becoming used to curt answers, indifference, and a lack of courtesy from the services staff, which included the front desk, waiters, bellmen, door attendants, and cleaners.

His first month was spent on walking around the property, investigating complaints, and interviewing as many employees as possible. He found some major problem areas. The employee locker room was in disgraceful condition. There was trash on the floor, no soap or towels in the restroom, toilet seats were missing, and locker doors were broken. Other employee areas were in similar disarray. West visited the employee cafeteria, where he found the food unpalatable and the utensils bent and dirty. In essence, he felt that the employees lived better at home than at The Court Arms. West could well imagine a room service waiter bringing fine food to a suite and then returning to a dungeon where he could not adequately or comfortably wash his hands.

When he questioned the personnel office, which was located at the rear of the hotel in the basement, about the orientation program, he was shocked to find out that the program consisted of signing a W-2 form and immediate assignment. The formal training program featured only on-the-job training for a three-day period and had no performance evaluation, except comments from the immediate supervisor. Moreover, a bulletin board planned for the outside of the personnel office had never been installed, and important employee notices were posted in a haphazard manner.

West soon discovered that a language barrier was partly responsible for poor communication. Five hundred employees out of 1,500 could not read, write, or speak English. Spanish was their primary language. Also, he found that employees in the same department and throughout the hotel knew their fellow members by face, not by proper name.

In his rounds of the front of the house, he noted that the desk clerks and reservationists had never seen a guest room, much less spent a night as a guest of The Court Arms. How could they effectively show enthusiasm about the rooms and special features to a prospective guest? In a similar vein, the managers of the six restaurants in the hotel ate only at their own restaurants. They neither knew about the merits (or lack of them) of the other five restaurants, nor had they investigated their competition outside the hotel. The hotel department heads also were unfamiliar with the internal workings of the other departments. Poor communication and coordination had led to many disruptions and embarrassments for the departments, and for the guests caught in between.

West had a monumental task in front of him. How could he achieve a smooth-functioning internal hotel team at The Court Arms, where the guests would be treated as well as the employees?

Source: Lundberg D E, Armatas J P. The Management of People in Hotels, Restaurants, and Clubs (Fourth edition). Dubuque Wm. C. Brown Company Publishers, 1980.

Questions for Discussion:

1. How could West motivate his service staff in order to instill a pride in their performance? Where should he start?

2. What role should the personnel department play in West's reorganization of and reemphasis on the employees?

名词解释(Key Terms)

1. 沟通：在个人或群体同另一个人或团体之间传递的信息。

Communication: The passage of information between one person or group and another person or group.

2. 信息发送者：沟通的发端者，他对信息进行编码和传递，也被称作信息编码者。

Sender: The originator of a communication, who encodes and transmits a message; also known as the encoder.

3. 信息接收者：沟通的收端者，他对信息进行解码，也被称作信息解码者。

Receiver: The recipient of a communication who decodes the message; also known as the decoder.

4. 编码：通过信息组建或加密以进行信息传递的准备过程。
Encoding: The process of preparing a message for transmission by putting it into some form or code.

5. 沟通渠道：信息从发送者流向接收者的传播媒介。
Channel: The vehicle through which a message flows from sender to receiver.

6. 下行沟通：信息在组织等级制度中自上而下传递，通常是从管理者至下级人员。
Downward Communication: Messages flowing downward in an organizational hierarchy, usually from superiors to subordinates.

7. 上行沟通：信息在组织等级制度中自下而上传递，通常形成反馈。
Upward Communication: Messages flowing upward in an organizational hierarchy, usually taking the form of feedback.

8. 平行沟通：信息在组织等级制度中由两个同级群体中传递。
Lateral Communication: Messages between two parties at the same level in an organizational hierarchy.

9. 晕轮效应：在绩效考核中，主管以下属的某一性状特点的评级来对该下属所有其他性状特点进行评级的行为。
Halo Effect: In performance appraisal, the problem that occurs when a supervisor's rating of a subordinate on one trait biases the rating of that person on other traits.

10. 工作群体：两个或两个以上的个人为实现目标所形成的社会交往。
Group: Two or more individuals engaged in social interaction to achieve some goal.

11. 凝聚力：群体成员之间的吸引程度。
Cohesiveness: The degree of attraction among group members.

12. 冲突：个人或群体意图抑制其他个人或群体实现目标的行为。
Conflict: Behavior by a person or group intended to inhibit the attainment of goals by another person or group.

13. 团队组织：由一个围绕着特定项目或产品而形成的团队成员组成的非传统组织结构。
Team Organization: A nontraditional organizational structure consisting of a team of members organized around a particular project or product.

复习思考题 (Questions for Review)

1. 哪些个人偏见会影响沟通？
What kinds of personal biases will affect communication?

2. 积极倾听的四个阶段是什么？每个阶段的重点是什么？
What are the four stages of positive listening? What is the key of each stage?

3. 积极倾听的反馈技巧有哪些？
What are the feedback skills of positive listening?

4. 谈谈非语言沟通的作用。
Discuss the influence of Non-Verbal Communication.

5. 简述团队的定义与特征。
Describe the definition and characteristics of teamwork.

6. 工作团队与工作群体的区别是什么？
What is the difference between team and group?

7. 简述饭店工作团队的类型有哪几种？
Describe the categories of hotel work team.

8. 团队的形成有哪几个阶段？
What are the phrases of the forming a team?

9. 团队的懒散性是什么？减轻团队的懒散性有哪些途径？
Define the laziness of a team. What are the methods to reduce laziness?

研究前沿 (Research Front)

The study investigated the role of communication satisfaction as a moderator strengthening the effect of three components of the expectancy theory (expectancy, instrumentality, valence) on work motivation in a hotel setting. High and low communication satisfaction groups respond differently to expectancy, instrumentality, valence, and work motivation. Employees who are highly satisfied with communication respond more positively toward motivation components, and they are more likely to perform well in their job when they are motivated. However, a series of confirmatory factor analyses of metric invariance indicated that there is no significant difference in the moderating effect between high and low communication satisfaction groups.

Communication should be managed collectively to motivate employees. Implications and suggestions for future research are provided to better explain the process of decision-making when hotel employees are motivated.

INTRODUCTION

The main purpose of this study is to examine the moderating role of communication satisfaction on the relationship between employee motivation and its determinants (expectancy, instrumentality, valence). Thus, this study extends the model by adding communication satisfaction as a moderator strengthening the process of employee motivation. Advanced statistical data analysis will also help in examining the moderator effect and will be used to provide validity and reliability as well as to enhance the understanding of theoretical development in research.

CONCEPTUAL BACKGROUND

In this study, communication satisfaction is proposed as a moderator to improve predicting hotel employee motivation because communication is important in strengthening good relationships between managers and employees. Thus, satisfaction with communication should increase the impact of expectancy, instrumentality, and valence on employee motivation.

Communication is probably the most central process in organizations (Frone & Major, 1988). Several studies posit that the perceived communication environment should be related to organizational outcomes such as work motivation, job satisfaction, and organization productivity or effectiveness. Communication satisfaction refers to satisfaction with communication linked to the employee's position in the organization (Mount & Back, 1999). The Communication Satisfaction Questionnaire (CSQ) was developed by Downs and Hazen (1977) to investigate the relationship between communication and job satisfaction. Eight factors were identified to explain communication satisfaction: communication climate, supervisory communication, organizational integration, media quality, coworker communication, corporate information, personal feedback, and subordinate communication. Mount and Back (1999) further examined communication satisfaction in the lodging setting by using a Communication Satisfaction Questionnaire (CSQ).

The main objective of this study was to examine the moderating role of communication satisfaction strength on the relationship between employee motivation and its determinants (expectancy, instrumentality, valence). A hypothesis was formed:

H1: The higher the level of communication satisfaction, the more positive are the effects of expectancy, instrumentality, and valence on hotel employee motivation.

METHODOLOGY

This study used convenience samples of hotel employees. Hotel employees from 56 hotels in several cities in a Midwestern state filled out the surveys. Most hotels were upper-economy and mid-scale hotels (such as Hampton Inn, Quality Inn, and Super 8), and few of them (Sheraton Hotel) were upper-scale hotels. A total of 1,450 surveys were distributed to employees in these participating hotels, and 301 were returned, yielding a response rate of 20.76%. Of the 301 returned responses, 12 were not usable because of missing data. Thus, 289 (19.93%) responses were used for analysis.

ANALYSIS AND RESULTS

The respondents were divided into a high communication satisfaction group and a low communication satisfaction group, based on their communication satisfaction scores. The high communication satisfaction group consisted of 146 respondents, and 143 respondents were categorized into the low communication satisfaction group. Based on the series of modeling tests, the two groups showed similar path coefficients among the variables; there was a non-significant moderating effect of communication satisfaction between these two groups. Thus, the proposed hypothesis was not supported: The higher the level of communication satisfaction does not have a positive effect on expectancy, instrumentality, or valence in hotel employee motivation.

DISCUSSION

Several studies posit that the perceived communication environment should be related to organizational outcomes such as work motivation, job satisfaction, and organization productivity or effectiveness. (Downs, 1977; Greenbaum, 1974; Hall & Goodale, 1986; Likert, 1973; Pinchus, 1986a, 1986b; Orpen, 1997; Porter & Roberts, 1993; Schuler, 1995). Other empirical research supports the hypothesized communication-job satisfaction relationship (Roberts & O'Reilly, 1974; Muchinsky, 1989; Sussman, 1974), and these studies suggest that high-quality communication is associated with relatively high levels of job satisfaction, whereas low-quality communication is associated with relatively low levels of job satisfaction. Frone and Major (1988) examined the moderating effect of job involvement on the relationship between perceived communication quality and job satisfaction in a sample of managerial issues. All these studies have indicated that communication is a direct predictor of job satisfaction or job outcomes. No study tested communication as a moderator. This present study verifies that communication satisfaction is not a moderator in the expectancy theory of employee motivation. However, communication might be a predictor for the expectancy theory, an idea that can be examined in future research.

Source: Chun-Fang Chiang, SooCheong (Shawn) Jang, Deborah Canter & Bruce Prince (2008). An Expectancy Theory Model for Hotel Employee Motivation: Examining the Moderating Role of Communication Satisfaction. International Journal of Hospitality & Tourism Administration, 9:4, 327–351.

第4章 招聘(Recruitment)

本章概要(Summary of This Chapter)

招聘是饭店人力资源管理工作中的一项重要的基础性工作,是饭店人力资源形成的关键,对于饭店人力资源的合理形成、管理与开发具有至关重要的作用。本章首先给出了招聘的含义,并说明了影响招聘工作的几大因素;随后,列举了招聘的渠道和方法,主要分为内部招聘和外部招聘两种,并分别说明了其优缺点;接着,阐述了人员甄选和录用的几个环节;本章最后介绍了成本效益评估和录用人员评估两种人员招聘评估方式。

Recruitment is a really important basic work in the hotel human resources management. It is the key to the formation of the hotel human resources management. And recruitment plays a vital role in the management and development of hotel human resources. This chapter first gives the definition of recruitment, and illustrates factors that influence the recruitment. Then, we list the recruitment channels and methods from internal and external aspects. And we also introduce their advantages and disadvantages respectively. Next, this paper discusses the personnel selection and employed process. At the end of this chapter we introduce two kinds of personnel recruitment assessment—cost-benefit assessment and hired personnel assessment.

开篇引例(Beginning Story)

As a longtime HR professional, Lisa Cruz was well aware of the importance of effective employee recruitment. If the Hotel Paris didn't get enough applicants, it could not be selective about who to hire. And, if it could not be selective about who to hire, it wasn't likely that the hotels would enjoy the customer-oriented employee behaviors that the company's strategy relied on. She was therefore disappointed to discover that the

Hotel Paris was paying virtually no attention to the job of recruiting prospective employees. Individual hotel managers slapped help wanted ads when they had positions to fill, and no one in the chain had any measurable idea of how many recruits these ads were producing or which recruiting approaches worked the best (or worked at all). Lisa knew that it was time to step back and get control of the Hotel Paris's recruitment function.①

第一节　招聘概述(Recruitment Overview)

招聘是饭店人力资源管理中的基础性工作,无论是饭店开业前的人员组织,还是饭店经营中人员的补充都离不开招聘工作。

一、招聘的含义(The Meaning of Recruitment)

招聘是指饭店根据人力资源计划和工作分析的结论,结合饭店的经营状况,及时地、足够多地吸引具备工作资格的个人补充饭店空缺职位的过程。员工招聘工作主要由招募、甄选、录用、评估等一系列活动构成(见图4-1)。

1. 招募

招募就是使潜在的合格人员对饭店的特定工作岗位产生兴趣,并前来应征该职位的过程。招募的主要工作内容包括:招聘计划的制订与审批、招聘信息的发布、接受应聘者的申请等。

2. 甄选

甄选则是通过一系列科学的方法,在招募过程确定的申请者进行选择,从中挑选出最适合饭店某一特定工作岗位的人员,并使之接受这一工作的过程。甄选的主要工作内容包括:评价求职者的申请和工作简历、面试、测试、个人材料的审查与调查、体检等。

3. 录用

录用是饭店最终决定雇用应聘者并分配其具体工作的过程。录用的主要工作内容包括:录用决策、通知被录用人、对落选者的回复等。

4. 评估

评估即饭店对招聘的成本以及招聘到的人员数量、质量进行评价的过程。

整个流程如图4-1所示。

---

① 加里·德斯勒. Human Resource Management (Tenth Edition). 北京:清华大学出版社.

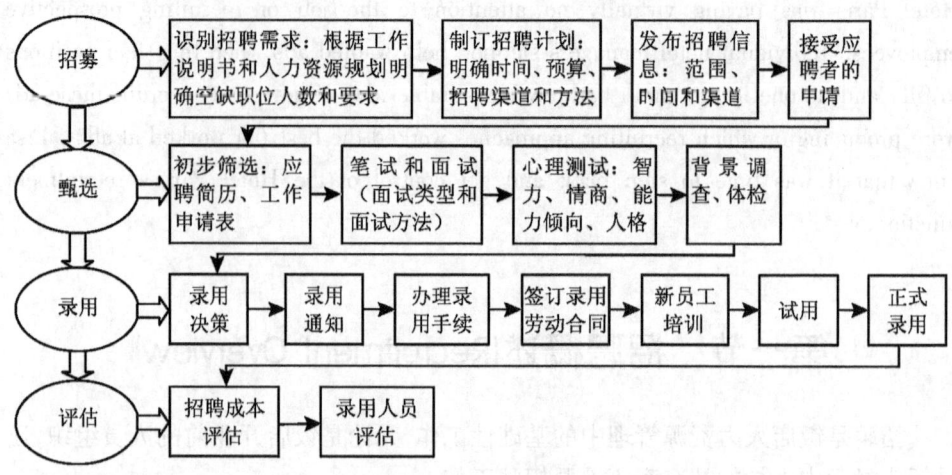

图 4-1 招聘流程

资料来源:田在兰.人力资源管理[M].广州:暨南大学出版社.2011:105.

通常,在大中型饭店里,招聘工作是由人力资源部门主持完成的。在小型饭店,招聘工作则可以由具体用人部门的经理来处理。

二、影响招聘工作的因素(Influence Factors of Recruitment)

饭店招聘工作能否获得成功,不仅取决于科学的招聘方法,而且还受到其他诸多因素的影响。这些影响招聘工作的因素归纳起来,主要可以分为外部环境因素和饭店内部因素两类。

(一)外部环境因素(External Environmental Factors)

1. 国家的法律、法规、政策

国家有关劳动用工的政策、法规从客观上对饭店招聘对象的选择和限制条件进行了制约。例如,《中华人民共和国劳动法》第12条规定:"劳动者就业,不因民族、种族、性别、宗教信仰不同而受歧视。"第13条规定:"妇女享有与男子平等的就业权利。在录用职工时,除国家规定的不适合妇女的工种或者岗位外,不得以性别为由拒绝录用妇女或者提高对妇女的录用标准。"第15条规定:"禁止用人单位招用未满16周岁的未成年人。"

2. 劳动力市场的供求状况

通常,把供给小于需求的劳动力市场称为短缺市场,而把劳动力供给充足的市场称为过剩市场。一般来说,当失业率比较高时,在饭店外部招聘新员工比较容易。相反,当某类人员短缺时,不仅可能引起其薪酬水平的上升,而且迫使饭店采取扩大招聘范围、放宽招聘条件等手段。

3. 行业的发展趋势

一个行业如果具有巨大的发展潜力,就能吸引大量的人才涌入这个行业,从而使该行业有比较大的选择。在我国,许多省市将旅游业作为当地的支柱型产业加以重点扶持、发展,现代饭店作为旅游业的一个重要组成部分,它对不同文化层次的人员几乎都有一定的需求。

(二) **饭店内部因素**(Hotel Internal Factors)

1. 饭店的形象和知名度

饭店是否在应聘者心中树立了良好的形象以及是否具有强大的号召力,将从应聘员工的心理方面影响着招聘活动。如一些知名度高或星级标准高的饭店,以它们在社会公众中的声望和条件,能很容易地吸引大批的应聘者。

2. 饭店所处的发展阶段

在饭店人力资源管理工作中,招聘职能的相对重要性,是随着饭店所处的发展阶段而变化的。由于饭店服务范围的扩大需要增加新的岗位和更多的人员,所以,处于发展阶段的饭店比成熟或下降阶段的饭店需要招聘更多的员工。此外,迅速扩大规模的饭店可以在招聘信息中强调员工有比较多的发展和晋升机会,从而吸引那些喜欢富有挑战性工作的人员。一个成熟型的饭店则可以强调其工作岗位的稳定性和所提供的高工资和福利。

3. 饭店的招聘政策

饭店的招聘政策影响着招聘方法。例如,对于要求较高业务水平和技能的工作,饭店可以利用不同的来源和招聘方法,这取决于企业高层管理者是喜欢从内部还是从外部招聘。目前,大多数饭店倾向于从内部招聘从事这类工作的人员,这种内部招聘政策可以为员工提供发展和晋升机会,有利于调动员工的积极性。

4. 福利待遇

饭店内部的工资制度是员工劳动报酬是否公正的主要体现,饭店的福利措施是饭店是否关心员工的反映,它们将从物质方面影响着招聘活动。

5. 成本和时间

由于招聘目标包括成本和效益两个方面,同时各种招聘方法奏效的时间也不一致,所以,成本和时间上的限制明显地影响招聘效果。招聘资金充足的饭店在招聘方法上可以有更多的选择,它们可以花大量费用制作招聘广告,甚至对一些高级管理岗位和某些稀缺的技术人才,如高级厨师、计算机网络工程师和财务总监等利用高级招聘机构代为其招聘。

时间上的制约也影响着招聘方法的选择。如果某一饭店正面临着扩大服务所带来的突发性需求,那么它就不会考虑去学校等单位招聘,因为学生毕业时间有一定的季节性,而且完成招聘需要比较多的时间。一般来说,许多招聘方法所涉及的时间是随着劳动力市场条件的变化而变化的。当劳动力市场短缺时,一方面应聘人的数目减少,另一方面他们愿意花更多的时间去比较和选择企业,所以一般招聘工作需要花较长的时间才能完成。

第二节 招聘的渠道和方法
(Recruitment Channels and Methods)

招募是及时地、足够多地吸引具备资格的个人并鼓励他们申请饭店中的工作岗位的过程。

从概念中可以看出,招募实际上是一个让人知道饭店的招聘信息,并诱导其决定申请该饭店职位的过程。这个阶段的主要工作是在明确招聘渠道和招聘方法的基础上,制订招聘计划及发布招聘信息。

一、招聘的渠道(Recruitment Channels)

饭店常见的招聘渠道包括内部招聘与外部招聘,相对应的招募来源也就有内部来源与外部来源之分。对于饭店来说,这两种招聘渠道也是各有利弊的,选择哪一类招聘来源取决于饭店的特点、饭店所在地的劳动力市场状况和计划招聘职位的性质、职务级别,以及饭店的规模等一系列因素。

(一)内部招聘(Internal Recruiting)

内部招聘是指通过内部各种渠道,选择适合待聘岗位要求的人员,其实质是饭店利用现有的员工来补充岗位空缺。当饭店出现岗位空缺时,优先从现有员工中物色人选。

1. 内部招聘的优点

(1)激发员工的内在积极性

当饭店实行内部招聘,从内部选拔人才时,员工就能感受到企业真正给自己提供了发展空间,就存在着晋升的可能与推销自己、引起组织注意和信任的希望,就能产生为取得更好的工作机会而拼搏的动力,这种政策产生的动力常常能够激发员工的积极性和创造性。

(2)迅速地熟悉和适应工作

内部员工比较熟悉饭店经营状况,熟悉企业的领导、同事,了解并认可企业的文化、价值观和其他硬件条件,因此能够很快了解工作流程并且适应工作环境,从而可以减少由于陌生而需要的时间和可能产生的失误。

(3) 保持企业内部的稳定性

从外部招聘新员工可能引起企业文化和价值观方面的碰撞,而通过内部获取将优质人力资源补充到合适岗位时,不会出现任何不稳定因素,可保持企业内部的稳定性。

(4) 尽量规避识人用人的失误,降低招聘风险

酒店对内部人员的品行与技能已经有了比较深入的了解,可以减少由于对求职者缺乏足够了解而带来的风险。

(5) 降低招聘成本

一次大规模的公开招聘,需要消耗相当多的时间和财力,内部选聘一般可以简化招聘程序,节约招聘测试费用,而且内部人员比外部人员所需要的职业定位时间更短,所需要的培训也更少。

2. 内部招聘的缺点

(1) 易产生"近亲繁殖"的现象

人员选择范围小的内部招聘途径容易形成企业内部人员的小帮派或非正式组织,当内部招聘渠道畅通时,非正式组织想推荐自己小圈子里的人员就成为一种必然。

(2) 可能引发企业高层领导的不团结

用人的分歧历来是在企业高层领导中最容易引起断裂的分歧,因为这涉及权力的分配,涉及个人核心班子的组成和个人威信的提高。因此,当出现用人分歧时,企业高层领导原来存在的不团结因素会更加明显化,而这种情况的产生是内部人才获取过程中最大的损伤。

(3) 缺少思想碰撞的火花,影响企业的活力和竞争力

通过内部招聘,企业一般不会产生思想碰撞,也就不会由于这种碰撞出现的不平衡而引发深层次的思考和继续碰撞。

(4) 营私舞弊的现象难以避免

由于彼此熟悉和了解,当一个崭新的机会来临时,不可避免地会出现托人情、找关系的现象,结果难以避免徇私情、走后门、官官相护或出现利益联盟的情况。

(5) 会出现涟漪效应

内部的每次人员调整,会出现一连串的内部波动,使得领导们不得不去接受本不该被移动的岗位和个人,从而给企业的工作带来损害。

(二) 外部招聘(External Recruiting)

外部招聘是饭店面向外部劳动力市场征集求职者以获取所需人力资源的过程。在内部补充机制不能满足饭店对人力资源的要求时,就需要考虑外部招聘。

饭店外部招聘的原因主要包括:没有合适的内部候选人;所需人员属于操作层或不同工种;外部人员能给组织带来新的理念和思维;饭店为发展业务或开拓新的业务,需要补充大量的人手,而内部招聘又解决不了。

1. 外部招聘的优点

(1) 选择余地大

外部招聘具有更为广泛的选择范围与更大的选择余地,可以从更多的求职者当中挑选适合本饭店要求的员工。

(2) 能够为饭店带来新的思想、观念,补充新鲜血液,增强饭店活力

外部招聘可以为饭店输入新生力量,给饭店带来新的思想、观念,新的文化和价值观,甚至新的人群和新的社会关系,给企业带来思想碰撞和新的活力,同时对饭店原有员工也有一定的鞭策作用。

(3) 减少人情影响

与内部招聘相比,外部招聘更容易避免原有人际关系网络等因素带来的影响,更有利于公平竞争。

(4) 扩大饭店的影响力

外部招聘是饭店对外界进行宣传的好机会,可以借助各种媒介,积极扩大饭店在求职者和公众中的影响,树立良好的外部形象。

2. 外部招聘的缺点

(1) 招聘成本高

无论是招聘高层次,还是中、低层次的人才,均须支付相当高的招聘费用,包括招聘人员的费用、广告费、测试费、专家顾问费等。

(2) 给现有员工以不安全感,影响内部员工的积极性

外部招聘,特别是非空缺岗位从外部招聘新员工,会使老员工产生不安全感,致使其工作热情下降,影响员工队伍的稳定性。

(3) 文化的融合需要时间

引入人才的新思想、新观念的同时也会带来对现有企业文化的挑战和思考,彼此的认同和相互吸引是事业成功的基础,而融合的时间会部分地影响工作的进展。如果新文化与原有文化无法融合,将会产生文化冲突。

(4) 需要更长的员工培训时间与工作适应期

新员工对岗位工作、饭店工作流程的熟悉,对与之配合的工作部门的熟悉,对上级、下属、同事的工作配合需要时间,饭店也需要时间对新员工进行相关工作的培训。

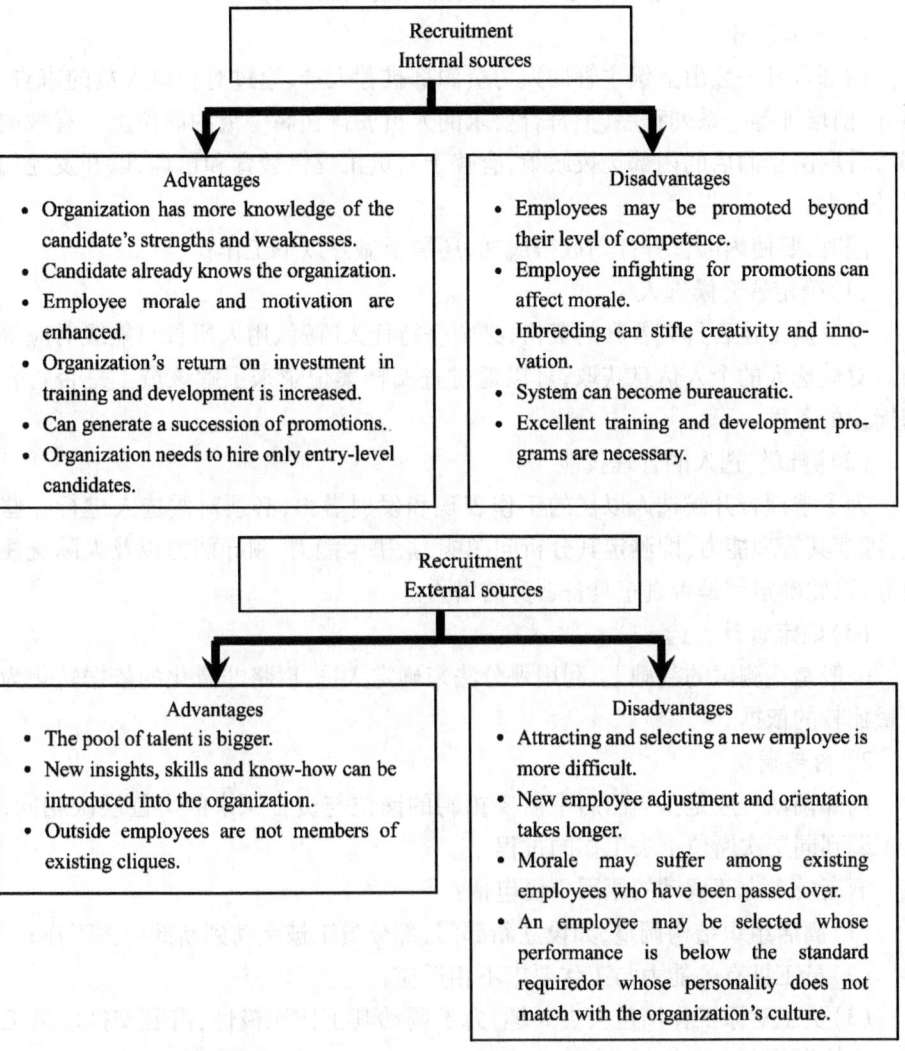

Figure 4-2　Recruitment (internal versus external sources)
Source: Stone R J. Human Resource Management (Fourth Edition). John Wiley & Sons Australia, Ltd.

二、招聘的方法(Recruitment Methods)

根据招聘的不同渠道,各自有不同的招聘方法和途径。

（一）内部招聘的途径（Ways of Internal Recruitment）

1. 内部晋升

内部晋升一般由上级主管向人力资源部推荐人选，通过对相应人员的审查、考核、岗前培训等一系列程序，把符合要求的人员安排在高一级的职位上。有效的内部晋升取决于酒店的内部选拔政策，有赖于对员工提供教育和培训，以开发他们的晋升潜力。

同时，要使内部晋升计划取得成功，还需要做好以下工作：

（1）确定晋升候选人

考察员工是否具有晋升的资格，必须坚持任人唯贤、用人所长与能级对应等原则。对候选人的个人信息获取，可以通过查阅档案记录来了解该员工是否符合待聘岗位的条件。

（2）测试候选人的管理技能

为了掌握晋升候选人以往的工作表现和发展潜力，必须对候选人进行一些测试，考察其管理能力，即测定其分析问题能力、决策能力、领导能力以及人际交往能力等，以此确定其是否真正具备晋升的潜力。

（3）确定晋升人选

一般是在测试的基础上，利用评分法来确定人选，以将非量化的依据转化为可定量比较的依据。

2. 内部调动

内部调动一般是指当酒店中需要招聘的岗位与员工原来的岗位层次相同，把员工调到同层次岗位上去工作的过程。

酒店员工内部调动的原因主要包括：

（1）酒店组织结构调整，如设立新部门，部分员工被调动到新部门去工作；

（2）员工拥有的能力与工作要求不相适应；

（3）员工对原工作岗位失去兴趣，为了调动其工作积极性，需要安排该员工到感兴趣的岗位上去工作；

（4）为了使员工成为多面手，增强他们的适应能力，对不同岗位上的员工定期地进行轮流换岗；

（5）员工在原工作部门出现了较为严重的人际关系问题，为了给他创造新的工作环境，对其进行工作调动。

3. 返聘

一些酒店由于一段时期经营情况不好，会暂时让一些员工下岗待聘，当情况好转时，再重新聘用这些员工。酒店业的淡旺不均现象，给酒店员工的合理配置提出了难题。在淡季，顾客数量锐减，酒店为了避免更多的经济损失可能不得不精减部分人员,但一旦旺季来临,或者酒店获得了新的发展机会,则会重新聘用暂时下岗的员工。重新聘用的方式能增强员工对酒店的归属感与忠诚度。

(二)内部招聘的方法(Approach to Internal Recruitment)

1. 工作公告和岗位竞聘

工作公告是内部招聘最常用的方法,尤其是对非管理层的职位而言。工作公告主要是通过布告、张榜的方式将现有工作空缺信息张贴在企业的布告栏上,让企业员工获知有关内部招聘的信息,工作公告中通常会对招聘工作的类型、职位说明、职位要求、薪资待遇、工作环境有一个简要的说明;所有具备资格的员工都可以申请竞聘该职位,人力资源部门或用人部门筛选这些申请,选中最符合条件的申请人进行面试。

通过工作公告可以让员工了解企业的职位空缺,提高企业内部选拔的透明度和公正性,可以对员工产生激励,提高其进取精神和减少员工流失。

2. 内部员工推荐

企业内部员工根据岗位的需要,通过推荐介绍的形式为企业找寻相关人才的方式。企业用人部门与人力资源部门对员工推荐来的人才进行相关的选拔与测评。内部员工推荐中最常见的是主管推荐,即当企业出现职位空缺时,可以要求部门主管提供一些他们认为适合此项工作的下属作为候选人。主管推荐这一方法受到了主管们的极大推崇,因为他们可以全权负责挑选那些即将成为他们下属的个体,他们可以了解潜在候选人的能力,特别是那些本在此部门工作并正在寻求晋升机会的人。然而主管决定推荐哪一名员工通常是很主观的,易受偏见和可能的歧视的影响,主管们可能会为了提拔他们的"亲信"而避开那些优秀的候选人,或者他们本身不了解某些人所具有的能力而忽视掉一些优秀的员工。

(三)外部招聘的途径和方法(Ways of External Recruitment)

1. 广告

招聘广告是外部渠道中使用较普遍的一种方法,它通过报纸、广播、电视和行业出版物等媒介向社会传递饭店的招聘需求信息,阅读广告的不仅有求职者,还有潜在的工作申请人,以及一些客户和一般大众。因此,饭店的招聘广告在一定程度上代表着公司的形象,需要认真实施。

借助广告进行招聘,饭店必须考虑两个关键的问题:

(1)广告媒体的选择

首先要考虑媒体本身承载信息传播的能力,即各种传播媒体的优缺点和适用范围。表4-1是各种广告媒体优缺点和使用范围的比较。

Table 4–1 Advantages and Disadvantages of the Major Types of Advertising Media

Type of Media	Advantages	Disadvantages	When to use
Newspapers	• Short deadlines • Ad size flexibility • Circulation concentrated in specific geographic areas • Classified sections well organized for easy access by active job seekers	• Easy for prospects to ignore • Considerable competitive clutter • Circulation not specialized—you must pay for great amount of unwanted readers • Poor printing quality	• When you want to limit recruiting to a specific area • When sufficient numbers of prospects are clustered in a specific area • When enough prospects are reading help-wanted ads to fill hiring needs
Magazines	• Specialized magazines reach pin-pointed occupation categories • Ad size flexibility • High-quality printing • Prestigious editorial environment • Long life—prospects keep magazines and reread them	• Wide geographic circulation—usually cannot be used to limit recruiting to specific area • Long lead time for ad placement	• When job is specialized • When time and geographic limitations are not of utmost importance • When involved in ongoing recruiting programs
Radio and television	• Difficult to ignore • Can reach prospects who are not actively looking for a job better than newspapers and magazines • Can be limited to specific geographic areas • Creatively flexible • Can dramatise employment story more effectively than printed ads • Little competitive recruitment clutter	• Only brief, uncomplicated messages are possible • Lack of permanence: prospect cannot refer back to it (repeated airings necessary to make impression) • Creation and production of commercials—particularly TV—can be time consuming and costly • Lack of special interest selectivity; paying for waste circulation	• In competitive situations when not enough prospects are reading your printed ads • When there are multiple job openings and there are enough prospects in a specific geographic area • When a large impact is needed quickly; a "blitz" campaign can saturate an area in two weeks or less • Useful to call attention to printed ads
Directories	• Specialized audiences • Long life	• Not timely • Often have competitive clutter	• Only appropriate for ongoing recruiting programs

第4章 招聘

续表

Type of Media	Advantages	Disadvantages	When to use
Direct mail	• Most personal form of advertising • Unlimited number of formats and amount of space • Names can be selected by geographical area, professional skills and other demographics, permitting precise targeting	• Difficult to find mailing list of prospects by occupation at home addresses • Cost for reaching each prospect is high	• If the right mailing list can be found, this is potentially the most effective medium—no other medium gives the prospect as much a feeling of being specially selected • Particularly valuable in competitive situations
Outdoor (roadside billboards) and transit (posters and buses and subways)	• Difficult to ignore • Can reach prospects as they are literally traveling to their current jobs • Precise geographic selectivity • Reaches large numbers of people many times at a low cost	• Only very brief message is possible • Requires long lead time for preparation and must be in place for long period of time (usually one to three months)	• When there is a steady hiring need for large numbers of people that is expected to remain constant over a long period of time
Internet	• Can target a global or local pool of labour • Increasingly not limited to high-tech positions • Short lead times and comparatively low cost • Job postings can target active job seekers • Banners, newsletters and email can target passive job seekers • Niche sites can target prospects with unique skills • An employment homepage can provide detailed employment information to prospects and serve as the centre of recruitment activities	• Prospects must be computer literate and/or have access to the internet • Increasing competitive clutter	• When there is a need to attract high-tech computer literate personnel or run highvolume recruitment campaigns • When a quick response is needed

Source: Bernard S. Hodes of Bernard Hodes Group (www.hodes.com).

在确定了媒体形式后,应进一步选择刊登招聘广告的具体媒体单位。主要考虑:

①媒体的定位：各种具体的传播载体都有其特定的消费群体定位，因此饭店应根据招聘人员的媒体消费特征选择其最可能接触的媒体。

②媒体的相关内容集中度：求职者在选择职位时，往往集中关注传播职位招聘信息量较大的媒体，便于选择比较。因此，饭店在选择媒体时，应选择招聘信息相对集中的媒体，尤其是在业界具有一定影响力的媒体。

③多种媒体并用：饭店在进行大规模的人员招聘时，或是人员招聘难度较大时，可以采用多种招聘方式，力求尽可能地覆盖目标人群接触范围。另外由于互联网的兴起，大量的在校学生和新一代知识人才都青睐网络带来的庞大的信息，组织可以借用网络形式实现招聘信息的传递，主要包括专业招聘网站、高校 BBS 以及饭店主页等。

(2) 如何设计广告

好的广告能吸引大量的求职者，同时广告制作也是一次绝好的宣传饭店形象的机会，有利于对外宣传饭店文化，容易使求职者产生对饭店的认同感。

饭店招聘广告的内容包含以下几个方面：

①广告题目。一般是"××饭店招聘""高薪诚聘"等。

②饭店简介。包括饭店的名称、性质、主营业务等，文字要简明扼要。

③审批机关。发布招聘广告一般要经过人力资源主管部门审批，一般是当地的人才交流中心。

④招聘岗位。包括岗位名称、任职资格、工作职责、工作地点等内容。

⑤人事政策。包括饭店的薪酬政策、社会保障政策、福利政策、培训政策等内容。

⑥联系方式。包括饭店地址、联系电话、传真、网址、电子信箱、联系人等内容。

一份好的广告应具备以下内容：

①使人过目不忘的广告词。

②说明招聘的岗位、人数、所需的资格条件等。

③能够起到宣传饭店的目的。

招聘广告的设计和构思，可以借鉴西方国家的 AIDA 方法。

A——attention，即广告要引人注意，善于利用各种技巧，如报纸的分类广告中，有意留白或为重要的职位进行单位的广告；

I——interest，即开发应聘者对职位的兴趣，这种兴趣可从职位本身去发掘，如未来的发展空间、收入、地理位置等；

D——desire，让求职者对空缺职位产生认同感和欲望；

A——action，即广告能让人马上采取行动。

2. 借助猎头

人员招聘，特别是高层管理者、重要中层岗位与尖端技术人员的招聘，是一项专业性和竞争性非常强的工作，有时酒店利用自身的力量往往难以获得合适的人才。因此,酒店会委托一些专业搜寻、网罗人才的"猎头"公司,凭借其人才情报网络与专业的眼光和方法,以及特有的"挖人"技巧,去猎取酒店所需的理想人才。猎头公司是酒店寻找高级经营人才和专业技术人才的服务机构,他们掌握着酒店业高级人才的资料,能够为雇主保密,能够帮助雇主一开始就接触到较为适合岗位要求的高素质求职者。

3. 校园招聘

学校作为培养各种各样人才的摇篮,是企业人力资源的重要来源。高校每年会为社会输送大量的专业人才,尽管学生的就业经验不足,但是他们扎实的基础知识、巨大的可塑性吸引了许多饭店企业到校园招聘。

校园招聘的优点体现在以下几个方面:

(1) 针对性强

可以根据企业的需要,选择学校、专业、特殊的专长等。

(2) 选择面大

学校是培养人才的基地,可供选择的人数多,具备各种专长的也大有人在,因此,选择的机会要比校园外的多得多。

(3) 选择层次是立体的

校园招聘有较低层次的中专、大专,也有中等层次的本科,还有较高层次的硕士和博士,这种选择的立体性只有校园招聘具备。

(4) 适宜进行战略性人才选择和储备部分优秀人才

由于校园人才的层次多、数量多,可供选择的机会多,便于企业进行战略性人才选择。

(5) 校园招聘的人才比较单纯,像一块璞玉,可以雕琢成各种精美的玉器

由于学生社会资历浅,思想单纯,因此接受能力和可塑性均强于其他来源的人才,如果培养、任用得当,人才对企业的认可度较高,忠诚度也较高。

校园招聘的缺点主要体现在以下几个方面:

(1) 由于没有任何工作经历,企业对应聘者今后可能的表现和绩效缺乏充分的把握。

(2) 由于学生缺乏工作经验,企业投入的培训成本高。

很多企业不喜欢招聘刚出校门的学生,主要是想节约培训成本,让别的企业培养3~5年,再想办法把较成熟的人员挖到自己的企业来。

(3) 由于学生常有眼高手低、对工作期望值过高的缺点,因此一年内跳槽的概率高,造成招聘成本高。

(4) 如果培养、任用不当,学生可能会不认可企业的文化和价值观,影响企业团队建设。

4. 网络招聘

21世纪是网络经济时代,网上招聘将成为企业招聘的主要渠道之一。

网上招聘的优点是:有多种类型的招聘网站可供选择,信息容量很大,不受版面容量的限制;可通过链接提供多层次、更详尽的信息;费用相对不高,覆盖面广、周期长、联系便捷等。

网上招聘的缺点是:容易导致招聘竞争的出现;有些招聘广告的真实性难以确认;网站的知名度、吸引到的求职者结构将在很大程度上决定招聘结果的有效性。

酒店通过网络招聘人才,既可以通过商业性的职业网站发布招聘信息,也可以在自己公司的主页上发布招聘信息。

5. 员工推荐

员工推荐对招聘专业人才比较有效。现在有很多公司逐渐认识到通过员工推荐的方法聘用现有员工的家属或朋友,有很多好处。

员工推荐的方法有如下优点:

(1)在推荐候选人的时候,他们对酒店的要求和候选人的条件都有一定的了解,会先在自己心目中进行一次筛选。

(2)被推荐者通过推荐者可以对酒店的基本情况、酒店文化等有一个基本的了解。而推荐者通常会认为被推荐者的素质与自己有关,只有在他们认为被推荐者不会给他/她带来不好的影响时,才会主动推荐。

员工推荐存在的主要问题是:

(1)易在酒店内形成"小团体",不利于管理。

(2)会使招聘工作取决于主管人的个人态度,而不是根据能力和工作绩效进行选择,从而影响招聘水平,尤其是在主管自己推荐的情况下。

(3)选用人员的面较窄。

6. 招聘会

随着我国人力资源开发及就业体制的建立与完善,人才市场的逐步形成与规范,各种人才见面会、交流会、应届生双向选择会等也相继增多。酒店可以抓住这种机会,广为宣传,塑造形象,积极网罗人才。同时,也可以收集同行业的人力资源供求状况与发展趋势,以便知己知彼,有的放矢。

第三节 人员甄选(Personnel Selection)

甄选,是指通过运用一定的工具和手段对已经招募到的求职者进行鉴别和考察,区分他们的人格特点与知识技能水平,预测他们的未来工作绩效,从而最终挑选出饭店所需要的、恰当的职位空缺填补者。

为了对应聘者的知识水平、能力、专业兴趣和个性特征等多方面的情况有比较全面和深入的了解，饭店应该借助于不同的方式来甄选出合适的人选。甄选已经成为饭店招聘工作的一个最重要的阶段。

一、初步筛选（Preliminary Screening）

初步筛选通常包括评价个人简历和审核工作申请表。初步筛选的目的在于透过简历和申请表的表面现象观察分析求职者潜在的危险信号。对显示出危险信号的申请者，应该在初步筛选中予以剔除。对于有希望的候选人，可以将发现的疑问记录下来，以备面试时进一步考察核实。

1. 个人简历的筛选

个人简历是应聘者自带的人格相关情况的介绍材料。在个人简历的筛选过程中，要注意以下几个问题：

（1）简历的内容是否完整。一份完整的简历一般要包括个人基本信息、受教育的经历、工作经历、工作业绩、性格特征和求职意向等。

（2）简历中个人的信息是否满足职位的要求。要重点考察应聘者的专业背景和工作经历是否和空缺职位相吻合。

（3）简历是否存在前后矛盾的地方。有些求职者为了得到工作机会，会在简历中虚构自己的工作经历，虚夸自己的工作业绩，或者回避一些关键性的问题。在简历中为了掩盖某一个信息，往往会出现自相矛盾的地方。

（4）简历的结构是否合理、设计是否美观。这些都能反映求职者的性格和习惯。

2. 工作申请表的筛选

工作申请表一般由饭店人力部门统一设计，用于考察应聘者的基本情况。

（1）考察求职态度。渴望得到工作、态度端正的应聘者都会认真地填写申请表，填写潦草或填写不完整的工作申请表被剔除的概率非常大。

（2）考察工作经历。在审查申请表时，可以重点了解应聘者的工作经历中所取得的成绩、担任的职务和运用的知识和技能等，对于那些频繁更换工作的应聘者要慎重考虑。

（3）考察申请表中一些可疑的地方。对于申请表中填写模糊或认为可能造假的地方要在面试中重点核实。

二、笔试（Written Examination）

笔试是一种最古老又最基本的选择方法，是让应聘者在试卷上笔答事先拟好的题目，然后根据应聘者答题的正确程度来评定成绩的一种甄选方法，这种方法主要通过测试应聘者的基础知识和素质能力的差异,判断该应聘者对招聘岗位的适应性。

笔试在员工招聘中有相当大的作用,尤其是在大规模的员工招聘中,它可以把员工的基本能力了解清楚,然后可以划分出一个基本符合需要的界限。通过笔试主要了解应聘者是否掌握应聘岗位必须具备的基础知识和专业知识,一般在甄选初期进行,成绩合格者才能继续参加下一轮的测试。

笔试的内容包括语言能力、专业技能、综合能力和心理素质等,其评价标准是速度和正确率。这种甄选方法的优点在于:花费的时间少、效率高、成本低,对应聘者的知识、能力、技术的考察可信度较高,成绩评价比较客观。缺点则是它不能全面地考察应聘者的工作态度、品德修养及其他一些隐性能力。

三、面试(Interview)

面试是通过测试者与应聘者双方面对面地观察、交谈等双向沟通方式,了解应聘者的心理素质、能力特征和个性品质的一种测试方法。面试是企业最常用的一种甄选方法,通过面对面的交流和沟通,双方都能加深了解,并能获得更多真实的信息。应聘者进一步了解企业,决定是否加入,同时企业在面试过程中考察应聘者更多方面的能力。

(一)面试的主要内容(Content of Interview)

面试时主要考察的信息和内容,一般需要根据具体的岗位来确定,面试大致包含以下一些内容:

(1)工作兴趣。申请动机;对该职位的了解程度;现具备哪些资格条件等。

(2)当前的工作状况。现在的职务;为什么要申请新的工作;如果被录用,何时能到岗。

(3)工作经历。最近工作的单位、地点、职务、职责、业绩等;曾经在哪些企业担任过何职,主要职责、待遇等;离职的原因等。

(4)教育背景。接受过何种教育、培训等。

(5)特长爱好。

(6)个人问题。是否愿意经常出差;自己的优缺点等。

(二)面试的类型(Type of Interview)

按照不同的划分方法,面试主要有以下几类:

1. 按照面试的结构划分

(1)结构化面试。是指提前准备好一系列问题和可能的答案,在面试过程中,根据应聘者的回答,给出相应的分数。结构化面试具有规范性、客观性及便于分析和比较的优点。如表4-2就是结构化面试中一个提问的提纲,值得注意的是并非表中的所有问题都要按次序一一提问,面试中可根据应聘者的表现跳过一些问题,也可以加上一些问题。

表4-2 结构化面试提问提纲

面试对象姓名		所在部门		申请职位	
面试地点		面试时间		面试人	
面试内容					
工作兴趣	1. 这一职位涉及哪些方面的工作 2. 你为什么想要做这份工作 3. 你为什么认为你能胜任这份工作 4. 你对待遇有什么要求 5. 你是怎么知道我们公司的				
目前工作情况	1. 如果可能,你什么时候能够到岗 2. 你现在的工作单位及工作职务情况如何				
工作经历	1. 请你简述你以前的工作经历,主要指职务及工作内容 2. 你所取得的主要工作成绩有哪些 3. 在以前的工作经历中,你一直是从事同一种工作吗 4. 说明你曾经从事过哪些不同的工作、时间及各方面的主要成绩 5. 你认为自己最适合做哪方面的工作?曾经在哪些方面有成就感 6. 你最初的薪水是多少?现在的薪水是多少 7. 你目前的求职意向是什么?要求薪水多少 8. 请简述以前几个工作的离职原因 9. 在选择新工作时,最看重的是公司的哪些方面				
教育背景	1. 你认为你所受的哪些教育和培训将帮助你胜任你所申请的工作 2. 对你受过的所有正规教育进行说明 3. 说明你工作以外的培训及学习情况				
个人问题	1. 你愿意出差吗 2. 你最大限度的出差时间可以保证多长 3. 你对加班的看法				
其他	1. 你认为你最大的优点是什么 2. 你认为你最大的缺点是什么 3. 你有哪些爱好和特长?你的性格特征如何 4. 你对以前工作单位满意的地方是什么?不满意的地方是什么 5. 你以前的上、下级及同事关系怎么样 6. 你对我们公司的印象怎么样?包括规模、特点、环境、竞争地位等 7. 你对申请的职位的最大兴趣是什么 8. 介绍一下你的家庭情况 9. 你认为对你的工作激励作用最大的因素有哪些 10. 你更喜欢独自工作还是协作工作				

资料来源:田在兰.人力资源管理[M].广州:暨南大学出版社,2011:123.

(2)非结构化面试。是指没有固定的格式,没有统一的评分标准,所提问题因人而异。面试官可以与应聘者讨论各种话题,可以根据应聘者对上一问题的具体回答来决定下一个问题问什么,还可以根据应聘者的回答进行追问,以了解更深入的信息。

(3)半结构化面试。是介于结构化面试和非结构化面试之间的一种面试方法。主要特征是提问可以不按固定的格式和程序进行,一部分问题是事先规划出来的一系列固定的问题,另一部分是可以根据实际情况随机提出来的。

2. 按照面试的过程划分

(1)一次性面试。是指对应聘者只进行一次面试就作出决策。

(2)序列面试。是指通过一系列连续的面试而为录用决策积累信息的方法,一般包括几轮面试,经过每一轮次的淘汰,最后作出录用决策。

3. 按照面试的组织方式划分

(1)一对一面试。由面试官和应聘者单独进行交流和沟通的面试方式。

(2)集体面试。由多个面试官同时对多个应聘者进行面试,这种方法有助于了解应聘者在参加集体活动时的人际关系能力,也可以节省面试时间。

(3)小组面试。由多个面试官对一个应聘者进行面试。面试小组成员包括人力资源管理部门的负责人和用人部门的负责人。小组面试的优点是为参与录用决策的人员提供了同等的机会审查应聘者。

(三)面试的主要方法(Ways of Interview)

1. 无领导小组讨论

是对一组人同时进行测试的方法,给讨论小组(一般由4~6人组成,不指定谁充当主持讨论的组长)发一个简短的案例,其中隐含着一个或数个待解决和处理的问题,以引导小组展开讨论。

这种方法通常没有人告诉任何一个小组成员他应该坐在哪个位置上,一般使用一张圆桌,以便每个座席的位置具有同等的重要性。在小组讨论的过程中,即使出现冷场、僵局的情况,甚至发生争吵,测评者也不出面干预,让应聘者们自发进行。

最后的测评结果,是由几位面试官根据小组中的每位应聘者在讨论中的表现及所起作用,按既定标准给予评分。这些标准包括主动性、宣传鼓励与说服力、口头沟通能力、企业管理能力、人际协调能力、自信、创新能力、心理承受能力等。应注意的是,这些素质和能力是通过应聘者在讨论中所扮演的角色(如主动发起者、指挥者、鼓动者、协调者、记录者、计时者等)的行为来表现的。

2. 公文处理

又称文件筐测试,在这种测评方法中,面对大量的报告、备忘录、电传、信函和其他材料,要求应聘者对所有的文件进行恰当的处理。例如,先处理那些对公司来说意义重大且急需处理的文件;对请示文件作出批示;回复信件等。由此可以测试应聘者的组织、计划、协调、分析、判断、分派任务的能力,处理问题的条理程度及收集和利用信息的能力。

公文处理法是经过多年实践检验的、有效的管理人员的测评方法。具体的步骤如下:

(1)发给每个应聘者一套文件汇编(由15~25份文件组成),包括下级呈上来的报告、请示、计划、预算,同级部门的备忘录,上级的指示、批复、规定、政策,外界用户、供应商、银行、政府有关部门乃至所在社区的函电、传真及电话记录,甚至还有群众检举或投诉信等,这些文件经常会出现在管理人员的办公桌上。

(2)向应聘者介绍有关的背景材料,并告知应聘者现在就是这个岗位的任职者,全权负责处理文件筐里的所有公文材料。应聘者根据自己的经验、知识和性格在给定的时间内去处理解决这些问题。

(3)最后,面试官根据既定的考评标准进行评判,最常见的考评标准有7个,即个人自信心、企业领导能力、计划安排能力、书面表达能力、分析决策能力、敢担风险倾向与信息敏感性,但也可以根据具体情况增减,如加上创造性思维能力、工作方法的合理性等。总之,应当将应聘者的岗位胜任能力与长远发展的潜质作为测评的重点。

3. 角色扮演

设置一个场景或一个具体事例,其中包含一系列尖锐的人际矛盾和冲突,让应聘者扮演某一角色去处理矛盾和冲突,通过观察应聘者在不同角色中的表现来评价其人际交往能力、思维敏捷性、情绪控制力及口头表达能力等。

4. 即席发言

给应聘者一个题目,让其稍作准备后发言,以了解应聘者的反应理解能力、语言表达能力、气质风度及发散思维能力等素质。

第四节 人员录用(Personnel Employment)

录用指最终确定相应职位的合格人选的过程。包括录用决策、体检、岗前培训、试用、正式录用等环节。

一、录用决策(Employ Decision)

录用决策主要是对甄选过程中获取的信息进行综合评价与分析,确定每一个候选人的能力特点,并根据预先设计的人员利用标准进行挑选,从而选择合适人员的过程。在对每个指标都进行类似的评价后,归结出应聘者在指标上的优缺点,并对照职位的要求作出判断。在作出录用决策时,应当充分考虑招聘的黄金法则——能岗匹配,最合适的才是最好的。

在许多企业中,录用决策一般是由人力资源管理部门具体负责决定,他们常常为用人部门提供经过筛选的候选人名单,由用人部门最终作出录用决策。

在作出录用决策后,人力资源部门就可以向被录用者发出录用通知,在录用通知书中,要说明报到的起止时间、报到的地点以及报到的程序等内容,同时对被录用者表示欢迎。

二、体检(Physical Examination)

身体健康是开展工作的基础,进行录用前的体检主要有以下四个方面的作用:
(1)确定求职者是否符合岗位的身体要求;
(2)建立求职者的健康记录,为未来的保险或员工的赔偿要求提供依据;
(3)降低缺勤率和事故,发现员工可能不知道的传染性疾病;
(4)体检资料还可以用于衡量员工的某些体力、能力特性是否与绩效水平相联系。

三、岗前培训(Pre-job Training)

岗前培训的目的在于向新员工介绍其工作环境及同事,能使其迅速熟悉业务流程,消除新员工对新工作、新环境及新同事的陌生感,激励新员工的士气。岗前培训包括熟悉工作内容、性质、责任、权限、利益、规范;了解企业文化、政策及规章制度;熟悉企业环境、岗位环境、人事环境;熟悉、掌握工作流程、技能等。培训时长根据具体情况而定。培训合格者方可上岗工作。

四、试用期考察(Probation investigation)

员工进入企业前,要与企业签订试用合同。试用合同是对员工与企业双方的约束与保障。试用合同应包括以下主要内容:试用的职位、试用的期限、员工在试用期的报酬与福利、员工在试用期的工作绩效目标与应承担的义务和责任、员工在试用期应接受的培训、员工在试用期应享受的权利、员工转正的条件、试用期企业解聘员工的条件与承担的义务和责任、员工辞职的条件与义务、员工试用期被延长的条件等。

试用的主要目的是为了通过工作实践考察录用人员对工作的适宜性,同时,也为试用的员工提供了进一步了解企业与所从事的工作的机会。试用期一般为3个月,特殊岗位的试用期为6个月,试用期工作优异者,经部门推荐、考核通过,可以提前结束试用期,正式录用。

五、正式录用(Formal Employment)

新员工的正式录用即通常所称的"转正",是指试用期满且试用合格的员工正式成为企业成员的过程。

正式录用过程中用人部门与人力资源部门应完成以下主要工作:员工试用期的考核鉴定;根据考核情况进行正式录用决策;与员工签订正式的录用合同;给员工提供相应的待遇;制订员工发展计划;为员工提供必要的帮助与咨询等。

第五节 人员招聘评估
(Personnel Recruitment Assessment)

招聘评估是招聘职能的最后环节,包括对招聘的成本、招聘到的人员数量与质量的评估。

招聘评估是招聘过程中必不可少的一个环节,它通过成本与效益核算能够使招聘人员清楚地知道费用的支出情况,区分哪些是应支出项目,哪些是不应支出项目,这有利于合理安排以后的招聘费用,为组织节省开支。

招聘评估通过对录用员工的绩效、实际能力、工作潜力的评估即通过对录用员工质量的评估,检验招聘工作成果与方法的有效性,有利于招聘方法的改进。

一、成本效益评估(Cost-Benefit Assessment)

招聘成本效益评估是指对招聘中的费用进行调查、核实,并对照预算进行评价的过程,招聘成本效益评估是鉴定招聘效率的一个重要指标。如果成本低,录用人员质量高,就意味着招聘效率高;反之,则意味着招聘效率低。从另一个角度来看,成本低,录用人员多,就意味着招聘效率高;反之,则意味着招聘效率低。

(一) *招聘成本*(Recruit Cost)

招聘成本分为招聘总成本与招聘单位成本。招聘总成本即人力资源的获取成本,它由两个部分组成,一部分是直接成本,包括招募费用、甄选费用、录用员工的家庭安置费用和工作安置费用以及其他费用(如招聘人员的差旅费、应聘人员的招待费等);另一部分是间接费用,包括内部提升费用、工作流动费用。招聘单位成本是招聘总成本与实际录用人数之比,如果招聘实际费用少,录用多,意味着招聘单位成本低;反之,则意味着招聘单位成本高。

（二）成本效用评估（Cost-Utility Assessment）

成本效用评估是对招聘成本所产生的效果进行的分析，主要包括招聘总成本效用分析、招募成本效用分析、人员甄选成本效用分析和人员录用成本效用分析等。计算方法是：

总成本效用 = 录用人数/招聘总成本

招募成本效用 = 应聘人数/招募期间的费用

甄选成本效用 = 被选中人数/甄选期间的费用

录用成本效用 = 正式录用的人数/录用期间的费用

（三）招聘收益成本比（Recruitment Benefit-Cost Ratio）

它既是一项经济评价指标，同时也是对招聘工作的有效性进行考核的一项指标，招聘的收益成本比越高，则说明招聘工作越有效。

招聘收益成本比 = 所有新员工为组织创造的总价值/招聘总成本

二、录用人员评估（Hired Personnel Assessment）

录用人员评估是指根据招聘计划对录用人员的质量和数量进行评价的过程，在大型招聘活动中，录用人员评估显得十分重要。如果录用人员不合格，那么招聘过程中所花的时间、精力和金钱就都浪费了；只有全部招聘到合格的人员才能说全面完成了招聘任务。

判断招聘数量的一个简单方法就是看职位空缺是否得到满足，雇用率是否真正符合招聘计划的设计。衡量招聘质量是按照企业的长、短期经营指标来分别确定的，在短期计划中，企业可根据求职人员的数量和实际雇用人数的比例来认定招聘质量；在长期计划中，企业可根据接受雇用的求职者的转化率来判断招聘的质量。

（一）数量评估（Quantitative Assessment）

录用员工数目的评估是对招聘工作有效性检验的一个重要方面，通过数量评估，分析在数量上满足或不满足需求的原因，有利于找出各招聘环节上的薄弱之处，改进招聘工作；同时，通过录用人员数量与招聘计划数量的比较，为人力资源规划的修订提供了依据。

主要从录用比、招聘完成比、应聘比三方面考虑。

1. 录用比 = 录用人数/应聘人数 × 100%

录用比例越小，说明录用者的素质可能越高。

2. 招聘完成比 = 录用人数/计划招聘人数 × 100%

招聘完成比等于或大于100%，说明在数量上全面或超额完成了招聘计划。

3. 应聘比＝应聘人数/计划招聘人数×100%

应聘比则说明招募的效果,应聘比越高,则招募信息发布的效果越好。

(二)**质量评估**(Quality Assessment)

录用员工质量的评估是对员工的工作绩效行为、实际能力、工作潜力的评估,它是对招聘的工作成果与方法的有效性检验的另一个重要方面,质量评估既有利于招聘方法的改进,又对员工培训、绩效评估提供了必要的信息。

录用人员的质量评估实际上是对所录用人员在甄选过程中对其能力、潜力、素质等进行的各种测试与考核的延续,也可根据招聘的要求和工作分析得出结论,对录用人员进行等级排列来确定其质量,其方法与绩效考核方法类似。当然,录用比和应聘比这两个数据也在一定程度上反映了录用人员的质量。

案例分析(Practice Case Analysis)

W Hotels—An Alternative Approach to Recruitment

Everyone in the hospitality industry knows that recruitment is a major headache. Turnover—at an average of 30% a year—is too high and with numerous hotels opening each month, finding and retaining good candidates is a tough task. For new hotels with vacancies in their hundreds, recruitment is a particular challenge.

One hotel company taking an innovative approach to staffing is W Hotels in Singapore, which has been holding a series of talent auditions in the region to meet the needs of upcoming hotels. The W, for example, needs to recruit 490 staff before its soft opening in December, and in August held a one-day audition that ran from 2∶00 to midnight. The event took place in a nightclub and applicants—or potential talent as the company prefers to call its employees—were entertained with DJs and dancers whilst sipping mocktails and waiting to be called for their one-on-one assessment.

The actual interview itself when it took place was also a typical with a more conversational approach adopted than used in the traditional recruitment process.

"Our goal for the event was to provide the potential 'staff' with a fun and entertaining experience, similar to the culture you would find at any of our W hotels," says Cary Gray, general manager of the W. The benefits of holding the event were two-fold, he says, first, in creating a buzz around the property—eight channels for live TV were at the event; and second, in immerging candidates into the W culture right from the start.

More than 800 candidates turned up on the day, but the event had a wider impact than predicted, with the number of calls of people interested in the vacancies trebling after the event based on word of mouth, says Gray. "To this day we are inundated with people looking for positions," he comments. "We try to screen people for those that really want W," says Gray. "A lot of the behavioural interview that we do involves finding out how much people know about W, how much research they've done, and whether or not they are aware about the brand."

While the event didn't entirely solve W's recruitment problems, it did go a long way to meet its staffing requirements, says Gray. He estimates the hotel filled between 180 and 200 positions on the day. "We had a total of 490 vacancies, had about 120 already and right now we're up to about 340," he says.

The W is not the first W hotel to try the talent audition approach to recruitment. The W Retreat & Spa Bali Seminyak also adopted the strategy earlier this year. It attracted some 900 applicants on the day, and of these, more than 400 people were recruited.

Craig Seaward, general manager of the W Retreat & Spa Bali Seminyak, believes that the unusual approach to recruitment helped to account for its high degree of success. "The Talent Show is designed with W vibe to bring out the personalities of the applicants. Personality is innate, it can't be inculcated," he comments. "It starts with the tone of our recruitment advertising, online and offline with a headline emphasizing that candidates do not necessarily need to come from the hospitality sector to fulfill positions available. The importance is a balance of talents with and without the background of hospitality," he adds.

Source: http://hma.hotelworldasia.com/content/case-study-w-hotels-%E2%80%93-alternative-approach-recruitment?page=0%2C0.

Questions for Discussion:
1. What's the innovation in the recruitment process of the W Hotels?
2. Which characteristic the W Hotels may focus on when they are having an interview? Experience, personality, or…?

名词解释(Key Terms)

1. 招聘:选择合格人选的过程。通过正式宣布或刊登广告及评估应聘者整个过程找到合格的应聘者来填充目前或未来的工作空缺。

Recruitment: It is the process of seeking and attracting a pool of qualified candidates for a job vacancy of a hotel and choosing the candidate who best meets the selection criteria.

2. 内部招聘:从企业内部找应聘者补充到空缺岗位上。

Internal Recruiting: The enterprise find candidate from internal to add vacancy positions.

3. 外部招聘:从企业外找应聘者补充到空缺岗位上。

External Recruiting: The enterprise find candidate from external to add vacancy positions.

4. 甄选:甄选是通过一系列科学的方法,在招募时确定的申请者中进行选择,从中挑选出最适合饭店某一特定工作岗位的人员,并使之接受这一工作的过程。

Selection: Selection is the process by which an organization chooses the person or persons from a list of applicants who best meet the selection criteria for the position available, considering current environmental conditions.

5. 录用:饭店最终决定雇用应聘者并分配其具体工作的过程。

Employ: The process that hotel finally decided to hire applicants and distribute specific work for them.

6. 人员招聘评估:饭店对招聘的成本以及招聘到的人员数量、质量进行评价的过程。

Evaluation: The process of hotel evaluate the cost of recruitment and the quantity and quality of hired personnel.

7. 面试:面试是通过测试者与应聘者双方面对面的观察、交谈等双向沟通方式,了解应聘者的心理素质、能力特征和个性品质的一种测试方法。

Interview: Interview is a kind of test method that the tester understands the psychological quality, ability and personality characteristics of applicants through communicating with them face to face or other two-way methods.

8. 招聘成本效益评估:它是指对招聘中的费用进行调查、核实,并对照预算进行评价的过程。

Cost Benefit Assessments of Recruitment: To evaluate the cost of the investigation and verification during recruitment and compare with the budget.

9. 录用人员评估:是指根据招聘计划对录用人员的质量和数量进行评价的过程。

Hired Personnel Assessment: The process of evaluating the quality and quantity of hired personnel according to the recruitment plan.

复习思考题(Questions for Review)

1. 简要说明招聘的定义及基本流程。

Explain the definition of recruitment and the basic process briefly.

2. 影响招聘工作的因素有哪些?

What is the influence factor of recruitment?

3. 比较内部招聘渠道和外部招聘渠道的优缺点。

Compare the advantages and disadvantages of internal recruitment channels and external recruitment channels.

4. 内部渠道和外部渠道的招聘方法分别有哪些?

What methods do internal channels and external channel recruitment have?

5. 人员甄选的定义和方法?

What is the definition and method of personnel selection?

6. 人员录用包含哪几个过程?

How many processes does personnel employed have? What are they?

7. 招聘评估包括哪几个方面? 如何进行相应的评估?

What respects does recruitment assessment have? How to do the assessment?

研究前沿(Research Front)

SOW HUP CHAN, OIMEIKUOK. A Study of Human Resources Recruitment, Selection, and Retention Issues in the Hospitality and Tourism Industry in Macau. Journal of Human Resources in Hospitality & Tourism, 2011,10: 421-441.

Through this study the authors examine hiring managers' attitudes regarding selection methods, vital skills sought in new employees, and why their employees quit. Completed questionnaires were collected from 135 employers. Applicants' resumes and interviews are the most frequently used selection methods. Consistent with literature, human relation skills are the most important skills employers seek. A major reason for employee turnover is due to salary. The findings suggest the need for discussion on creative human resource approaches and a program to increase employee commitment. Implications for management are included.

...

The purpose of the authors in this study was to examine the recruitment, selection, and retention issues in the hospitality and tourism industry in Macau. The specific objectives were to:

1. Determine how employers in the hospitality and tourism industry assess their applicants;
2. Identify what skills employers value most in the selection process;
3. Identify the reasons behind the employee turnover in Macau.

The findings provide insights into understanding hiring attitudes toward recruitment in a tight labor market.

...

Recruitment

Recruitment is the process of generating a pool of capable people applying to an organization for employment (Gold, 2007). Employers who want to fill a vacancy quickly or are unwilling to invest in the recruitment process maybe less discriminating in the quality (or quantity) of the applicants (Russo, Rietveld, Nijkamp & Gorter, 2000) while employers who made greater efforts in the recruitment process activate more search channels than employers who did not (Russo et al., 2000). Firms are more discerning when the cost of a mistake in recruitment is high (Russo et al., 2000).

Initial Assessment Methods

Employers in different countries prefer different selection methods. Reference checks are the most frequently used selection method in the United States (Rynes, Orlitsky & Bretz, 1997). For recent university graduates, employers in the United States prefer to evaluate the educational achievement of the applicants or assess their abilities through a trial work period (Rynesetal. 1997). Initial interviews, reference checks, and application forms are the most popular methods in the United Kingdom (Hodgkinson, Daley & Payne, 1995) while the application form is the most popular in Australia, with about 94% of organizations using it (Carless, 2007). The employment interview is one of the most widely used selection methods (Ryan, McFarland, Baron, & Page, 1999) especially for entry level hospitality employees in the United States (Martin & Groves, 2002). Although the validity and reliability of interviews have been disappointing (Gold, 2007), applicants prefer interviews to other selection instruments (Posthuma, Morgesin & Campion, 2002). Background checks are used less than reference checks and graphology is not considered a viable means of assessing one's character, abilities, and performance (British Psychological Society, 1993). Nevertheless, graphology is widely used in Western Europe (particularly France and Switzerland) and Israel (Heneman & Judge, 2006; Sharma& Vardhan, 1975). The use of genetic screening is not widespread due to its high cost and legal concerns of employers (Heneman & Judge, 2006).

Interviews, resumes, and work samples were the best-rated and most favorably appraised methods among students and employees in Greece (Nikolaou& Judge, 2007). Similar results were found in Western Europe and the United States (Anderson & Witvliet, 2008). Hausknecht, Day, and Thomas (2004) also noted that interviews, resumes, work samples, and references were perceived favorably by job applicants.

Substantive Assessment Methods

Reducing the number of finalists for a job is time consuming. A useful selection device is one that "provides information on who will be a good employee" (Ryan & Tippins, 2004, p. 308). For instance, job knowledge tests may be inappropriate for an entry-level position if they test knowledge easily acquired on the job and not needed at the time of hire (Schmitt & Chan, 1998).

The high costs involved in developing and managing structured interviews explains its moderate level of usage (Heneman & Judge, 2006). Job candidates are in favor of interviews—whether they are structured or unstructured (Hausknecht et al., 2004) and react negatively if they are not given the opportunity to be interviewed. Personality tests, which can help to ensure a match between the personality type of the applicant and the job, are in low use (Heneman & Judge, 2006). While both performance tests and work samples have a high degree of reliability and validity in predicting job performance, both tests measure what applicants can do not what they will do (Schmitt & Chan, 1998). Both of these tests are expensive to conduct (Heneman & Judge, 2006).

Previous studies revealed that cognitive ability tests are very effective hiring and recruitment strategies (Ryan & Tippins, 2004). Although ability tests are the most effective way to predict job success, only between 15% and 20% of companies use some sort of ability test (Rowe, Williams & Day, 1994). Carless (2007) reported that only a small proportion of companies use drug tests (14%), integrity tests (10%), physical ability tests (8%), and vocational interest inventories (8%).

Although selection and recruitment practices vary from country to country, there is limited literature on samples from China where the culture is quite different. While the problems faced by the hospitality and tourism industry in attracting, recruiting, and retaining adequately trained and motivated staff are well documented (Barron, 2008), and most turnover in hotels in Hong Kong occurs in the first few months of employment (Lam, Lo, & Chan, 2002), there are no discussions regarding the criteria or selection methods used. Thus, the first research question investigated by the authors was: How do local employers assess applicants?

Communication and Employability Skills

Communication skills are vital for career success, however there are relatively few studies of employers' perceptions of the communication skills of the new hires from 1990 through 2002 (Stevens, 2005). From available studies, Moody, Stewart, and Bolt - Lee (2002) revealed that the top five skills sought by employers are communication (oral and written), computer literacy, interpersonal/social, critical thinking/leadership (tied), and teamwork. Employers favor the resume and interview methods to demonstrate these skills, and they felt a portfolio was useful in providing evidence of the skills sought (Moody et al., 2002). Consequently, Moody et al. (2002) suggest that instructors provide students with explicit instruction on developing resumes and portfolios.

Many employers rate communication skills as the most desirable abilities when hiring new employees (Maes, Weldy, & Icenogle, 1997). While employers are looking for good technical skills in their recruits, they are also looking for strong soft skills, often called "people skills", which are typically hard to observe, quantify, and measure (Coates, 2006). Examples of soft skills include problem solving, teamwork, collaboration, planning, leadership, and presentation skills, as well as knowledge of transferable information technology(IT) and adaptability. Although some of these skills can only be determined once individuals start their job, other skills can be determined before recruitment. While many employers placed emphasis on the values of a person's intrinsic qualities and less on examination results, Teo (1993) revealed that public sector employers seem to place more importance on examination results than private sector employers.

In sum, prospective employees should be aware of various skills that might influence their chance of being short-listed during the recruitment process. Thus, the second research question was stated as "What skills do employers value most in the selection process?"

Employee Turnover

Employee turnover refers to an employee's exit from an organization (Taylor, 2007). Studies on turnover showed that pre-hire predictors are related to both turnover and job performance (Barrick & Zimmerman, 2009). Employees and job applicants with intention to quit may lower their performance level even when they remain in the organization (Meyer, Stanley, Herscovitch & Topolnytsky, 2002). The ability to assess applicant—organization fit, in addition to more embedded social links, will likely increase the probability that employees will remain with the organization (Barrick & Zimmerman, 2009).

Previous research also showed that employers use money to attract, retain, and motivate employees to achieve organizational goals (Milkovich & Newman, 2002). While the undesirable consequences of pay dissatisfaction may lead to turnover, employees may also be lured away when offered higher salaries by another organization. This suggests that only highly committed employees choose to remain with their organizations. Since pay satisfaction is positively related to organizational commitment (Tang & Chiu, 2003), is pay the major reason leading to turnover in Macau? The third research question was stated as "What are the reasons leading to turnover in Macau?"

METHODOLOGY

The lists of skills and attributes used for this study were derived from previous studies (see, for example, Albrecht & Sack, 2000; Kavanagh & Drennan, 2008; Okeiyi, Finley & Postel, 1994; Tanyel, Mitchell, & McAlum, 1999; Tas, 1988) and textbooks (Heneman & Judge, 2006). Three specialist skills (job-related technical skills, related work experience, and business knowledge skills) and nonverbal communication were also added. The skills studied include communication and interpersonal communication skills, job-related technologies, human relations, and problem solving abilities. Selection methods include initial assessment, substantive assessment, and contingencies.

The Questionnaire

A questionnaire was designed which consists of five parts. Part 1 consists of 16 questions about the respondents' perceptions of the importance of skill and attributes as employment criteria. A five point Likert scale was used to evaluate each skill: 5 = Extremely Important, 4 = Very Important, 3 = Important, 2 = Slightly Important, and 1 = Not Important. Part 2 of the questionnaire asked how the skills in Part 1 are best demonstrated by the job applicant, while Part 3 of the questionnaire asked for employers' perceptions of the initial screening and criteria used in evaluating job applicants. There are six questions on initial screening, six questions on initial assessment, and ten questions on substantive assessment. The same five point Likert scale used in Part 1 is used in this section. The last two questions in Part 3 on contingent methods are questions with dichotomous "Yes" or "No" answers. Part 4 of the questionnaire consists of four dichotomous questions concerning staff turnover, while Part 5 consists of four questions on demographics.

Respondents and Data Collection

The respondents were hiring managers directly involved in selecting and hiring employees for hotels, travel agencies, restaurants, and trading (souvenir) companies. Researchers were asked to randomly select and make contact with the human resource (HR) department of companies listed in a local business telephone directory in order to identify 200 employers who had either recruited new staff or experienced turnover in the past six months. The person answering the phone at the business was then asked for the name and contact information of the hiring manager. The researchers then established contact with the hiring manager directly to invite their participation in the survey. One hundred and thirty-seven hiring managers agreed to participate in the study. An appointment was then made to deliver the survey questionnaire to each of these managers who were then asked to complete a short, two-page questionnaire. Each questionnaire was delivered by hand by the researchers and was collected right after completion. The major reason for this procedure was to ensure that the survey was not completed by a secretary or someone else.

Data Analysis

The data collected were analyzed using the SPSS version 15. Descriptive statistics, such as frequencies and mean scores, were calculated for each item.

RESULTS

Demographic Profile of Respondents

Two hundred employers met the criteria for the study. Although they were all invited to participate in the study, only 137 agreed to complete the questionnaire. Two questionnaires were discarded due to too many missing variables. The valid response rate was (135/200) 67.5%. All the respondents were hiring managers from hotels (51), trading companies (40), travel agencies (27), and restaurants (17) with employee size ranging from 40 to 400. Specifically, 28 were HR professionals while the others were line managers in information technology, marketing, accounting, and customer service departments. Two thirds of the respondents were female (63%). A majority of the participants were under 45 years old (73.4%) and held managerial positions (60%).

CONCLUSIONS

The authors found in this study that the resume and recruitment interview are the most frequently used selection and assessment methods. Attitude, interest, values, and preference inventories are most important during the substantive stage. Employers also value human relation skills, oral communication, and listening skills. The findings here suggest that job applicants should frame their resumes to meet the expectations of employers, project an appropriate attitude and interest in the position, and demonstrate their communication skills during the job interview. Pay was a major reason for employees to quit their jobs. Employers in Macau experienced difficulty in retaining their workforce, and they are willing to recruit staff without the needed experience to meet their hiring needs.

IMPLICATIONS

The implications for the HR managers are as follows: First, localization should be considered since most (if not all) the senior positions are filled by foreign workers, especially in the casino hotels. The localization process can enhance employee commitment and reduce turnover. Second, HR managers might need to make cross boarder strategic alliances with contractors and sub-contractors for various activities that can be managed off-site including hiring employees in ZhuHai to handle back-office work, such as accounts, or to complete mundane tasks, such as folding dining table napkins. Such alliances with organizations in mainland China, to a certain extent, can lower the tight labor market situation. Third, since turnover is often caused by the lack of careers, inadequate salaries, or low job satisfaction, HR managers may find it useful to increase their employees' job satisfaction and organizational commitment, conduct formal exit interviews to identify reasons for high turnover, and to undertake comprehensive HR planning and approaches to examine turnover to ensure effective HR utilization that contributes to quality service. There is also a need to adopt creative approaches for fast tract employees, as well as training for all staff, enhance the work environment, and increase remuneration. HR managers should offer development training for their employees rather than only job related training. This can benefit the organization while increasing organizational commitment among the employees.

Furthermore, HR managers might gain from implementing talent management strategies "to ensure that the sector is able to recruit, retain, support, and develop personnel of the highest quality appropriate to the diversity of work and employment situations that exists within the sector" (Baum, 2008, p. 725), as well as consider the use of low skilled migrant labor as a means to provide temporary solutions to some of the staffing problem.

The findings also have important implications for educators, students, and policy makers. Colleges and universities have a pivotal role to play in the training and development of future hospitality and tourism managers. Job search strategies and more communication-related courses, such as interpersonal communication skill courses or human relation courses, must be incorporated in the undergraduate curriculum. Change in the secondary school level curriculum can also, to a certain extent, help provide necessary skills for the hospitality and tourism industry, while balancing the skills in demand for other sectors. Students should know what to include in their resumes and frame the resumes to match the desired position. Students should also attend university instead of grabbing high paying jobs with poor long-term prospects, since more employers prefer to recruit staff without needed experience rather than to recruit staff with lower academic qualifications. Because part-time work has shown to have benefits for both industry and students (Barron, 2008) and that "the casual, part-time employee of today might be tomorrow's manager" (p. 738), perhaps policy makers may want to allow foreign students who are currently barred from employment to engage in casual or part-time work. Such an approach may put a break on the drastic increase in salaries in some sectors while providing students with necessary experience before joining the workforce. More importantly, with no technically trained graduates being produced, such as chefs and with only one government sponsored technical school which trains only dealers, Macau needs a clear, concise policy on the use of foreign labor and the development of local labor.

LIMITATIONS AND FURTHER RESEARCH

Several limitations of this study are to be noted. First, the cross-sectional data was largely based on information provided by the employers for the last position filled, which are generally entry-level, front-line in nature. Second, the findings can only serve as reference for other small populated economies that rely on the hospitality or tourism industry and other tight labor markets in the region. Replication of this study in different settings can validate the findings and allow for comparison. It is recommended that a replication of this study be longitudinal and include higher-level positions to determine appropriate recruitment strategies at various organizational levels. Factors such as the channels of recruitment not covered in the present study should also be investigated.

Future researchers may investigate HR managerial capabilities to derive benefits, such as cost, accessibility, etc. to meet Macau's HR requirements by exploring and exploiting the abundance of human resources across the borders in Mainland China and Hong Kong. Such research might provide answers to unanswered questions and unresolved issues concerning local HR needs in a tight labor market and more importantly, contribute to HR management theory.

第5章 培训(Training)

本章概要(Summary of This Chapter)

培训是饭店人力资源管理的最重要内容之一,无论对顾客、员工乃至饭店自身都具有十分重要的意义,因此,任何饭店都必须重视对员工的培训工作。培训并不是一个单一的事件,而是一个循环往复的过程。本章首先介绍了饭店培训的含义、作用及特点,然后着重讨论了培训的程序。实施培训的方法有许多种,例如,讲座、案例分析、角色扮演、行为模仿、商业游戏、敏感性培训、工作轮换等,这些方法的适用情境及优缺点各有不同。

Training is one of the most important aspects of hospitality human resource management. It has a significant meaning to not only the hotel itself, but also its stakeholders, such as staff and customers. As a result, a hotel must pay much attention to training. Training is not a single incident, but a cycling progress. This chapter first introduces the concept, impact and attributes of hospitality training program. Then the procedures of training are discussed. There are plenty of methods to carry out a training program, for example, lecture, case study, role playing, behavior modeling, business game, sensitivity training, job rotation, etc. Differences exist among the applicable situations and relative merits of these methods.

开篇引例(Beginning Story)

One day, Mr. Geller, who lived in X-hotel, went to its restaurant for lunch. When he got out of the elevator, the attendant standing at the elevator door politely nodded and said, "Hello, Sir." Mr. Geller smiled and responded, "Hello." When he went into the restaurant, the receptionist said the same word, "Hello, Sir." Mr. Geller just nodded with a smile as a response. After a good meal, Mr. Geller decided to have a short walk in the yard of X-hotel. Just stepping into the gate of the yard, he received the same word from a waiter, "Hello, Sir." Mr. Geller nodded subconsciously and went right to the yard. Then he got the same "Hello, Sir" from the same waiter after a short while when he was going to step out of the yard gate. At that time, Mr. Geller had become out of patience and went straight back to his room without any response. The attendant was still standing at the elevator door serving guests in and out of the elevator, and said "Hello, Sir" with an honor when she saw Mr. Geller coming over. Mr. Geller can not conceal his discomfort any more. He went upstairs with a frown pretending that he did not hear what the attendant had said.

A couple of days later, a complaint letter was put on the desk of the hotel general manager. Mr. Geller complained in that letter: "I really do not understand how your hotel has trained your staff. I encountered several attendants in a short noon time. And every single attendant kept repeating the same 'Hello, Sir.' without any difference. Could there be anything else? …"

第一节 饭店培训概述(Training Overview)

一、饭店培训的含义(The Meaning of Training)

饭店培训通常出于一定的目的,有计划、有组织地通过讲授、训练、实验和实习等方法向受训人传授饭店服务、管理的知识和技能,以及企业文化,使受训人的行为方式在理论、技术和职业道德等方面有所提高或改善,从而保证受训人能够按照预期的标准或水平完成承担或将要承担的工作与任务。培训是饭店人力资源管理的重要内容之一,是维持整个饭店有效运转的一种重要手段。

准确理解饭店员工培训的含义可以从以下四个方面入手:

1. 饭店培训是为实现饭店的经营目标服务的

饭店首先应当有利于饭店经营目标的实现。倘若仅仅为培训而培训是不可能收到良好效果的,管理者必须从饭店的功能着手,找出对员工进行培训的具体目标。如果一项培训活动无法对饭店的经营目标产生积极的影响,这项培训就没有实施的必要。培训是帮助饭店实现其经营目标的一种手段,因此,管理者需要将培训与有助于实现组织目标的其他方法及途径相比,以判断培训是否是成本最小或障碍最小的方式。当饭店实施一项员工培训计划时,必须详尽、准确地分析培训所需耗费的成本、所能取得的收益。这样做能够纠正实际培训工作的偏差,使培训工作得以有效促进饭店经营目标的实现。

2. 饭店培训是员工职业发展的助推器

现代人力资源管理认为,员工作为组织成员,不但要为实现组织目标而努力,而且还会为增加自身人力价值而努力,提高自己的职业素质能力,把自己推向更高的职业发展阶段。真正有效的培训活动不但能够促进饭店经营目标的实现,而且能够提高员工的职业能力,拓展员工的发展空间。因此,饭店培训是员工职业发展的助推器。

3. 饭店培训是一种管理工具

把饭店培训看成是一种管理工具,是因为它不是在消极地约束员工的行为,而是在积极地引导员工的行为。组织行为理论认为,一个人的工作绩效取决于他的工作行为,而他的工作行为又由这个人在具体工作情境下所选定行为目标决定。饭店管理者希望通过培训促进饭店经营目标的实现,这个过程必须通过影响员工在特定工作情境下的行为选择完成。如果接受培训之后,员工的工作绩效有所改善,那就是通过行为目标和方式的改进实现的。把饭店培训看作一种管理工具,也就是要通过培训塑造员工在服务工作中的合理行为。

4. 饭店培训是一种重要的投资方式

与传统的人事管理不同,现代人力资源管理把员工视为一种资源。饭店的培训活动,在增加受训人人力价值的同时,也增加了饭店拥有的人力资本价值。在知识经济时代和信息社会里,饭店资产的增加不仅意味着物质资产规模的扩大,更重要的是资本增值能力的提高,以及对物质资本吸引力的增强。而这些,离开人力资源都无法实现。许多著名的饭店之所以舍得对培训进行大规模的投资,就是因为意识到了这一点。

二、培训的作用(The Effect of Training)

开篇案例反映出饭店员工只知道如何工作是远远不够的,由于从事饭店工作需要与形形色色的客人打交道,员工必须掌握熟练的工作技巧并且具备提供良好服务的能力。培训是使饭店员工更为有效工作的重要手段之一,培训对工作程序进行描述,有助于员工掌握工作技巧,从而胜任不同层面的工作。

事实上,培训不仅对员工自身具有十分重要的影响,而且对饭店整体及饭店人力资源管理的其他方面也具有非常巨大的作用。

(一)培训对饭店员工的作用(the Role of Training for Hotel Staff)

1. 提高员工的职业素养和技能水平

员工培训能使员工了解岗位工作的要求,通过提高员工各方面的职业素养和专业技术水平,使其达到任职资格的要求,使个人和饭店双受益。通过培训,新员工可以比较快地适应新环境,掌握操作技能;原有员工能够不断补充新知识、及时学到新的服务技能,从而更加适应工作发展的需要。

2. 改进工作行为

员工培训可以确保员工掌握正确的工作方法,改变错误或不良的工作习惯。饭店很多服务工作都有一定的浪费与损耗,未经培训的员工造成的损耗会更大。在饭店业的一些研究中发现,未受过培训的员工所造成的事故数量是受过培训员工的数量的3倍。

3. 有助于员工的职业发展

无论是新员工还是在职员工,经过一段时间的培训,会掌握工作的最优方法和技能,这就意味着其就业能力的增强。不仅如此,如果员工确实德才兼备,那么培训则可以帮助员工晋升到更高级的职位。

此外,培训工作还有利于增强员工的自信心,减轻工作压力,以及培养员工的成就感等。

Example

No matter senior management or cleaners, all new staff of Disney Land must participate in a traditional induction training lasting two days. As a part of the training program, new staff are taken to the "Magic Kingdom" to see how experienced staff work. They will ask the new staff how to deal with the relationship with customers, which helps Disney spread the service ideas to the new staff.

After the two-day welcoming new comers activity, new staff will go to their own position. They are greeted by their supervisors and experienced trainers. Training courses designed according to the position are given and administrative staff from Human Resource Department will supervise the process of the training.

Source: Hiebeler R, Kelly T B, Ketterman C. Best Practices: Building Your Business With Customer-focused Solutions. New York: Simon & Schuster, 1998.

(二)员工培训对饭店的作用(the Role of Training for Hotel)

1. 传播企业文化

员工培训能使员工对企业文化、饭店的经营目标和服务理念有深刻的体会和理解,能培养和增强员工对饭店的认同感。

2. 提高饭店管理效率

员工培训能改进员工的工作行为,提高员工完成任务的质量水平,因而可以让管理者从日常琐碎的事务中解脱出来,不再陷入补救错误、更正失误的情况中,可以有更充足的时间从事更重要的管理工作。

3. 建立优秀的团队

当接受到合适的培训后,员工会有一种被企业重视的感觉。经过培训后,他们会主动应用所学到的新技能,提高个人工作绩效。培训能够增强员工的自觉性与责任心。另外,一些研究证实,在饭店行业,受过培训的员工的流动率只是未受培训员工的流动率的一半。因此,培训通过培养优秀的员工、降低员工流失率,而为企业建立并保有了优秀的工作团队。

4. 建立良好的口碑,提高顾客忠诚度

经过培训,饭店员工的职业素养与技能水平得到提升,从而能够为顾客提供更高质量的产品和服务。顾客会感到物有所值,其满意度会相应提高,重复消费的可能性也大大提高。从这个角度而言,员工培训有助于饭店提高顾客忠诚度,并建立良好的品牌形象。

综上所述,员工培训同饭店管理的各方面都息息相关,它是饭店人力资源管理体系中不可缺少的方面和环节。表 5-1 对饭店培训的益处进行了总结。

表 5-1 培训的益处

对员工的益处:
·提高员工的职业素养和技能水平
·改进工作行为
·有助于员工的职业发展
·增强员工的自信心
·减轻工作压力
·培养员工的成就感
对饭店的益处:
·传播企业文化
·提高饭店的管理效率
·建立优秀的团队
·建立良好的口碑,提高顾客忠诚度

三、培训的特点(Characteristics of Training)

培训是受训人通过指导活动获取知识、提高技术、改进工作态度的一个过程,它有别于以应试教学为主要特点的学校教育。饭店培训的特点和规律与其行业特征有密切的关系。

1. 全员性

饭店培训具有全员性的特点。一家饭店可以有几十种工作岗位,各工种之间的技术含量有时存在巨大差异,因此,凡是在职的饭店员工,无论是一般服务员,还是经营管理者,无论是资深的老员工,还是阅历较浅的年轻员工,都有要求和接受培训的权利和义务。

2. 继续性

培训属于继续教育范畴,它的目的在于提高员工运用知识、技术和科学方法解决实际问题的能力。现代饭店的培训理念是"终身培训",接受过常规服务培训的员工,在工作中随着环境的变化和顾客需求的变化,以及物质生活水平提高带来的消费档次的提升、消费模式个性化,等等,都迫切需要继续接受再培训,以适应新旧服务内容和形式上的交替,提高服务水平、质量和顾客满意度。

3. 实用性

饭店培训必须与实际工作紧密结合。培训必须是为解决实际工作中可能遇到的所有问题,为提高饭店服务效率、顾客满意度和员工队伍素质而进行的,真正做到有的放矢。强调饭店培训实用性的另一个方面,就是要提供必要的超前培训。只有为客人提供超值的服务和实现特色经营,饭店才有可能在激烈的市场竞争中取胜,而必要的超前培训则是制胜的有效手段。

4. 多样性

饭店培训具有多样性的特点。一方面,饭店对员工进行的培训是一种多岗位、多层次的训练活动。它包含的内容极其丰富,涵盖了客房服务、餐厅服务、社交礼仪、烹调知识、酒水知识、市场营销、消费心理,以及管理知识和计算机应用技术等许多方面。另一方面,由于培训的指导思想是理论联系实际,坚持学以致用、因材施教、讲求实效,因此,培训必须根据不同类型、不同层次职位的要求采取灵活多样的方式。

5. 成人性

饭店培训的对象虽然在性别、年龄、岗位和受教育程度等方面存在差异,但都属于成人,针对他们的培训,一方面存在着"年龄较大,机械记忆力减退;各种干扰因素较多,容易分散精力"等困难;另一方面,我们还应明确,他们需要的培训内容应是"学习目的明确,理论联系实际,而非空谈理论"。

四、培训的对象(Training Objects)

由于不同类别的员工在工作性质、工作方式等方面大相径庭,因此,培训的侧重点也有不同,由此可以划分出不同的培训对象。

(一)根据员工进入企业组织的先后顺序,培训对象可分为新员工和老员工(New employees and experienced employees)

饭店在招聘新员工的时候,虽然运用各种考试、测评等科学方法,挑选出符合招聘条件、有发展潜力的人员,但是,所录用的新员工并非一开始就具备完成规定员工所必需的知识和技能,也缺乏在特定集体中进行协作的工作态度和行为习惯。为使他们尽快融入到组织中去,尽快掌握必要的知识、技能和应具备的服务意识,必须对他们进行培训。同时,饭店是在一个不断变化的经济、技术、文化环境中生存和发展的,必须不断调整自己,以适应环境,否则,必然会在激烈的市场竞争中被无情地淘汰。老员工的知识、技能和服务意识,也必须不断与组织的发展相适应。只有员工不断更新知识,不断提高技能,才能使本企业保持竞争力,这同样需要通过培训实现。

(二)根据员工在饭店中的地位和作用,培训对象可以分为不同的层次和类型(Different levels and types)

1. 部门经理及以上人员

部门经理的知识、能力及行为方式对本部门的经营状况影响极大,甚至会直接影响到整个饭店的经济效益。从这个意义上说,所有部门经理及以上人员都有必要参加培训。

一般来说,部门经理都有丰富的工作经验和优秀的才能,因此,对他们的培训主要是达到以下目的:

(1)使他们更加有效地运用自己的经验,发挥自己的才能。

(2)帮助他们及时发现和理解饭店外部环境和内部条件的变化。

(3)帮助他们提高和完善工作中的专门技能。如处理人际关系的技能,主持会议、授权、沟通等方面的技能。

(4)对于新上任的经理人员,应帮助他们迅速了解饭店的经营战略、方针、目标、饭店内外关系,等等,以使他们尽快适应工作。

2. 基层管理人员

基层管理人员,如领班、经理助理等在饭店中处于一个特殊的位置。他们既是饭店整体利益的代表,又是其下属员工利益的代表,很容易发生角色冲突和矛盾。从实际情况看,饭店中大多数基层管理人员过去都从事具体的业务性和事务性的工作,在管理方面经验不足。在他们担任基层管理职务后,必须通过培训尽快掌握必要的管理技能,明确自己的新职责,改变自己的工作观念,熟悉新的工作方法。

3. 专业人员

在饭店的财务部、工程部和计算机部门一般有会计师、工程师等各类专业技术人员。这些人都有自己的业务范围,掌握着本专业的知识和技能。在现代企业中,团队工作方式日益普遍,如果各类专业人员局限于自己的专业领域,彼此之间缺乏沟通与协调,势必会妨碍团队的工作。培训的目的之一,就是让他们了解别人的工作,促进各类人员之间的沟通协调,使他们能从饭店整体出发开展工作。专业人员参加培训的另一个重要目的,是紧跟时代的发展,不断更新专业知识,及时了解各自领域内的最新动态和最新知识,与社会经济技术发展相适应。

4. 一般员工

一般员工是饭店员工队伍的主体,他们负责完成具体的服务工作任务。对一般员工的培训,主要是依据工作说明书和工作规范的要求,明确权责界限,掌握必要的服务技能和技巧,培养与饭店发展相适应的工作态度和行为习惯,使之不仅能有效地完成本职责工作,而且能在饭店中不断发展自己。

第二节 培训程序(Training Process)

培训程序,也可以称为培训周期,因为培训往往是一个循环往复的过程而并非一个单一的事件。

培训周期始于需求评估或发现问题,通常表现为实际行为与预期结果之间存在差异。在饭店中,这种差异的表现形式可能是多种多样的。例如,客人投诉客房不整洁、抱怨办理入住登记或退房手续时等候时间过长、对员工服务进行投诉,等等,这些都是对这种差异的反映。但是客人只是提供事实,而不会告诉企业究竟问题出在哪里。大多数情况下,培训需求源于主管或员工的判断而非客人的投诉。

培训程序的第二步是确立培训目标。培训目标是指员工在培训后应当了解或做到的事情。由于培训需求的不同,培训目标不尽相同,例如提高服务质量、提高工作效率、降低成本,等等。

第三步是建立培训标准。培训标准是指衡量培训是否有效的准则,实际上,就是考察受训人培训是否合格的标准。

第四步是选择并测试受训人。受训人可以是新员工、在职员工或潜在员工。明确受训人之后,需要对受训人的情况进行预测。这一步骤包括了解受训人当前的知识、技能及能力水平,调查结果可以为后续培训方式的选择和培训计划的制订提供依据。

第五步是培训实施。培训实施首先要选择合适的培训方式和方法,应当依据培训的目标、标准及受训人的当前情况选择恰当的培训方式。要在先前的培训步骤都完成之后,依照制订好的培训计划实施培训。

最后一步是对整个培训计划进行评价。培训计划评价是对培训是否有效的实现了预期的目标进行评估。

但是,即使本次培训效果很好,整个培训过程也不会就此停止,在实际工作中,客人对饭店和饭店员工、饭店对员工以及员工对自身的要求都会不断提高,因此会不断出现新的培训需求,从而促使饭店进入下一轮培训周期。

一、设计及实施培训需求评估(Design and Imply Training Needs Assessment)

任何培训的第一步都是需求评估,需要识别员工为做好本职工作、发展职业道路、使企业实现业绩目标而必须掌握的知识、技巧和能力。需求评估应该从组织、任务和行为、个人三个方面入手分析。每个培训计划都会对企业整体产生影响。例如,为了提高餐饮部的服务效率,对服务员培训一种较快速的写单方法,但是除非对厨师也进行培训,使其能够认读这种订单,否则服务效率并不会得到提升。因此,培训需要考虑饭店整体的需求,培训目标需要与饭店整体的文化和战略相匹配,否则期望的培训目标将难以实现。对任务和行为进行分析是指将工作任务分解为知识、技能和能力的过程。任务和行为分析能够发现员工当前的工作情况与工作的实际要求间存在的差异,从而有助于培训计划的设计。培训计划有时是针对部门或饭店整体的,有时是集中在需要培训的个别员工身上的,因此,进行个人分析目的是明确个人在工作中的优缺点,从而了解应该为不同的员工提供何种不同的培训。

表5-2列举了实施需求评估的11种方法,其中没有哪种方法是具有普适性的,应当针对不同的情况选择适当的需求评估方法。

表5-2 需求评估方法

·咨询委员会
·工作要求
·工作抽样
·工作绩效衡量
·态度调查
·技能测试
·绩效档案
·顾客反馈
·问卷调查
·离职访谈
·关键事件

资料来源:Woods R H. 饭店业人力资源管理(第三版). 张凌云,马晓秋,主译. 北京:中国旅游出版社,2003.

1. 咨询委员会

咨询委员会通常由评估工作任务和行为的经理人员和员工代表组成,他们需要比对寻找工作要求与员工实际工作情况之间的差异,评估方法一般由委员会中的员工代表提出。以饭店客房部为例,客房部的咨询委员会成员应包括客房部助理经理、前台经理、预订部经理以及各部门员工。咨询委员会的优点是评估得出的需求结果一般都非常符合企业的实际需要,但缺点是委员会中的员工代表向管理者提出的反对意见作用有限。

2. 工作要求

工作要求是指将工作描述中要求的知识、技能和能力与员工目前的工作表现进行比较,寻找二者之间的差距,从而确定培训需求。这种比较通常由部门经理进行,效果可能会优于咨询委员会。

3. 工作抽样

工作抽样是由专业分析师对工作表现进行系统的观察和评价,分析师只从旁观察而不参与其中。工作抽样的优点是分析师实际观察了工作进行的过程而不仅仅是听取汇报或查看结果,因此能够得出更准确的培训需求。这种方法的缺点是聘请分析师需要耗费额外的费用,并且为了保证结果的准确性,分析师必须观察大量员工的工作,这一过程需要耗费大量时间。

4. 工作绩效衡量

工作绩效衡量同工作抽样一样,也需要聘请专业分析师,不同之处在于工作绩效衡量需要分析师在观察工作的同时参与工作实践。通过直接参与,分析师能够更加直接地了解工作需要的知识、技能和能力。但是除了需要花费额外的费用和大量时间外,有些工作还需要特殊的技能,例如厨师,这样的工作很难找到一个分析师能够在未经培训的情况下参与每一项工作,因此并非所有的工作都可以采用这种方法。

5. 态度调查

并非所有的培训都旨在改进员工的具体工作技能,特别是对于饭店而言,改善员工对客人的态度和行为方式更加重要。态度调查可以有效地确定改进服务态度和行为的必要时机。态度调查也可以看出员工对工作、同事和管理者的好恶之处。这种调查有利于通过培训提高员工的满意度,降低员工流失率。但其缺点是不适用于技能方面的培训。

6. 技能测试

技能测试是一种最为通用的培训需求评估方法,可以检验员工完成一项工作的能力。这种方法对确定与技能有关的培训需求十分有效,但是不能应用于行为培训的需求评估。

7. 绩效档案

绩效档案是指包括出勤率、销售额、顾客投诉、推荐和生产率等的报告,可以用于判断个人培训需求。由于相关的信息和数据是在员工日常工作过程中记录的,因此调查绩效档案是确定培训需求最经济的方法,但是由于绩效档案中没有员工的行为记录,因此这种方法不适用于评估员工的行为培训需求。

8. 顾客反馈

当客人投诉时,有些饭店经理或者业主就能够判断需要对员工进行培训了。但是研究发现,许多客人很少投诉,而是在不满意后不再光顾,甚至向周围的人传播不良的口碑。这样一来,除非饭店主动向客人征求意见或建议,否则不能单凭投诉来判断是否存在培训需求。

9. 问卷调查

用问卷调查的方式来收集培训需求信息的优点是可以方便经济地获得大量的数据和信息,这种方法除了可以用来判断员工的培训需求之外,也可以对管理者的培训需求进行评估。

10. 离职访谈

通常情况下,员工在离职时愿意向其他人述说一些自己过往的经验和教训,这经常能够使管理者了解一些平时无法得知的内幕消息,特别是与员工流动相关的问题,这些信息可以作为评估培训需求的依据。但是有研究表明,除非离职员工确信谈话内容是保密的,否则在离职访谈过程中他们并不愿意提供真实的信息,因为这可能关系到他们未来的职业发展和人际交往。因此,选取与企业无关的第三方或电脑调查系统,确保员工能够匿名提供信息是一种比较有效的离职访谈方式。

11. 关键事件

关键事件评估方法要求企业管理者或外聘专业分析师观察并记录员工在工作过程表现很好或很差的重要事件,经过一段时间的资料收集,可以明确培训需求。这种方法对带有案例研究性质的培训方式非常有效,关键事件可以成为出色的培训教材。但是关键事件不可能总在需要时就立即发生,观察者常常要花费很长一段时间等待关键事件出现。

二、确立培训目标(Establish Training Goal)

首先,培训目标应当与组织目标保持一致。培训内容中有一部分是对组织管理理念和组织文化的培训,一般来讲,如果培训与企业的管理理念和企业文化不一致,培训是不会有成效的。例如,20世纪60年代有许多企业为员工提供培养个人独立性的培训,希望提高员工的创新能力,但是后来大部分企业发现,培训结束之后员工并没有将所学应用到实际工作中去。这是因为这些企业的文化和价值观不提倡个人的突出性而是强调团队合作精神,这种培训只能以失败告终。这表明,饭店只有将其企业文化和价值观融入到培训过程中,培训才会更有效。

另外,具体的培训目标可以按照培训内容的不同划分为4种:反应式、学习式、工作行为式和结果导向式。

反应式目标,是指是为了提高员工对饭店情感的培训,如安排员工参加健身活动就属于反应式培训项目。这些培训项目的结果通常直接使受训人受益,而对企业发展具有间接作用。

学习式目标是指在培训中学习知识和技能,并以此作为培训的最终目的。比如饭店为餐饮部的服务员提供葡萄酒知识培训及葡萄酒销售和服务的技能培训。

第三种培训目标与工作行为培训有关,例如常常用员工接待客人时的热情友善程度作为衡量服务质量的一个标准,因此饭店会制订一些以积极为客人服务为目标的培训计划。

结果导向式目标,是指培训以改进个人或团体工作为目的,这些工作通常是可量化、易于培训前后进行效果评估的,如提高饭店客房部服务员的工作效率、减少厨房的浪费、增加回头客的数量,等等。结果导向式目标是最常见的一种培训目标。

有些培训的目标是单一的,有些培训同时包含多个目标,比如饭店为提高客房部服务员的工作效率而对其进行工作行为培训,成绩优异者可以获得奖励,这个培训项目就结合了反应式、工作行为式和结果导向式三种培训目标。

三、建立培训标准(Establish Training Standards)

饭店在进行一项培训时,要实现预期的效果,除了准确评估需求、明确目标之外,还必须建立一套完善的衡量标准,即衡量培训是否达到预期目标的准则。维尔京群岛度假村酒店在使用的一套培训计划中,对培训的每一个阶段都设定相应的知识技能和行为准则作为考评受训人是否合格的标准。例如,食品服务培训部门的标准包括受训人能否知道如何高效地摆台、跑单和上菜等,考评时要求受训人在规定时间内独立完成整个工作流程。

培训标准必须是具体的、可量化的,否则无法有效衡量培训是否实现预计的效果。

四、选择及测试受训人(Choose and Test Trainee)

饭店培训成功的另一决定要素是选择合适的员工参加培训,可以在明确培训需求和目标之后就进行选择,也可以随着培训的不断进行随时选择员工加入或退出。维尔京群岛度假村酒店曾使用过这种边培训边选择受训人的方法。旅游业是维尔京群岛的主要经济支柱之一,为了发展旅游业,在政府的资助下,维尔京大酒店进行这项培训的目的是把岛上的居民培训成为合格的前台接待员,受训人都是没有任何饭店工作经验的本地居民。培训分为几个阶段,每个阶段侧重不同的知识和技能培养。一共有100人参加了这次培训,培训共进行8周,每周由不同的培训师讲授培训内容。每周培训结束后,培训师和培训总监及饭店经理开会评估每个受训人的表现,得出统一的结果后,培训总监会和每个受训人面谈,总结上一周的进步情况并提出下一周的目标。上一周没有进步的受训人会收到一张书面通知,对下一周的努力方向给出建议,如果下一周仍不能达到要求则会被淘汰。到最后这100人中总共有75人通过了培训结业[①]。

如果不了解受训人当前的知识、技能和能力水平,很难对其培训前后的表现进行比较,也很难对培训效果进行评估。因此,在选择完合适的受训人之后,饭店管理者有必要测试受训人的当前水平。

测试可以选用对比实验的方法。可以将饭店员工分为两组,一组参加培训,另外一组不参加培训,参加培训的一组称为实验组,不参加培训的一组称为对照组。分别在培训前和培训后对两组员工进行能力测试,通过测试结果比对,饭店管理者可以更确切地了解培训效果。当然受训人知识、技能和能力水平的提高还受到其他诸多因素的影响,不能完全归功于培训。

五、实施培训计划(Imply Training Plan)

在明确培训目标和标准、选择适合接受培训的员工之后,培训人员需要制订详细的培训计划并密切关注每一个培训步骤的实施。由于技术的进步,实施培训的方式不断更新,现在饭店业既增添了新式的培训方法也保留着传统的培训手段。不同类型的培训、不同的受训人、不同的培训目标和培训环境要求选择不同的培训方式。本部分主要介绍了饭店最常用的一些培训方式,培训方式通常分为两大类:脱岗培训和在职培训。

(一)脱岗培训(Off-job Training)

脱岗培训是指在工作场地之外的培训,主要包括讲座、仿真培训、远程培训、案例分析、角色扮演、行为模仿、商业游戏、敏感性培训等。

讲座是最常用的脱岗培训方法之一,由专题专家或培训师进行个人演讲,与一群受训人分享知识和信息。这种方法的优点是可以在短时间内向大量的人传递大量的信息,因此是非常经济的方式。但缺点是以单向交流为主,缺乏双向沟通,不能满足不同层次听众的要求,而且除非演讲人非常有经验,否则容易造成枯燥乏味

---

① Woods R H. 饭店业人力资源管理(第三版). 张凌云,马晓秋,主译. 北京:中国旅游出版社,2003.

的课堂气氛。

仿真培训是指利用模拟器虚拟地在工作以外的环境中再现工作情境的培训方法。模拟培训有时非常适用于饭店，如培训员工使用收款机、入住和退房系统等电子设备。这种方法的优点是不会被正常工作中的事务干扰，可以在短时间内集中完成培训，但往往成本较高。

随着互联网和远程教学技术的普及，远程培训这种培训技术得以发展。这种方法允许受训人以个人节奏安排学习，培训的效果通过笔试或电脑测试进行评定。这种可以自由安排学习时间的方式较受员工欢迎，因此培训的效果通常很好，但一般需要饭店在初期投入较高的培训资金。

案例分析是指将商业环境中具体事件的细节提供给受训人，让受训人从资料中发现问题并提出解决方案的培训方法。这种培训方式能够培养受训人的判断性思维并且易激发受训人展开讨论，但受训人提出的解决方案仅仅局限于案例本身，由于在实际决策时面临的是复杂多变的环境，因此这些解决方案可能缺乏实际意义。

案例分析通常只是阅读案例，然后进行讨论分析，而在角色扮演过程中受训人能够亲身感受真实的或夸张的工作场景。例如，在教授酒水服务技能时，培训师可以要求一名受训人扮演酒吧服务员，另外一名受训人扮演醉酒的客人，两人模拟表演酒吧服务员拒绝为已经喝醉的客人提供更多酒水时的对话。这种方法最大的优点是使受训人有机会站在对方的角度观察和感受事物，投入情感从而获得实际操作培训中难以体验的东西。但在使用这种方法时必须充分考虑受训人的性格情况，一些外向、热衷交际的人会喜欢角色扮演这种方式，而性格内向的人对这种在众人面前表演的形式会感到尴尬或不安。

行为模仿先向受训人展示一个或几个示范人物，受训人可以观察示范人物在特定环境中的行为表现，然后再由受训人进行模仿表演，饭店培训人员可以根据受训人的行为表现不断提供反馈及修正建议。这种方法用实际的展示替代了简单的口头描述，对饭店管理者的人际关系交往技巧培训十分有效。

商业游戏为受训人创造一个模拟的商业环境，使其通过处理各种问题得到培训，这种方法趣味性强，涉及许多现实工作中存在的问题，但是受训人有时会专注于获胜，而忽略了培训的真正目的。

敏感性培训最早由科特·列文等学者提出，常用于4至10人的小组培训。培训过程中每一个受训人都要面对其他小组成员的行为，并在小组讨论中分享自己的感受。这种方法常用于人际关系交往技巧的培训，其优点是能够让受训人了解自己行为引致他人的感受，但如果缺乏恰当的协调控制，容易引发人际矛盾。

(二)在职培训(In-job Training)

顾名思义,在职培训是在实际工作过程中进行的,是一种非常适合饭店业的培训方式,主要包括工作指导培训和工作轮换等。

工作指导培训首先会列出完成一项工作的所有步骤和程序并指明正确操作需注意的关键动作或行为,然后要求受训人按照既定顺序完成的培训方法。这种培训主要适用于可分解步骤的技能性工作,如操作机器或准备食物等。培训师可以利用工作手册或视频录像等向受训人提供培训,工作指导培训的培训师可以是部门主管,也可以是指定的一线员工。

工作轮换,又称轮岗工作,即要求受训人从一个岗位换到另一个岗位。这种方法常用于饭店管理人员培训,让他们在上任前在每个岗位都工作几周,优点是使其了解各个不同岗位的工作及员工状况,以便于上任后开展管理工作。

在职培训是一种非常有效且经济适用的培训方法,但是如果培训人指派不当,培训效果可能会受到影响。另外,这种边工作边接受培训的方式一方面使得受训人没有足够的时间掌握培训内容,另一方面可能会影响正常工作的进行。

Tips for Common Training Programs

- Encouraged behaviors will repeat.
- Once behaviors achieve the standards, they need consolidated immediately.
- Behaviors without consolidation but simple repetition will be very bad.
- The impact of threat and punishment is unsteady. Sometimes it may affect the process of learning.
- Sense of success due to improved performance of learning is the best reward and it will lead to improvement of other aspects.
- The value of extrinsic rewards depends on the presenters. If the presenter has a high status, the value of the extrinsic reward will be great. If not, it will be low.
- The progress of learning depends on trainee's own goal.
- Trainees will be more active to the programs which have involved them before.
- Arbitrary leaders will make trainees rely on him (or her) and feel upset about the team.
- Too strict discipline will make trainees feel obedient, upset and silent. Easy discipline will make trainees be more active and creative.
- People's self-confidence, creativity and evaluation ability will be frustrated by excessive criticism and failure.

- Frustrated people will be less participative, objective and rational.
- People with less achievement cannot focus on learning.
- People will be innovative when they face interesting and challenging problems.
- The best way to help people form a common concept is to repeat it under different situations.
- Spending time recalling past material and then repeating will improve learning effectively.
- People always remember new information which corresponds to their attitude.
- Trainees will use what they have learned if they encounter the similar situations in a short time after learning.
- The best time to learn something is that it is felt useful.

Source: Mondy R W, Noe R R. Human Resource Management, US: Prentice Hall, 1996.

六、评价培训计划(Evaluation of Training Plan)

　　饭店的管理者当然希望所有的培训都能达到预期的效果,但事实上,并非所有的培训计划都是成功的,大量的事实证明由于员工在接受培训后没有进步甚至表现退步,而导致许多企业的培训投入成为一种资源浪费。因此,在培训实施后,及时对培训效果进行评价、发现失败的原因是十分必要的。评价培训计划是指系统地收集做出有效的培训决策所必需的说明性和评价性的信息。这一步骤可以真正使饭店了解培训对员工的帮助作用到底有多大,因此评价培训计划是培训过程中不可或缺的部分。

　　评价培训计划是否达到了预期的培训目标的最直接有效的方法是依据培训标准比对受训人在培训前和培训后的表现,以判断现状是否得以改善。另外,受训人表现的变化可能由其他因素导致,因此只找到变化所在是不够的,有效的培训计划评价必须明确变化是否是由培训引起的,如果这一点无法明确,饭店管理者就不能承认培训的效果。

案例分析(Practice Case Analysis)

Background

The M. V. Star of the Orient is a 14,000-ton cruise ship that was built in 1977. The ship is Greek-registered and Hong Kong-owned. It had spent ten years cruising from Miami before 1989, and was transferred to the Southeastern Asia cruise circuit in 1989. This circuit involves programs which are between 7 and 12 days from Singapore, calling at Penang, Phuket, Bali, Cebu, and Ho Chi Minh City.

The ship has cabin capacity for 720 passengers in double and family berths. The on-board facilities, renovated and themed before the transference from Miami, include many sporting, leisure, and recreational options (both organized and free-standing) for guests. There are five passenger restaurants on board:

- The China Seas—a themed Cantonese restaurant
- Star of the Orient—a mixed Asian family restaurant
- The Moulin Rouge—a continental cabaret restaurant and supper club
- The Mermaid—a 24-hour coffee shop and family eatery
- The Seaburger—a fast-food grill

In addition, there are six bars and five retail outlets on the ship. Land-based programs with local guides are scheduled at each port-of-call.

The cruise market is very mixed, creating some product and service management problems. The market consists of, about equal proportions, Japanese, European, North American, and regional (mainly from Hong Kong and Singapore) guests.

Except for some of the European and Japanese officers, the ship's technical and maritime crew are recruited locally. Service and hospitality staff, who have direct contact with customers and are in food-related jobs, are recruited to cope with the cultural diversity of the customer markets. Currently, the origin of service and hospitality staff is as follows:

- Regional   35%
- Japanese   20%
- European   25%
- US/Canada   20%

Staff work on the basis of three months on and three months off. Labor turnover between cruises is currently over 30%.

Problem

The Director of Training, in cooperation with all departmental heads, has recently completed a comprehensive Training Needs Assessment with the service and hospitality areas in order to counter and overcome some poor customer feedback. Common skill and attitudinal deficiencies among service and hospitality staff have been identified and prioritized as follows:

- Customer care skills
- Language skills (Japanese and German)
- Personal hygiene
- Currency/Cash handling
- Supervisory skills
- Safety/Emergency procedures

Source: Go F M, Monachello M L, Baum T. Human Resource Management in the Hospitality Industry, NY: John Wiley & Sons, Inc., 1996.

Questions for Discussion:

1. Please explain the priority of the skill required.

2. You sit on the ship's Training Committee, which is chaired by the Director of Training and has representation from all departments on the ship. You and other members of your group are required to prepare a Training Plan, utilizing both shore-and ship-based facilities, to meet the identified training needs.

名词解释(Key Terms)

1. 入职教育:入职教育是为新员工对饭店和他们的专项工作进行介绍。

Orientation: Orientation is an introduction of the hotel and their specific tasks to the new staff.

2. 培训程序:也可以称为培训周期,因为培训往往是一个循环往复的过程而并非一个单一的事件。

Training Procedure: Training procedure, also called training cycle, is a circulating process consisting of several steps rather than one single incident.

3. 需求评估:需求评估或发现问题,通常表现为实际行为与预期结果之间存在差异,是培训计划的第一步。

Needs Assessment: Needs assessment, or problem recognition, usually manifests various differences between the actual behavior of hotel staff and the organization's predicted result. It is the first step of training.

4. 培训目标：培训目标是指员工在培训后应当了解或做到的事情。

Training Objective: Training objective is a series of things that hotel staff are able to understand or complete after the training program.

5. 培训标准：培训标准是指衡量培训是否有效的准则。

Training Criteria: Training criteria is the standard used to evaluate whether the training is effective or not.

6. 培训评价：培训评价是对培训是否有效地实现了预期的目标进行评估。

Training Evaluation: Training evaluation is to assess whether the training program has achieved the predicted objective effectively or not.

7. 组织分析：培训需要考虑整个饭店的需求，培训目标必须契合整个饭店的组织文化和战略。

Organizational Analysis: Training needs to consider the whole hotel's demand. Training objective must match the whole hotel's organization culture and strategy.

8. 个人分析：个人分析专注于员工个体的优缺点，从而饭店经理可以为不同的员工安排不同培训项目。

Individual Analysis: Individual analysis focuses on an individual worker's advantages and disadvantages so that the hotel manager can arrange different training programs for different workers.

9. 反应式目标：是指为了提高员工对饭店情感的培训。

Reaction Objective: Reaction objective is to reinforce staff's emotions or feelings to the hotel through training.

10. 学习式目标：是指在培训中学习知识和技能，并以此作为培训的最终目的。

Learning Objective: Learning objective is to develop hotel staff's knowledge or skills.

11. 行为式目标：是指在培训中改进员工的工作行为。

Behavior Objective: Behavior objective is to improve hotel staff's job behavior through training.

12. 结果导向式目标：是指培训以改进个人或团体工作为目的。

Result Objective: Result objective is to improve the quality of individual or team work.

13. 脱岗培训:脱岗培训是指在工作场地之外的培训。

Off-job Training: Off-job training is a kind of training program arranged outside the work field.

14. 在职培训:在职培训可以使受训人在实际接触特定工作时,通过观察、交流或者协助有经验的员工提高相关知识、技能和能力。

On-job Training: On-job training allows trainees to develop relevant knowledge, skills and abilities by observation, conversation or assisting experienced workers, and so on when they are actually engaged in a specific task.

复习思考题(Questions for Review)

1. 饭店对员工进行培训的意义是什么?

What is the significance of hotel's training program?

2. 请说明饭店培训的步骤。

Please state the steps of hotel's training program.

3. 请列举培训需求评估的方法。

Please list the methods of training demand evaluation.

4. 饭店培训目标一般分为哪几种?

How many kinds of hospitality training goals are there, and what are they?

5. 常用的培训方式有哪些,它们各自的特点是什么?

Please state and illustrate the common ways of training.

研究前沿(Research Front)

Posttraining Self-Efficacy, Job Involvement, and Training Effectiveness in the Hospitality Industry

INTRODUCTION

Training has become a huge investment in organizations. Both theory and practice have improved dramatically over the last few decades in demonstrating training effectiveness. Research has identified various factors that contribute to the effectiveness of training programs. Pretraining self-efficacy was identified as one critical cause.

Training processes can be usefully arranged on a timeline with three distinct phases: pretraining, training, and posttraining; much previous research has focused on self-efficacy before or during training. Different with existing research, the current study focuses on the effects of posttraining self-efficacy on training effectiveness. More specifically, the objective of the current study is to investigate the influence of training acquisition and job involvement on posttraining self-efficacy and the relationship of posttraining self-efficacy and training effectiveness. It is suggested in this study that the degree to which an individual perceives him or herself to have acquired useful knowledge in training will affect the individual's perceptions of self-efficacy. This relationship depends in part on the extent to which the individual is involved in their job. Individuals who perceive a higher level of self-efficacy consequent to training will be more likely to translate their learning into behaviors in the workplace. Hence posttraining self-efficacy is considered to be an important factor in translating training initiatives into work behaviors. The conceptual model is shown in Figure 1.

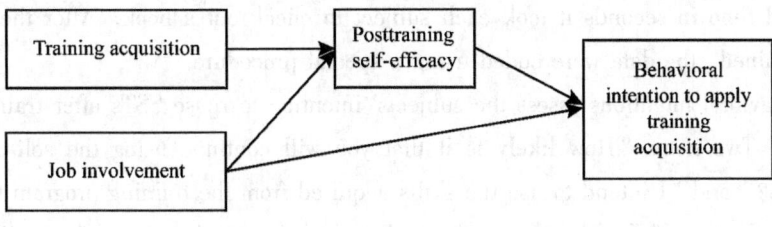

Figure 1

METHODS

Hypothesis 1. Training acquisition positively influences posttraining self-efficacy.

Hypothesis 2. Posttraining self-efficacy positively leads to trainees' behavioral intentions to apply training acquisition.

Hypothesis 3a. Posttraining self-efficacy fully mediates the effects of job involvement on trainees' behavioral intentions to apply training acquisition.

Hypothesis 3b. Posttraining self-efficacy partially mediates the effects of job involvement on trainees' behavioral intentions to apply training acquisition.

To test the hypotheses, the researchers conducted a laboratory experiment in the context of training students to use self-checkout machines (SST) in a university library. Thus the training focuses on service procedures and capabilities, which became a simulation of hospitality training.

Sample

Research participants were 87 college students within the hospitality management major enrolled at a large northeastern university. Participants were recruited from several courses and were offered course extra credit in return for their voluntary participation. All 87 participants took part in and completed all requirements of the research process.

Measures

Posttraining self-efficacy was measured in terms of the participants' expectations after training that they could successfully operate an SST. An eight-item scale was revised for the purpose of the current study. The eight items were scored on a 7-point Likert-type scale anchored by "strongly disagree" and "strongly agree".

Job involvement evaluates the centrality and importance of the job for employees and a nine-item scale was adapted.

Training acquisition evaluates trainees' learning outcomes. To measure training acquisition, the researchers recruited and asked three coders to record the number of trials and time in seconds it took each subject to check out a book. After the records were obtained, the data were coded using a special procedure.

Behavioral intentions assess the subjects' intention to reuse SSTs after training and one trial. Two items "How likely is it that you will continue using the self-checkout machines?" and "I intend to use the skills acquired from the training program to check out books by myself." were measured on a 7-point Likert scale ranging from "likely" to "unlikely" and from "strongly disagree" to "strongly agree", respectively.

Result

A path analysis based on a series of regression analyses was conducted to test hypotheses. The results showed that Hypothesis 1 and Hypothesis 2 are supported. However, job involvement has a significant direct impact on behavioral intention. Hence, Hypotheses 3a and 3b are not supported. The tested model is shown in Figure 2.

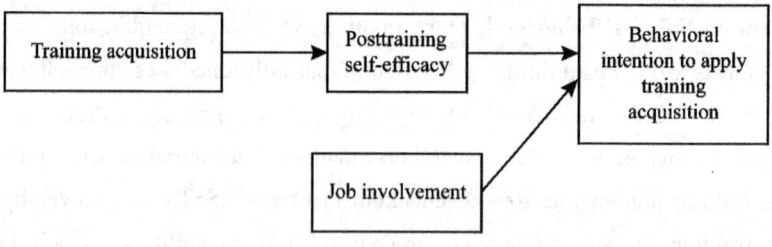

Figure 2

CONCLUSIONS AND FUTURE RESEARCH

The study provided adequate evidence that in the context of hospitality training, posttraining self-efficacy is a critical factor influencing the transfer of training acquisition to training application, and that job involvement has distinct effects on training transfer. Based on the conclusions, future research is needed on the following topics. First, future studies should explore the effects of posttraining self-efficacy on real behaviors in the workplace instead of behavioral intentions. Second, future research can perhaps test a "holistic" model of training motivation before, during, and after training. Finally, further testing on the independent model of job involvement in the context of hospitality training is needed.

Source: Xinyuan Zhao, Karthik Namasivayam. Post training Self-Efficacy, Job Involvement, and Training Effectiveness in the Hospitality Industry. Journal of Human Resources in Hospitality & Tourism, 2009, 8:137 – 152.

第6章 评估和辅导
(Evaluation and Coaching)

本章概要(Summary of This Chapter)

员工绩效评估是管理人员的重要职责之一,对饭店的发展具有深远的意义。管理人员把员工实际工作表现与工作标准加以比较,如果员工的实际绩效高于期望的工作标准,则应给予奖励;如果实际绩效低于期望的工作标准,就意味着员工要尽力改进这一差异。本章首先描述了绩效评估的作用,并讨论了有效评估的障碍及存在的问题。饭店进行绩效评估的方法有很多种,常见的为比较法、图表尺度评价法、行为锚定等级评价法、行为观察评价法、叙述文章、关键事件和目标管理等。最后,本章还展示了辅导的原则、目的等。

Employee performance evaluation is one of the most important duties of managers and has a profound meaning to the development of hotels. Managers compare the employees' actual performance with work standard. If the staff's practical performance is above the expected standard of work, manager should reward the staff. If the staff's practical performance is lower than expected, that means the staff needs to try to narrow the difference. This chapter first describes the benefits of employee performance evaluation and then discusses the barriers and the existing problems of effective evaluation. There are many methods to evaluate employee's performance. Comparison, graphic rating scale, behaviorally anchored rating scale, behavioral observation scale, narrative essay and management by objective are some common employee performance evaluation methods. At the end of this chapter, the principle and purpose of coaching are showed.

开篇引例(Beginning Story)

It is time for ×× hotel to evaluate the performance of every staff which makes both managers and staffs become nervous. × × hotel uses forced distribution method to eliminate staff. By the end of the year, each department's employees will be divided into A, B, C, D and E five level according to the employee's performance. Each level respectively takes proportion of 10%, 20%, 40%, 20% and 10%. If one employee is ranked at the last level once the wage of his or hers will drop one level. If one employee is ranked at the last level twice he or she will have to take part in off-duty training and can only get basic living expenses during the training. After the training there will be a test. Managers determine whether to let the employee be on duty or not according to the result of the test. If the employee is ranked in the last 10% again after on duty, he or she will be fired. Many managers and employees in × × hotel are not agree with this kind of performance evaluation. Mr. White, manager of finance department, takes great pains to do evaluation every year. Finance department is a functional department. Everyone in this department has no mistakes and works very well. So it is inappropriate to rank anyone the last level. Last year, Wendy asked a few days off for private reasons and was late for work several times. But in fact she didn't delay her work. At last Mr. White had no idea but rank Wendy the last level. Wendy is still minding that business now. Who should be ranked the last level this year? It is a big problem.

Do you think fiancé department should use forced distribution method to eliminate staffs? Why?

第一节 绩效评估的益处
（Benefits of Performance Evaluation）

绩效评估是一个按照事先确定的工作目标、工作时间和衡量标准，考察员工实际完成的绩效情况的过程。绩效评估包括工作结果评估和工作行为评估两个方面。工作结果评估是对饭店员工在饭店中的相对价值或贡献程度进行评估。工作行为评估则是根据饭店员工在绩效周期内表现出来的具体的行为态度进行评估。评价一个雇员或管理者的业绩总是困难的，但是对饭店企业而言，饭店的组织目标与绩效和员工个人的目标与绩效之间有着紧密的联系（详见图6-1），因此员工绩效评估本身是非常重要的。绩效评估可以给员工、管理者和管理层带来诸多益处，满足饭店各种不同的需要。饭店管理者可以根据绩效评估的结果为员工提供有针对性的培训。绩效评估还能为薪酬管理、饭店内部的员工流动、员工的奖惩等提供依据。

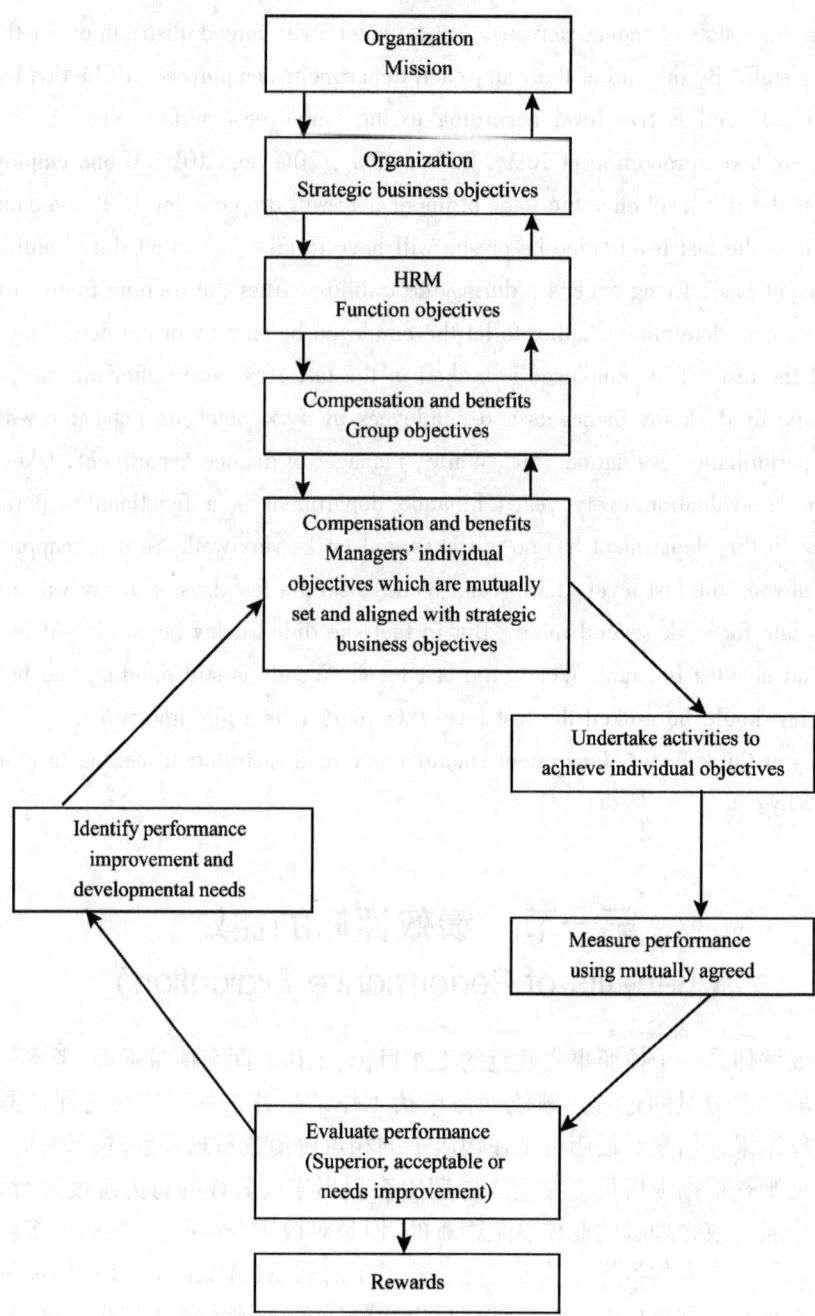

Figure 6-1 The Strategic Link Between Organizational Objectives and Performance and Individual Objectives and Performance

Source: Asia Pacific Management Co. Ltd, 2001.

一、反馈意见(Feedback)

绩效评估最重要的作用之一是提供反馈意见。饭店管理者根据评估结果与员工保持经常性的工作情况沟通,这能防止员工对自己的表现评估不当。饭店员工一般都想知道自己的表现如何,如果他们不能定期地得到反馈,便很难对自己的工作表现有一个准确的把握。策划周密的业绩评估能帮助员工识别自己的优点和需要改进的地方。饭店管理者通过绩效评估,对于饭店员工在工作中取得的成绩以及员工在某一方面的卓越能力,将给予认可和肯定。同时,评估人能通过绩效评估明确指出员工在工作中的不足以及工作能力方面的缺憾,以便员工在下一次评估之前做出改进。

二、员工培训及发展(Staff Training and Development)

通过绩效评估,饭店管理者可以发现员工的长处和不足、优势和劣势,从而根据实际情况明确哪些员工或管理人员需要进行培训,哪些可以获得提升,哪些部门需要进行整体培训。例如,餐饮部全体服务员需要接受新的电脑点菜系统的培训。有效的员工培训必须针对员工目前的表现、业绩和素质特征与其所在岗位的岗位规范、组织发展要求等方面的差距进行,并以此合理地确定培训目标、培训内容,选择相应的培训方法。而绩效评估恰恰能帮助饭店发现这些差距,从而制订培训计划。

此外,绩效评估还可用于辅助员工建立远期事业发展规划。绩效评估能使管理者识别并认可员工个人对工作改进做出的贡献和努力。对业绩的合理公正的评估可以使员工明确其未来的努力方向,鞭策员工不断进行自我完善。并且,根据以往的绩效评估结果,饭店管理者能为员工长期的发展计划提供有益的建议。因此在某种程度上,绩效评估能督促员工制定具体的职业发展战略和实施进程,从而有助于员工的职业发展。

三、决策工具(Decision Tools)

饭店业的管理层可以通过评估过程获得大量的信息。评估可以通过区分业绩的好坏帮助人力资源决策,包括提升、纪律规范、培训或激励。作为一种管理工具,业绩评估可以有效地将奖惩制度与工作表现联系起来。以奖励为主、惩罚为辅,奖惩结合,这历来是饭店管理中的激励原则。对于那些忠于职守、踏实工作、表现良好的员工会得到好的绩效评估结果,这个结果将使他们获得精神和物质上的奖励;而对于那些不负责任、工作怠慢、表现低劣的员工则要给予相应的惩戒。

四、培训、政策或计划的评估(Evaluation of Training, Policy or Plan)

培训结束后,饭店要对培训效果进行评估,这有助于了解培训的有效性。饭店在员工培训中的投资是否有回报,往往体现在受训员工的工作表现和工作业绩上,而这些信息往往需要通过绩效评估获得。评估过程中经理和员工的近距离接触,使双方可以就一些相关目标、政策或计划的问题进行探讨。评估过程中经理可以从员工那里了解哪些政策和计划不像计划的那样有效。从这种意义上说,评估也可用于新政策实施后的效果测评。①

综上可见,经常地、客观地对员工进行业绩评估是非常重要的。

Table 6–1 A Ranking of the Uses of Performance Appraisal From A Survey of 256 Companies

Rank	Function of Appraisal	Percentage
1	Merit increases	91
2	Performance results/feedback/job counseling	90
3	Promotion	82
4	Termination or layoff	64
5	Performance potential	62
6	Succession planning	57
7	Career planning	52
8	Transfer	50
9	Manpower planning	38
10	Bonuses	32
11	Development and evaluation of training programs	29
12	Internal communication	25
13	Criteria for selection procedure validation	16
14	Expense control	7

Source:Fombrun C J and Laud R L. Strategic Issues in Performance Appraisal:Theory and Practice. No. 6 (November-December 1983):23 – 31.

---

① Woods R H. 饭店业人力资源管理(第三版). 张凌云,马晓秋,主译. 北京:中国旅游出版社,2003:208.

The most common decisions based on evaluation objectives concern compensation, which includes merit increases, employee bonuses, and other increases in pay. As far as employees are concerned, this is one of the primary objectives of performance appraisals. Thus, the term merit review, or merit evaluation, can be found in organizations using the performance appraisal to determine pay increases. Staffing decisions constitute another evaluation objective of performance appraisal, because the managers and supervisors must make decisions concerning promotions, demotions, transfers, and layoffs. Past performance appraisals normally influence which employee is most deserving of a promotion or other desirable job change. As Table 6-1 illustrates, the evaluation objectives of compensation decisions (merit increases, bonuses) and staffing decisions (promotion, termination, succession planning, transfer, manpower planning) dominate the common uses of performance appraisal systems, with seven of the top ten uses.[①]

第二节　有效评估的障碍及常见问题
(Effective Evaluation Barriers and Common Problem)

如前所述,绩效评估是饭店人力资源管理活动中的一项系统工作,在具体实施过程中会受到各方面因素的影响,从而使评估面临诸多问题,影响绩效评估的准确性和合理性。下面我们将指出有效绩效评估的一些障碍和常见问题。有效评估的障碍包括来自评估标准、评估人和被评估人等方面的障碍,常见的错误有最近印象型错误、固守过去错误、光环效应型错误、偏松错误、偏紧错误和中庸型错误等。

一、有效评估的障碍(Effective Evaluation Barriers)

(一)评估人缺乏技巧(Lack of Skill)

评估人是饭店绩效评估制度的具体执行者,是评估工作的具体实施者,因此,其专业性会对评估结果产生影响。然而,由于饭店业工作的繁忙性,评估人可能本身没有正式接受过进行绩效评估的培训。有时甚至评估人自己都没有被评估过。如果饭店要求评估人去进行工作表现的评估,但又不对评估人进行培训,这意味着这种评估几乎是无效的。

---

① Carrell M R, Kuzmits F E. Human Resource Management(Second Edition). Merrill Publishing Company, 1989:176.

(二)评估标准不当(Improper Evaluation Standard)

绩效评估所遵循的标准直接决定着评估结果。因此,评估标准的恰当性至关重要。一方面,评估同一职位工作绩效的标准在一定时期内应保持一致性,同时,不同评估人员对同一职位的员工的评估标准要保持一致。一般而言,评估标准的设定要以评估职位的职位说明书和职位规范为依据,不能随意改变评估标准。另一方面,评估标准要正确、合理和有效。在设定具体评估项目时要使其与所评估职位的特点相适应,在各项目的设置上也要考虑该职位主要职责和次要职责的关系。评估人员应避免评估内容与工作无关或非常复杂冗长使得员工不知如何作答,不仅如此,还应避免相关人员不知如何使用评估中得到的信息去策划改进员工工作表现的行动。例如,饭店负责打扫公共区域卫生的员工一般文化水平都不高,因此让他们填写的评估表应该设计得浅显易懂,并且,对他们进行评估时,具体操作能力的权重要大于组织协调能力的权重。而对于饭店主管等高级管理人员的评估则恰恰相反,应使组织协调能力的权重大于具体操作能力的权重。

(三)评估程序和频率不当(Improper Program)

在实际运营中,一些饭店的绩效评估程序是毫无条理的,经理只是在对员工实行纪律时才想起业绩评估,而不是把它作为获益性机会。有些饭店只是凌乱和偶尔地对员工进行评估,而不是有规律并经常性地开展业绩评估。通常情况下,对员工的正式业绩评估每年至少要做一两次,并且要经常性地开展非正式评估,这可以使员工得到不断的反馈来改进他们的工作。

(四)唯恐激怒员工(Afraid of Anger Employee)[①]

祝贺员工有突出的工作表现是一件容易并惬意的事情。然而,指出员工的工作未达到工作标准就不容易了。评估人员在评估工作表现不佳的员工时恐怕激怒他们,或违心地不按实际情况来进行评估。这种评估损害了业绩评估的目的,并失去了改善饭店经营管理状况的机会。

当评估工作表现欠佳的员工时,应把重点放在指正员工的工作缺点上,而不应针对该员工。决策应是行业性的,而不应卷入个人恩怨。在业绩评估中,应罗列具体事例,避免笼统的表述。最终提示员工采取哪些具体步骤来提高业绩。

当业绩评估与薪资增加挂钩时,员工常在接到不满意的工作反馈时对评估人员发难。员工们常认为他们的实际工作表现比工作标准要强,这就要求要充分强调工作标准的可衡量性,保留准确的数据,并在整个评估过程中不断向员工提供反馈。

(五)没有跟进(No Follow-up)

在一些饭店,评估者只是停留在填充业绩评估表并把它们归档上,并没有充分

---

① Kavanaugh R R 等著. 饭店业督导(第三版). 宿荣江,主译. 北京:中国旅游出版社,2002:163.

地发挥绩效评估的作用。在实际工作中,一些评估者不把绩效评估表给员工看,也不及时地把信息反馈给员工。为了使工作表现评估真正起到作用,必须使员工参与整个过程,而且必须使用评估得到的信息提高员工的绩效。

饭店管理者必须不断跟进员工的绩效评估。采用的跟进方法包括辅导、咨询或再培训来帮助员工提高工作表现。如果评估完成后很快被遗忘,对员工进行的评估和讨论就没有任何意义了。

绩效评估不应该有偏见,应该公平地对待每一个员工,但管理人员很难做到在任何时候都完全没有偏见。相关的培训能使评估者们尽可能客观和公正地主持评估。虽然不可能绝对地避免错误的出现,但可极大地减少错误的出现率。下面介绍在绩效评估过程中常见的几种错误。

二、常见错误(Common Appraisal Problems)

(一)最近印象型错误(Recency Error)

一般来说,人们对最近发生的事情印象会比较深刻,而对于远期发生的事情印象会较为淡薄。因此,在具体的考评工作开始之前的较短时期内,员工的表现会对评估结果有较大影响。例如饭店经理倾向于给那些在评估前一两个星期表现较为出色的员工偏高的评估;但对于那些过去表现一直较好,但在近期内犯了较为严重错误的员工,评价往往偏低。解决这一问题较为有效的方法是,加强对被评估者平时工作中关键事件的观察和记录,必要时可建立员工的个人档案。

(二)固守过去错误(Past Anchoring Error)

管理人员倾向于根据过去的评估来评估员工目前的工作表现。如果员工过去的评估分数高,而目前的得分本应低于这个数值,但管理人员可能会因为过去的分值而给员工一个偏高的分数。同样,尽管过去评估得分较低的员工目前工作表现突出,管理人员也可能会依据过去的低分值而给员工一个偏低的评估分数。

(三)光环效应型错误(Halo Error)

当饭店管理人员根据员工的单一特性、举止或行为而积极评价员工时,常产生光环效应型错误。员工的某些工作表现出色时,另一些可能是不合标准或勉强合格,但光环效应常使管理者根据员工的某些出色表现而判定其全部工作。

(四)偏松错误(Leniency Error)

有些饭店管理人员给员工打分时多给几分同情分。比如,从1分到5分给饭店员工打分(1=最差,5=最好),大多数管理人员的打分会在中点附近。由于存在同情打分现象,打分结果可能比实际情况显得好。

(五)偏紧错误(Severity Error)

与偏松错误相反,有些经理打分过于严厉,打分结果可能远离5而趋向1。

（六）中庸型错误（Central-tendency Error）

在进行员工绩效评估时，很多饭店管理者不考虑员工的真正业绩，只取中间值打分，这就犯了中庸型错误。例如，如果从 1 到 7 作为打分标准，那么饭店评估者很可能既避开较高的 6 分和 7 分，也避开较低的 1 分和 2 分，而把大多数员工都评定为 3 分、4 分和 5 分这三个等级上。有些评估系统要求评估者说明给予极高或极低评分的原因，这通常会导致中庸型错误。评估者会用接近平均值的评价来避免可能的争议或批评。

Summary: If a hotel manager overemphasizes the employee's most recent behavior, this results in a "recency effect error". The cunning employee uses this bias by ensuring, just before appraisal time, that they submit some outstanding piece of work, come to work early, leave late and appear highly motivated. The manager is overimpressed by the dramatic improvement in the employee's performance, evaluating only this segment of work rather than the employee's performance over the full review period. The halo error or effect is a "tendency to rate high or low on all factors due to the impression of a high or low rating on some specific factor."[1] Research shows that people with good attendance records are viewed as intelligent and responsible. Similarly, workers with poor attendance records are considered poor performance, even though the tardy person may produce work of far greater quantity and quality than the punctual employee.[2] A leniency error occurs when managers rate their employees consistently high.

第三节 评估过程和方法
(The Appraisal Process and Methods)

一、绩效评估过程(The Appraisal Process[3])

The appraisal process (see Figure 6-2) begins with the establishment of

---

[1] Bernardin H J, Beatty R W. Performance Appraisal: Assessing Human Behavior at Work. Boston: Kent Publishing, 1984:140.

[2] Schermerhorn J R, Hunt J G and Osborn R N. Managing Organizational Behavior(5th ed). John Wiley & Sons, 155.

[3] De Cenzo D A & Robbins S P. Human Resource Management (Fifth Edition). John Wiley & sons, 327-328.

performance standards in accordance with the hotel's strategic goals. These should have evolved out of the hotel's strategic direction. These performance standards should also be clear and objective enough to be understood and measured. Once performance standards are established, it is necessary to communicate these expectations; it should not be part of the employees' job to guess what is expected of them. Too many jobs in hotel have vague performance standards, and the problem is compounded when these standards are set in isolation and do not involve the employee. It is important to note that communication is a two-way street: Mere transference of information from the manager to the employee regarding expectations is not communication!

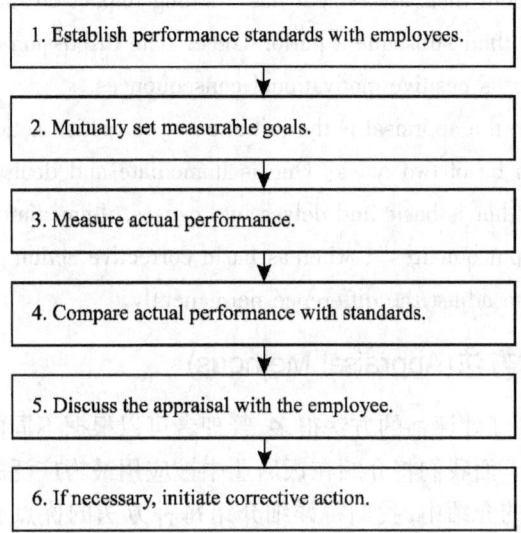

Figure 6 – 2　The Appraisal Process

Source: De Cenzo D A & Robbins S P. Human Resource Management (Fifth Edition). John Wiley & Sons, 327 – 328.

The third step in the appraisal process is the measurement of performance. To determine what actual performance is, it is necessary to acquire information about it. We should be concern with how we measure and what we measure. Four common sources of information are frequently used by managers regarding how to measure actual performance: personal observation, statistical reports, oral reports, and written reports. Each has its strengths and weaknesses; however, a combination of them increases both the number of input sources and the probability of receiving reliable information. What we measure is probably more critical to the evaluation process than how we measure, since the selection of the wrong criteria can result in serious, dysfunctional consequences. And what we measure determines, to a great extent, what people in the hotel will attempt to excel at. The criteria we measure must represent performance as it was mutually set in the first two steps of the appraisal process.

The fourth step in the appraisal process is the comparison of actual performance with standards. The point of this step is to note deviations between standard performance and actual performance so that we can proceed to the fifth step in the process—the discussion of the appraisal with the employee. One of the most challenging tasks facing managers is to present an accurate appraisal to the employee. The impression that employees receive about their assessment has a strong impact on their self-esteem and, very importantly, on their subsequent performance. The discussion of the appraisal can have negative as well as positive motivational consequences.

The final step in the appraisal is the initiation of corrective action where necessary. Corrective action can be of two types: One is immediate and deals predominantly with symptoms, and the other is basic and delves into causes. Immediate corrective action is often described as "put out fires", whereas basic corrective action gets to the source of deviation and seeks to adjust the difference permanently.

二、绩效评估方法(Appraisal Methods)

在饭店行业中,绩效评估的方法很多,管理者可以根据不同的评估目的来选择不同的评估方法。下面我们将介绍在饭店业中被应用最为广泛的一些绩效评估方法。各种评估方法的介绍中,我们将详细介绍每种方法的优点和缺点。这将有助于评估人更好地理解饭店业的具体评估系统。

(一)比较法(Comparison Method)

饭店绩效评估中的比较法(CM)是指通过对员工之间的相互比较,来确定其在工作绩效中的水平。这种方法在饭店行业中有其操作的限制性。因为饭店不同部门从事的工作不同,相同部门不同岗位的员工所做的工作也不相同,因此很难或不可能保证对比的持续性、公平性和客观性。而且员工希望得到的是对自己工作能力的测评,而不是把自己和他人做比较的结果,这会对员工造成心理压力,让他们在感情上接受比较困难。比较法中常使用的四种方法是:简单排列法;交叉排列法;对比排列法;比例分类法。

1. 简单排列法

要求饭店管理人员对员工从最好到最差进行排序,即评估者根据平时对员工的工作能力、工作态度等方面的总体印象,对员工的工作绩效从高到低进行排序。其好处是排序方法简单,评估结果是将员工从好到差排成一个连续的序列,结果简单易懂。但这种方法的缺点有:当员工的绩效水平接近时难以排序;不能区分不同性质的工作,只能针对一个或少量几个的工作要求进行排序;与薪酬制度挂钩困难等。

2. 交叉排列法

交叉排列法是简单排列法的改进型,在优缺点方面与简单排序法类似,两者只是在如何进行排序方面有差别。这种方法要求评估者首先列出所有被评估员工的名单,然后根据评价因素从中挑选出最好的,然后再找出对比最鲜明的最差的;将最好的列于榜首,最差的列于榜尾。再在剩下的员工中挑出次优者和次劣者;分别置于首二和尾二,以此类推,直到将所有员工评价排序完毕为止。

3. 对比排列法

这种方法是将全体员工逐一配对比较,按照配对比较中被评为较优的总次数来确定名次。即饭店管理人员将员工两人编成一组,根据评估要求轮流编组进行比较;考评者只需在每组中选出较优者,较优者得2分,较差者得0分,如果两人不相上下,则各得1分。最后,将每位员工得到的分数相加,就能够排出顺序。当被评估的员工人数太多时,需要比较的次数太多,这种方法也就不可行了。

4. 比例分类法

比例分类法是按照事物"两头小、中间大"的分布规律,先确定员工绩效的等级比例,然后评估者按照员工个人的相对优劣程度将所有员工按照该比例分配到各个等级中。例如,如果将饭店员工分成优、中、劣三等级,则分别占30%、40%和30%;如果将饭店员工分成优、良、中、差、劣五个等级,则每等级分别占5%、15%、60%、15%与5%(如图6-3所示)。

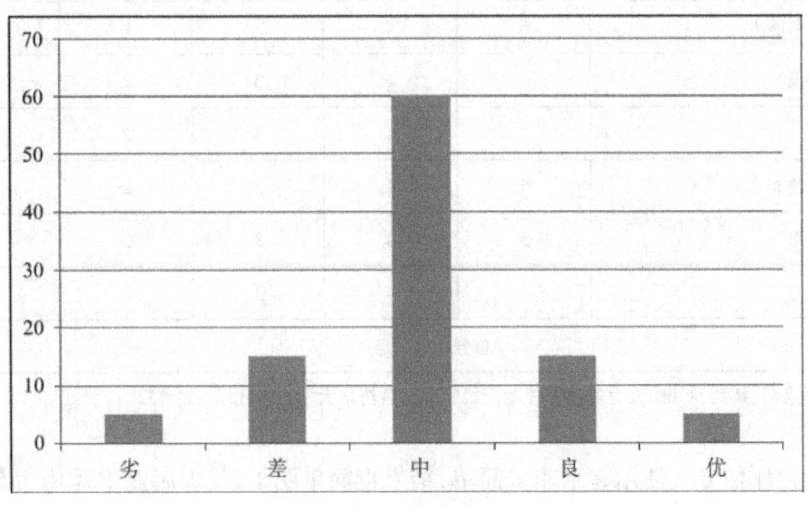

图6-3 比例分类法

从饭店管理者的角度看,交叉排列法和对比排列法可以找出员工队伍中对饭店最有价值和最没价值的员工,但无法了解到为什么一个员工比另一个员工更有价值,更有价值到什么程度。

(二) 图表尺度评价法(Graphic Rating Scale Method)

图表尺度评价法(GRSM)常用于饭店钟点工。这种方法是对工作的 10 到 15 项内容进行从 1 到 5 的评价计分。这些内容包括工作特点、工作质量、工作数量、独立性、出勤率、人际关系能力、工作知识、解决问题能力等。所有的计分最后加总得出员工的整体得分。表 6-2 是某饭店进行员工绩效评估时所用的图表尺度评价表。

表 6-2 图表尺度评价表

考核日期： 年 月 日

考核人：		职务：		所在部门：	
被考核人：		岗位：		所在部门：	
考核要素	评价尺度				
绩效内容	优异	优秀	值得表扬	一般	较差
工作特点	5	4	3	2	1
工作质量	5	4	3	2	1
工作数量	5	4	3	2	1
独立性	5	4	3	2	1
出勤率	5	4	3	2	1
人际关系能力	5	4	3	2	1
工作知识	5	4	3	2	1
创造性	5	4	3	2	1
解决问题能力	5	4	3	2	1
团队合作	5	4	3	2	1
沟通能力	5	4	3	2	1
总分					

资料来源:卿涛,罗键.人力资源管理概论[M].北京:清华大学出版社,2007:232.

这种评估方法使用起来非常简单,结果也简单明了,是饭店业中运用得最普遍的工作绩效评估技术之一;但这种评价可能会犯偏松错误、偏紧错误和扩大化错误,而且评估人可能觉得评价内容标准不好理解,如人际关系怎么评判?每个评估人对独立性的理解可能不一样。

这种方法的另一个问题是各个评价内容的重要性不同,每个评估人对每个内容的重要性看法也不同,如有的评估人认为出勤率是最重要的评估因素,而有的评估人认为工作质量是最重要的评估因素。不同的看法使评估人的评价标准也各不相同。

(三)行为锚定等级评价法(Behaviorally Anchored Rating Scale)

行为锚定等级评价法(BARS)和图表尺度评价法一样,也是评估人用连续等级计分的方法对员工进行评估,只不过这种方法是根据员工工作中的关键事件或具体行为进行评估。关键事件是管理者捕捉并记录下来的工作相关细节,并通过细节的综合形成工作的整体描绘。通常用于 BARS 的关键事件,是由管理人员和员工共同讨论得出的,更容易让员工接受,表6-3给出了一个行为锚定等级评价的范例。

开发一项行为锚定式评估量表的过程是相当复杂的。主要需经历以下几个步骤:第一,收集大量代表工作中的优秀和无效绩效的关键事件。第二,将所收集到的关键事件划分为不同的绩效维度,确定评估员工工作绩效的重要维度,列出维度并对每一个维度进行定义。第三,把那些被专家们认为能够清楚地代表某一特定绩效水平的关键事件作为指导评估者评估员工工作绩效的行为事例的标准。第四,为每一个维度开发出一个评估量表,用这些行为作为"锚"来定义量表上的评分。

Table 6-3 Behaviorally anchored rating scale for an employment officer

	EMPLOYMENT OFFICER	
Superior performance	7	Could be expected at all times to be developing, implementing and refining selection procedures and their own interviewing techniques to the highest professional standard.
Very good performance	6	Could be expected to have an excellent knowledge of the company, its products and job vacancies, and to be accurate and thorough in matching applicants with jobs.
Good performance	5	Could be expected to interview in depth and treat applicants with courtesy and respect and inform them fully about the job, the company and its products.
Acceptable performance	4	Could be expected to talk with an applicant about the job, their interests etc., and to cover key questions regarding suitability.
Marginal performance	3	Could be expected to show little personal interest in the candidate and possess only basic knowledge about the job, the company and its products.
Poor performance	2	Could be expected to keep applicants waiting, interview haphazardly and have little or no knowledge about the job, the company and its products.
Unsatisfactory performance	1	Could be expected to disclose confidential information about applicants, be rude, ask questions that are not job-related and keep applicants waiting.

Source: Stone R J. Appraising employee performance, Action Report No. 26. Rydge Publications, Sydney, 1985.

The research on BARS indicates that while it is far from perfect, it does tend to reduce rating errors. Possibly its major advantage stems from the dimensions generated, rather than from any particular superiority of behavior over trait anchors.① A major drawback with BARS is that they take a great deal with management time and effort to develop. In addition, because separate rating forms must be developed for different jobs, their use is restricted to a minority of big organizations with generic jobs performed by large numbers of incumbents.②

(四)行为观察评价法(Behavior Observation Scale)

行为观察评价法(BOS)是20世纪末期针对行为锚定等级评价法(BARS)的缺点而开发出来的。因为后者对一个员工只能有一个评判,而研究人员认为BARS不能准确地评估那些表现时好时坏的员工。BOS不是单纯地以关键事件为评判标准,而是要求评估人根据关键事件标准观察员工表现出的这种行为的频度。现在,这种方法在饭店行业中也得到广泛的应用。例如,在评估中餐厅服务员与团队中其他人合作时,让评估人标出员工是"经常"还是"从不"与人合作得很好。与BARS相比,BOS更加客观,能够提供更全面的反馈信息(Table 6 – 4 is a sample BOS for an employment officer)。

Table 6 – 4 Behavior observation scale for an employment officer

EMPLOYMENT OFFICER
1. Gives the applicant a clear description of the job
(almost never)　1　2　3　4　5　(almost always)
2. Gives the applicant a clear description of the pay and benefits offered
(almost never)　1　2　3　4　5　(almost always)
3. Conducts in-depth interviews with applicants
(almost never)　1　2　3　4　5　(almost always)
4. Treats all applicants in a non-discriminatory and courteous manner
(almost never)　1　2　3　4　5　(almost always)
5. Undertakes thorough reference checks
(almost never)　1　2　3　4　5　(almost always)
Total score
5 ~ 9: Needs improvement
10 ~ 14: Acceptable
15 ~ 19: Good
20 + : Superior

Source: Stone R J. Human resource management(4th ed). John Wiley & Sons Australia, Ltd. 2002:289.

---

① Murphy K R and Pardaffy V A. Bias in Behaviorally Anchored Rating Scales: Global or Scale Specific. Journal of Applied Psychology (April 1989), 343 – 346.

② Nankervis A R and Leece P. Performance appraisal: two steps forward, one step back?. Asia Pacific Journal of Human Resources, Volume. 35. No. 2, 1997:85.

(五)叙述文章法(Essay Description)

叙述文章法(ED)是评估者用短文的形式对员工绩效进行简单描述的一种绩效评估方法,是饭店常用的绩效评估方法之一。这种方法更关注员工在工作中的特别事件,而不是每日的常规表现。最理想的情况是评估人能认真写出评估文章,全面概括评估对象的表现,包括以后改进方向的建议。好的评估文章能弥补量化评估方式的不足。

Some hotels may use an essay description to try to determine performance levels (see Table 6-5). A manager may be asked to describe, in their own words, the employee's performance (covering the quantity and quality of work performed, job know-how, human relations skills, strength and weaknesses, and so on). The major problems associated with this approach are subjectivity and the impact of the manager's writing skills on the impression conveyed in the report.

Table 6-5 Example of essay description performance appraisal format

Name:
Position:
Department:
Date started on job:
Date of last rating:
Date of this rating:
Appraisal of performance:
————————————————————————
————————————————————————
————————————————————————
Suggestions for development:
————————————————————————
————————————————————————
————————————————————————
Prepared by: Position:
Signature:

Source: Stone R J. Human resource management(4th ed). John Wiley & Sons Australia, Ltd. 2002:289.

(六)关键事件法(Critical Incident Method)

关键事件法(CIM)是通过对员工日常工作中那些会对部门的整体工作绩效产生积极或消极影响的重大事件的考核来确定员工绩效的方法。以关键事件为标准进行业绩表现评估的饭店管理人员会保留员工的个人记录,其中主要记载特定情况下的员工行为。这种方法对饭店企业尤为适用。

例如,饭店服务员在下雨天把自己的伞借给客人。这种方法的优点是员工参与性强,设计成本低,操作比较容易等。这种关键事件也可以成为一种象征性的目标,要求其他员工学习的典范。如培训录像中可以演播一名西餐厅服务员把客人落在餐桌上的手机送还给客人。这类关键事件能很好地描绘出企业希望员工表现出的行为和对顾客服务的关注。

这种方法的一个不足之处是经理必须仔细记录所观察到的关键事件,并且考核结果无法在员工之间进行比较,也很难与薪酬挂钩。

(七)目标管理(Management By Objective)

目标管理法(MBO)始于管理大师德鲁克的《管理实践》一书中。德鲁克认为每一项工作都必须为达到总目标而展开。

与其他方法不同的是,目标管理(MBO)需要员工和饭店经理/或主管双方一起开会探讨大家共同的目标,为达到这个目标而制订的计划,以及实施手段。一般来讲,MBO 系统要求这种会议定期进行以评价进展情况,最后根据目标的实现情况对员工进行评估。

目标管理法的其中一种形式是使用工作细则(具体工作岗位的任务)和工作细述(具体解释每项工作)。上述两种工具是在培训阶段中制定的,应有效地使用它们来对员工进行客观的评估。评估者和员工对工作的优点和应改进的地方应达成共识,应向员工分发工作细则和工作细述,以使员工能参照并达到相关的工作标准。

有些饭店管理者和学者强烈认同这种方法,认为这既是一种可行的业绩评估方法,也能体现出良好的管理理念。但也有些人认为这种方法有欠缺:如管理成本很高,容易产生忽视饭店长远发展目标的现象,缺乏必要的行为指导等。另外在目标管理系统中,也很难评估不同员工的不同目标的实现程度,因为有的员工设定的目标比其他人的要困难。这给比较排列员工的评估人又出了个难题。

(八)关键绩效指标法(KPI)

关键绩效指标法(Key Performance Indicator)是目前在饭店业中运用最广的考核方法之一。它把对绩效的评估简化为对几个关键指标的考核,把关键指标当作评估标准,把员工的绩效与关键指标作出比较进行评估,在一定程度上可以说是目标管理法与帕累托定律的有效结合。

确立关键绩效指标的要点在于流程性、计划性和系统性,其基本的操作流程如下:

(1)确定企业级 KPI。明确企业的战略目标,并利用头脑风暴法和鱼骨分析法等找出企业的业务重点,再进一步确定这些关键业务领域的 KPI,即企业级 KPI。

(2) 分解出部门级 KPI。各部门的负责人依据企业级 KPI,确定实现目标的工作流程,分解出各部门级的 KPI,以便确定评价指标体系。

(3) 分解出个人的 KPI。各部门的负责人和相关员工一起再将 KPI 进一步细分,分解为更细的 KPI 及各职位的业绩衡量指标。这些业绩衡量指标就是员工考核的要素和依据。

(4) 设定评价标准。一般来说,指标指的是从哪些方面衡量或评价工作,解决评价什么的问题,而标准指的是各个指标分别应该达到什么样的水平,解决被评价者怎样做的问题。

(5) 审核关键绩效指标。为了确保拟定的关键绩效指标能够全面、客观地反映被评估对象的绩效和可操作性,需要审核多个评价者对同一个绩效指标进行评价的结果是否能取得一致,这些指标的总和是否可以解释被评估者 80% 以上的工作目标等问题。

关键绩效指标法是企业战略目标的层层分解,致力于使员工绩效行为与企业目标要求的行为相吻合,既有利于企业战略目标的实现,也有利于组织利益与个人利益达成一致。但是关键绩效指标法也有其自身的不足之处,例如,关键绩效指标更多是倾向于定量化的指标,这些定量化的指标是否真正对企业绩效产生关键性的影响,如果没有运用专业化的工具和手段,是很难界定的。另外,如果过分地依赖量化的考核指标而不考虑人为因素和弹性因素容易产生一些考核上的争端和异议。

(九) 360 度反馈评估法(360-Degree Feedback Evaluation Method)

360 度反馈评估法(360-Degree Feedback)也称为全方位反馈评价法或多源反馈评价法,主要是针对酒店的员工进行自上而下、自下而上、本人的、平级的以及来自酒店外部顾客的全方位的考评,更多的时候是用于管理人员的绩效评估。这种方法是目前比较流行的绩效评估方法,很多大公司都采用这种方法进行绩效评估,例如英特尔公司、波音公司、杜邦公司,等等。

360 度评估进行前要进行细致策划,在实施时要考虑下列建议:

(1) 反馈必须是不记名的、保密的,只有公司在一定级别以上的管理人员可以看到评估者的信息。

(2) 要考虑到评估对象的任职时间长短,评估人和评估对象的一些历史背景资料是必要的。

(3) 反馈资料要由专家进行数据分析。

(4) 一定要做后续工作,在收到反馈资料后制订行动计划并实施。

(5) 量化评估和陈述评估结果,单有数字不能说明太多问题。

(6) 避免疲劳评估,不要同时对每个人都进行评估。

尽管360度评估非常流行，它也有一些局限性。由于360度反馈评估法涉及的信息渠道比较多，因而在有关考评数据和信息的收集过程中，需要耗费大量的时间、人力、财力和物力，并且，数据处理和信息处理的成本也比较高。并且，该方法参考与被评估者有工作关系的每一个方面的意见，因此，意见反馈者的评价公正与否将会直接影响到所提供信息的公正性与准确性，这就要求参评人员有较高素质。

Reading Material

Joe Malik is the manager of a team of engineers at AT&T in New Jersey. Joe is an individual who prides himself on recognizing his strengths and weaknesses. He makes every attempt to capitalize on those strengths, and works fervently on developing efforts to overcome the weaknesses. His biggest problem, he thought, was his temper. In the past, Joe just blew his stack—and it was no surprise to anyone when Joe flew off the handle at work. He understood that this interfered with his work and with relationships he had on the job. Understandably, Joe has been working very hard to overcome this problem. No 360-degree appraisal was needed to confirm that was a problem.

Although an active believer in getting and receiving feedback, Joe was startled to learn that his employees viewed him as having a bigger problem. A function of his temperament, Joe thought? No, his employees thought Joe had no vision for where the group was heading!

Team members reported to Joe that whenever any of them asked about the future plans for their work group, Joe would just "scrunch up in his chair." Everyone perceived this as Joe's way of evading the question—a tough one at that. Moreover, his body language indicated to these employees that he may know some unsettling news, and just didn't want to share it. Fear became rampant! Sadly, though, their perceptions were furthest from the truth. Interestingly enough, Joe prided himself as being a visionary. How else could he manage a group of professions developing prototypes for the phone systems networking system? Unfortunately, Joe kept his vision to himself. Through AT&T's 360-degree evaluation process, Joe was able to appreciate and understand the results of his behavior. Joe now knows that his employees have a strong desire to understand where they are going, and what his future plans for the units are. He now communicates such information to team members regularly. As a result, team members are less frustrated, and Joe has overcome one of his shortcomings.

By providing this constructive feedback through the 360-degree appraisal, team members' needs are being better met. As for Joe, he still scrunches up in his chair, but not because he doesn't know the answer to employee questions. That's just Joe, and it doesn't bother his employees any longer!

Source: O'Reilly B. 360-Feedback Can Change Your Life. Fortune, 1994: 64-65.

（十）平衡计分卡（Balanced Score Card）

平衡计分卡（BSC）由美国的戴维·诺顿（David Norton）和罗伯特·卡普兰（Robert Kaplan）于20世纪90年代初创立。在他们研究平衡计分卡之前，Analog Device（简称"ADI"）公司最早于1987年就进行了平衡计分卡实践尝试。由于其具有的强有力的理论基础和便于操作的特点，一经提出便迅速得到广泛的应用。目前，平衡计分卡是饭店业最常用的绩效评估方法之一。平衡计分卡是从财务、顾客、内部流程、学习和成长四个维度关注其他绩效，并把公司的战略目标转化成具体的目标和评价指标，从而形成的一套完整的、全面的绩效管理体系。表6-6是ADI公司的第一张平衡计分卡。

表6-6 ADI公司的第一张平衡计分卡

	财年××年		第一季度		第二季度		第三季度		第四季度	
	标杆	实际	标杆	实际	标杆	实际	标杆	实际	标杆	实际
财务指标										
资本收益率										
营业收入增长										
利润										
……										
客户服务										
及时交货										
供货时间										
次品率										
……										

续表

	财年××年		第一季度		第二季度		第三季度		第四季度	
	标杆	实际	标杆	实际	标杆	实际	标杆	实际	标杆	实际
内部										
生产周期										
流程错误率										
产能										
……										
新品开发										
新品导入										
新品订货量/率										
员工流动比率										
……										

资料来源:http://wiki.mbalib.com/wiki/%E5%B9%B3%E8%A1%A1%E8%AE%A1%E5%88%86%86-E5%8D%A1.

平衡计分卡的框架如图6－4所示。

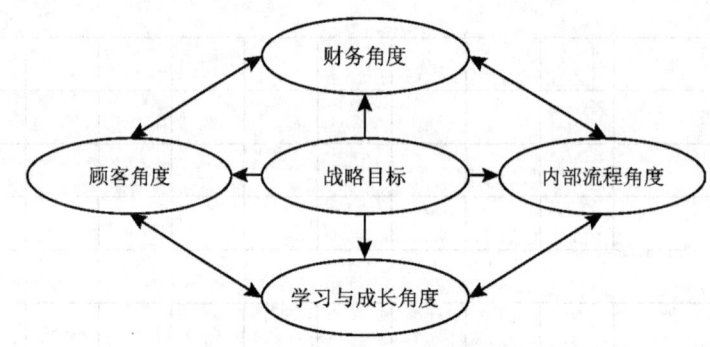

图6－4 平衡计分卡框架

资料来源:张德.人力资源开发与管理(第三版).北京:清华大学出版社,2007.4.

1.财务视角:从股东角度来看企业增长、利润率及战略

回答怎样满足股东的需要问题。企业经常的直接目的是为股东创造价值,尽管战略不同,阶段不同,但财务目标是最终的目标。财务指标反映实施战略之后是

否对改善经营结构产生贡献,常见的是销售收入、投资收益率、经济附加值等。

2.顾客视角:从顾客角度来看企业创造价值和差异化的战略

要达成财务目标,必须满足顾客什么样的要求? 产品的质量、性能和服务等方面如何满足要求,包括顾客满意度、顾客保持率、新顾客争取率。

3.内部流程视角:使各种业务流程满足顾客和股东的优先战略

要使股东和顾客满意,我们应该具备什么优势? 例如改善流程、创造新产品/服务;降低成本、提高质量。

4.学习与成长角度:如何持续创造价值

不断提高能力,适应环境变化和激烈竞争的需要。优先创造一种支持公司变化、革新和成长的气候。包括人、系统和组织程序。例如员工发展、技术改进、新产品销售比率、流程再造等。

平衡计分卡的设计思想是以学习与成长作为企业发展的驱动力,通过内部流程优势满足顾客需要开拓市场,最终实现企业的财务目标。其逻辑是:(1)如果组织拥有学习与发展能力,就会获得优于竞争对手的内部流程。(2)如果获得优于竞争对手的内部流程,就会获得更满意的顾客。(3)如果获得更满意的顾客,就会实现公司的财务目标。平衡计分卡的功能主要表现在:(1)阐明了企业的战略方向。(2)建立起了目标与手段之间的因果关系。(3)使个人、团队工作与组织目标协调起来。(4)把企业战略目标落实到具体工作绩效上。

第四节 绩效评估的主体
(Who performs the Evaluation)

很多饭店管理人员仅简单地指派工作负责人对员工进行绩效评估,绝大多数情况下的评估由主管进行;但这些人可能与所评估的员工的实际接触很少。发生接触也大都是在特定情形下,真正的互动接触可能更少。如同衡量工作的标准是多种多样的,绩效评估的参与者也是多方面的。由于饭店中岗位的复杂性,仅仅凭借一个人的观察和评价是很难对员工做出全面的绩效评估的。饭店业发展到现阶段,员工绩效评估已经较为完善,许多饭店参与评估的人员包括直接主管、同事、下级员工、员工自己以及顾客等。

一、直接主管评估(Supervisor Evaluation)

直接主管的评估是评估员工绩效的传统方法。在绝大多数情况下,直接主管是执行这项任务的最佳人选,原因如下:第一,直接主管有机会直接观察员工的实际工作绩效。第二，主管负责管理一个小团体，当由其他人员评估下属时，他的权威性会受到伤害。第三，下属的培训和发展是每个管理者工作的重要组成部分。正如前面所说的，员工工作绩效评估与员工发展息息相关。

从另一个角度看，员工的直属主管又不一定是适合于评估的人选，因为他们往往会重视员工的某些方面而忽视了其他方面，甚至有些主管会为了加薪和升职而蓄意操纵评估结果。

二、雇员的同事评估(Peer Evaluation)

有研究表明雇员的同事评估是最好的评估方法，因为这可以制造员工同事接触的机会，这对饭店企业的团队合作非常重要。由于同事经常从不同角度来观察绩效，因此，同事评估能提供比上司评估更正确和真实的信息。同事在评估一个员工的优缺点的同时，能够很容易观察到员工各方面的能力。同事评估结果往往和直接主管评估结果、顾客评估结果之间有高度的相关性。然而，雇员的同事评估要求同事之间能经常看到对方的表现，并且同事之间是高度互相信任的。

三、下级员工评估(Subordinate Evaluation)

尽管目前很少有饭店会把员工评价与经理的任职联系得很紧密，但这是一种值得借鉴的绩效评估方法。在评价管理者时，员工是非常有发言权的，因为他们经常和其上司接触，最了解上级的领导能力、授权、团队协调能力、口头表达能力和对下属的关注程度等。为了避免潜在的麻烦，下级员工评估应该采用匿名的方式，并综合考虑多人的评估结果。

四、自我评估(Self-evaluation)

如果员工了解自己的目标及用于评价的指标，他们就可以进行很好的自我评估了。很多人都知道自己在工作中哪些方面做得好，哪些是需要改进的。这种方法可以提高员工的参与度，给予员工一个思考自身优缺点的机会。当需要饭店上级管理者和一线员工一起建立未来的工作目标或者员工个人发展计划时，这种方法尤为适用。

五、顾客评估(Customer Evaluation)

顾客评估曾经被饭店管理者认为是最好的评估方法，因为他们的满意是服务的最终目标，顾客评估也有助于明确培训需求。现在，仍然有很多饭店通过顾客评估来获得员工绩效评估。但是收集准确的顾客评估是很困难的，很多客人根本不填顾客意见卡，除非他们对服务特别不满或特别满意，其结果是顾客评估可能强调两极而不是一般水平。

第五节　辅导(Coaching)

通过前面的论述我们已经知道有几个因素是影响业绩评估的,管理人员有很多选择机会,选择评估方法,选择评估人等。

培训能使员工学会如何及为什么要根据工作标准来完成工作。管理者提供的辅导则能使员工把在培训中学到的技巧付诸实践。在辅导的过程中,管理者应说服、改正并激励员工更有效地工作。通过正面的表扬能获得预期的结果。

辅导不同于咨询和实行纪律。辅导的目的在于向员工提供反馈并帮助员工改善工作表现。如果员工因为不理解如何来完成工作而犯了错误,这时则需要展开辅导。但如果是明知故犯,那就需要我们采取纪律措施。

在任何计划周密的辅导中,管理者应至少关注并解决三个问题:
第一,需要解决的具体问题。
第二,管理者与员工之间的关系。
第三,员工的综合发展。

这种计划周密的辅导应在形式和方式上与面试相似。管理者在辅导的过程中应获得事实,提供公正的反馈,表示对员工心情的理解并策划改进措施。通过计划周密的辅导过程来解决工作问题,并增进辅导与员工之间的关系。辅导最终能帮助员工更有效地工作。

辅导一般是围绕着解决问题这一重点,即针对员工在工作中遇到的问题或工作表现不佳所造成的问题而采取相应的措施。

一、辅导的原则(Principle of Coaching)

工作辅导是一项重要的管理者活动。员工的态度和工作表现很大程度上受到管理者的工作方式、管理者对员工的态度和管理者本身工作表现的影响。如果管理者的行为显示出对员工的工作表现不闻不问,员工本人对工作也不可能非常关注。如果管理者期望工作达到既定的工作标准,员工也就会按此标准工作。只有当管理者创造了能使员工身心投入的工作氛围后,辅导才能起到作用。

（一）员工参与(Employee Involvement)

要想使辅导成功,员工必须积极参加目标的设置并致力于目标的完成。员工越是积极地参与问题的评估和措施的制定,他们就越能增强使命感,从而增加成功的可能性。管理者应鼓励员工积极参加管理者过程并征询员工意见,以帮助他们解决问题。

（二）相互理解（Mutual Understanding）

饭店的员工必须了解双方在讨论的问题主题。为确保这一点,应让员工用自己的语言确定问题的症结。然后,重述员工的见解以证实员工的理解力。做不到这一点,管理者和员工双方可能抱着截然不同的观点和解决措施而结束讨论。

（三）聆听（Listening）

管理者不仅要善于谈吐,更重要的是能聆听他人的意见。在辅导的过程中,如果能聆听员工发表的意见,双方都会从辅导的过程中受益。允许员工描述工作的问题,能获取员工的建议和他们对与工作有关的问题的见解。

二、辅导的目的(Aim of Coaching)

管理者进行辅导的目的是改进员工的行为和态度,包括改变工作局面、员工的工作态度,改善员工技巧或改变员工的工作目的。

（一）改变工作局面（Change Work Situation）

管理者可以改变自我的行为或领导方式;重组工作人员搭配来改变员工的行为或调整遇到问题的员工的工作组合;改变工作资源或条件。从事这些工作变化的管理者能帮助员工调整行为举止。

（二）改变员工工作态度（Change Work Attitude）

管理者使员工确信能准确了解到公司的运营目的、目标、面临的挑战等问题情况,从而帮助员工转变对待工作的态度。此外,管理者能指出员工如何才能有效地工作从而达到个人目标。不论员工是否达到既定的工作标准,管理者都应提供正面的反馈意见。

（三）改善员工的技巧（Improve Skills）

管理者能帮助员工学到更多的工作技巧,并使员工知道如何解决普遍性的问题。这有助于改善员工的态度和自重感(自信心、积极态度、自我尊重感)。

（四）改变员工的工作目的（Change Work Purpose）

管理者能帮助员工设置他们能达到的工作目的。管理者应经常审视工作表现标准。如果标准设置过高或员工对自己的要求过高,员工可能往往会感到失望。因此要帮助员工设立能达到的短期目标。

三、设置辅导目标的原则（The Principle of Setting Goals）

辅导的总目标是要改善员工的工作表现。只有与员工共同制定出工作目标,才能达到这一目的。为员工设置辅导目标看似是一件简单的事情,每个人都有过制定目标的经历,但是如果上升到技术层面,饭店管理者必须学习并掌握SMART

原则。

所谓 SMART 原则,SMART 是 5 个英文单词首字母的缩写。

目标必须是明确的(Specific)。所谓明确就是要具体、清楚地说明想要达成的行为标准,而不是抽象的语言和内容。

目标必须是可以衡量的(Measurable)。衡量性就是指应该有一组明确的数据,作为衡量是否达成目标的依据。

目标必须是可以达到的(Attainable)。目标是要被执行人能够承担和接受的,确保制定出高标准的目标,但也应是可行的。

目标必须和其他目标具有相关性(Relevant)。目标的相关性是指实现此目标与其他目标的关联情况。如果实现了这个目标,但与其他的目标完全不相关,或者相关度很低,那这个目标即使被达到了,意义也不是很大。

目标必须具有明确的截止期限(Time-based)。目标的时限性就是指目标是有时间限制的。应牢记在制定最后期限时应保留出足够的完成工作任务的时间。

为员工设置的工作标准数目也需着重考虑。员工一般在同一时期只能完成五至九项工作目标。这是一般可行的目标设置的范围,因为员工完全能在其固定的岗位上去努力完成这些目标。超出这个范围就意味着员工会感到工作的盲目性或认为目标设置过高。

四、辅导的类型(The Type of Coaching)

辅导有非正式和正式两种。

(一)非正式辅导(Non-official Coaching)

非正式辅导通常发生在员工的实际工作岗位上。它可贯穿于日常工作的始终。非正式辅导的目的是指出员工的工作行为是否达到工作标准。如果员工的工作未达到工作标准,管理者应该展示正确的工作程序,并解释错误的程序为什么是行不通的。

当你想要员工始终如一地坚持按工作标准操作时,你应随时关注员工的行为,并随时在恰当的时间表扬你的员工。当场表扬员工的长处是行之有效的手段,员工最有可能重复受到正面表扬的行为。在辅导的过程中,你应向员工说明并重述你的期望值,直到他们了解并记住为止。重述期望值能鼓励员工去学习,并能提醒员工时刻遵循既定的工作标准。应该注意的是,在重述期望值的过程中,不应该以威胁的口吻来评述员工工作表现与员工标准之间的差距。相反,应具体强调员工的工作不当之处,并解释应该如何改进。设身处地地为员工着想,有的时候能达到事半功倍的效果,管理者们不妨使用"远距离观察",而不是寸步不离地监控员工的一举一动。

(二)正式辅导(Official Coaching)

正式辅导常在岗位之外私下以面谈形式进行,着重于涉及那些影响员工工作表现的知识、技巧或态度问题。正式辅导还被称为工作表现改进商讨。管理者应该制订日常计划并正式记录所商讨的事宜。正式辅导包含提问型和非提问型两种基本面谈模式。

提问型面谈是指用直接提问来展开面谈,常被用来发出或接收情况与信息,但有时也涉及情感和态度问题。非直接型提问面谈指不拘形式的探讨问题方式,目的在于分析员工的态度对工作的影响。管理者往往以泛泛的问题或陈述作为开场白,然后让员工充分地发表自己的看法。在非提问型的面谈中,员工有时会隐藏或掩饰自己的真实想法,管理者应尽量创造开诚布公、相互理解的氛围,真心实意地倾听他们的想法。非提问型面谈要求管理者具备很高的沟通技巧。

如果可能的话,正式辅导应在安静、避开众人的场合中进行面谈,个人办公室或会议室都是不错的选择。辅导的起步应平缓,在面谈的起初应给员工足够的时间认真考虑问题,消除他的恐惧和迷茫,尽可能以积极和关心的态度讨论问题。可以多询问员工对解决问题的方案的意见,并认真做简要记录,让员工有受重视的感觉。最后,管理者应以积极的、关心的方式结束讨论,并强调自己对员工能力的肯定以及对其改进工作的信心,并愿意随时提供帮助。

辅导结束后,管理者应主动跟进,并经常观察员工的工作表现。对于员工做出的改进要给予及时的肯定和鼓励,在员工需要帮助时适时伸出自己的手。必要时要提供进一步的辅导,这一后续辅导要在下一次正式评估之前进行。

案例分析(Practice Case Analysis)

The Performance Evaluation of XXX Hotel

In the meeting room of ×××hotel, Mr. Smith, CEO of ×××hotel, is carefully listening to the implementation information about performance evaluation last year. There are two decisions making him troubled. One is that according to the performance evaluation result, employees who were ranked in the last level are the most hard-working employees in the hotel. Whether these people should be demoted and cut salaries according to the original examining plans or not? How to adjust the next stage inspection plan as a more effective one? The other is that Human Resource department suggests buying a set of human resources management software to improve the efficiency of the statistical work. But can a set of software truly have effect on performance evaluation improving?

× × × hotel was set up 4 years ago. In order to evaluate and incent all levels of staffs better, it has established a set of performance management system while introduced market mechanism of employing. The human resource manager said this system details the traditional few indexes—morality, ability, industry and performance. At the same time it highlights work performance. The design is focusd on refining the traditional few indexes into 10 measurable indicators and details every indicator into 5 levels. Meanwhile, it qualitatively describes level definition. Managers just need to correspond employees' actual behavior to description, and then assess achievement by accumulating corresponding scores.

But something strange happened. The original more outstanding and active employees' performance evaluation results are often rank behind most staffs. Some employees who are not active but make few mistakes always rank in the front. And some managers are not understanding the method of ranking performance evaluation result, therefore they are against this kind of method in their hearts. Despite all the bugs of the system, the present performance evaluation has made some achievements synthesizing all aspects. All the departments can perform well. The only thing need to make sure is how to implement the punishment measures on people who were ranked at the end of evaluation result. If these people were demoted and cut salaries, there is no doubt a batch of employees who work as hard as them will be harmed. But if these people were not punished which may damage the seriousness and continuity of assessment system easily. Another problem is that, in this examination, statistical tools are relative far behind that makes assessment achievements statistics too big work. There are only 3 staff in HR department. They have to statistic more than 200 people's performance evaluation scores. And they need to talk with these people respectively. So during the whole evaluation month all staffs in HR department are doing this work, while other things are delayed.

Mr. Smith decides to invite the managers of finance department, human resource department and F&B department to the office to get a deep understanding of actual situation.

After Mr. Smith explains the reasons briefly, Emily, manager of F&B department, first replies, "I think this assessment plan needs to adjust as soon as possible, because it doesn't really reflect our actual work. Take my department as an example, we are mainly responsible for serving customers directly. In order to ensure customers satisfied we can't have an error or we may lost a customer. But on the performance evaluation table there is a question 'Does he/she always harm the benefit of customers'. It is really improper."

Eric, manager of finance department, then says, "In my department, our work is finished basically all according to specifications and standards. Filling tables and making accounts allows no risk at all. How can the work reflect innovation ability? If we don't have this content, should we sign the highest or the lowest scores? I think there is another problem should be pay attention to. We continue to use the traditional democratic appraisal way in this evaluation. I have no doubt about the department internal personnel evaluation. But actually I doubt whether it is proper to be scored by people in other departments. Our financial work often offends people. Is it justice to let people who were offended by our work to evaluate our work?"

Questions for Discussion:
1. What's the problem of ××× hotel's performance evaluation system?
2. How to design a performance evaluation system that can adapt to different positions?

名词解释(Key Terms)

1. 交叉排列法:在评估过程中,评估者在所有参加评估的员工中按照工作表现从最佳员工依次排列至最差员工的方法。

Alternative Ranking: It is a kind of employee performance evaluation method by which the assessors line employees from the best one to the worst one according to their performance during the process of assessment.

2. 行为观察评价法:计分方法的一种,评估人找出员工达标行为的次数。

Behavioral Observation Scales: It is a kind of scoring method—the assessors find out the number of standard behaviors committed by employees.

3. 行为锚定等级评价法:计分方法的一种,评估人对员工某些特定行为的展示进行评分。

Behaviorally Anchored Rating Scale: It is a kind of scoring method—the assessors score the certain behavior of employees.

4. 关键事件:工作分析技巧之一,以捕捉和记录实际工作中的事件作为基础,将这些支离的事件组合后形成描述实际工作要求的完整画面。这种方法尤其适用于服务行业规范描述、培训或业绩评估的标准。

Critical Incident: It is one of job analysis skills, based on capturing and recording the events on actual work, forming the complete picture of depicting actual work demand after combined these bitty events. This method is especially suitable for service industry standard description, training or performance evaluation standards.

5. 比例类法:管理人员评估中所使用的两头小、中间大的统计曲线方法。

Forced Distribution: It is a statistical curve method used by managers in employee performance evaluation.

6. 图表尺度评价法:评价方法的一种,评估人根据一些具体可测知的标准为员工打分。

Graphic Rating Scale: One of the evaluation method—the assessors score for employees according to some specific and measurable standard.

7. 光环效应错误:管理人员在工作表现评估或面谈中只根据员工单独的一次性积极表现来作出评估。

Halo Error: Managers make assessment only according to employees' one-time positive performance in the employee performance assessment or interview.

8. 偏松错误:业绩评估或访谈中的一种错误,经理或访谈者给员工的评价过于正面化。

Leniency Error: It is a kind of mistake during performance evaluation or interview. The managers or interviewers give the employee a exaggerated positive evaluation.

9. 偏紧错误:业绩评估或面谈时的一种错误,经理或接见者对员工的评价过于严厉。

Severity Error: It is a kind of mistake during performance evaluation or interview. The managers or interviewers give the employee a exaggerated strict evaluation.

10. 目标管理:业绩评估系统之一,经理与员工见面,一起确定具体工作目标,一段时间后双方再次会面评估目标的完成情况。

Management by Objective: It is one of the employee performance evaluation systems. The managers meet with the staff and determine the specific work target together. After a period of time they gather together and assess the completion of work target.

11. 叙述文章:评价系统中的一种,评估人写下叙述性描述形容每个员工的优缺点。

Essay Description: It is one of the employee performance evaluation systems. The evaluator writes narrative essay to describe the advantages and disadvantages of each employee.

12. 对比排列法：在员工之间进行工作表现、行为、技巧或知识的比较，从而得出工作表现评估的结果。

Paired Comparison: Compare performance, behavior, skill or knowledge between employees to get the result of employee performance.

13. 固守过去错误：业绩评估时的一种错误，经理或接见者根据以往的评分评价员工。

Past Anchoring Error: It is a kind of mistake during performance evaluation. The managers or interviewers assess employees according to former score.

14. 业绩评估：经理和员工之间的会面，其目的是评估员工的业绩表现、行为、知识和能力。

Performance Appraisal: It is a meeting between managers and employees which is on target to assess the performance, behavior, knowledge and ability of employees.

15. 预测有效性：预测值在多大程度上符合未来的行为。

Predictive Validity: To what extent predicted meet future behavior.

16. 最近印象型错误：管理人员主要根据员工最近的工作表现或行为而作出工作表现评估的错误方式。

Recency Error: It is a kind of mistake during performance evaluation. Managers make assessment just according to recent performance or behavior of employees.

17. 简单排列法：用单一的方法排列所有的员工，也被称之为直接排列法。

Simple Ranking: Rank all employees with a single method, which is also called direct ranking.

复习思考题 (Questions for Review)

1. What's the benefit of doing performance appraisal?
开展绩效评估的益处有哪些？

2. What's the obstacle of effective performance appraisal?
有效的绩效评估的障碍是什么？

3. What common errors should we avoid during performance appraisal?
进行绩效评估应避免哪些常见的错误？

4. Please list several methods of performance appraisal and compare the difference.
列举绩效评估的几种方法并比较它们的不同。

5. Generally who will take part in the performance evaluation?

一般而言,绩效评估的主体包括哪些?

6. How often do you think hotels should do employee performance evaluation? Why?

你觉得饭店多长时间进行一次评估比较合理? 为什么?

7. In your opinion, what is the strength and weakness of hotels do employee performance evaluation?

你认为饭店进行绩效评估的优劣势有哪些?

研究前沿(Research Front)

In recent years, the significant meaning of employee performance evaluation has been realized by more people. More scholars begin to pay more attention to employee performance evaluation research. Developed countries have done deep research and validly applied on employee performance evaluation. Some scholars discussed the relationship between the awareness of fairness in employee performance evaluation and the degree of work-respected. More people have studied induces and system of employee performance evaluation. Some new technology and method have also been introduced into employee performance evaluation.

Source: George A & Dimitrios K. Human Resource Evaluation in Hotel Units. Management, 2012,7:17-34.

This paper presents and analyzes the performance appraisal systems and the human potential development in hotel units. It concentrates on the hotel units system to prove the importance of human resource evaluation in hotel units. HR evaluation analysis is presented through relevant theoretical background on the evaluation method and the presentation of the practical problematical issues in order to create an image for a whole evaluation system of HR in Greek hotel enterprises.

…

Performance Appraisal

One way to review the performance and potential of staff is through a system of performance appraisal. It is important that members of the organization know exactly what is expected of them, and the yardsticks by which their performance and results will be measured. A formalized and systematic appraisal scheme will enable a regular assessment of the individual's performance, highlight potential, and identify training and development needs. Most importantly, an effective appraisal scheme can improve the future performance of staff and planned career progression (Mullins, 2005; Pfau et al. 2002). A comprehensive appraisal system can provide the basis for key managerial decisions such as those relating to allocation of duties and responsibilities, pay, empowerment and levels of supervision, promotions, training and development needs, and terminations (Mullins, 2005; Stein, 1991).

...

Evaluation of Human Resources of Hotel Enterprises

What is meant by the term evaluation of performance of human resources (Aspridis, 2004), is the procedure of clarification and recording of performance and qualifications of employees (but also of the total of service), in relation to the demands of the position they hold and the potentials of progress that are presented to them. The evaluation of human resource performance needs to be clarifying and comparative. It has to be informative and consultative and administrative.

The main purpose is re-supplying of results to responsible people who are in charge of decision making, in order to avoid past mistakes in the future, because if the employees know on what basis their performance is being measured, in relation to their expectations, it will become better. Every evaluation system must be correlated with the whole human resource development system. It has to be specific and simple in order to become accepted by the evaluators and the evaluated people without significant reactions. Implementation of an evaluation method is based on the realized choice which it is not always possible to found in objective criteria, because it can be affected by the person's familiarization with only some techniques, with personal experience and generally with personal beliefs and considerations. Every evaluation method needs to be objective during the results countdown, to be clear for its application to be easygoing. It is necessary to approach the special operating conditions of the organization, meaning another method for building companies and another for service providing organizations. Additionally, the selected method depends on the number of staff that every organization employs, the usage of modern technology and, finally, the organizational economic sizes.

Single human resource performance evaluation system can be considered perfect and ideal. What has been pursued a priori is its effectiveness and its contribution to the capabilities development of employees, which makes them more productive. Usually, it is required to be fully specialized and adapted to each organization's needs, either public or private sector, and to be renewed in fixed time periods according to every organization's and its employees' targets. An important role in the evaluation system evolution is played by the personal employment of every employee and the time period in which that person occupied, since nobody can evaluate in the same way the routine and target-placing works. For this reason, targets will be renewed in fixed time periods.

...

The evaluator should not to compare the employee according to himself, should not consider himself as a judge or police officer, whose aim is to judge and control his subordinates as well as imposing penalties instead of helping them to improve their performance, and not to be limited exclusively to in the employee's reaction on critical occasions, but also to take into consideration the total image of the employee as it is being shaped during the evaluation period. With the completion of the human resource evaluation procedure and by defining its meaning the total of results can be assessed. Whichever method is utilized there, will be implemented an ultimate phase, that of the results evaluation during which the responsible people of the system are to control if and to what extent the system is effective or not, evaluating produced data quality and overtaking stereotypes and partial positions. Whatever the results may be, satisfying or not, a re-supply of the system will exist for future evaluations. If, on the contrary, errors emerge, it is essential that the changes to be made are specified in order to avoid error repetition and re-planning of the system from the controversial point or even from the beginning.

In order to overcome all problems, wherever they are caused, it is essential for the appropriate system planning to exist by using those personnel evaluation methods, mainly through pre-agreed target placing and the institution of objective evaluation criteria. Good relations and the creation of a mutual trust climate between supervisors and subordinates are required, because without them, an efficient personnel evaluation system cannot exist. Improving the communication procedure with the interview method and through the usage of specific methods and interview techniques adds a plus to the evaluation system. Finally, full justification of evaluation reports from the evaluators and the existence of a second evaluator, assist in error decrease.

Evaluation of human resource in hotel units

The first hotel unit that was studied belongs to a large group of companies, which consists of one of the largest non-commercial shipfleets as well as other enterprises, mostly in Europe, except from hotel units. It is considered to be one of the most ancient and larger hotel chains in Greece, with five hotel units in Athens, Corfu, Chios and Thessaloniki. In the frame of human resource development, evaluation is being introduced as the first step-phase of this policy. Evaluations are realized once a year, during December, for every permanent employee. In extraordinary situations, and when it is considered worthwhile, a direct order from the General Manager has been given. This evaluation can concern all or part of the personnel. The evaluation does not take into consideration seasonal personnel, for whom brief details are being kept by their direct supervisors for future usage. The evaluation is being realized by the direct supervisor of each employee and is later submitted, in a sealed envelope, to the present Personnel Manager. Evaluation forms of every employee are kept in the Human Resource Division and are dealt with as strictly confidential. For the completion of the evaluation forms, direct collaboration of the evaluator and the evaluated person is needed for at least two months. The direct supervisor is obliged to invite for an evaluation interview every one of his subordinates. During the interview, the evaluation results are to be analyzed and measures in order to improve employee performance are to be decided.

Criteria grading is alphabetically numbered. As "Very Good"—grade 4, is characterized an employee who responds exceptionally to work demands. As "Good"—grade 3, is characterized an employee who fully responds to work demands but does not respond from extra capability or desire. As "Average"—grade 2, is that employee who does not fully meet to the work demands. As "Inadequate"—grade 1, is judged that employee who does not entirely respond to work demands, and direct improvement is demanded in order to further evaluate his existence in the company. As the final evaluation mark, an average of every criteria mark is being extracted. Evaluation consists of two forms. The first one concerns personnel and the second specialized executives. As for executive evaluation, the criteria are personnel management, influence, communication, interpersonal relations development, planning, data and information analysis, decision making, business development and self-control. From the moment that the HRM collects all evaluation forms, it is obliged to notify and brief the General Manager for the evaluation results. According to those, the General Manager has to make decisions on educational-training matters, succession programming, re-organization of duties and, finally, personnel renewal.

During the last years, factual evaluation for all personnel has been conducted. Evaluators have taken specialized seminars the with aim of achieving a unified evaluation procedure. Company's aims include full utilization of the present performance evaluation system, and evaluation results announcement to each employee through individual interview. In addition, the company focuses on the implementation of an informal promotions system with allocation of new and more responsible duties and finally, progression possibilities and human resource succession at all levels. Also, the company is occupied with connecting the human resource evaluation system to the remaining systems (like payroll and productivity bonuses, progression, training and informal promotions system).

The second hotel belongs to the universal group of a large, universal hotel enterprise which has 147 hotel units globally, with 49,904 rooms. In Greece, this hotel offers 543 rooms of which 60 luxurious suites and one presidential suite. In 2007, it was presented with the distinction of being *Greece's Leading Business Hotel*. The specific hotel disposes of a full human resource performance evaluation system. Evaluation is realized every semester and annually, and concerns supervisors and the rest of personnel. The main evaluation criteria are total evaluation of performance, primary performance targets, leadership capabilities, according to the hotel's international practices and *winning way*. Specifically, supervisors are evaluated on business formation, work quality, communication capability, credibility and other factors. Moreover, the rest of the personnel are evaluated on criteria such as work knowledge, work quantity and quality, interest, cooperation with colleagues and more. Evaluation is realized by the direct supervisor, while there is the possibility of self evaluation of the evaluated people. The final judgment springs from conversation and the mutual decision of both evaluators and evaluated people. More specifically, we refer to leadership and human resource development, and that interest is shown in action and in results. Furthermore, interest is directed towards the market, change procedure and full comprehension of employment and finally towards strategy. On occasions when the evaluation has negative results, problem sources are being investigated, which among others can be personal, family, professional, lack of education and knowledge and finally, lack of will.

Final thoughts

It is a fact that the majority of Greek enterprises consider human resource performance evaluation as an essential element of Human Resource Management, in order to achieve the best possible results during the production process. The aim of all companies is, through evaluation systems, to develop a good working environment, to avoid leaking to other companies, especially the antagonist ones, and to increase total productivity and business profitability.

Almost every hotel enterprise utilizes a special form for their personnel evaluation, which takes place at least once a year and includes its total. Evaluation is realized by two evaluators, who are always the direct supervisors of the evaluated employee. Primary evaluation aims are promoting executives to superior positions, their pay progression, formatting a career plan and training for all those employees who experience problems. The basic element for adopting the appropriate evaluation system is the hotel unit size, because in a small unit with few employees a typical evaluation system, cannot be implemented, such as the one that is implemented in large hotel units. On these occasions, an informal evaluation system is being utilized. Through employee evaluation, it is possible for their weak points to be revealed (which they have to improve) as well as ascertaining their capabilities (which can lead to progression potentials). In order for the evaluation to be realized, it is necessary to set up a committee from the hotel's managerial executives, which will be based on quantitative criteria to achieve more objective evaluations. These evaluations have to be realized in fixed time periods, meaning, once or twice per annum, in order not to have too long an intervening time, and for the employee image to be more fully presented (Laloumis and Roupas, 1996).

Moreover, it is possible for self-evaluation to exist as a method, where the employee will be invited to answer a series of questions like "In which field of your work are you more efficient?" or "Do you have some special abilities/capabilities that you do not use in your present work?" Thanks to evaluation, the company can focus on the reward and progression potentials of human resource. Evaluation through re-supplying makes it possible to achieve important results both for the individual and the organization in total and to be connected by motivation.

According to employees themselves, the aim of human resource performance evaluation is the amelioration of the training provided the demand from superiors to pose targets for their employees and finally to have the evaluation results published through a re-insert of data. Criteria marking should be accompanied by arithmetic characterizations which will be fully determined and will not create suspicions for doubts, so as to better present the existing employee image and total impression. In each criterion, it is essential for a gravity factor to be given so that the phenomenon of total evaluated criteria leveling does not appear. Specifically from zero (0) (who does not perform his work and whose performance is lower than expected) to four (4) (is far above the expected, and exceptional performance is achieved which is also continuous).

Employee effectiveness must also be estimated in mid-term time points of the year, such as in 3-month or 4-month periods, and not only at its end, through supervisors and employees meetings with an aim to critically evaluate realized work and ensure continuous briefing of subordinates by their supervisors for their evaluation results. At this point it would be useful to mention benchmarking, which is based on comparing the enterprise with others which are considered to be points of reference. It is possible to implement this technique in the company's interior. It is been implemented systematically by enterprises that wish to evaluate their product's performance and favor the initiative, creativity and innovation spirit (Roux, 2007).

...

An evaluation system to be successful must be adaptive in real organizational facts and not simply transplanted as a simple foreign model copy. In some multinational companies, that have branches in Greece, evaluation is realized through the prototype form which is in the native language. For the best possible results to be achieved there is continuous and constant communication between their representative in Greece and the company's owner abroad. In this circumstance, the basic problem that surfaces is that of mutual communication and its presented difficulties. Human resource evaluation is easy in the case when the supervisor has individual and separate meetings and conversations with each of his subordinates during the year. The evaluation must be addressed to the total of the executives' personal and professional development. The hotel units executives' evaluation procedure should consist of a series of procedures that have as their target to form a total employee image.

...

Conclusion

It is comprehensive in the fact that hotel units' amelioration receives special meaning and especially their human resource improvement in the large hotel units. Hotel human resource consists of the most important criterion for service users' satisfaction. What is needed necessarily is adequate knowledge of personnel around customer service related matters, excellent communication between customers and personnel and to comprehend customers' problems and, finally, to be friendly towards them. In order to achieve all these aims, human resource evaluation is necessary (Fergadis, Siskos and Maninou, 2006).

It is necessary for a controlling mechanism of evaluation to be created, so that its weaknesses and its problems of application are located and its continuous improvement will be ensured. All of the above have no value at all if there is no interest in better performance by the employees. And last but not least, we do not have an ideal system of performance appraisal in hotel units because of the organizational policies.

For an effective system of performance evaluation, in hotel units, it is necessary to accept the criteria of the system, which should be explicit and predetermined and should be adapted to the real data. The criteria should provide an accurate picture of the employee performance. A system of evaluation has to be created, so that its weaknesses and the problems of application are found, its continuous improvement is ensured and the complete acceptance of workers in hotel units is gained. Last but not least, the system of performance evaluation must review performance formally at least annually, and will form a new organizational culture in the hotel sector.

第7章 饭店薪酬与福利管理
(Compensation Management and Welfare Management)

本章概要(Summary of This Chapter)

饭店薪酬与福利管理是饭店人力资源管理的重要内容。本章从饭店薪酬的概念出发,详细分析和介绍了饭店薪酬的五大基本形式——工资、奖金、津贴、福利和股权,并进一步探讨了饭店薪酬体系设计的基本原则和基本流程。福利作为饭店薪酬的基本形式之一,在饭店人力资源管理中扮演着重要的角色。本章从法定福利和弹性福利两个方面分析了饭店员工福利的内容,并详细介绍了饭店福利的具体形式。

Hotel compensation and welfare management are important contents of the hotel human resource management. This chapter starts with the concept of hotel compensation, and gives a detailed analysis of the hotel compensation's five basic forms—wage, bonus, allowance, welfare and equity, and further discusses the basic principle and basic process of hotel compensation system design. As one of the hotel compensation basic forms, welfare management plays an important role in the hotel human resources management. From two aspects of the legal welfare and elastic welfare, this chapter analyzes the content of hotel welfare, introduces the detailed forms of hotel welfare.

开篇引例(Beginning Story)

The Ambiguous Ownership of Tips[①]

Mr Nerva was a waiter at the Heaven and Hell restaurant. He and some of his colleagues took their employer to court because they believed they had not been paid the minimum rate laid down by the Wages Council for their sector. The employer claimed that the minimum had been paid, once the distribution of tips paid by customers adding sums to their cheques or credit card payment had been taken into account. They did not include cash tips which the employer conceded could not be treated as part of employees' wages. The employer claimed that the tips in question were distributed on a weekly basis, irrespective of whether the card sum/cheque had cleared, and ignoring the commission to the credit card company (i.e. the employer was effectively underwriting that percentage). Mr Nerva argued that the customers did not intend their tips to go to make up basic pay. Mr Justice Mance ruled in the employer's favour, saying that customers who tipped by cheque or credit card could not know how the money was distributed and, as far as the law is concerned, they are leaving it to the employer to decide how the sum should be paid out; it is, in effect, the property of the employer with customers only having a "general hope and expectation" that the tip be passed on.

Mr Saavendra worked at a London restaurant where his contract said his pay was a standard rate "plus service". Each customer had a 15 percent service charge added to their bill and this was distributed to employees according to their position in the staff hierarchy. Because of recessionary pressures, the employer decided to allocate the service charge only partly to staff, reserving some for the restaurant. Mr Saavendra was unhappy both because takings were down (reducing the service charges available for distribution) and because those service charges that were collected were being skimmed by the employer. He claimed unlawful deduction of wages under the terms of the 1986 Wages Act. The Employment Appeal Tribunal agreed that while the employer had the right under the contact to allocate the service charge to the employees, he could not reserve a portion for the restaurant as the contact said that the service charge was for the employees and the latter had not given their agreement to the employer's new action. The employer had therefore unlawfully deducted employees' wages.

---

① Industrial Relations Law Reports. 1995;200.

第一节 饭店员工激励理论
（Hotel Staff Incentive Theory）

激励本来是心理学的概念，是指激发人的行为动机的心理过程，即通过各种客观因素的刺激，引发和增强人的行为的内在驱动力，即内驱力，使人达到一种兴奋的状态，从而把外部的刺激内化为个人自觉的行动。现在将这一概念引入饭店人力资源管理中来，赋予了其新的含义：激励是一种精神状态或力量，起着加强、激发推动动机和行为的作用，并引导饭店员工的行为指向饭店的目标。所以，饭店员工的激励是饭店人力资源管理的重要课题。

20世纪30年代以来，出现了许多有意义的激励理论，本节主要针对饭店员工的激励，探讨了两种主要的激励理论——内容型激励理论和过程型激励理论。内容型激励理论集中研究行为的一些特定变量，包括内在需求和外界条件，由此确定在工作环境中推动个人行为的那些特定需要和使行为持久的那些特定奖酬。过程型激励理论力图测定那些解释行为的主要变量，但集中点置于动态上，说明力量的方向、大小、持久等多方面与变因相关的情况，其主要变因是鼓励、推动、强化和期望。

一、内容型激励理论（Content Type Incentive Theory）

（一）马斯洛的需求层次理论（Maslow's Hierarchy of Needs Theory）

1943年美国心理学家亚伯拉罕·马斯洛将人类行为的动力从理论上和原则上进行系统化的整理，提出了需求层次理论。该理论将人的需求分为5个基本层次，即生理需求、安全需求、社交需求、尊重需求和自我实现的需求（如图7-1），认为只有低层次的需求得到满足后，人才会有动因去追求高一层次需求的满足。

1. 生理需求

亦被称为自然需求，是人类最基本、最强烈、最原始的一种需求，包括对食物、水、氧气、睡眠、住所、性行为等人类生存和种族延续所必需的各种需求。这些需要是个体感受到的强烈的驱力，这种生理的驱力是最强大的，优先于其他任何需要。

2. 安全需求

当生理需求基本上得到满足之后，安全需求就上升到主要的位置。主要包括对人身安全、生活稳定、免遭痛苦、威胁或疾病的需要。在饭店中这种需要包

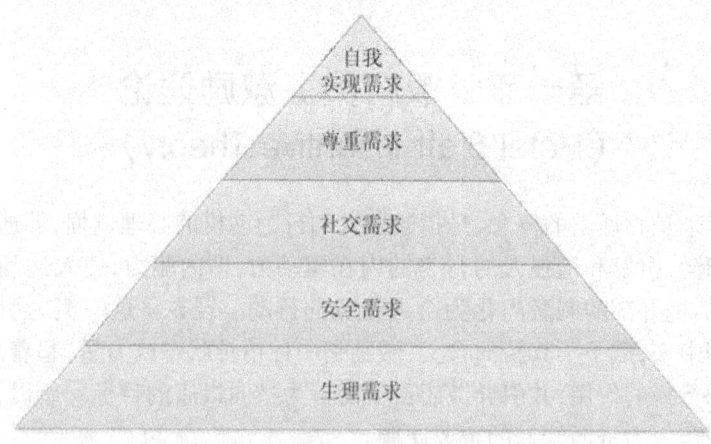

图7-1 马斯洛的需求层次

括员工需要的工作保障、等级晋升、工作环境的安全、劳保、保险、退休计划和解雇费等。

3. 社交需求

在生理和安全需求得到满足后,人最关心的就是被人接纳、被人爱并且被认为富于吸引力,这就是所谓的社交需求,主要包括对同伴、爱和归属感的需求。社交需要程度往往与一个人的经历、受教育程度、信仰等有密切联系,所以,社交需求比生理和安全需求更细腻、更难以捉摸。在饭店中这种需求可以通过工作团体、团队及饭店组织的活动来满足。

4. 尊重需求

当社交的需要获得了一定的满足之后,就会产生受尊重的需要,是指人们希望自己有稳定的社会地位,有追求名利的欲望,要求个人能力、成就得到社会的承认等。马斯洛区分了两类受尊重的需要:来源于别人对自己的尊重和来源于自己对自己的尊重。别人对自己的尊重包括承认、接纳、名誉、地位、威信和欣赏,而自尊感包括自信心、独立、适应、能力、成就和自爱。在饭店中,这种需求包括个人名誉、认同感、头衔、奖励、地位象征、职责、提升和夸奖。

5. 自我实现需求

马斯洛认为在前4个需求都满足后,人的需求会侧重于自我实现的满足,力求发掘自己的所有潜能,实现个人的理想、抱负,是人们努力实现个人最大愿望的一种需求。从饭店人力资源管理的角度讲,帮助员工实现自我,意味着必须做到人尽其才,达到人与岗位或工作的最佳组合。为满足自我实现的需求而采取的途径是因人而异的。

根据马斯洛的需求层次理论,每个人都有需要,且每个人的需要都不相同,其满足程度也都不同。这就使饭店管理者必须认真思考这样一些问题:对员工的需要假设(即员工将要满足的是什么需要)、满足程度假设(即能否满足和满足多少)是否正确,采取何种途径加以满足。虽然马斯洛的理论不能为报酬计划提出明确的解决方案,但可以帮助饭店管理者思考如何激励员工。

(二)赫茨伯格的双因素理论(Herzberg's Two-factor Theory)

"双因素理论"是由美国学者弗雷德里克·赫茨伯格提出的关于影响员工积极性的因素的理论。赫茨伯格认为,使员工满意与不满意的因素是两类不同性质的事务,即员工有两种不同的需求,保健因素和激励因素。第一组需求指维持需求或不满意因素;第二组需求指满意因素。

1. 保健因素

保健因素具备后,并不意味着员工对本职工作就一定抱有积极的态度,保健因素不能让员工对工作环境感到满意,其对员工工作满意程度的作用是"有之未必然,无之必不然"。如果缺乏保健因素,员工会感到不满意。在饭店工作中,保健因素通常包括:饭店工资制度、领导和员工之间的关系、劳动环境、行政管理、福利政策以及工作安全等。

2. 激励因素

激励因素可以让员工感到满意,能够激发员工的工作积极性和创造性。激励因素与员工的满意度有着很强的相关性,这方面要素的缺乏会引起员工的不满意。在饭店工作中的激励因素包括:成就感、认同感、责任感和晋升机会等。

双因素理论对饭店工作丰富化和工作扩大化提供了理论指导;激励因素可以从饭店员工内心激发积极性和创造性,为饭店激励工作指明了一条通往成功的途径;双因素理论使饭店管理者清楚看到员工所处的心理状态及其影响因素,使管理者在人性认识的过程中又向前迈进了一步。

(三)麦克莱兰德的成就需要理论(McClelland's Need and Achievement Theory)

哈佛大学心理学家麦克莱兰德于1961年在《获得成就的社会》一书中,提出了"成就需要"理论。该理论认为人有三种需求:成就、权力和联系。

1. 成就需求

对成功有一种强烈的欲望。具有较高成就需求的员工会成为好的管理者,因为这些人的特点是选择中等风险程度、需求具体的业绩反馈,具有处理问题的责任感,倾向于设立不太扎眼的目标,具有较强的组织和计划能力。激励这部分员工,饭店需要为他们创造让他们开创、执行和完成工作的机会。

2. 权力需求

有较高权力欲,希望担任领导和控制别人,对领导权的渴求。不同的人对权力的渴望程度也不同。较高权力需要的人喜欢支配、影响他人,喜欢对别人"发号施令",并愿意替他人负责,注重争取地位和影响力。在很多的饭店企业中,这个需求是有积极意义的。

3. 联系需求

与他人建立亲近、合作和友善的人际关系的需要,是寻求被他人接纳和喜爱的一种愿望。具有强烈联系需求的员工渴望友谊,喜欢合作而不是竞争的工作环境,倾向于与他人进行交往,愿意为他人着想,希望与他人建立良好的沟通与理解,和谐的环境会给他们带来内心的愉快和满足,通常他们对环境中的人际关系更为敏感。具有强烈联系需求的员工更适合于社交或人际交往要求高的工作。

麦克莱兰德研究表明,企业家表现出相当高的成就需求和相当大的权力需求,但联系需求则十分低。经理人员一般表现出较高的成就需求和权力需求,则联系需求较低,但高或低的程度没有企业家那样显著。而且小公司的总裁普遍具有非常高的成就需求,而大公司的总裁只有一般的成就需求,但对权力和联系需求的追求比较强烈。

Tips

The McClelland theory believes that the manager can be divided into three categories: Institutional type manager, personal powerful type manager and contacting type manager. Institutional type manager may be in power demand more than contacting demand, who has higher self-control. Personal powerful type manager needs more power than contact, who is willing to accept social communication. Contacting type manager needs contact more than power, who is interested in social communication. Related research proves that Institutional type manager and personal powerful type manager are more efficient in management, because they have more desire for power.

资料来源:编者整理

二、过程型激励理论(Process Type Incentive Theory)

(一)预期理论(Expectancy Theory)

美国心理学家和行为科学家维克多·弗鲁姆 1964 年在《工作与激励》一书中提出了期望理论。期望理论的基本假设是:人之所以能够从事某项工作并达成组织目标,是因为这些工作和组织目标会帮助他们实现自己的目标,满足自己某方面的需要。

在假设的基础上,弗鲁姆指出了影响人们行为的三个关系变量及其内在联系:

1. 期望几率

某一行动将导致一个预期绩效的概率,即一个人对于目标实现的可能性所作的估计,它与个人能力、绩效目标有很大关系。

2. 目标价值

当达到目标时满足需要的价值或效用,它与一个人的价值观有密切的联系。

3. 关联性

绩效和报酬之间的关系。期望几率和目标价值的乘积决定激励力的大小,即激励力 = 目标价值 × 期望几率。

在三种关键变量的基础上,弗鲁姆还提出了人的基本期望模式。(见图7-2)人们总是希望通过自己的努力或行为,在工作中取得良好的业绩,并因此而获得物质和精神奖励,而奖励也应该能够满足个人的某种需要,然后又回到新的起点,开始下一轮循环。

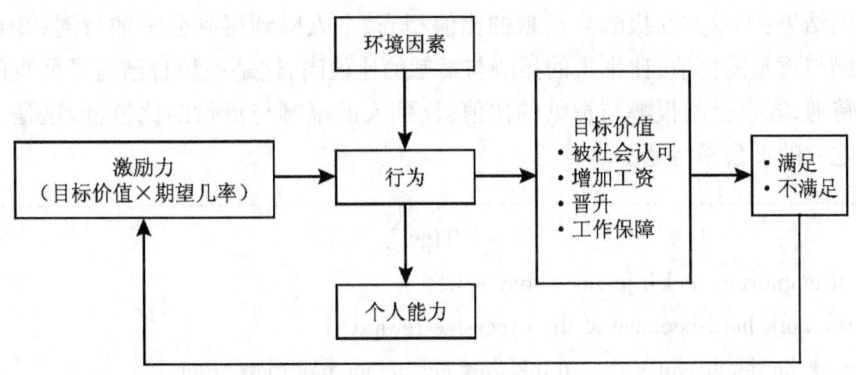

图7-2 基本期望模式

为了提高目标对人的吸引力和激励力,必须处理好三对关系:

1. 努力—绩效关系

只有当员工认为他只要付出适当的努力就能取得他预期的高水平的工作成绩时,激励才能奏效。即目标实现的概率越高,激励效果就越好。

2. 绩效—奖酬关系

有效的激励只有在员工坚信他们的工作成绩会使他们获得很高程度的奖励或回报时,才会出现。

3. 奖酬—个人需要关系

要使某一奖酬或回报成为具有较高影响力的激励因素，它就必须在员工的心目中有比较高的价值，即员工只有在发现奖励内容正是他所渴求的目标时，才会尽最大努力去工作，以实现愿望，这时激励的效果最好。

（二）公平理论(Equity Theory)

J.斯泰西·亚当斯于20世纪60年代提出了公平理论，该理论基于交换原理（即人们期望得到的回报是他们的贡献或投入的交换），主要探讨了工作报酬分配的合理性、公平性对职工积极性产生的影响。

公平理论指出：当一个人做出了成绩并取得了报酬以后，员工不仅关心自己所得报酬的绝对量，而且关心自己所得报酬的相对量，即与他人所得报酬的比较。员工要进行与他人的比较来确定自己所获报酬是否合理，比较的结果将直接影响员工今后工作的积极性。

这种公平比较有两个角度：①横向比较——把自己付出的劳动和所得的报酬与他人付出的劳动和所得报酬进行社会比较；②纵向比较——对自己现在付出的劳动和所得报酬与自己过去劳动和所得报酬进行历史比较。这种公平比较有三种可能的结果：①双方的报酬与贡献的比值相当，个人感到得到公平的待遇；②自己的报酬与贡献的比值，比别人的报酬与贡献的比值高，这是一种自己占了便宜的不公平待遇；③自己的报酬与贡献的比值，比别人的报酬与贡献的比值低，这是一种自己吃亏的不公平待遇。

Tips

If employees feel injustice, they will：
(1) not work hard because of the excessive reward;
(2) work harder because they think they get higher pay than others;
(3) advise others not to work hard to restore fair;
(4) advise others work to harder to restore fair;
(5) adjust the view of fair;
(6) change reference people.

资料来源：编者整理

（三）强化理论(Reinforcement Theory)

强化理论是由美国心理学家B·F·斯金纳提出，该理论的前提依据是人们对刺激有条件反射，在工作中，强化理论认为员工的行为受过去的经验影响，影响过程是一个简单的四阶段模型(如图7-3)。

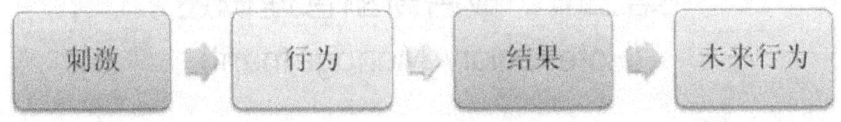

图7-3 斯金纳的强化理论

强化理论认为人的行为是可以塑造的,具体地讲,人的行为可以通过内部和外部因素,而使之重新塑造、成形和改变。强化可以分为四种类型:

1. 正强化

饭店经理通过对行为的奖励,鼓励所希望的行为。通常是饭店管理者用某种有吸引力的结果,如认可、赞赏、增加工资或奖金、提升等创造一种令人满意的环境,以表示对某一种行为的奖励和肯定,使这种行为可能重复发生。

2. 负强化

饭店经理通过解除处罚或令人不快的刺激(如批评)鼓励所希望的行为。

3. 消除

饭店经理通过忽视某种行为而抑制它。是指取消正强化,对某种期望不出现行为不予理睬,以表示对该行为的轻视或否定,该行为长期得不到正强化便会逐渐消失,变得不可能发生。

4. 惩罚

饭店经理通过惩罚员工的行为抑制这种他不希望看到的行为的再度出现。是指用某种带有强制性、威胁性的结果,如批评、降薪、罚款、开除等,制造一种令人不满意、不愉快的环境,以示对某一种不符合要求的行为的否定,降低这种行为重复发生的可能性。

Tips

Application of reinforcement theory should be paid attention to:
(1) Emphasizing the wanting behavior (such as to reward this behavior) so as to encourage employee behavior. If pay incentive system of the enterprise cannot in fact awards this wanting behavior, the system may be counter productive.
(2) Eliminating the practice that may have both effects on enterprise desirable behavior and undesirable behavior, if the wanting employee's behavior can not be emphasized, then they won't have similar behavior.

资料来源:编者整理

第二节 饭店薪酬管理概述
(Hotel Salary Management)

在现代社会,劳动还是人们谋生的手段,对物质生活的追求仍然是人们的第一需要。对饭店员工来说也不例外,薪酬直接影响到员工工作积极性的调动与发挥,因此,薪酬是饭店人力资源管理必须要研究的内容。

一、饭店薪酬的概念(Hotel Salary)

薪酬的概念来自于西方的经济学和管理学。美国的薪酬管理专家米尔科维奇定义薪酬为:雇员作为雇佣关系中的一方所得到的各种货币收入,以及各种具体的服务和福利之和。而美国学者约瑟夫·J·马尔托奇奥在其著作《战略薪酬》一书中,将薪酬界定为:雇员因完成工作而得到的内在和外在的奖励,并将薪酬划分为外在薪酬和内在薪酬。兰德尔·S·斯库勒将薪酬分为货币薪酬和非货币薪酬,其中货币薪酬包括基本薪水(变动工资和奖金),以绩效为基础的报酬(股票期权、红利、绩效工资和奖励工资),公共保障(社会保障、失业救济、伤残补贴),企业保障(养老金、储蓄、失业福利、保险),带薪休假和生命周期福利等;非货币薪酬包括职业报酬(保险、自我发展、职业弹性、收入增长机会)和社会报酬(身份象征、表扬和肯定、享受责任感、友谊)。

广义的饭店薪酬包括经济性的报酬和非经济性的报酬。经济性的报酬指能够直接或间接地以金钱形式来衡量的与经济有关的报酬,主要包括工资、奖金、福利待遇和假期等,也叫货币薪酬;非经济性的报酬指个人对企业及对工作本身在心理上的一种感受,也叫非货币薪酬。我们认为狭义的饭店薪酬是指个人获得的以工资、奖金以及金钱或实物形式支付的劳动回报。本书探讨的主要是基于狭义饭店薪酬的概念。

Tips

Four tasks are involved in an efficient compensation structure:
(1) it ensures that sufficient number of people are attracted to work in the organization from the external labour market;
(2) it encourages the internal labour market to function effectively so that promotion and training incentives exsit to motivate staff;
(3) it ensures that feelings of inequity are not engendered;
(4) it allows for the development of new jobs evolved through reorganization or the introduction of new technology (and, of course, facilitates the scope for removing old positions no longer of relevance to the organization).

资料来源:编者整理

二、饭店薪酬的基本形式(The Basic Form of Hotel Salary)

饭店薪酬的基本形式主要包括工资、奖金、津贴、福利和股权等。

(一)**工资**(Wages)

工资有广义和狭义之分,广义的工资包括货币形式和非货币形式的报酬;狭义的工资是指以货币形式付给饭店员工的报酬,如果报酬的表现形式是实物而非货币,人们称为福利。从总体上讲,工资大致可以分为基本工资和激励工资两大部分。

1. 饭店工资支付形式

饭店工资支付形式,大多是根据所在地最低生活费标准和员工的工作效率来规定的,并且从减少劳动纠纷的角度出发,以劳资协议方式来执行。工资支付形式主要包括计时工资制、计时奖励工资制、计件工资制、计点奖励工资制等,其中计时工资制和计件工资制是最为常见的工资支付形式。

(1)计时工资制

"计时工资"是至今采用最为普遍的工资支付形式,是根据员工的计时工资标准和工作时间来计算工资用以支付员工劳动报酬的形式。所有按照员工工作时间长短来支付员工工资报酬的制度都属于这一基本类型。按照这种工资制度,员工工资收入是他的工作时间和工资标准的乘积。其计算公式为:$W = R \times H$,其中,W:工资额,R:工资标准,H:工作时间。计时工资制根据计算的时间单位不同,可分为小时工资制、日工资制和月工资制。

计时工资制之所以被广泛采用,主要原因是:简单明了、计算简便,奖惩不十分严格。其最大的特点是并不鼓励员工把注意力仅仅集中在提高产品的数量上,更注重的是产品的质量。饭店业属于服务性行业,服务是难以用数量来衡量的,服务质量才是饭店生存的基础。因此,这种注重产品质量而不注重数量的计时工资制在酒店业得到了广泛的应用。其缺点是没有重视员工内在潜力的发挥,不利于调动员工的工作积极性。

Tips

Advantages of time rate system are that they: (a) encourage retention of human resources through the stability associated with employees' knowledge that they will gradually improve their rewards because of the incremental nature of pay; (b) are easy to administer and allow the employer to accurately predict total labour costs; and (c) ensure quantity of output is not emphasized to the detriment of quality, and cost advantages to the employer accrue over time as employees enhance main skill and efficiency.

The principle disadvantage of time-rate systems is their inability to reward more productive workers through the motivation that might come from output-based rewards.

资料来源:编者整理

（2）计时奖励工资制

计时奖励工资制是以计时工资制为基础，并有所发展和修正，主要变化在于员工的小时工资率将定期根据总体工作情况加以重新修订。采用这种工资制度，员工的实际收入是根据其基本工资率和其他若干部分的奖金百分比综合计算的，这些方面包括：员工工作数量、质量、可靠性、各方面能力、出勤情况等。

这种工资制度的优点是员工的收入很容易计算，同时又能满足鼓励员工、提高服务质量的需要，而且，员工的实际收入不取决于单一的因素，而是综合评判，因而容易反映出员工的实际工作业绩，在员工心理上形成一种相对公平感。目前，我国很多饭店、餐厅等都是以此为基础，采用修订式的计时奖励工资制度。

（3）计件工资制

计件工资制是指员工的收入根据他所完成的合格产品或服务工作的数量来决定的，而不是以工作时间为单位来计算。每件工作或服务项目都预先确定了单价，称为计件单价。其计算公式如下：$W = N \times U$，其中，W：工资额，N：每件工作的单价，U：工作的件数。

计件工资制的优点是：能准确反映员工实际付出的劳动数量，能有效激发员工的劳动积极性，促进劳动生产率的提高，且计算简便。但计件工资制也有其不可克服的局限性，如容易出现片面追求产品数量而忽视产品质量的现象。而且，容易使员工工作过度紧张，不利于员工的身心健康。因此，饭店不适于在所有部门和岗位采用这种工资形式，但在某些时候可以灵活参考此种计件工资方式，如旅游旺季，客人多而客房服务员不足的情况下，可以规定工资额按照所清扫的客房数来计算；餐饮部服务员的工资按照其服务客人数来计算等，以此来刺激员工的工作积极性。

Tips

Advantages of piece work system are that according to the employee's work achievement to pay, it (a) brings out strongly incentive remuneration and can make people feel justice. What's more, it (b) induces people to care more about their work, arouse the enthusiasm and promote the improvement of labor productivity.

The biggest limitation of piece work system is the phenomenon of the one-sided pursuit of products quantity and ignorance of the products' quality, and what's more, it is easy to make workers overstrain, so it is not conducive to the physical and mental health of employees.

资料来源：编者整理

(4)计点奖励工资制

计点奖励工资制是一种长期使用的刺激工资制度。按照这种工资制,个人完成一项工作所节约的时间部分,按一定百分比提取奖金。其计算公式为:$W = (H \times R) + [(S-H)R]P$,其中,H:实际工作时间;S:标准工作时间;P:奖金百分比;R:每小时工资额。

这种工资制度的优点是:员工的奖金按具体工作时间来决定,如工资需要调整,只改变奖金率就可以了;由于员工奖金部分是根据对某项工作标准时间的节约而确定的,因此可以成为直接影响员工工作态度的积极因素,对员工心理上的影响比计件工资制的影响还要大,有利于鼓励员工改进工作,提高效率。

2.饭店工资等级制度

工资等级制度是根据工作的复杂程度、精确程度、负责程度、繁重程度和工作条件等因素,将各岗位的工资划分等级,按等级确定工资标准的一种人力资源管理制度。工资等级制度的形式,归纳起来主要有:能力工资制、岗位(职务)工资制、结构工资制和岗位技能工资制等类型,其中结构工资制和岗位技能工资制是饭店业中比较常见的。

(1)结构工资制

结构工资制是把员工的工资划分成若干个组成部分,构成动态性的工资结构模式,用工资分解的方式,确定和发挥各部分工资各自不同的功能,克服了传统工资制度中将员工的工作年限长短、技术水平高低、劳动态度优劣、贡献大小等因素混杂在一起,用混合式方法确定工资标准而带来的一些弊病。

结构工资制,一般有以下几个组成部分:

①基础工资。基础工资是员工工资收入中的基本部分,是维持劳动力简单再生产,保障员工基本生活条件的工资收入。

②岗位(职务)工资。岗位工资按照各个岗位的工作繁简、劳动量轻重、责任大小和劳动条件等因素决定的工资,是结构工资制的主要组成部分。

③技能工资。技能工资是根据员工的综合能力而确定的工资,它主要是弥补岗位薪资的不足,鼓励员工钻研技术、提高技能,也是对员工智力投资的补偿。

④工龄工资。是根据员工工龄的长短和每年工龄应计的工资额来确定工资,是对员工工作经验和劳动贡献的积累所给予的补偿,是随着工龄的增长而逐年增长的。

⑤奖励性工资。是以基础工资和岗位(职务)工资为基础,使员工的收入和饭店的发展、经济效益及本人贡献大小相结合,联产、联利,多超多得、少超少得、不超不得。

以上五个组成部分,各饭店可根据实际情况和分配需要,做出侧重点不一的具体规定,项目上可增可减,并可以适当进行调整。

> **Tips**
>
> Features of structure wage system are that salary structure is corresponding with the labor structure, and wage structure can reflect the employee's contribution, give play to all sorts of functions, especially the adjustment function.
>
> What's more, it will contribute to implement salary grading management, and avoid customer service "one size fits all" disease.

资料来源:编者整理

(2)岗位技能工资制

岗位技能工资制是以劳动技能、劳动责任、劳动强度和劳动条件等基本劳动要素评价为基础,以岗位工资、技能工资为主要内容的基本工资制度。从本质上说,它也是结构工资制中更为规范的一种具体形式。岗位技能工资制是由岗位工资与技能工资两大单元组成。岗位工资是根据员工所在的岗位或所担任的职务、所在职位的责任轻重、劳动强度大小和劳动条件优劣而确定的工资;技能工资是根据不同岗位、职位、职务对劳动技能的要求和员工所具备的劳动技能水平而确定的工资。

岗位技能工资制有以下的特点:

①全面反映员工的劳动差别。由岗位工资和技能工资两大单元组成,比较全面地反映了劳动者潜在、流动、凝结三种形态劳动差别的统一。

②从动态上反映了劳动差别和报酬差别。岗位技能工资制的特点是随岗位、技能变化而变化,实行"易岗易薪,技变薪变"的原则,这种对应关系,使饭店的薪酬体系始终处于动态均衡之中。

③报酬与效益挂钩。岗位技能工资制较好地反映了按劳分配在市场经济条件下的实现特点,使劳动差别经过市场鉴定,通过经济效益反映出来,使工资收入不仅与劳动差别相适应,而且与经济效益相适应。

④为严格绩效考核提供了科学的依据。通过岗位测评实现劳动测评,使不同质的劳动量化,成为可比劳动。这种劳动差别的科学测评,使按劳分配进入规范化新阶段,同时,也为严格绩效考核提供了科学的依据。

⑤有利于饭店基础管理工作的加强。岗位技能工资制的关键是岗位测评,要做到对员工劳动量的科学评估,就必须有扎实的基础工作。同时,劳动量的评估必然要求整个基础管理和考试、考核制度的健全和完善。

(二)奖金(Bonus)

奖金是指支付给员工的超额劳动报酬和增收节支的劳动报酬,是对员工超额劳动的一种补偿。奖金作为基本工资制度的一种辅助形式,具有灵活性、及时性和明显的激励作用等,特别是在鼓励员工在生产过程中提高质量、节约材料和经费以及技术革新等方面发挥着重要的作用。

1. 奖金的类型

奖金表现形式包括红利、利润分享和奖金等。

(1)根据奖金的发放周期可划分为月奖、季奖和年奖。

(2)根据一定时期内发奖次数划分,有经常性奖金和一次性奖金。

(3)根据奖励范围来划分,有个人奖和集体奖。

(4)根据奖励的条件来划分,有综合奖和单项奖。其中,综合奖是对员工的劳动贡献和劳动成绩进行全面评价后统一计奖;单项奖只对劳动成果中的某一方面进行专项考核,单项奖的主要形式有节约奖、安全奖、超额奖等。

2. 发放奖金的基本原则

(1)及时性原则

是指在员工的工作成绩出现后及时加以肯定或发放奖金,这样不仅能够发挥奖金的功效,而且还增强了员工对奖金的重视。

(2)合理分配奖金额度的原则

要使奖金起到激励作用,在发放过程中必须做到"两头挂钩",一是要把奖金的提取与饭店的经营成果密切联系起来,二是要把奖金的分配同员工的劳动贡献相结合,以超额劳动作为评奖、发奖的唯一尺度,同时要了解员工的心理,选择最佳奖励形式。

(3)最大限度地发挥奖金效价的原则

发放奖金的形式要多样化,要因地制宜、因人而异;将发放奖金与精神奖励有机结合起来,这样既满足了人们的生理需求,又满足了尊重、成就、发展提高等高层次的需求,从而提高奖金的效价。

Tips

Three note conditions of bonuses: first, the bonus conditions should be appropriate, that is to say, staff could take efforts to achieve the conditions, so the conditions can neither too high nor too low; Second, before making incentive system hotel managers should fully understand the desire of employees; Third, the number of bonus should be enough to produce incentive effect.

资料来源:编者整理

3. 采用奖金奖励的工作要点

(1) 制定奖励指标

要对饭店不同部门制定有针对性的奖励指标,如对于房务餐饮部等一线服务部门,可在成本节约、操作规程、劳动纪律、顾客投诉等方面设立奖励指标;对于营销部来说,客房销售量、利润率才是重要的奖励指标。

(2) 明确奖励范围和奖励形式

实施奖金奖励,必须明确受奖人员、奖励幅度和奖励周期。如与饭店整体经济效益和社会效益有关的奖励,可采取年度奖的形式;而质量奖、顾客满意奖等可采取月奖或季奖形式。

(3) 明确计奖单位

饭店中按劳动特点不同可以大致划分为两类计奖单位:独立计奖单位,指计奖指标明确的单位,如营销部、餐饮部等;平均计奖单位,指劳动成果不能准确计量的单位,如酒店中的职能部门、后勤部门等。

(4) 确定奖金总额

可以按照饭店超额利润的一定百分比提取奖金;也可以按客房销售量、成本节约量等来确定相应的奖金总额。

(5) 制定奖金分配方法

在对各岗位进行劳动评价的基础上,根据岗位贡献大小确定奖金系数,最后根据个人完成任务情况按系数进行奖金分配。

(三) 津贴(Allowance)

津贴是指为了补偿饭店员工特殊或额外的劳动消耗和因其他特殊原因支付给职工劳动报酬的一种工资形式,包括补偿员工特殊或额外劳动消耗的津贴、保健性津贴、技术性津贴、年功性津贴及其他津贴。

习惯上,人们把属于生产性质的称为津贴,属于生活性质的称为补贴。津贴、补贴的种类、发放范围和标准等,一般由国家统一规定。对国家没有统一规定的,饭店可以根据生产工作需要,在政策允许的范围内,自行设立一些津贴、补贴项目。

根据津贴不同的实施目的,津贴可以分为三类:地域性津贴、生活性津贴和劳动性津贴。

1. 地域性津贴

是指由于饭店员工在艰苦的自然地理环境中花费了更多的生活费用而得到的补偿。比如林区津贴、艰苦生活津贴、高寒地区津贴等。

2. 生活性津贴

是指为了保障饭店员工的实际生活水平而得到的补偿。由于员工的收入是货币性工资收入,货币性工资收入会受到物价上涨因素的影响。为了弥补物价上涨造成的员工生活水平下降,就会有肉食补贴、副食补贴等津贴。另外,由于工作而造成的员工家庭生活开支分离而产生生活费用的增加,也应有相应的津贴,如出差补贴等。

3. 劳动性津贴

是指从事特殊性工作而得到的补偿。如饭店员工夜班工作的夜班补贴,厨师在高温环境工作的高温津贴等。

Tips

Allowance is a supplement form of the worker's wage, and it has the following several characteristics:

(1) Allowance is a compensatory remuneration. It reflects not the labor itself, namely labor quantity and quality difference, but the difference of working environment and conditions.

(2) Allowance is oneness. Most allowance is based on a specific condition, just for a specific purpose or the only thing.

(3) Allowance has greater adaptability, can change along with the work environment and the labor condition changes. That is, it can be increased or be reduced, even be relieved.

资料来源:编者整理

(四) 福利(Benifits)

在饭店薪酬体系中,工资、奖金和福利是三个不可或缺的组成部分,分别发挥着不同的作用。工资具有基本的保障功能,奖金具有明显而直接的激励作用,福利的作用则是间接而深远的。我国饭店员工的福利主要包括法定福利和企业福利等内容,员工福利的形式包括经济性和非经济性福利。具体将在本章第四节饭店福利管理进行详细讲解。

(五) 股权(Equity)

1. 股权的定义

以饭店的股权作为对员工的薪酬,即让员工持有饭店的股票,使之成为饭店企业股东,将员工的个人利益与饭店利益联系在一起,以激发员工通过提升饭店企业长期价值来增加自己的财富。

2. 股权薪酬的作用

作为一种长期激励手段,在饭店企业中采用股权这种薪酬形式,能够让员工为饭店长期利润最大化而努力。股权的作用主要表现为以下几个方面。

(1) 有利于减少代理成本

股权薪酬使员工成为饭店企业股东,使所有权和经营权在一定程度上得到融合,从而在一定程度上缓解了代理问题,有利于减少委托人的监督支出和剩余损失,从而减少代理成本。

(2) 有利于减少饭店企业中的短期化行为,提高长期效益

股权薪酬使员工获得饭店业绩不断增长的长期收益,促使员工兼顾饭店短期和长期目标。由于股权收益可能远大于年薪,也促使员工更注重长期目标,从而有效减少员工的短期化行为和虚增短期利润的行为。

(3) 有利于吸引和留住人才

一方面,在饭店效益不断增长的情况下,股权薪酬能给员工带来丰厚的收益,从而成为一种吸引人才的激励方式。另一方面,由于股权薪酬往往同时伴有股票持有期的约束条件,如果提前离去,员工可能会失去全部股权收益,因而大大增加了员工的退出成本,留住了优秀人才。

第三节 饭店薪酬体系设计
(Hotel Salary System Design)

饭店要想吸引和留住高素质的人才,必须建立一套公平、规范、有效的薪酬支付体系,即要进行科学的薪酬设计。

一、饭店薪酬设计的基本原则 (Fundamental Principle of Hotel Salary System Design)

(一) 战略原则 (Strategic Principle)

饭店的薪酬制度要与饭店的发展战略相一致,能反映出饭店的战略需求,并把这种需求转化为对员工的薪酬激励。

(二) 公平原则 (Equal Principle)

饭店的薪酬制度首先要让饭店内部员工对其表示认可,让他们觉得与饭店内部其他员工相比,其所得薪酬是公平的。为此,饭店薪酬管理者必须经常了解员工对饭店薪酬体系的意见,并采用透明、公平和富有竞争性的薪酬体系。其次,公平性还体现在与其他同类型的饭店相比,本饭店所提供的薪酬也应该是适

当的。

(三)激励原则(Incentive Principle)

要根据员工的能力和贡献大小适当拉开其收入差距,让能力强、贡献大者获得较高的薪酬,充分调动他们的积极性,让低职位、低薪酬者产生努力工作、积极上进的动力,使饭店的薪酬制度达到最大激励员工的目的。

(四)竞争原则(Competitive Principle)

指该饭店的薪酬在饭店业同行中是富有吸引力的,在人才竞争激烈的形势下,可观的薪酬可以达到吸引和留住优秀员工的目的。

(五)成本控制原则(Cost-control Principle)

饭店是劳动力密集型企业,人力成本占据了饭店经营成本的很大一部分,饭店要考虑人力资本的投入产出比率,在薪酬设计时要进行人力资本核算,把人力资本控制在一个合理的范围内,这是近年来饭店业普遍进行的开源节流、减员增效的重要举措。

(六)合法原则(Legal Principle)

薪酬设计要遵守国家的法律法规,如禁止雇用童工、最低工资限制、必需的保险项目,等等。

Tips

Hotel compensation strategy should include:

(1) Core values, such as, the understanding of the hotel staff's nature, the overall recognition of the value of employees, and also the value recognition of management backbone which contains senior management personnel, professional and technical personnel and marketing talents, etc;

(2) Hotel basic compensation system and distribution principle;

(3) Hotel compensation allocation policies and strategies, such as distribution basis and scale standards of wage, bonus and welfare, etc.

资料来源:编者整理

二、饭店薪酬设计的基本流程（The Basic Process of Hotel Salary System Design）

图7-4 薪酬设计的过程步骤

（一）工作分析(Job Analysis)

工作分析是确定薪酬的基础。结合饭店的经营目标，饭店管理层要在业务分析和人员分析的基础上，理清各部门的职能和相关职位的关系，人力资源部门和各部门主管合作编写出工作说明书。通过这一步骤将明确饭店各岗位的职责、组织的架构和所需员工的技能等情况，即会产生清晰的饭店岗位结构图和各岗位的工作说明书。

Tips

There are six steps for job analysis:
(1) to determine the purpose of job analysis information;
(2) to collect the background information of the job, then to design organization chart and work flow chart;
(3) to choose the representative job to analysis;
(4) to collect job analysis information;
(5) to review collected information with the people who you work with;
(6) to write job description and job specification.

资料来源：编者整理

（二）职位评价(Job Evaluation)

职位评价重在解决薪酬的对内公平性问题，其目的是要将工作岗位的劳动价值、劳动者的劳动贡献与工资报酬三者有机地结合起来，通过对职务劳动价值的量的比较,来确定饭店的工资结构,以达到薪酬的内部公平性。职位评价包括在确定各职位工作内容的基础上对其进行相互比较,即对职位薪酬因素进行比较、分析、衡量。而职位评估方法是一项非常重要的工作,对薪酬方案的设计具有极其重要的意义,常用的职位评估方法有以下几种:

1. 排序法

排序法是一种非常简单的工作评估方法,是指依据"工作复杂程度"等总体指标,对每个职位的相对价值予以排序。主要有以下几个步骤:

获取工作信息。首先进行工作分析,要对每个岗位做好工作规范,说明"岗位总体情况"。

选择等级参照物并对具体工作划分职位等级。在实际运作中,常见的是按部门或不同的工种进行排序,比如,服务员、领班经理助理等,这就避免了将不同的职业放在一起比较。

选择薪酬因素。不论选择了多少薪酬因素,最好向评估人员仔细解释这项薪酬因素的具体含义,以确保评估工作的一致性。

对岗位进行排序。最简单的做法是给每个等级建一套索引卡片,每套卡片都对岗位有一个简短的说明,然后把这些卡片按其代表的岗位的价值从低到高进行排序。为了取得更为精确的结果,可以采用"交替排序法"。

综合排序结果。对岗位排序时,通常还要分别使用几种等级标准,因此,排序工作完成后,饭店人力资源部只需要简单地取其平均值。

排序法的优点是简单易操作、省时、花费小;缺点是在实际运用中过分依赖"主观估计"的因素,只适合规模小、岗位少的小型饭店,对于大型饭店不适合。

Tips

Job ranking also sometimes known as the "factor comparison" method, job ranking involves:

Establishing a set of characteristics associated with task performance—for example, minimum level of education required, level of task complexity, level of responsibility;

Using agreed job descriptions, ranking all jobs on a scale (usually 1~5) on a whole job basis.

This last point is important, for those involved in the job evaluation process are being asked to consider the absolute value of a job, on its own merits, without recourse to analysis of the actual constituent elements of the job but with reference to a set of general job characteristics.

资料来源:编者整理

2. 归类法

归类法也被称为职位分级法,是指将每一个工作与事先设定的等级或级别进行比较,它把所有的岗位分成若干组,工作内容相似的小组称为"类",工作内容除了复杂程度接近以外都不一样的,就称为"级"。

具体步骤为:首先,选择薪酬要素,制定同岗位薪酬要素数量,或基准有关的类别或级别说明书;然后,根据这些薪酬要素,就可以得出"分级说明书";最后,由饭店人力资源部门审评所有的工作说明书并给每个岗位确定合适的级别或类别。

归类法的优点简单易行,比排序法准确些,而且新工作很容易被归入这种分类体系中;缺点是仍然难于进行精确评比,而且工种的复杂多样会使定级非常困难。

Tips

The advantages of both job ranking and job classification are that:
(1) They are relatively easy to understand;
(2) The methods employed are generally easy to perform (although where many jobs are involved, the paired comparisons method can be cumbersome without a computer applications system);
(3) They are usually inexpensive to perform and install.

The disadvantages of both job ranking and job classification are that:
(1) The possibility that, as "whole job" methods, important differences between jobs are ignored and jobs may be inappropriately classified; An over-reliance, following from the above point, on the collective knowledge of the job evaluators involved in the evaluation process—evaluators are unlikely to be familiar with the details of all the jobs to be classified;
(2) A tendency to rigidity and inflexibility such that subsequent grading systems predicated on job evaluation are "set in stone", risking the possibility that they come to be regarded as unfair by job holders as well as giving rise to ambiguities where certain jobs appear to straddle particular grades.

资料来源:编者整理

3. 要素计点法

要素计点法可能是工作评价中最常用的一种方法,是一种比较复杂的量化岗位评估方法。首先要求确定多个薪酬要素,每个要素要分成几个等级;其次,这些要素的等级都是工作的现实情况。其中分值法是使用最广泛的岗位评估方法。具体操作步骤如下:

（1）确定要评估的岗位组。饭店中岗位繁多，最实际的做法是将这些岗位按照不同的工作性质，分成不同的岗位组，对于每个岗位组提出一个方案。

（2）收集岗位信息。工作分析做得比较出色的饭店，此时可以直接利用在工作分析中得出的工作说明书。

（3）选择薪酬要素。岗位不同，选择的薪酬要素也不相同。要素可以包括受教育水平、身体素质要求、技能水平，等等。

（4）界定薪酬要素。通过仔细界定，以确保在比较、权衡、应用这些要素的时候能保持一致。

（5）确定要素等级。可根据工作的复杂程度为每个要素确定5个等级，每个要素的等级可以根据具体情况确定，但要确保能够清楚区分岗位水平。

（6）确定要素的相对价值。确定每个要素的权重，不同的岗位，同一种要素的重要性不同；不同的要素在同一岗位中的重要性也不相同。

（7）确定各要素及各要素等级的分值。首先将岗位的总分值确定，然后对于每个要素，最高水平的就是这个分值，其他层次的按照等差的形式类推。

（8）编写岗位评估手册。完成上述工作步骤后，把所得到的结果汇编成册，便于使用。

（9）将岗位列等。每个岗位都能够按照要素进行评估以确定其分值，按照结果将其列等。

要素计点法的优点在于易于解释和评估，缺点是建立一个分值评估方案是一个非常复杂的过程，一般需要聘请咨询公司进行，很少有企业在内部员工中能找到这种专业人士。

Tips

Points ranking system was generally accepted as the most widely used method of job evaluation. It relies on the identification of job characteristics or factors which are believed to be (a) applicable to the analysis of most or all jobs in the organization; and (b) differentiate such jobs. These characteristics or factors can be broken down into various sub-factors and then degrees or levels. Typically, such factors/sub-factors include skill, knowledge, responsibility, degree of decision-making, job complexity and requirement for problem solving. Points are awarded to each degree/level and the factors/sub-factors are weighted in terms of their predetermined overall importance. Each job description is scored against each factor and a total points score calculated for each job description. Grades (and thus the remuneration structure) are generated from a comparative analysis of all job descriptions as scored.

资料来源：编者整理

4. 要素比较法

要素比较法常用于那些关键工种,即被评估小组认为是对企业最重要的工作,如餐厅里的厨师、迎宾员和服务员。它需要分析比其他的方法更多的薪酬要素,要素比较法实质上是对排序法的一种改进。它需要多次选择薪酬指标,并据此对岗位多次排序,然后把各个岗位的各序列分数加权得出一个总体序列分。

要素比较法首先要确定与薪酬分配有关的评价要素,并给这些要素定义不同的权重和分数。它的优点在于是一种精确、系统、量化的岗位评估方法,并且对于每个岗位都是进行相互比较以确定其相对价值;缺点在于它的复杂性,往往难以向员工解释评定的结果。

(三)*薪酬调查*(Salary Survey)

薪酬调查是通过各种正常的手段,来获取相关饭店各职务的薪酬水平及相关信息。饭店薪酬调查的目的,主要是为了保证薪酬水平具有竞争力,薪酬调查在确定员工薪酬时起着关键的作用。薪酬调查需要了解和掌握本地区、本行业的薪酬水平,特别是竞争对手的薪酬状况。同时要参照同地区同行业的其他酒店的薪酬水平,及时制定和调整本酒店的薪酬结构和对应工作的薪酬。这项工作主要包括薪酬调查的渠道,即从哪里获得数据,包括酒店之间的相互调查、委托专业机构进行调查、从公开的信息中了解等;如何实施,即要调查些什么、怎样调查和处理所收集的数据等。实施薪酬调查一般可分为确定调查目的、确定调查范围、选择调查方式、整理和分析调查数据等四个步骤。

(四)*薪酬定位*(Salary Positioning)

在薪酬调查的基础上,需要做的是根据本饭店经营状况确定薪酬水平。影响饭店薪酬水平的因素有很多。从外部环境看,国家的宏观调控、通货膨胀、行业特点和行业竞争、人力资源供应状况等都可能对饭店的薪酬水平产生不同程度的影响。在饭店内部,盈利能力、支付能力和员工的素质要求是决定薪酬水平的关键因素。此外,所需人才的稀缺程度、饭店的品牌效应和综合实力,也是重要影响因素。

在薪酬设计时有个专用术语叫 25P、50P、75P,意思是说,假如有 100 家企业(或职位)参与薪酬调查,薪酬水平按照由低到高排名,第 25 位排名以前的代表低位薪酬(25P),第 50 位排名左右代表中位薪酬(50P),第 75 位之后的代表高位薪酬(75P)。

> **Tips**
>
> Considering the positioning of salary, the hotel can choose salary leading strategy or the salary following strategy. The leader of the salary is not necessarily the brand loudest company, because the brand loudest company need not spend the highest wages, but can depend on its comprehensive advantages to find the best talent. And the rising stars who has much money are most easily to use high salary strategy. Because these companies are in the rapidly developing stage, investors are willing to use money to buy time, hope to quick close the gap with the giant company through digging the first-class talent.

资料来源:编者整理

(五)薪酬结构设计(Salary Structure Design)

在国外,许多饭店在确定员工的薪酬时,往往要综合考虑三个方面的因素:一是职位等级,二是个人的技能和资历,三是个人绩效。在薪酬结构上与其相对应的,分别是职位薪酬、技能薪酬和绩效薪酬,也有的将前两者合并考虑,作为确定一个人基本薪酬的基础。

薪酬结构又称为薪酬模式,就是指在薪酬体系中,工资、奖金、福利、保险、津贴等所占的份额和比例。这5种薪酬形式的组合会形成不同的薪酬结构,通常有3种模式,即弹性模式、稳定模式、理性模式。

1. 弹性模式

这种模式的薪酬主要是根据员工近期的工作绩效决定。在弹性模式下,奖金和津贴的比重要大一些,福利、保险的比重要小一些,并且在基本工资的部分,也常常实行绩效薪酬或销售提成等形式。这种模式有较强的激励功能,但是员工缺乏安全感,比较适合饭店迅速发展阶段。

2. 稳定模式

这种模式的薪酬主要取决于员工工龄与饭店的经营状况,与个人的工作绩效联系不多,这种模式的薪酬的主要部分是基本工资,奖金所占比重较小,而且主要依据饭店经营状况,并结合员工基本工资水平按一定比例发放或是平均发放。这种模式对员工而言有比较强的安全感,但缺乏激励功能,比较适合业务正常发展的成熟型饭店。

3. 理性模式

这种模式需要管理者根据饭店的经营目标和工作特点及收益情况,合理地进行薪酬组合,既要有弹性,能激励员工提高工作绩效,还应具有稳定性,这种模式的薪酬结构,通过较低的基本工资、与成本控制相结合的奖金以及标准的福利待遇水平,实现其控制成本的目标,比较适合业务没有增长或出现衰退的饭店。

(六)薪酬实施与调整(Salary Implementation and Adjustment)

1. 预算

薪酬预算主要有两种方法:一是从饭店的每一位员工未来一年薪酬的预算估计数字,计算出整个部门所需的薪酬支出,然后汇集所有部门的预算数字,编制饭店整体的薪酬预算。二是饭店的高层管理者首先决定饭店整体的薪酬预算额和增薪的数额,然后再将整个预算数额分配到每个部门,各部门按照所分配的预算数额,根据本部门内部的实际情况,将数额分配到每一位员工。

2. 沟通

及时、有效的沟通是保证薪酬制度顺利执行的因素之一,薪酬制度的合理与否在很大程度上取决于员工是否满意。饭店人力资源部可以利用薪酬制度问答、员工座谈会、员工满意度调查、内部刊物等形式,充分介绍饭店的薪酬政策。

3. 支付

薪酬支付的标准应该是公开化的,薪酬管理要坚持公平的原则,而员工对于薪酬的公平感来自于管理人员将正确的薪酬标准传达给员工;薪酬支付的时间要有所选择,调动员工积极性的手段之一就是对他们良好的工作绩效给予及时的奖励;要确定合理的支付方式,计时制支付方式是将薪酬与工作时间进行直接联系,计时制可分为小时薪酬、周薪酬和月薪酬。

4. 调整

薪酬制度在执行的过程中,由于各种因素的变化,必须不断地加以调整,因为僵化不变的薪酬制度将会使其激励功能大大退化。对薪酬的调整主要包括奖励性调整、根据生活指数调整、根据效益调整和根据工龄调整。

第四节 饭店福利管理
(Hotel Welfare Management)

饭店员工福利是指饭店为了使员工保持稳定、积极的工作状态,根据国家或地方有关法律、法规或政策,结合饭店经营管理的特点和经济承受能力,向员工提供的各种非工资和奖金形式的利益和优惠措施。近年来,随着饭店业的发展和员工待遇的提高,越来越多的饭店意识到福利待遇的重要性,竞相采用各种形式的福利措施使员工满意。

一、饭店员工福利的内容(The Concept of Hotel Staff Welfare)

法定福利待遇是国家或地方政府通过法律、法规和有关政策的形式,要求企业为员工提供的最基本的福利。在我国,根据《中华人民共和国劳动法》的有关规定,企业必须为员工提供的福利有:

(一)法定福利(Mandated Welfare)

1. 非工作时间报酬

(1)工作内的休息时间,包括工作期间定时短暂休息,如:员工饮水时间、员工解决个人生理要求的时间。

(2)每周休假。我国实行劳动者每日工作时间不超过 8 小时,每周至少休息 2 天的工时制度。

(3)节假日。员工在法定节假日享受有带薪休假,如:春节、元旦、国庆节、劳动节等。

(4)年休假。我国劳动法规定,在企业连续工作 1 年以上的员工,享受带薪年休假。

(5)探亲假。我国凡在单位工作满 1 年的员工,如果与父母或配偶不在一起,可享受一次探亲假。

2. 社会保障制度

为了保护劳动者的权益,国家建立社会保障制度,设立社会保障基金,使劳动者在年老、患病、工伤、失业、生育等情况下获得帮助和补偿。社会保障基金根据保险类型确定基金来源,并实行社会统筹。企业必须参加社会保障,定期为员工缴纳保险费。目前,我国的社会保障项目主要有养老保险、工伤事故补偿、失业保险、生育保险、医疗保险和住房公积金。关于这些社会保险的具体内容和实施,有非常详尽的法律规定。

(二)弹性福利(Flexible Welfare)

饭店结合本行业特点和企业的经济效益为员工提供的,除法定以外的其他福利,属于企业福利。企业福利是多种多样的,既有货币形式,也有实物形式。同时,企业福利也会给企业带来重要的效益。因此,饭店必须选择适合本企业特点的福利组合,以确保组织目标的顺利实现。随着社会经济的发展,饭店福利管理也越来越灵活,出现了自助式福利。所谓的自助式福利也称为弹性福利,是指由饭店员工自行选择福利项目的福利管理模式,但自助并不意味着员工可以完全自由地进行选择,有一些项目是必选的,如法定社会保险等。自助式福利的几个类型:

1. 附加型自助福利

附加型自助福利是最普遍的弹性福利制,是指在现有的福利计划之外,再提供其他不同的福利措施或扩大原有福利新项目的水准,让员工去选择。例如某家酒店原先的福利计划包括房租津贴、交通补助费、意外险、带薪休假等,如果该酒店实施附加型弹性福利制,可以将现有的福利项目及其给付水准全部保留下来当作核心福利,然后再根据员工的需求,额外提供不同的福利措施,如国外休假补助、人寿保险等,但通常都会标上一个"金额"作为"售价";每个员工则根据自己的薪资、服务年资、职务高低或家眷数等因素,发给数目不等的福利限额,员工可用分配到的限额去认购所需要的额外福利。

2. 资助福利账户

饭店员工每年可以从其税前收入中,拨出一定数额的款项作为自己的"支出账户",并以此账户选购各种福利项目的福利计划。为保证"专款专用",一般规定账户中的金额不能跨年度使用,也不能以现金形式发放,而且不能挪作他用。

3. 福利"套餐"型

福利"套餐"型是指由饭店同时推出不同的福利组合,每一个组合所包含的福利项目或优惠水准都不一样,员工只能选择其中一个弹性福利制。在规划此种弹性福利制时,饭店可以根据员工群体的背景(如婚姻状况、年龄、有无眷属、住宅需求等)来设计。

4. 浮动福利制

前几种自助福利模式允许饭店员工对福利项目或福利组合进行选择,但是无论如何选择,福利总的水平与固定福利的水平相当。浮动福利制不仅允许饭店员工对福利项目和组合进行选择,而且允许对福利支付水平进行选择,如果饭店员工选择的福利支付水平低于固定福利水平,差额部分可以现金方式转入直接薪酬;反之,如果饭店员工选择的福利支付水平高于固定福利的水平,差额部分可以从员工的直接薪酬划转。

Tips

Self-help welfare effectively improves employees' satisfaction and has obvious advantages to attract employees, so it is promoted widely in all over the world. Of course, self-help welfare also has shortcomings.

First of all, implementing self-help welfare cannot achieve the purpose of controlling labor cost, and it is a challenge for hotel standardization management; Secondly, this kind of design and implementation needs a lot of time and energy, and it is possible to work out the reasonable combination of welfare on the basis of seriously extensive discussion and communication between organization and employee.

资料来源:编者整理

二、饭店福利的形式（Forms of Hotel Welfare）

（一）经济性的福利（Economic Welfare）

(1) 额外货币收入。如春节、中秋或国庆节等特殊节日的加薪。

(2) 企业年金。一般由有能力的企业自愿建立，由企业和个人按照一定的比例缴纳费用，进入员工个人年金账户，由员工在退休后领取。企业年金作为企业对员工的一项福利保障措施，补充了社会基本养老保险保障水平的不足，也成为资本市场的重要参与者。

员工变动工作单位时，企业年金个人账户资金可以随同转移；员工升学、参军、失业期间或新就业单位没有实行企业年金制度的，其企业年金个人账户可由原管理机构继续管理；员工或退休人员死亡后，其企业年金个人账户余额由其指定的受益人或法定继承人一次性领取。

(3) 利润分红。这是饭店根据利润状况，通常以一次性奖励的方式让员工共享企业的盈利。利润分红与奖金的区别在于：前者是在饭店盈利的条件下，对员工的一种额外嘉奖；后者主要是为了补偿员工的超额劳动。

(4) 股票赊购。是指饭店为主要管理人员担保贷款，鼓励其购买本饭店的股票，并享受股利分红。这种方式有利于调动管理人员努力工作的积极性，争取最佳效益，从而获得更高的股票利润。股票赊购在国外一些大型饭店管理集团是一种比较常见的福利措施。

(5) 住房福利。主要包括单身宿舍、夜班宿舍、廉价公房出租或出售、发放购房补贴等。我国饭店业员工都比较年轻，大多是合同工，住房问题尤为突出。住房问题在某种程度上行直接关系到员工的积极性和流动率，帮助员工解决住房问题已成为稳定员工队伍的重要措施。

(6) 饮食福利。主要包括免费工作餐、工间免费饮料（茶水、咖啡或冷饮）。

(7) 医疗保健福利。主要包括公费医疗（全部或部分）、免费定期体检及防疫注射、免费或优惠疗养等。

(8) 退休金福利。包括退休金、公积金（按月抽取员工基础工资的一定比例，饭店同时提供一定补贴，积累到员工退休时一次发还；若提前离职，饭店发还其自供部分，还可以按规定对不同服务年限发给不同部分补贴）及长期服务奖金（工龄到规定年限时发给）等。

(9) 带薪假期福利。带薪假期福利指除每周两天及法定节假日和病假、产假以外，饭店根据年度营业规律，每年在经营淡季安排员工若干天休假日，时间长短通常按员工在本饭店服务年限的不同而有所区别。饭店业的服务性质决定了假期的重要性，很多员工都非常珍惜饭店所提供的假日。

（10）教育培训福利。包括在职或短期脱产培训、公费进修（业余、半脱产或脱产）、专业书刊购买报销、为愿意来本饭店工作的大学生提供专项奖学金等。

（11）文体娱乐福利。主要包括有组织的集体文娱活动（如误会、郊游、趣味运动会等）、饭店自建文体设施（如阅览室、棋牌室等）。

（12）其他生活性福利。一些饭店还会结合本行业的特点为员工提供免费洗澡、理发、发放生日礼物（礼金）以及市内上、下班公交费补贴等其他生活性福利。

（二）非经济性的福利（Non-economic Welfare）

1. 咨询服务

饭店为员工提供免费的个人职业生涯发展设计（给予分析、指导和建议、提供参考资料等）、员工心理健康咨询（过分的工作负荷与压力导致的高度焦虑或精神紧张等心理症状的诊疗）等。这种属于福利性质的咨询服务常见于国外一些规模比较大的饭店管理公司。

2. 工作环境保障

工作环境保障作为一种福利措施，在饭店中可以应用的内容包括将人体工程学原理用于工作环境的设计（如总服务台的使用设计、厨房设备的规划等），扩大工作反馈渠道，饭店内部晋升政策（即有高一级职位出现空缺时，首先考虑从内部下级员工中选拔），员工参与的民主化管理等。

案例分析(Practice Case Analysis)

'Zero-hour' contracts at Burger King—a Christmas carol with a difference①

As organizations increasingly recognize the importance of flexibility, there are as we have already noted, a range of strategies to achieve flexible working. The improved responsiveness to market uncertainties and variability of demand can be crucial, although organizations also need to be aware of some potential difficulties and risks in the use of flexibility. This can be seen in issues like a loss of stability, continuity, commitment and quality, as well as creating possible employee resentment.

These issues are nicely illustrated by the case in December 1995 of Burger King, when they attracted opprobrium from a range of politicians, trade unionists and newspapers (for example, they just missed out on the Observer's new Friend of Scrooge

---

① Bowcott O. Burger King backs down and pays up. The Guardian. December 6, 1995:4. Caterer and Hotelkeeper, Burger King pays out £106,000 to staff. January 4, 1996:6.

Award for businesses in the vanguard of corporate selfishness). The case arose out of the seemingly inappropriate use of 'zero-hour' contracts by a number of Burger King outlets. 'Zero-hour' contracts are an extreme form of temporal flexibility, which have been seen in a range of service sector industries, and in particular the hospitality and retail industries. The use of temporal flexibility can be important to organizations in allowing for the adaptability of working-time patterns to reflect work pressures and variability in customer demand. However at its most extreme level, 'zero-hour' contracts mean that there is no formal commitment made by employers regarding the number of hours the contract holder (i.e. the employee) will work. Instead, the employee is effectively 'on-call', working only for those periods that the employer calls upon them to do so. Clearly, while such arrangements provide a very high level of flexibility for the employer, they offer little in return for the employee, other than a lack of continuity and predictability.

The case of Burger King generated a high level of adverse publicity for the company due to the fact their use of 'zero-hour' contracts resulted in apparent abuse by a number of managers. The example which attracted the most publicity was that of a Glasgow student, who regularly earned £ 1 for a five hour shift, even though he had been led to believe that he had been hired for £ 3.10 an hour. The reason behind such low wages was the practice of asking staff to 'clock-off' to take unpaid breaks when business was slack. Immediately business picked up staff were asked to 'clock-on' again, to meet these short-term changes in demand. When these practices were revealed there was a public outcry, and, after a campaign led by the Labor Party and the trade unions, Burger King were forced to pay £ 106,000 in compensation to 900 workers, who had been affected by these practices. Even though Burger King had argued that this 'misuse of rostering' was not company practice or widespread within the company, they agreed to the compensation. Subsequently, Burger King have told managers in both franchised and company outlets that 'clocking-off' staff during quiet periods is unacceptable and had now become a dismissable offence. Nonetheless the publicity generated by the case reflected badly on Burger King as an employer, especially when it was revealed that global sales for the previous year were £ 5000 million, and Grand Metropolitan the owners of Burger King had made a profit of £ 912 million. Burger King were held up as exemplifying the fact that low pay and poor employment practices are not simply found in small organizations—not really the image that any organization wants to be portraying to the world. Furthermore, agreeing to the compensation payment did not necessarily rectify the bad publicity. Though the compensation payments were welcomed, Ian McCartney, the Labor Party's Employment spokesman commented, somewhat sardonically, that 'Scrooge has backed down just in time for Christmas' and suggested that under a future Labor government such 'zero-hour' contracts would be made unlawful.

Questions for Discussion:
1. How do you think of the 'zero-hour' contracts at Burger King?
2. Considering catering enterprise's characteristics of Burger King and the staff compensation management, how to solve the problem of Burger King?

名词解释(Key Terms)

1. 内容型激励理论:该理论集中研究行为的一些特定变量,包括内在需求和外界条件,由此确定在工作环境中推动个人行为的那些特定需要和使行为持久的那些特定奖酬。

Content Type Incentive Theory: This theory focuses on the study of some specific behavior variables, including internal demands and external conditions, which determines those specific needs promoting individual behavior in work environment and those specific rewards making behavior lasting.

2. 过程型激励理论:该理论力图测定那些解释行为的主要变量,但集中点置于动态上,说明力量的方向、大小、持久等多方面与变因相关的情况,其主要变因是鼓励、推动、强化和期望。

Process Type Incentive Theory: This theory refers to trying to determine the main variables of interpreting the behavior, but focuses on dynamic, and suggests the direction of the strength, size, lasting and other aspects related with variable reasons, and the main variable reasons are encouraging, promoting, strengthening and expecting.

3. 马斯洛的需求层次理论:该理论是动机理论的一种,认为人有5种基本需求层次:生理需求、安全需求、社交需求、尊重需求和自我实现的需求。

Maslow's Hierarchy of Needs Theory: This theory is one of motivation theories, considers that people have five basic need levels: physiological needs, security needs, social communication needs, respected needs and the self-actualization needs.

4. 赫茨伯格的双因素理论:认为使员工满意与不满意的因素是两类不同性质的事务,即员工有两种不同的需求,保健因素和激励因素。

Herzberg's Two-factor Theory: This theory thinks that there are two different types of affairs making employee satisfaction and dissatisfaction factors, that is, employees have two different kinds of needs—hygiene factors and incentive factors.

5. 麦克莱兰德的需求——成就理论:该理论认为人有三种需求:成就、权力和联系。

McClelland's N-Achievement Theory: McClelland's N-Achievement theory considers that people have three requirements: achievement, power and contact.

6. 预期理论:是激励理论的一种,指出了影响人们行为的三个关系变量及其内在联系——期望几率、目标价值、绩效和报酬之间的关系。

Expectancy Theory: Expectancy theory is one of incentive theories, points out three relational variables influencing people's behavior and the inner link of three relational variables—expected chance, target value, the relationship between the performance and reward.

7. 公平理论:是指与其他人相比,员工觉得受到公平或不公平的待遇。

Equity Theory: Equity theorymeans thatcompared to others, the staff feel the fair or unfair treatment.

8. 强化理论:是由B·F·斯金纳创立的理论,认为人们会对刺激有条件反射,反复强调巩固会引导人的行为。

Reinforcement Theory: Reinforcement theory founded by B. F. Skinner thinks that people will have the conditional reflection to stimulate, and reiterated emphasis will guide the behavior.

9. 饭店薪酬:指个人获得的以工资、奖金以及金钱或实物形式支付的劳动回报。

Hotel Salary: Hotel salary refers that the individual gets labor pay, which includes salary, bonus, money or physical pay form.

10. 计时工资制:根据员工的计时工资标准和工作时间来计算工资用以支付员工劳动报酬的形式。

Time Rate System: Time rate system is to pay the employee according to the staff's hourly wage standard and working hours.

11. 计时奖励工资制:以计时工资制为基础,并有所发展和修正,主要变化在于员工的小时工资率将定期根据总体工作情况加以重新修订。

Time Rate Reward System: Time rate reward system is on the basis of time rate system, major changes in employee hour wage rate will regularly be revised according to the general working condition.

12. 计件工资制：指员工的收入根据他所完成的合格产品或服务工作的数量来决定的，而不是以工作时间为单位来计算。

Piece Work System: Piece work system refers that the salary of the employee is decided by the number of complete qualified products or service, not by calculating working hours.

13. 计点奖励工资制：一种长期使用的刺激工资制度。按照这种工资制，个人完成一项工作所节约的时间部分，按一定百分比提取奖金。

Piece Work Reward System: Piece work reward system is a kind of long-term stimulation wage system. According to this wage system, staff can get a certain percentage of extraction bonus when he save some time to finish a work.

14. 结构工资制：把员工的工资划分成若干个组成部分，构成动态性的工资结构模式，用工资分解的方式，确定和发挥各部分工资各自不同的功能。

Structure Wage System: Structure wage system is to divide the employee's salary into several parts, and form a dynamic model of the wage structure. Using this wage decomposition way will give full play to the different function of each part of salary.

15. 岗位技能工资制：以劳动技能、劳动责任、劳动强度和劳动条件等基本劳动要素评价为基础，以岗位工资、技能工资为主要内容的基本工资制度。

Job Skills Wage System: Job skills wage system is based on labor skills, labor responsibility, labor intensity and working conditions, and consists of post salary, skill-based salary.

16. 职位评价：通过对职务劳动价值的量的比较，来确定饭店的工资结构，以达到薪酬的内部公平性。

Job Evaluation: Job evaluation is based on comparing the amount of different jobs' labor value to determine the hotel wage structure, in order to achieve the internal fairness of salary.

17. 薪酬调查：通过各种正常的手段，来获取相关饭店各职务的薪酬水平及相关信息。

Salary Survey: Salary survey is to get the hotel salary level and related posts' information through the various kinds of normal means.

18. 薪酬结构：又称为薪酬模式，指在薪酬体系中，工资、奖金、福利、保险、津贴等所占的份额和比例。

Compensation Structure: Compensation structure also known as compensation mode, refers to proportion and scale of wage, bonus, welfare, insurance, allowance in the compensation system.

19. 饭店福利:指饭店为了使员工保持稳定、积极的工作状态,根据国家或地方有关法律、法规或政策,结合饭店经营管理的特点和经济承受能力,向员工提供的各种非工资和奖金形式的利益和优惠措施。

Hotel Welfare: The hotel welfare refers to interests and preferential measures of various staff salaries and bonuses, is to make the employees keeping stable, positive working state, according to the national or local laws, regulations or policies, combined with the characteristics of the hotel management and hotel economic bearing ability.

20. 自助式福利:也称为弹性福利,由饭店员工自行选择福利项目的福利管理模式。

Self-help Welfare: Self-help welfare also called elastic welfare, is meant to the welfare management mode chosen by hotel employees.

21. 附加型自助福利:在现有的福利计划之外,再提供其他不同的福利措施或扩大原有福利新项目的水准,让员工去选择。

Additional Self-help Welfare: Additional self-help welfare means that besides the existing welfare programs, the hotel provides other different welfare measures or expands original welfare level of new projectsto let the employees to choose.

22. 资助福利账户:饭店员工每年可以从其税前收入中,拨出一定数额的款项作为自己的"支出账户",并以此账户选购各种福利项目的福利计划。

Funding Welfare Account: Funding welfare account refers that the hotel employees can dial out a certain amount of money every year from its income before tax to form their "spending account", andon this account to choose and buy all kinds of welfare projects.

23. 福利"套餐"型:由饭店同时推出不同的福利组合,每一个组合所包含的福利项目或优惠水准都不一样,员工只能选择其中一个弹性福利制。

"Package" Welfare Type: "Package" welfare type is point to that hotel provides different welfare combination forms, each combination form contains different welfare projects, but the staff can only choose one kind of the elastic welfare.

24. 浮动福利制:不仅允许饭店员工对福利项目和组合进行选择,而且允许对福利支付水平进行选择。

Floating Welfare System: Floating welfare system means that the hotel allows staff not only to choose welfare projects, but also to choose welfare pay level.

复习思考题 (Questions for Review)

1. 什么是饭店薪酬？它有哪些基本形式？

What is the hotel compensation? What are the basic forms of compensation?

2. 在我国饭店中，有哪些形式的工资制度和福利制度？请分别说明它们的特点和适用范围。

In Chinese hotel industry, how many forms of compensation system and welfare system? Please respectively indicate their characteristics and applicable scope.

3. 简述职位评估的各种方法。

Please briefly introduce the work evaluation methods.

4. 饭店薪酬体系设计应遵循哪些原则？包括哪些步骤？

What are the principles of hotel compensation design? How many steps does hotel compensation design include?

5. 我国饭店企业员工福利有哪些？

How many welfare do the hotel employers have?

研究前沿 (Research Front)

Wage Differentials in the Lodging Industry: A Case Study[①]
Sheryl Kline Yu-Chin (Jerrie) Hsieh

ABSTRACT. Salary compensation programs are widely used as a tool to attract, retain, and motivate employees in the hotel industry. The development of a sound compensation plan is a critical component of any successful business. This study investigated the pay differential from different perspectives by using the data collected by the California Hoteland Lodging Association (CHLA), the largest state level hotel association in the United States. The results indicated that full service hotels offer higher base pay in positions such as General Manager, Resident Manager, and Executive Housekeeper as compared with limited service hotels. When accounting for hotel size only, hotels with more than 300 rooms offered higher base pay than their counterparts in

---

① Journal of Human Resources in Hospitality & Tourism, 2007, 6(1): 69-84.

several but notall managerial positions. The findings serve as a reference for human resources administrators in the state of California to develop their pay system. Pay differential rates were calculated to see the wage gap between different managerial positions. The results also provide a base salary referenceto those looking for a job in the lodging industry.

KEYWORDS. Compensation, salary, wage, hotel management

INTRODUCTION

Hotel wage compensation programs are widely used as a tool to attract, retain, and motivate employees. The development of a sound compensation plan is critical to the credibility of the management and success of a business. Several reasons highlight the importance of an effective pay system in the industry.

One is high employee turnover rate within the lodging industry. Many researchers have found that pay affects both employees' decision to leave and their level of job satisfaction (Ghiselli, Lalopa, &Bai, 2001; Peppard&Boudreau, 1995). Second, the lodging industry is a service industry. The quality of the service depends upon the quality of the employees. Pay has been used to attract and keep the best employees. Third, in the hospitality sector, labor costs which include salary and benefits, average about a third of total revenue and 43 percent of all operating expenses (Quek, 2000). Sound management practices require that employers pay competitively, but not excessively. This makes it critical for companies to develop a pay system that balances theneeds of the employees and the needs of the employer to minimize labor costs.

To be effective, a company's pay system should include four things: (1) A sufficient level of rewards to fulfill basic needs; (2) equity with the external labor market; (3) equity within the organization; and (4) treatment of each member of the organization in terms of his or her individual needs (Lawler, 1989). Among those factors, equity is probably the most important. Based on equity theory, people in social exchange relationships believe that rewards should be distributed according to the level of individual contribution (Adams, 1965; Walster, Walster & Berscheid, 1978). People tend to determine what they and others deserve to be paid by comparing what they give to the organization with what they get out of the organization. If they regard the exchange as fair or equitable, they are likely to be satisfied. When individuals perceive that their ratio of inputs to outcomes is not equal to that of their comparative referents, they are likely to be dissatisfied and may end the inequitable relationships by leaving their organizations (Werner & Ones, 2000). High performers who feel that their pay is too low may leave the organization. As a result, the company loses its productive talents. If dissatisfied employees stay, they may react by withholding efforts in order to restrict output or lower quality. A pay differential is the difference in pay, either within the same department, across departments, or among organizations.

A pay differential determined by internal equity is the salary at one level divided by the salary at the next level, irrespective of job content of function. Pay differentials reflect the relative worth of these positions to the organizationand are not related to the individual's or job incumbent's knowledge, skills, and abilities (Tang, Chiu, &Luk, 2000). There is nothing that can destroy the morale of a group of employees faster than the belief that the pay structure is inequitable. The purpose of this study is to investigate the pay differential from different perspectives by using the data collected by the California Hotel and Lodging Association (CHLA) in 2000. The data were chosen because CHLA is the largest and most influential state lodging trade association in the United States and in the world. The data were randomly selected from the hotels in California and represent diverse segments of the lodging industry.

This research focused on the following questions:

1. In terms of hotel segment, do luxury hotels pay their managers more than their counterparts? What are the pay differential rates?

2. Do larger hotels pay their managers more than smaller hotels? What are the pay differential rates?

3. What are the pay differential rates between General Manager and other managerial positions?

REVIEW OF WAGE AND SALARY SYSTEM PRACTICES

According to Wheelhouse (Jackson & Schuler, 2003; Wheelhouse, 1989), the goal of the wage and salary program is to help the company attract and keep qualified employees, provide equal pay for equal work, reward good performance, control labor costs, and maintain a cost parity with direct competitors. An employee's base pay refers to the wage or salary he or she receives, exclusive of any incentive pay or benefits (Jackson&Schuler, 2003). In establishing base pay, two pieces of information are required. One is the information about the job itself and its relative value within the organization. The other is the market information about what other employers pay for the job. Most lodging companies employ the following administration activities to establish their wage and salary system (Tang et al., 2000; Wheelhouse, 1989).

1. Job analysis is the systematic collection of information about jobs in order to develop job descriptions, resulting in job specifications.

2. Job evaluation is comparison of jobs by a systematic procedure such as ranking; jobs point factor technique is used to provide a set of criteriafor differentiating jobs for the purpose of wage determination. Job evaluation assists in maintaining internal equity in the pay rates among jobs.

3. Choosing appropriate survey data for comparison of pay rates to those of your company. Special attention should be paid to those hospitality operations that are geographically close to yours, and that provide similar products/services, because they may draw employees away from your operation.

4. Developing a wage and salary structure of grades, classifications or rates of pay. To do this, the jobs are categorized in terms of compensable factors obtained from the job analysis: the skill required, job responsibilities, effort, working conditions and job requirements. The philosophy, mission statement and organizational goals will influence which factors are weighted more than others.

5. Developing wage and salary budgets (including annual merit or improvement pay).

6. The appraisal of individual employees for purposes of salary adjustments.

7. Making changes in a wage and salary grade, classification, or rate of pay.

METHODOLOGY

This research examined data from the employee compensation survey conducted by the California Hotel and Lodging Association (CHLA) in 2000. The target population was all the hotels in the State of California, USA. Three thousand hotels from the target populations were randomly selected to participate in the study. To increase the response rate, postcard reminders were sent to the non-respondents three weeks after the first questionnaires. Two hundred fifty-seven questionnaires were returned, yielding a response rate of 8.5%, which is quite consistent with the response rate from the studies conducted in the lodging industry (David, Grabski, &Kasavana, 1996; Reid & Sandler,1992). Of the respondents, 34 of them were bed and breakfast properties. Due to the fact that bed and breakfast operations are slightly different from other hotel operations, this type of property was excluded them from the data set. In addition, five cases were deleted due to participant errors. A total of 218 usable data were included in this study for analysis.

RESULTS

The results of the ANOVA showed that there were statistically significant base pay differences in General Manager's minimum and maximum salaries, Resident Manager's maximum salary, and Executive Housekeeper's minimum/maximum salaries among six types of hotel segments.

In terms of the hotel size, significant salary differences were found in General Manager minimum/maximum salary, Resident Manager maximum salary, Controller maximum salary, Reservation manager minimum/maximum salaries, Director of Maintenance minimum salary, Director of Sales minimum/maximum salaries, Sales Manager maximum salary, Executive Housekeeper minimum/maximum salaries, Human Resources Manager maximum salary, Chief Engineer minimum/maximum salary, Food & Beverage Manager minimum/maximum salaries, Executive Chief minimum salary.

CONCLUSIONS

The results partially supported hypothesis one and two and suggested that full service hotels offer higher base pay for positions such as General Manager, Resident Manager, and Executive Housekeeper than limited service hotels. In the full service category, full service-"luxury" hotels were found to offer a higher maximum base salary in the three positions but not a higher minimum salary. For example, the full service-moderate hotels offered higher starting salaries for Executive Housekeepers (2,801.75 vs. 2,768.52) and General Managers (6,191.45 vs. 6,169.38) than the full service-luxury hotels did.

This illustrates that full service-luxury hotels had a larger salary structure range and consequently, more flexibility in salary.

Perhaps due to their limited operations and scale, limited service hotels may have a less flexible salary structure. Pursuing a position such as General Manager, Resident Manager, and Executive Housekeeper in a full service hotel offers more potential for increasing a manager's base salary.

In terms of a General Manager's minimum/maximum salary, the full service hotels paid almost double that of limited service-budget/economy hotels (the differential rate was 1.89). In terms of the Executive Housekeeper's minimum/maximum salary, the differential rates between full service hotels and limited service-budget/economy hotels were 1.55 and 1.72. It was noted that full service-luxury hotels paid five times more than the limited service-budget/economy hotels. It is possible that in many full service hotels, the Resident Manager, in addition to overseeing the daily operations of the hotel, has to serve as General Manager during the latter's absence.

Hotels with more than 300 rooms offered higher base pay than their counterparts for such positions as General Manger, Resident Manager, Controller, Reservation Manager, Director of Maintenance, Director of Sales, Executive Housekeeper, Human Resources Manager, Chief Engineering, and Food and Beverage Manager.

With the exception of the Executive Chef position, it was found consistently that larger hotels (with more than 300 rooms) paid more than small and medium-sized hotels. The average minimum salary for the Executive Chef in small hotels was 4,657.14, against 3,489.85 in large hotels. This is the only position that yielded a result where a smaller property paid more than a larger property for the same position. Due to the nature of the data, this study does not have the information to describe why this is the case for the executive chef position. However, one could speculate that it may depend on the nature of that position within small hotels such as the chef may serve as both food and beverage manager and chef.

Medium-sized hotels did not pay more than the small hotels in these positions. According to the results, small hotels paid higher base salaries than medium-sized hotels for positions such as General Manager (minimum/ maximum base salary), Resident Manager (minimum/maximum base salary), Director of Maintenance (minimum base salary), and Food and Beverage Manager (minimum/maximum base salary).

The largest pay differential rate among the different hotels was found between medium-sized hotels and large hotels with regard to the Resident Manager's maximum salary (the differential rate was 2.84). Another large pay differential rate was found between small hotels and large hotels with regard to the General Manager's maximum salary (the differential rate was 2.33). The pay differential rate was smaller between small and large hotels for positions such as Reservation Manager (minimum pay, where the differential rate was 1.21), Chief Engineer (minimum pay, differential rate 1.35), and Food and Beverage Manager (minimum pay, differential 1.33).

The types and the size of the hotels do matter when comparing lodging managers' base pay. Managers at the larger, more complex hotels tend to be paid more. A possible explanation is that the larger the hotels, the more complexity the operations are. Consequently, managers are required to take more responsibilities and have more experience or capabilities. The types of services describe the quality and service level of a hotel. It was evident that hotels with greater complexities, such as luxury and first class hotels, pay their managerial employees the most.

In terms of career path, the greatest pay differential between General Manager and the department heads was found in the Executive Housekeeper, followed by Front Office Manager. General Manager earned almost twice as much the Executive Housekeeper, and 1.5 times as much the Front Office Manager. The smallest pay gap was found between General Manager and the Director of Sales. The pay differential rates were between 1.09 and 1.16.

IMPLICATIONS AND LIMITATIONS

The findings provide a hotel industry pay profile and contribute to the understanding of pay structures and pay differentials in the lodging industry by examining the empirical sample. The results can also serve as a reference for human resources administrators in the state of California to develop their pay systems and avoid pay inequity. The results also provide a base salary reference to those looking for a job in the lodging industry. The pay differential between General Manager and the entry level job can provide information regarding the compensation reward a person will have when developing his or her career path.

However, this study has several limitations. Due to the secondary data, many missing data were found in bonus and benefits. Hence, this study only focused on base pay or wage. An inclusive approach that investigates the whole compensation package is suggested for further study. Future studies should include benefit packages that delineate the medical, dental, insurance, retirement, andvacation compensation. Also, due to the unique nature of the hotel industry there are additional benefits relating to the field. Many hotel companies offer meals, free or reduced rates on hotel room, housing and dry cleaning as part of management's benefit packages.

The sample was also limited to the hotels in the state of the California. The base pay may vary among hotels located in different geographical regions due to the different living costs in different areas. This research provides a case study of one state at a point in time. The generalization of this study was limited to the state of California. Future research can collect national data to increase the generalization and make a regional comparison.

第8章 纪律和人员流动
(Discipline and Turnover)

本章概要(Summary of This Chapter)

大部分员工积极表现并希望领导满意他们的工作,他们想通过努力工作保住自己的饭碗。但为什么饭店行业的员工流动比例比其他行业高出那么多呢? 在失业率很高的情况下,饭店行业仍然面临人员短缺的问题。本章首先重点探讨饭店员工的高流动率的原因及解决方案。纪律的实行是饭店管理的一项重要技巧,合格的饭店管理者应了解何时执行纪律并如何使员工识别问题的起因,从而制订可行的解决方案。本章的第二节将帮助饭店管理者学会如何更好地采取各种纪律措施——使员工在工作中保持高效。

Most employees try to make a positive performance and hope their leaders are happy with their work. They want to work hard to keep their jobs. But why is the turnover ratio in hospitality industry much higher than other industries? Though the unemployment rate is high, the hotel industry still faces the problem of staff shortages. This chapter first discusses the reason of high turnover ratio in hospitality industry and how to solve the problems. The implementation of the discipline is an important skill of hotel management. A qualified hotel manager should know when to implement discipline and how to make the staff identify the cause of the problem, so as to formulate feasible solutions. The second section of this chapter will help hotel managers learn how to make employees keep high efficiency through taking various disciplinary measures.

开篇引例(Beginning Story)

In the middle of June 2011, Gloria, the new general manager of ××× hotel was very worried after reading the report which was send by human resources department about the human resource situation in recent 3 months. The report showed that last three months the employee turnover actually reached as high as 40%, which is really unfavorable to the future development of the hotel. ××× hotel is located in the center of the business district in Hangzhou. It is only ten minutes' drive from the hotel to the airport and train station. The building style of the hotel is quite special with magnificent lobby lounge, more than 100 luxurious guest rooms and all kinds of entertainment and leisure facilities. And decoration of the coffee shop is really elegant. At the same time ××× hotel hasmany different kinds of conference rooms which are equipped with international standard and fully functional audio-visual equipment. In November 2010, a new hotel that has the same star as ××× hotel and is opposite to ××× hotel started business. According to the human resources manager, many employees have flowed to the opposite hotel. If you were Gloria do you know how to reverse the situation?

第一节 饭店人员流动
(Turnover of Hospitality)

在市场竞争日趋激烈的今天,饭店业经历了从硬件设施的竞争到价格的竞争再到服务品牌的竞争,最后都归结在人才的竞争。这与其自身劳动密集型的本质特点密不可分。在市场经济条件下,人才流动是绝对的。但是,饭店业的人员高流动率一直是令饭店经营者头疼的问题,流动率一直居高不下,这对饭店正常经营运转有很不利的影响。而面对这样的现实状况,留住优秀人才成为饭店越来越关心的问题,也将是本章的一个重点内容。

一、饭店人员流动情况(the Overview of Employee Turnover)

由于饭店业的门槛低、退出成本小以及随着职业选择几率的增加,饭店业的从业人员在饭店业内与其他行业间转换工作岗位、变换职业角色的行为,已经成为人力资源市场化的普遍现象。饭店行业已经成为员工流动最频繁的行业之一。饭店业的员工流动率一直处于较高的状态,这种状况既影响了员工招聘,增加了人员招聘的工作量,更影响了对员工的培训投入,饭店投入大量的培训费用都随着员工的流失而浪费。这样就导致了饭店对招聘的把关不严,培训不到位,引起了饭店经营管理的一系列问题。因此,饭店员工队伍的不稳定,人才流失严重,是饭店管理人员所面临的一个非常棘手的问题。

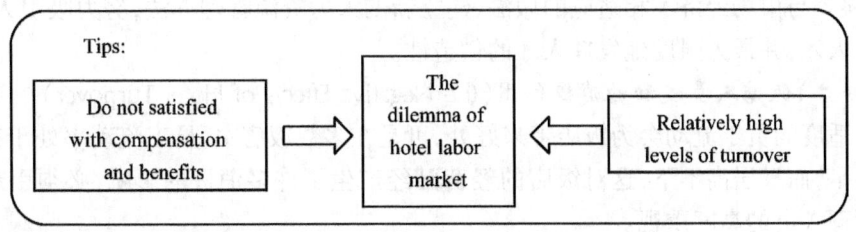

Figure 8-1　The Dilemma of Hotel Labor Market

资料来源:编者整理收集

在讨论饭店人员流动时,我们需要正确地认识人员流动。任何一个行业都需要一定人员流动,流动率是指在一定时期内从业人员的调入、调出之和与从业人员平均人数之比。要想保证企业的正常运营,既要确保企业能吸引新的人才,注入新的血液,还要保证流动率维持在一个稳定的范围内。因此,我们要从全方位的角度去看待人员流动问题,合理的流动率也是企业继续生存的重要保障。

(一)饭店人员流动的积极作用(the Positive Effects of Hotel Turnover)

人员流动作为市场经济劳动力资源配置的一种实现方式,具有重要的作用。从整个社会的角度来看,它有利于实现人力资源的合理配置,从而提高人力资源的使用效率;从饭店的角度来看,适度的人员流动,可优化饭店内部人员结构,使饭店充满生机和活力。适度的人员流动的积极作用主要体现在以下几个方面:

1. 为饭店清除"朽木",提供更多的优秀人才资源

一些心怀异志的员工,即使暂时留在饭店也不会给饭店带来好处,他们对自己所处的饭店已经不再忠心,工作会不认真,他们会拖整个部门的后腿,而且影响其他员工的工作士气,更为严重的是,他们在对客服务时出现错误,极有可能会损坏饭店的形象。因此,表现不好的员工的流动,不仅可以清除部门中的"朽木",而且大量不合格人才的流动,为饭店挑选人才提供了更加充分的资源。

2. 人员流动有利于更好的人才开发和有效利用

对饭店来说,任何一个总经理不管他有多么聪明,也无法做到让每个人才资源都合理利用。人才的每一次流动都是智力和能力的一次开发和提升,当新的人才进入饭店后,必须学会掌握新的知识、开发自己的潜能、提高自己的水平。人员的流动也为新的人才以及饭店内部优秀的员工晋升创造机会。

3. 人员流动会为饭店带来新的变化,为饭店管理提出新课题

即使是优秀的员工离开,也是为引进新人创造了机会。新人会给饭店的运营带来新的想法。如果每个岗位的流动都处于停滞的状态,企业的发展就会处于停滞的状态,最终只能走向倒闭。另外,高员工流动会促使现代饭店按照市场经济要

求,摒弃与市场经济不相适应的做法,建立新的人力资源管理办法,努力吸引人才,留住人才,并最大限度地发挥人才的创造性。

(二)饭店人员流动的消极作用(the Negative Effects of Hotel Turnover)

适度的员工流动会为饭店带来好处,可是在多数饭店中,员工流动率处于很高的水平,而且居高不下,这对饭店的经营已经产生了许多消极的影响,必须引起饭店管理人员的高度重视。

1. 高流动率为饭店造成财务损失

饭店人员高流动率会为饭店带来高的培训费用和经营成本,而且相对老员工,新员工由于技术生疏,会影响饭店的经营,这样就会影响到饭店的收益。由于饭店从业人员的技能、态度对培训的依赖性很强,一名饭店员工从进店培训、轮岗培训、到具体部门培训,直到成为熟练工,饭店是需要支出一笔不小的花费的,员工流动过于频繁,饭店就需要承担很大的人员培训成本。同时,由于新员工对服务技巧和对饭店的设施操作技能生疏,就会引起很多非自然损耗,增加饭店的经营成本,不到位的服务会导致客源的流失,影响饭店的经营绩效。成本增加,收入减少,使得饭店造成了财务损失。

2. 高流动率造成饭店服务质量不稳定,损害饭店品牌

由于饭店行业属于服务行业,要求其从业人员与顾客直接交流,工作经验在员工服务时有很重要的影响。工作经验丰富的员工能够更好地处理各种突发状况,而这种状况是在基础的入职培训中很难预见的。顾客对服务质量的感知是由服务人员的服务技巧决定的,而员工的高流动,尤其是熟练工的频繁离职,会直接造成饭店服务质量下降,影响饭店形象。而且高的流动率在饭店内部会引起依旧在职员工的士气,造成饭店人心浮动。从饭店外部来看,饭店的信誉也会受到一定程度的负面影响。高流动率往往被视为是员工对饭店的不满,对于优秀人才的吸引也带来了很大的挑战。

3. 高流动率会降低管理效率

高流动率对饭店内部的管理也提出了很严峻的挑战,人员的频繁流动使得管理人员不断地面对新的员工,这就使得他们重新熟悉这些员工,继续开发合适的管理手段。当管理人员找到了有效的管理方法后,而员工已经离职,这样就浪费了管理人员的时间,大大降低了管理效率。

二、人员高流动率的原因(the Reason of High Turnover Rate)

饭店人员流动的原因是多方面的,本节主要就社会因素、饭店因素两个方面进行归纳分析。(见图 8 - 2)

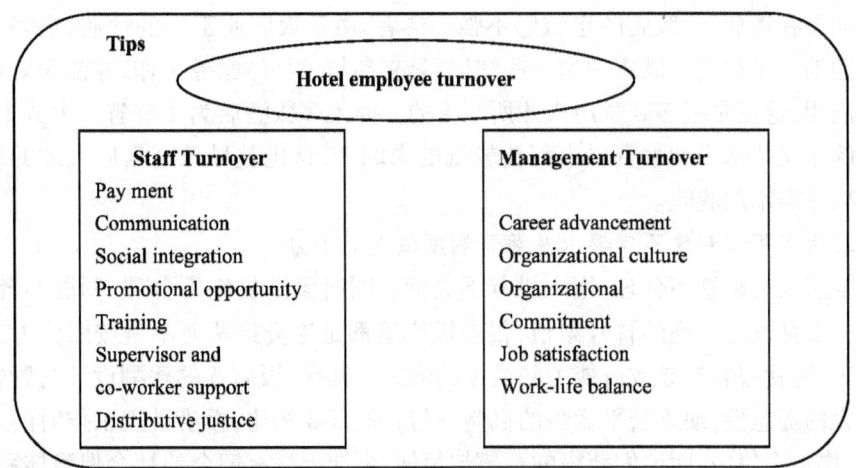

Figure 8-2 Hotel Employee Turnover

资料来源:编者整理收集

(一)社会因素(Social Factors)

1. 人才供需不平衡

改革开放后,饭店业的飞速发展使得饭店人才供不应求。饭店业是劳动密集型的行业,它的容量是决定人员流动的客观基础。在20世纪80年代,我国饭店多数是属于国营性质的,主要负责对外接待,而且饭店数量很少、岗位有限、人员饱和,想跳槽也难。而目前饭店数量迅猛增加、规模也扩大,国外饭店和本土饭店的竞争激烈,对人才需求量大大增加,客观上为人才流动提供了条件。

2. 职业观念原因

饭店职业的特殊性,导致饭店人才难求而且流动率高:一是因为饭店属于服务性行业,在中国传统观念的影响下,全社会对饭店职业的理解存在偏见,从事饭店行业常被认为是"伺候"客人,低人一等。而且饭店行业被认为是"吃青春饭"的行业,这无疑增加了饭店从业人员的社会压力,导致了多数人不会将饭店业的工作列入长久的职业发展规划。二是目前社会上的就业面更为广泛,对于具有众多技能的高素质饭店人才,他们完全能够在其他领域发挥自己的才能,越来越少的人愿意留在饭店,他们会选择一些社会定位相对较高的职业,技术含量较高的行业,这也是导致大量高素质饭店人才外流的一个重要因素。

(二)饭店本身原因(Hotel Facters)

1. 进入壁垒过低,不重视高素质人才

进入壁垒低是饭店业的一个最显著的特点,入职员工良莠不齐,很多服务员只要有初中以上的文化程度,进行简单的培训都直接上岗,这种情况招到的员工很难

长时间留在饭店,对饭店的忠诚感不强。再者,由于饭店业工作的性质,很多工作对经验的要求很高。酒店中的一些知识,只有参与了具体服务工作,才能很好地掌握和应用,这正是很多高学历人才所缺乏的。而大多数酒店为了节省人力成本,更加青睐于文化水平和薪资要求都比较低的求职者,这也就导致高素质人才的培养和饭店业需求的脱轨。

2. 饭店管理制度不完善以及薪酬制度缺乏竞争力

饭店人员配置不合理,用人机制不灵活。同时激励机制不合理,制度不健全,员工一般都没有合理的晋升渠道,很多饭店里都是论资排辈而不是按照能力来提拔员工,这就很容易导致有能力的员工的流失。其次,饭店业的薪酬设计与管理带有很大的随意性,缺乏公平竞争的机制。与其他行业相比,饭店员工工作时间不稳定,工作强度集中,而他们获得的薪酬却很低,再加上没有健全的社会保障体系,员工的跳槽就更加频繁。

三、人员高流动率的解决措施(Methods of Solving High Turnover Rate Problems)

针对员工流动的现状和原因,我国饭店行业在降低员工流动率、培养员工忠诚度方面也做出了很大的努力,除了关注流动现象外,很多饭店企业缺乏具体的解决办法,当然也有一部分企业制定了旨在降低流动率的一些措施。大部分成功降低了流动率的企业都是从积极的角度考虑这个问题的,因此用于降低员工流动率的措施被称为保留计划(retention program)。

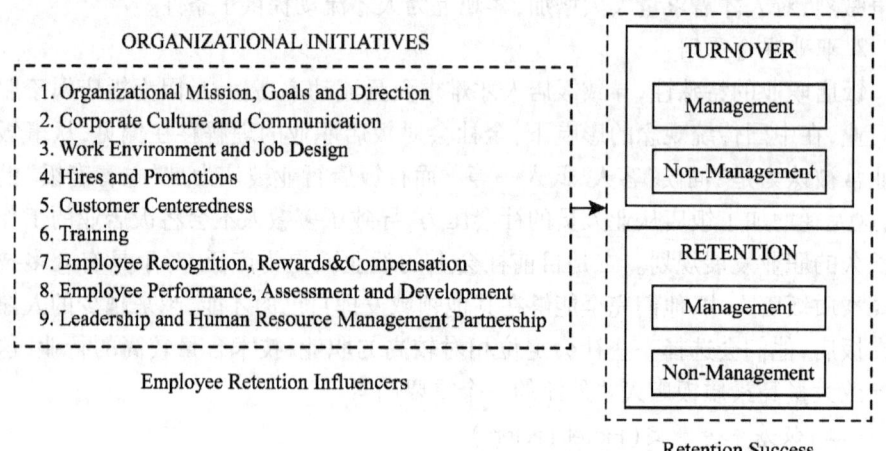

Figure 8-3 Hotel Employee Retention

Source: International Journal of Contemporary Hospitality Management, Vol. 21 No. 4, 2009: An exploratory study of US lodging properties' organizational practices on employee turnover and retention.

流动不可能完全消除,其实这种结果也并不是经理所需要的,新员工能带来新思维和活力,因此一定程度的流动性是必要的。

(一)短期解决方案(Short-term Methods)

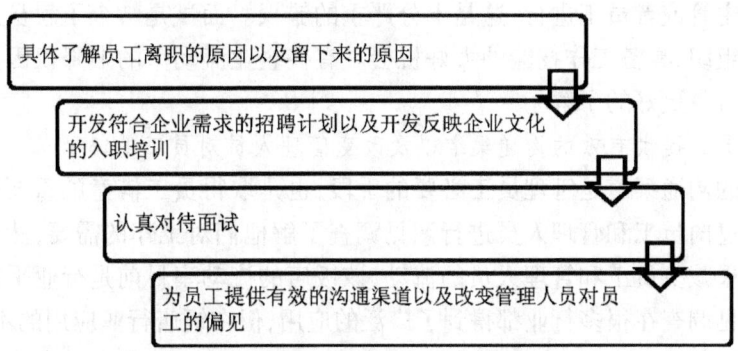

图 8-4　员工流动短期解决方案

1. 具体了解员工离职的原因以及留下来的原因

很多饭店企业不知道他们员工为什么离开,很少有企业能正确掌握员工流动的相关资料,并用于解决问题。进行离职面谈是十分有必要的,可以从中了解到员工为什么离开,并找出饭店自身的原因,在今后的工作中进行改进。最好是对离职员工建立起一套记录档案,记录他们离职的原因,这些资料是招聘新员工时的有用信息。其次,还可以了解一下在职员工留下来的原因,了解他们喜欢在饭店工作的原因以及对饭店哪些方面感到满意,并在今后的发展中继续保持这些优势方面,而且要不断改进,使其成为留下员工的重要因素。其中,态度调查是了解员工为什么留下来的最简单有效的方法。调查内容包括了解员工对他们工作或者工作环境的感觉看法。但这种调查也会产生一个问题,员工的回答并不一定是真诚的,因为有员工担心管理人员会因反面意见而打击报复。如果用第三方咨询公司收集分析数据,这个问题可能就解决了,因为员工会觉得第三方会保护员工利益的。

2. 开发符合企业需求的招聘计划以及开发反映企业文化的入职培训

很多雇主用"混日子的雇员"(warm body)来填补工作急需的空缺而犯有过失。虽然雇主们知道这些员工不会长待的,但是他们实在没有选择余地,要么雇这些人,要么就没人干。要医治"混日子的雇员"的症状,管理人员必须发掘出员工品性中成功的方面,另外可以借助于有创意的招聘计划。开发反映企业文化的上岗引导:上岗引导培训计划应介绍企业的文化,而很多企业只是简单地让新员工跟着老员工干,而老员工很少能了解企业希望新员工了解的东西,结果是这种不符合企业文化的不良上岗引导使员工流动现象反复出现。

3. 认真对待面试

面试潜在员工是一件很严肃的事情，面试进行的好坏直接决定了今后几年内企业的员工流动率。很多经理不认真对待面试过程，甚至把这件事交给了一些没有经验的主管或者员工进行，这是十分严重的错误。面试是一个了解员工是否适应企业的组织、具备工作技能的大好机会。有些企业流动率的下降仅因为企业对面试人进行了更好的了解。

4. 为员工提供有效的沟通渠道以及改变管理人员对员工的偏见

良好的沟通渠道是管理员工必要的手段，也是取得员工满意的重要基础。马里奥特通过向员工和管理人员进行意见调查了解他们对工作的需要，然后再用这些调查结果减少员工和管理人员的流动，该饭店的流动率目前是行业平均水平的一半。意见调查在很多行业都得到了广泛的应用，但在饭店行业应用的不多，因为很多饭店经理担心这种调查会让员工产生不切实际的幻想，事实上有这种担心的经理根本没认真考虑员工流动率的问题。因此，改变管理人员对员工的偏见也是至关重要的。管理人员很少真正地知道员工到底需要什么，一般管理人员都觉得员工首要关注的肯定是钱。虽然薪酬是一个重要部分，但如果薪酬可以满足员工的正常需求，员工更多的会将注意力放在其他方面，例如工作环境以及氛围。让管理人员不带偏见地了解员工的真正需求有助于员工的开发保留计划。

其实面对员工的流失，解决的方法有很多，以上几个只是笔者认为比较有效的措施。在处理员工离职时，管理者有着很重要的作用。他们要认识到员工的流动是正常现象，不能对申请离职的员工有怨恨或者别的看法，应该摆正态度，了解具体的情况，妥善处理问题，从细节发现饭店存在的问题，积极改进不合理的制度，争取能为减少员工流动率做出一定的贡献。

（二）长期解决方案(Long-term Methods)

短期解决方案侧重于收集和使用信息解决当务之急，长期方案侧重于企业组织的变更，让企业能对员工更有吸引力。这些方案一般较费时费钱，费用的投入是由流动的严重程度和企业对变化的需求而决定的。

员工流动长期解决方案：

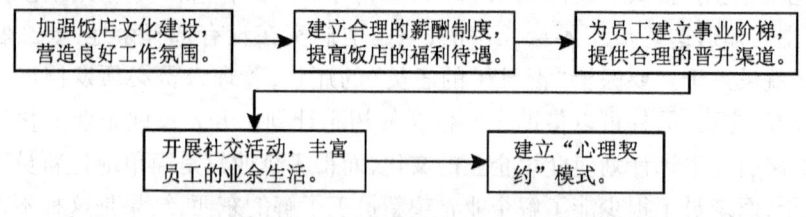

图 8-5 员工流动长期解决方案

1. 加强饭店文化建设,营造良好工作氛围

饭店企业文化价值是饭店员工共同拥有的价值观、饭店精神、经营哲学等,是饭店的灵魂所在。饭店文化的建设也是增强饭店凝聚力、调动员工积极性的有效途径。如若企业的主要价值观是"管理人员与员工一道工作",在这种企业中管理人员会卷起袖子与员工一起洗碗、服务客人或者干任何需要他做的事。也有些企业的主要价值观是"管理人员监督指导员工工作",在这种企业中,管理人员具有一定的权威,可以不必亲自动手。利用饭店文化的微妙性来管理员工,规避制度的刚性所带来的对人的冷漠,从而从整体上提高员工的素质,增强饭店竞争力。建设饭店文化对外可以树立良好的社会形象,对内可以形成强大的凝聚力,增强员工对企业的认同感和责任感,自然就会减少员工的流动。

2. 建立合理的薪酬制度,提高饭店的福利待遇

合理的薪资制度不仅影响到酒店在人才市场的竞争力,而且也是留住员工的一个基本保障。饭店的薪酬结构设计要让员工的薪酬水平与其贡献成正比,通过对员工的绩效考核,使岗位之间的晋升或降级有量化的考核标准,使员工的精力集中到努力工作、提高工作业绩上来。薪酬不仅是员工的劳动所得,还代表着员工自身的价值以及酒店对员工工作的认同,甚至对其个人能力、品行和发展前景的认可。所以,薪酬激励是一种复杂的激励方式,它是员工努力工作的主要动力。其次,饭店良好的福利待遇也可以降低员工的流失率以及调动员工的积极性,保证服务质量,提高饭店经济效益。饭店应为员工提供必要的福利性补贴,如提供宿舍、适当的交通补助、医疗保健、带薪假期以及人身保险等。另外,饭店应制定合理的奖金分配制度,把奖金、能力和工作绩效挂钩,激励员工工作的积极性,使员工树立起"我以饭店为家""我以饭店为荣"的意识。虽然短期中产生了一定的成本,可是从长远来看,这些忠诚的员工会是饭店更宝贵的财富。

3. 为员工建立事业阶梯,提供合理的晋升渠道

员工积极努力工作是十分重要的,但管理岗位毕竟是有限的,大多数的员工只能在普通的工作岗位上努力,不可能都得到升迁的机会,因此饭店要帮助员工进行多重职业发展的帮助以满足员工多重需要。具体来讲,饭店可针对酒店员工不同需要,深入地进行调查研究,了解核心员工需要层次和需要结构的变化趋势,实施多重职业发展路径,从职务提升、工作重新设计、技术等级提升等多方面进行尝试,使员工有可能选择一条适合其核心能力和价值观的职业道路,保证其获得职业发展的成就感和促进个人成长,提供公平合理的晋升渠道。

4. 开展社交活动,丰富员工的业余生活

饭店开展适当的社交活动,不仅有助于员工之间以及员工与领导的沟通,而且这也是增强企业人性化管理的体现。在保证员工基本的需求基础上,和谐的工作

氛围也是留住员工的一种有效手段。现在工作和生活压力都很大,尤其饭店业的旺季是在节假日,而且工作强度相对较大,员工很容易疲劳和厌烦,以致对工作和饭店产生不满。在饭店中开展适当的社交活动,例如举行各种棋牌比赛、与同行的交流会以及组织大家出去进行短途旅游等都会激发起员工对工作和企业的热爱和认同。

5. 建立"心理契约"模式

心理契约是员工和饭店之间在相互期望的基础上形成的一种并没有直接表达出的无形关系。这种无形关系能反映员工和饭店之间的物质期望,如饭店期望员工努力工作,提高绩效;员工则希望饭店能够给他提供优厚的物质待遇。同时,心理契约还能体现饭店和员工之间的无形期望,如个人希望在饭店中有良好的工作环境和工作氛围,使自己得到最充分的自我价值实现;饭店则希望员工能够对饭店忠诚,维护饭店的形象,视饭店为自己的另外一个家。

建立良好的心理契约,可以增强员工对饭店的信任和依赖,也可以降低员工流失率、保证员工队伍的稳定。同时,还可以影响员工的绩效表现,满足员工的个人需要。以劳动契约和心理契约为双重纽带的战略合作关系,构建饭店与员工关系的新模式,是饭店人员流动管理的有效方式。

第二节 纪律管理(Discipline)

无规矩不成方圆,这条准则适应各种组织,大到整个人类社会,小到每个家庭。尽管人性化管理成为21世纪的管理的热点,但是一个组织的正常运行绝对离不开有效的纪律管理和监督。良好工作业绩的取得有赖于管理以及非管理人员对纪律的遵守。大多数员工希望能够在一个组织良好、培训有道、纪律严明的组织中任职。员工会从纪律中受益,而从无序中只会受损。尽管员工并不一定希望受到处罚,但是他们却希望受到适度的监管。而组织也正是从员工对纪律的遵守中得以正常运行。

因此,对劳动密集型的饭店行业来说,高效的纪律管理更是必不可少,本节重点介绍纪律管理在饭店行业的运用。

一、纪律的含义(The Meaning of Discipline)

纪律是一种必不可少的管理工具,但是也是最难运用的,很多管理者在过程中不能前后一致或者公平地运用。有些人把纪律当作一种严格处罚过去的不当行为的手段,而不是保证企业将来正常运行的工具,其实这些人不知道纪律也可以用于鼓励企业希望看到的行为。

实际上,纪律和惩罚有着本质的区别,让我们来看一下纪律的具体定义。

纪律是指要求人们在集体生活、工作、学习中遵守秩序、执行命令和履行自己职责的一种行为规则。如果每个人都遵守规则、规章,工作有序地进行,那么我们就说这个部门或公司的纪律良好。如果员工不遵守规则、规章,不能够履行自己的义务,完不成分内的工作,导致整个公司或者组织工作无法进行,员工相互争斗,一片混乱,那么我们就说这里的纪律差。

以上是纪律的一部分,而纪律还有另一层意思,即为保证员工行为有序,遵守规则而采取的行动。如果员工违反规则,相应的管理或监督人员就可以以纪律处治他们,以保证他们以后能遵守规则。纪律制裁的方法视政策和具体情况而定。如果员工的自律性强,那么就不必经常用纪律制裁他们。

保持组织良好的纪律是组织健康发展的基础,因此有效的纪律管理也成为饭店人力资源管理的重要内容。

二、纪律管理的方法(The Methods of Discipline Management)

纪律管理是指管理者按照事先确定的行为规则,组织和监督在纪律约束范围内的人员规范行为,以确保工作顺利进行。它可以是消极的和抑制性的,通过惩罚来严格纪律,这种方法是基于 X 理论对员工和管理风格为依据的;相反,纪律管理也可以是积极的和具有建设性的,通过提供情况予以纠正性培训的方式,这相应的就是以 Y 理论为基础。无论哪一种情况,纪律都是一种力量,可以促使个人或团队遵守政策、规则、规章和程序的要求,以达到组织的既定目标。

(一)消极的纪律管理(Negative Discipline)

消极的纪律管理(negative discipline)指的是依靠外部的力量或影响来改变员工的行为。这种力量也许可以使一个人的外在表现发生变化,表面上服从管理,但并非精神和情感上的变化。或者说它对于人的变化只会发生在一段时间内不断进行惩罚的情况下。消极的纪律管理不能过度使用,并且最好是在积极的纪律管理失效时使用。但遗憾的是,许多组织几乎只使用消极的纪律管理,尤其是在饭店这种劳动密集型的行业,很容易导致员工的恶意服从(malicious obedience),大大影响了组织的有效运行。红热炉法和递进(分级)纪律法是两种比较常见的消极纪律管理方法。这两种方法强调对员工违反纪律后的处罚,是被动的反应式的,纪律在错误行为之后起作用。

1. 红热炉法(hot-stove rule)

反映了一种传统的管理思维模式,将企业的规章制度比作红热炉,若操作不规范,碰到了红热炉,你会被烫伤。从企业角度讲,如果你违反了纪律,将受到纪律处分。

在采用红热炉法时,为了保证其更有效地发挥作用,应该注意以下几点:首先,一碰红热炉就立即被烫伤,即惩罚一定要及时。即触犯纪律的行为一经发生必须及时做出反应,这样才能将纪律和行为紧密联系起来。员工才能清楚地知道是哪种行为不符合规章制度,在下次可能会犯同样的错误时,回想起这次惩罚后能够及时地停止。

其次,饭店要有明确的规章制度,制定一套人人都知道、都明白的规定,并且说明违反每条规定将带来的后果。即有明确的警告,经理必须提出明确的规定并适时提醒员工,如果违反规定"会被红热炉烫伤的",会受到惩罚的。

再次,纪律处分行为必须连贯一致,给予一视同仁的惩罚,即不论谁碰了红热炉都会被同等程度地烫伤。而且还要保证处罚对事不对人,即纪律必须与行为联系起来,而不是与人联系起来。

最后,纪律处分和程度必须与触犯纪律的严重性相当,把握好适度原则。不宜过重,打击员工继续为企业服务的信心;也不能太轻,否则员工会不够重视,还可能继续触犯纪律。

这个系统看起来非常合理,对所有员工都是平等的,规则与纪律处分都有一一对应的关系,但这个系统也有一个问题,就是绝对平等,红热炉会烫伤每一个碰到它的人,即不论个人和情况是否相同一律如此,缺乏一定的灵活性,一名因病而旷工的员工和刻意逃班的员工如果处理不当,可能同样程度地被烫伤。

2. 分级处罚法(progressive discipline)

与红热炉法类似,不过在红热炉法的基础上进行了一些改善,这个方法的前提是明确和完整的行为定义,即什么样的行为会受到处分,会受到什么样的处分。根据分级惩处法,工作拖拉一次的员工可能受到口头警告,拖拉两次可能受到书面警告,三次停职,这样的纪律处分依据行为程度递进。

这种方法很常见,大部分递进纪律包括四个层次:

由于红热炉法和分级惩处法能够很好地规范企业的运行,经理们一般都喜欢用这两种方法。两种方法都要求依据法规明晰,强调连贯一致性和处分的公平性。但是,这两种传统方法都只能起到短期效果,因为这些处分只针对行为,而不针对行为的根源,违反纪律只是一种现象,不是理由。

同时,常常采用消极的纪律管理方法的管理者往往是死守教条的人。他们很在意自己惩罚别人的权力和控制的责任,所以他们按书本的章程做事,如果违规,就要惩罚。这种严格纪律的方式最大的特点就是僵化和一成不变。此外,使用惩罚管理纪律的管理者往往有绵绵不断的纪律问题。这种消极的纪律管理方法以 X 理论为依据来对员工进行管理,使用这种方法多年来,从来没有使违反纪律的员工

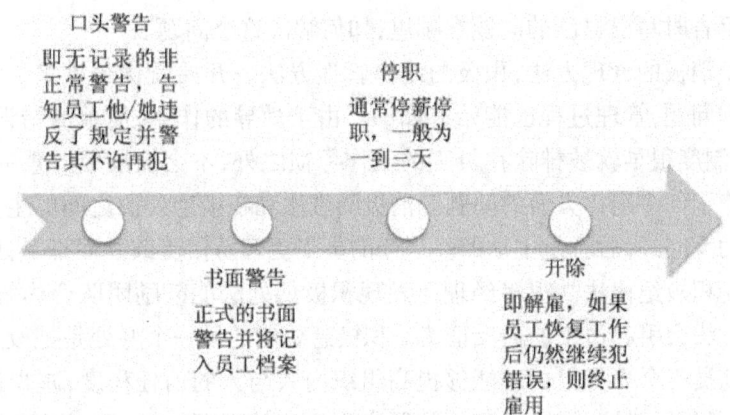

图 8-6　递进纪律的四个层次

变得顺从、合作。它不能鼓励员工转变,不能帮助员工向好的方向努力,也容易造成员工和老板之间的敌对关系和明争暗斗的权利争夺,这对工作气氛和员工工作热情极为有害。因此,组织光靠这些消极的纪律管理是很难得到员工的青睐的。

(二)积极的纪律管理(Positive Discipline)

积极的纪律管理(positive discipline)通过激活内部的动力来促进员工情感上的满足而不是情感上的抵触,倾向于预防或积极正面的行为。它能给员工提供更大的自由,同时在最少地动用正式权威的情况下带来协作和和谐。主管和员工之间会进行适度的沟通。当团队目标和程序为员工所共知,并且已经成为个人行为的基础时,积极的纪律管理就可以最大限度地发挥作用。它往往是管理者有效应用激励、领导和沟通的结果。积极的纪律管理还会有意识甚至是无意识地使用同级的压力来增加管理的效果。

这种管理方法的典型代表是预防(积极)纪律法,这是一种积极的方法,侧重于指导员工的行为,倾向于预防或积极正面的行为是这种方法与传统方法的区别,这个方法针对生产效率低下的根源,而不是违反纪律的表象。主管与员工之间的"横向"沟通,是一种成人之间的沟通,强调如何解决问题而不是处罚。这个方法的内涵是提起员工的重视,调动起员工的主人翁意识,给他或者她改正的时间和机会。

积极惩处法是把纪律实施的重点放在认识和强调好的行为而不是坏的行为,这类纪律行为的步骤包括:口头提醒、书面提醒、带薪停职反省、开除。

除了最后一步开除,其他阶段都是强调鼓励员工向好的方向转变,整个过程都在提醒员工应该干什么而不是什么做错了。这个做法的目的是让员工仔细思考自己行为中哪些是该做的,哪些是不该做的,如何改进并提高工作效率。有些经理要求员工在反省时写出自己的问题在哪里,如何解决这个问题。

相对于消极的管理方法,积极的纪律管理方法一开始就优越许多。它更易于较早地处理问题,管理过程也能始终如一。由于教导的作用,简单的错误、违反规章、政策和制度很早就被排除在员工的工作习惯之外,不会发展成严重的问题,从根本上杜绝了许多纪律方面的问题。消极的方法和积极惩处法之间的主要区别是前者是被动反应式,后者是主动的。当今的员工更容易接受鼓励而抵触处罚,他们更容易接受积极纪律法。很多经理还发现积极惩处法能鼓励团队合作解决问题,而消极的方法会引起员工的逆反情绪。积极惩处法的另一个好处是把改进工作的责任转移到员工个人身上。这能够提高组织内人与人的信任程度,减少诉讼发生的可能性。积极惩处法能让经理在问题产生之初就提醒员工,这时的问题比较容易纠正,这一点对大部分企业都是非常有益的。此外,积极的纪律管理方法能减少成本,减少违纪事件,降低人员流动率,减少错误,提高工作水平。营造一个有利于提高生产效率、鼓舞员工工作热情的工作环境和良好的工作氛围。而惩罚式的纪律管理方法会增加成本,削弱员工的工作积极性,引起员工的敌对情绪和破坏行动。积极的纪律管理是一种把充满敌意的员工转变为负责、能干的员工的方法。这对整个企业的有效运行起着至关重要的作用。

在实施手段和方法中,消极的纪律管理与积极的纪律管理的不同见下图:

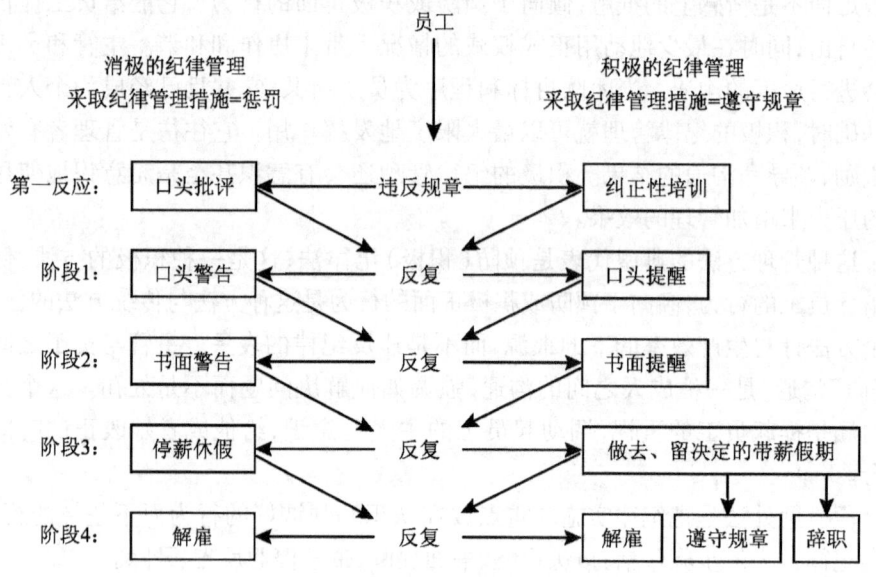

图 8-7 消极管理与积极纪律管理的不同

资料来源:杰克·E·米勒,玛莉·波特,凯伦·埃克·多蒙德. 酒店督导. 大连:大连理工出版社,2002:255-256.

在员工犯错误时,消极的纪律管理方法的第一反应就是进行口头批评和责备,这就为员工形成了一定的压力,而积极的方法则是进行相应的纠正性培训,指出员工错误的地方以及改进的方法,以期员工不会因为技术或者技巧问题再犯同样的错误。

在阶段1时,消极的纪律管理方法会给予员工口头警告,告知员工违反规定而且警告其不许再犯。而积极的方法则是进行口头提醒,需要管理人员友好地指出员工违反规定的地方,告诉他违规的严重性,制定规定的原因,遵守规定的必要性。

阶段2是若员工再次违纪,两种方法分别是书面警告和书面提醒,这次是口头警告的深入,相对较为正式,但是积极的管理方法不只是对员工进行警告,还要与员工进行讨论和协商,试图和员工进行更多的沟通,了解犯错的真正原因,帮助员工进行改进。

阶段3是对反复违纪的员工的一个初步的处罚。消极的纪律管理是会直接将员工进行停薪休假,一般是一到三天。积极的纪律管理方法是给员工做去留决定的带薪假期。在假期期间,让员工自己决定是回公司并遵守公司的规章制度还是离开公司,而且要明确指出,如果再次违纪就将被解雇。

阶段4则都是解雇。如果员工恢复工作后继续犯错,就会被解雇。虽然结果相同,但是过程的不同还是对饭店的管理很有帮助的,在采用积极的纪律管理方法后,员工被解雇也不是饭店的责任,因为饭店已经给了他很多次机会,不断地给予他帮助和足够的改进空间。

三、纪律管理的过程(The Process of Discipline Management)

实行纪律的过程应能为饭店业运营产生积极的回报。否则将导致紧张的人际关系、较差的工作表现、潜在的诉讼或工会争端,并使管理者和员工双方倍感不快。管理者应该时刻牢记:采取纪律措施的目的是改变员工的行为,而并非惩罚对方。整个实行纪律的过程应投放在查找问题的症结和制订最佳解决方案上。较为有效的方式是争取员工的参与和承诺——而这并不能通过批评、责备或指责员工而获得。

下面的七个步骤是处理严重违纪行为或者不太严重但屡次发生的违反操作规定或不符合工作要求的行为。它们适用于任何一种纪律管理方法——积极的或消极的,同时也适用于纪律管理过程的任何一个阶段。

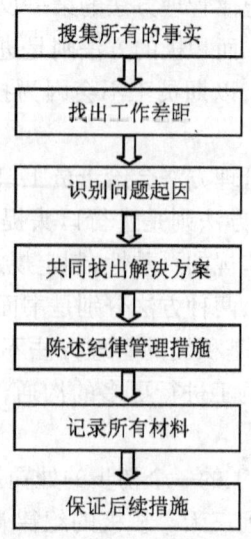

图 8-8 纪律管理的步骤

第一步,搜集所有的事实。一旦发现员工的不良行为,搜集到相关的事实,征询所有涉及的员工和目击者,记下所有情况。尽量把别人说的事实和主管看法区别开,考虑问题时也要区别对待事实和主管看法。避免在全面掌握情况之前妄下定论。可以参考以下问题作为指导:

员工这样做的原因,是故意的吗?还是意外事故?是不了解情况还是误解造成的?

是否有特殊情况?比如严重的个人问题或者工作上的危机?

违纪的程度是否严重?员工认错的态度是否真诚?

该员工过去是否有同样的违纪行为?是初犯还是重犯?

第二步,找出工作差距。在与员工面谈时应首先核查问题的起因,讨论员工的实际工作表现与管理者的期望值之间的差距。员工必须清楚地意识到自己工作的缺点或偏差。如果管理者与员工已进行过定期的同一问题的探讨,则应总结员工目前采取或未采取的行动,向员工表明其行动是否有任何的积极改正。

在描述员工工作表现的差距时应尽量具体。应尽量避免使用类似下列的提示:"你的工作表现极差""你需要好好干"或"你应改变自己的态度"等笼统的评价。这种笼统的评价忽视了问题的真正具体内在原因,所以没有任何效果。此外这种评价只是在指责员工。管理者应着眼于未达到期望值的工作表现;而不应只注重员工的态度,更不应指责员工的性格。例如:不应只对员工讲"你很粗鲁",而应说:"当客人走来问你问题时,你背向客人是很不礼貌的。"如果管理者把注意力集中在员工的行为而并非其本人时，便能帮助员工保持自尊。这样员工能去除戒备之心，客观地与管理者讨论问题。在整个过程中，切记不可威胁、争论或发泄怨恨。这些行为只能使人偏离目标——即纠正员工的行为而并非惩罚员工。

确切地使员工了解管理者的期望值。如果员工的行为不符合公司的政策和规章制度——应向员工解释相关的政策和规章制度。简单地以"因为政策"回答员工并不能坚持工作的标准——至少员工不这样看问题。应向员工解释政策的重要性和与工作的关系性，大多数政策都有其存在的道理。

作为管理者，向员工解释你对问题的看法是十分必要的。如果员工感到低于标准的工作表现对于管理层无关紧要，他就会对纪律措施不屑一顾。而如果向员工说"我对你背向客人感到失望，你损坏了公司的声誉"会更有效。表明自己的感受更能激发员工坦言，同时还能帮助员工找到自己的问题并意识到解决问题的重大责任。

第三步，识别问题的起因。要求员工解释其行为。在员工做自我解释的过程中，应仔细并客观地聆听。使用聆听技巧来鼓励员工，如"对""继续讲""我明白"或者频频点头。最后要求员工总结错误所在，双方应对问题的起因达成共识。

饭店管理者的目的是达成对问题起因的共识，以使员工参与共同找出解决方案。应真诚地倾听任何可能与问题有关的情况解释，而且要透过现象看本质。鼓励员工进一步提供情况，不论听到何种信息，都应在适当时积极地点头并表示明白了，绝不要打断员工的谈话。采用"何时"或"如何"这类启发性问题能强调具体情况的探究，避免使用指令性的提问。

第四步，共同找出解决方案。在与员工讨论问题的起因后，接下来就需要弥补已犯下的错误，争取使企业或者客人的损失最小。而在寻求解决方案时，员工作为当事人是最了解情况的，如若能够悉心听取员工的意见，加上管理者合理的指导和意见，就可取得最佳方案。员工虽然犯了错误，如果态度诚恳，此举不仅可以事半功倍，而且让员工将功补过，还能激励员工继续工作的热情，一举两得。

第五步，陈述纪律措施。员工触犯了纪律，必要的处罚一定要有的，在采取行动时，一定要保证行动的合理性，以免引起其余员工的不满。要做到这一点必须考虑在类似情况下，别人是怎么做的，必须保证没有歧视性行为。在确定采取某种惩罚措施时，根据具体情况需要，如有必要应与其他部门或者上司进行商榷。

在确定具体的惩罚措施后，还应保证采取合适的行动，比如书面警告，或与员工一起用以下步骤制订一项改进方案。

向员工说明管理者要采取的行动，用严肃的、实事求是的语调说话，不要带有报复或气愤的意味。并且说明，如果违纪行为再次发生会有什么后果。

让员工确定一些他自己所能采取的行动以防止此类事情再次发生，确定一个完成改进的日期。

结束时用鼓励的语气表明对员工的信任,相信他能改进工作,解决问题。还要表达真心希望看到他进步的原因,以积极口吻结束谈话。

第六步,务必确定所有的材料都有记载,书面记录是很有必要的。首先,如果员工对企业的惩罚起诉,或出席事业补偿听证会,企业就需要书面材料打官司;其次,记录的过程帮你更客观地看待情况,把注意力集中到与工作有关的事情上;再次,书面材料通常包括员工的改进方案,所以可以帮助员工进步;最后,书面记录可以为以后出现类似错误的情况提供借鉴,以及合理的解决方案。

第七步,保证后续措施。管理者在尽全力帮助员工努力达到企业对他的期望时,也要警惕新的违纪或捣乱行为的发生。如果员工没有达到管理者的期望,就必须采取相应的措施。

 案例分析(Practice Case Analysis)

Rita's trouble with discipline management

Rita is a leader of the waiters in a bachelor bar. The bar specializes in serving cocktails. What's more, this bar also provides some special food except drinks, and it is a great choice of young people. This bar is located in the business center of Shanghai; with the fashionable lifestyle of metropolitan young people, the bar is quite popular, and of course, the business is booming. As a department leader, the main responsibility of Rita is to supervise a large number of part-time workers. Before her promotion, she was one of them. Those part-time employees are very active, all of them are post 80s, and have their own strong personalities. They admire the freedom of their work and their personalities. They consider themselves as the independent operator of this bar, instead of part-time staff or submissive staff.

Most of them rarely pay attention to many rules of the bar, such as "get to work on time", "take break on scheduled time", "no frippery jewelry and weird clothes are allowed to wear during working time", and "no smoking and drinking during duty time" and so on. They always break the rules. However, their working efficiency is extremely high, and they are welcomed among the guests. In Rita's mind, working efficiency and guest satisfaction are the most important, so that's why Rita ignore the behavior of these staff, and sometimes she even connives them.

One day, her boss, Sam, who just took office and is responsible for the entire bar, called her into his office for a "friendly chat", he gave her a cup of coffee and paused for a moment, then straight into the main theme.

"Well, Rita, I have to tell you that there are many discipline problems in the team you are responsible for, too many staff ignored the rules, they broke rules frequently, and made a lot of trouble," he said, "the waiters serving food and kitchen staff have to abide by those regulations, they do what the rules says and pay much attention to them, what the rules forbidden they never do it. If not, those offenders will face disciplinary punishment. Well, when they see what your team member did, they feel angry and unfair. You may know those cocktail waiters always drink in staff room, and smoking with guests, they didn't wear uniform instead of various fancy clothes and jewelries. What's more, they are frequently late for work and leave early, let the other people do their job during their working hours. What they did made other employees very angry. And I'm sure you can understand their feelings."

"Well, I know this phenomenon, but I think their feeling is not my problem." Rita said.

"I think it is." Sam said, "And now I ask you to make clear regulations for working hours and the provisions of smoking and drinking, and make sure they are effective and being implemented. Of course, I will be glad to help you, but specific rules are made by you. You can think about it today and I suggest we meet again tomorrow to discuss your plans, and set up some improvement goal together. OK?"

Rita dumbfounded, "listen to me, Sam," she said, "anyone in my team could find a same kind of job in 5 minutes in anywhere in the city, so do I! Improve? They already had very good work performance, as to the way they did the job, they like it that way!"

"What you said I know," Sam said, "but others don't like. And, it has become a serious problem. Even some guests noticed and complained, this problem has already affected other employees, influenced our business in the bar. Rita, calm down and think about it, tomorrow we will talk about it again."

Rita's first reaction is to resist and anger, but she knew it is no good to her, she would rather stay here than change job. She is proud to be a supervisor, and the salary in here is very decent and the highest in the city, colleges are friendly, and also working environment is comfortable. Then she has to face the situation and deal with the problem, actually toughest problem is how to let her staff abide by the rules?

Questions for Discussion:

1. Which kind of common mistakes did Rita make? What led to the consequence?

2. What do you prefer do when there are conflicts between keeping thriving business and implementing regulations? Try to tell us why.

3. Do you think it is feasible that we make different regulations in different sections? Why?

4. What do you think about Sam's way of dealing with the problem? How did his "chat" go? What risk did he take?

5. What should Rita do now?

6. What reactions do you think Rita's staff will have to her supervisor style? How to prevent the resignation of employees? What should she do if employees ask for resignation?

名词解释(Key Terms)

1. 人员流动:员工离开一个企业或一个工作单位。
Turnover: Employees leave a company or a work unit.

2. 保留计划:用于减少人员流动的计划。
Retention Program: A plan that used to reduce personnel flow away.

3. 积极的纪律管理:通过激活内部的动力来促进员工情感上的满足而不是情感上的抵触,倾向于预防或积极正面的行为。
Positive Discipline: To promote the meet of the staffs' emotion by activating the internal motivation other than emotional conflict. This kind of discipline management tends to prevent or be positive behavior.

4. 消极的纪律管理:指的是依靠外部的力量或影响来改变员工的行为。
Negative Discipline: Refers to rely on outside force or influence to change the behavior of employees.

5. 渐进处罚:根据员工违纪行为的轻重程度递进的纪律处分方式,处分由轻到重,从口头警告到书面警告,到停职,最后到开除。
Progressive Discipline: It means punish staffs depending on the indiscipline degree. The penalty can from light to heavy, from oral warning to written warning and finally to the fire.

6. 红热炉法:实施纪律处分的一种方法,对每一起违反纪律的行为进行立即处分。

Hot-stove Approach: A kind of method that used to implement disciplinary action. To conduct immediate sanctions for each behavior of violate discipline.

7. 纪律:纪律有两层意思,一是指要求人们在集体生活、工作、学习中遵守秩序、执行命令和履行自己职责的一种行为规则。纪律的另一层意思指为保证员工行为有序,遵守规则而采取的行动。

Discipline: The discipline has two meanings. One is a kind of behaviour rules that ask people to abide and carry out orders and perform their duties in the collective life, work and study. The other refers to take action to ensure employees' behaviors and abide of the rules.

复习思考题(Questions for Review)

1. Why staff turnover rate is so high in the Hospitality Industry?
饭店业员工流失率高的原因有哪些?
2. How to solve the problem of high turnover rate in the Hospitality Industry?
如何解决饭店业员工高流动率的问题?
3. What is the meaning of discipline?
什么是纪律?
4. Compare hot-stove rule method with progressive discipline.
对比一下红热炉法和分级惩处法。
5. What's the advantage of positive discipline compared to negative discipline?
与消极的纪律管理相比,积极的纪律管理有什么优点?

研究前沿(Research Front)

The purpose of this study was to examine the effects of scarcity of resources, favoritism, and organizational support as antecedents on organizational politics perceptions of frontline staff and the effect of these perceptionson their turnover intention in Cypriot hotels as its setting.

Hypothesized model of perceptions of organizational politics

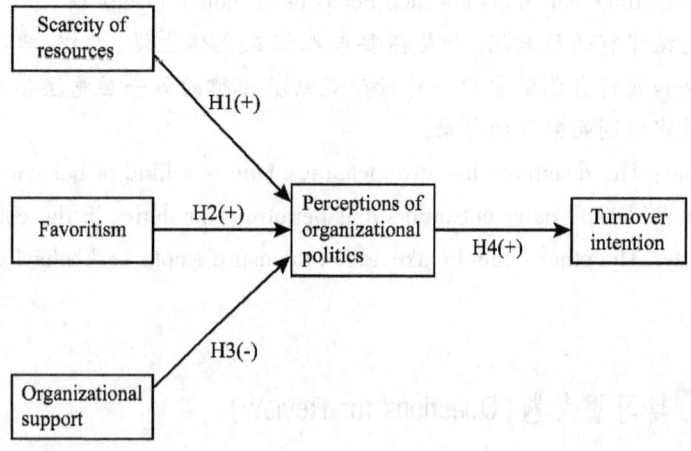

Figure 1

Methodology

To test the proposed model, a survey of frontline employees was conducted.

Constructs and measures

As outlined in the model, relationship between five constructs-favoritism, organizational politics, organization support, scarcity of resources and turnover intention was tested. Measurements for the seconstructs were adopted from the existing measures that had been used in the relevant literature. Forall items, a five-point response scale was used, ranging from 1 – strongly disagree to 5 – strongly agree.

Survey instrument

To test the proposed model a questionnaire was used, consisting of two parts. The first part consistedof 19 items relating to favoritism, organizational politics, organizational support, scarcity of resources, and turnover intentions. The second part of the questionnaire consisted of demographic questions-gender, education and organizational tenure. Education and organizational tenure were measuredusing four-point categorical scales. Gender, on the other hand, was dichotomous variable (1 = male and 2 = female). The questions were initially prepared in English and then translated to Turkish usingthe back-translation method (McGorry, 2000). Thequestionnaire was designed for self-completionand pilot tested on a convenience sample of 15 supervisors. As a result of pilot-test, no reason wasfound to change the survey instrument. Pilot-testing did not indicate any problems with the clarity of question. It was revealed that there was ten minute required to complete the questionnaire and it was considered acceptable.

Data analysis

The Statistical Package for Social Sciences Version 18 was used to explore the data. As for statistical techniques, firstly, reliability (Cronbach's alpha) and validity tests were conducted. Next, mean scorewas employed to observe average responses. The exploratory factor analyses were performed in orderto test the assumptions for issues of dimensionality and convergent validity and correlation analysis was carried out in order to ascertain the strength and the direction of association between the items. Finally, in order to test the proposed model outlined in Figure 1, regression analysis were carried out.

Results

Psychometric properties of the measures

The exploratory factor analyses were performed in order to test the assumptions for issues of dimensionality and convergent validity. There was a reasonable fit of the five-factor measurement model tothe data. To test construct reliability, Cronbach's alpha coefficient was used…In order to test whether the distribution of values was adequate for conducting analysis, the Kaiser-Meyer-Olkin (KMO) measure of sampling adequacy was used and all constructs exceeded the threshold value of 0.50 (favoritism = 0.810, organizational support = 0.727, scarcity of resources = 0.659, organizational politics = 0.918, and turnover intention = 0.645) as suggested by Field (2000). In addition, Bartlett's test of sphericity measure indicated that the multivariate normality of theset of distributions was normal for the all constructs, showing a significant value, $p = 0.000$ (<0.05). Therefore, the data was appropriate for conducting the factor analysis (Hair, Anderson, Tatham &Black, 1998). In observing the commonalities, all item loadings were found to be significant following threshold of 0.50 recommended by Barclay, Thompson, and Higgins (1995).

Correlation analysis results

The mean value ranged from 1.90 to 3.78 and the standard deviation from 0.84 to 1.31. Specifically, favoritism was positively associated with politics perceptions ($r = 0.893$, $p < 0.01$) and turnover intention ($r = 0.542$, $p < 0.01$), meaning that frontline supervisors perceived more politics when favoritism dominated their organizational environments which, in turn, increased their turnover intentions. On the other hand, organizational support was negatively correlated with organizational politics

($r = -0.865$, $p < 0.01$). This result reveals that organizational support decreases political behaviors. Scarcity of resources has positive correlation with politics perceptions ($r = 0.701$, $p < 0.01$), such that political behaviors increase in the work environment where resources are scarce. Also, politics perceptions was positively correlated with turnover intention ($r = 0.573$, $p < 0.01$). This suggests that supervisors' perceptions of politics increase their turnover intentions.

Model test

Pairwise and multiple variable collinearity were inspected by collinearity diagnostics in SPSS prior to analysis. The tolerance values were found well above the commonly accepted threshold value of 0.10 (Hair, Anderson, Tatham ôc Black, 2005) and none of the variance inflation factor (VIF) values exceeded 10.

Hypothesis 1 suggested that scarcity of resources (SCAR) is positively associated with perception of organizational politics (POP). The results of path analysis lent empirical support to this relationship. Hypothesis 1 was therefore supported. Hypothesis 2 predicted that favoritism (FAVO) exerts a significant positive effect on supervisors' politics perceptions. The effect of favoritism on politics perceptions was both significant and positive. Hypothesis 2 was therefore supported. Hypothesis 3 stated that organizational support (OS) has a significant negative influence on supervisors' politics perceptions. According to the results of the path analysis, the negative effect of organizational support on politics perceptions was significant. Hypothesis 3 was therefore supported. Scarcity of resources, favoritism, and organizational support jointly explained 85% of the variance in perceptions of organizational politics. Finally, hypothesis 4 suggested that politics perceptions have positive impact on supervisor's turnover intentions (TINT). The results of the path analysis also provided empirical support for this hypothesized relationship. Hypothesis 4 was thus supported. Politics perceptions explained 32% of the variance in turnover intention.

Discussion and conclusions

Based on the recent extant literature findings, insufficient empirical attention has been devoted to the impacts of scarce resources, favoritism, and organizational support on employees' politics perceptions which, in turn, affects their turnover intentions (e.g., Poon, 2003; Kacmar et al., 1999; Kwon, 2006; Arasli ôc Tumer, 2008; Valle & Perrewé 2000; Cropanzano et al., 1997). Thus, the aim of this study was to measure the effects of scarce resources, favoritism, and organizational support as antecedents onfrontline supervisors' perceptions of organizational politics and, in turn, their influence on intention to quit employment. To this end, an integrative model of aforementioned impacts and relationships was developed and tested. All hypothesized relationships were supported.

...

The findings concerning the effect of favoritism on politics perceptions are concordant with the study hypothesis and previous research (e. g., Adams, 1965; Kwon, 2006). The current empirical evidence shows that discriminating work environment is dominant in hotel sector in North Cyprus, where hotel executives have been practicing unfair actions in personnel recruitment, selection, appraisal, promotion and disciplinary procedures. In other words, the hotel executives have been engaged in unfair activities under the pressure of favoritism. Consequently, working in an unfair competitive environment encourages employees to exhibit political behaviors characterized by manipulation and self-serving behaviors. They might withdraw from the job mentally, become uncommitted to their hotels and lose interest in their work involvement, cooperation with their coworkers and coordination in their hotel's activities.

The results of the path analysis also demonstrate that organizational support has a significant negative effect on politics perceptions. This relationship is consistent with that of Hochwarter et al. (2003). The current result claims that support by the hotel managements in the form of rewards, performance feedback, skill variety, autonomy, job security, training, salary, supervisory support, empowerment, teamclimate, rewards and career opportunities make supervisors to perceive less politics in their working environments. Moreover, there is a positive relationship between organizational politics and turnover intention. Results of this study bring empirical support to the proposed relationship. This result suggests that working environment prevalent with politics leads supervisors to harbor thoughts of quitting.

Managerial implications

The employees are vital sources of tourism and hospitality firms' success and competitive advantage (e. g., Pfeffer & Sutton, 2006; Wirtz, Heracleous & Nitin, 2008). Owing to the unfavorable impacts of employee turnover, it is crucial for hotel owners and managers in service setting to be aware of how to keep star performing employees to achieve organizational goals in the long run. The findings of this study conjure up some practical implications and offer normative guidelines that can be usedin managing frontline supervisor turnover. Contingently, the prominent implication of this study is that management must revise the existing policies or take decisive steps to devise new policies and procedures to generate a work environment where politics is minimized.

As already alluded to, as most of the islands economies. North Cyprus is an island country with small business market, where the economy depends mainly on agriculture and tourism. Consequently, the job market is very competitive with limited job opportunities and incentives such as promotion, payrises, social insurance, fringe benefits, pension funds, training, and career opportunities. This, in turn, triggers the spread of organizational politics. Hotel owners/managers should be aware of this and allocate their limited resources in a transparent manner that benefits everyone. In addition, they should establish a control mechanism in order to efficiently use organizational resources and new policies and procedures may be needed to punish arrogance and unfair practices.

The current study demonstrates that favoritism provides benefits solely to the relatives and close friends rather than the organization as a whole. Society of North Cyprus, as a small island country, is characterized by multiple social connections of each member through political party membership orassociation, kinship relations and close friendships. The hotel executives in Northern Cyprus generally tend to hire, promote or reward their relatives or acquaintances instead of looking for professional knowledge, training, and skills of applicants. Such practice is more frequent for supervisory and managerial positions that require more job experience, skills and knowledge. This kind of favoritism may lead really skilled and high performer employees or supervisors to be demoralized and to neglect their responsibilities and minimize their real working performance (Arasli & Tumer, 2008). Since the job opportunities are limited because of scarce resources and current economic stagnations in the hospitality industry in North Cyprus, supervisors may not think of leaving their jobs even if they are not happy with their jobs. But, working in an environment dominant with favoritism practices may lead supervisors to exhibit manipulation and self-serving behaviors (politics) in the form of establishing close ties with hotel executives and their relatives or close friends in order to secure their positions rather than by showing real performance. Thus, in the long term, favoritism paralyzes the human resource practices, organizational efficiency, and organizational trust between the staff which, in turn, negatively influence customer service quality. Hotel management needs to be aware that higher level of perceived justice lead staff to be more responsible involved and committed to their organizations(Harris, Andrews & Kacmar, 2007).

The present study also reveals that organizational support decreases supervisors' politics perceptions. Exclusively, a supervisory position is crucial and role modeling in hospitality organizations. They have a close control over employees at the time of service offered to customers. Hereby, the hotel executives should spend time with supervisors through socialization and job training actions. Supportive organizations are seen as taking pride in their personnel, paying and rewarding them fairly, looking after their needs and caring their career development and general satisfaction at work. Organizational goals and policies should be devised to support the supervisors or employees in their jobs. Executives should hire mentors who are additional models for perceived organizational support and job autonomy and provide functions in the categories of vocational support and role modeling (Lankau, Garlson& Nielson, 2006). As a result, if hotel organizations desire to maintain a work environment where supervisors can cope with difficulties related with organizational politics. They should establish justice and teamwork climate in personnel, offer career opportunities, job security, performance feedback, training and delegate authority when necessary.

The last finding of this empirical research is that organizational politics enhance the supervisors' turnover intentions. Hotel executives should mitigate the impact of politics perceptions on turnover intentions which may turn to real turnover. Replacing employees may be costly and time consuming, both, inrecruiting and training employees to reach optimal levels of performance over time (Gollins & Smith, 2006). Additionally, high levels of employee turnover may impede the quality, consistency and stability of services that organizations provide to customers (Trevor of Nyberg, 2008) and, in turn, detrimentally affect customer satisfaction with the services provided by the organization (Lin & Chang, 2005).

Limitations and future research directions

Although this study has contributed to the current body of research into organizational politics and its consequences, expanding it to different cultural setting, it is not without limitation.

Firstly, the cross-sectional design of this study does not permit to make causal inferences. Futurestudies conducting longitudinal designs would be helpful in establishing causal relationships. Equally important, as organizational politics are complex, the future studies might benefit from a qualitative approach to provide richer insights into the antecedents and outcomes associated with organizational politics. Second limitation presents the reliance on self-reported data from frontline supervisors. Such data are prone to common-method variance (Doty & Glick, 1998). To minimize common-method variance, future research should use multiple-informants and, for instance, measure organizational politics perceptions from both management and employee side. To cross-validate our findings and extend the scope for further generalizations, replication studies between other samples of hotel personnel in North Gyprus are also needed. Likewise, future research might examine these relationships indifferent service settings such as restaurants, travel agents and airlines. In addition, inclusion of controlvariables (gender, education and tenure) in the model would enhance the understanding concerning their moderating roles on the perceptions.

Source: Mustafa Daskin & Murat Tezer. Organizational politics and turnover: An empirical research from hospitality industry. Original Scientific Paper, 2012,3:273-291.

第 9 章 压力、健康、EAP 与职业发展
(Pressure, Health, EAP and Career Development)

> **本章概要(Summary of This Chapter)**
>
> 本章内容重点聚焦于工作个体在组织工作过程中会产生的压力的种类，形成压力的原因，由于压力的产生造成的对心理以及对工作绩效的影响，通过对压力的管理，使员工压力转化为员工健康，提高工作效率。其次介绍了员工帮助计划在组织中的运用，并协助员工进行职业发展规划，促进个体和组织的有效发展。
>
> This chapter focuses on the types of pressure of individuals in the organization during work process, the causes of pressure formed, the impact on mental and job performance due to the pressure caused by stress and try to transfer the work stress into employee-wellness through stress managementso as to improve work efficiency. Secondly, it also introduces the operation of Employee Assistance Program in the organization, to assist staff to make career development planning, and promote the effective development both for individuals and organizations.

开篇引例(Beginning Story)

Stress Levels and Stress Sources of Executives around the World

A common stereotype in the United States is the highly stressed, top-level business executive (Friedman, Hall, & Harris, 1985). Is this characterization accurate, and if so, are high-level managers in other nations similarly stressed? The first question—"are executives highly stressed?"—does not have an easy answer. For example, many executives constantly work under such stressful conditions as work overload, high levels of responsibility, and interrole conflict. The finding that executives have a higher rate of certain types of ulcers than certain blue-collar workers attests to the existence of executive stress (Hurrell, Murphy, Sauter, & Cooper, 1988).

The answer to the question of whether executives worldwide experience similar stressors is also not complete clear. There is some indication, however, that executives in different nations experience different types or sources of stress. For example, executives in less developed countries such as Nigeria and Egypt seem to experience a great deal of stress due to lack of autonomy, while those from more developed countries, such as the U.S., and the United Kingdom, experience greater stress from work overload (Cooper & Hensman, 1985).

An interesting study by Kirkcaldy and Cooper (1993) found some evidence that work stress for executives may be modified by preference for leisure activities—and that preferred leisure activities may be related to culture. For example, managers from Germany, who tend to prefer nonaggressive leisure activities, experienced less job stress than British managers, who typically prefer aggressive leisure activities.

Overall, such studies seem to indicate that while job stress is universal, the amount of stress experienced, and the sources of the stress, may vary depending on country or culture.

第一节 工作压力与健康
(Working Pressure and Health)

一、工作压力(Working Pressure)

(一)工作压力与压力源(Working Pressure and Stressor)

1. 压力的定义

压力是指当环境或内在要求超出个体的适应性资源时所出现的生理或心理上的紧张状态。

工作压力的定义存在着一定的分歧,一般从以下三种模式来界定。

(1)以刺激为基础的模式

工作压力是作用于个人的力量或刺激,从而导致人的紧张反应,压力是人对外界的刺激所引起的生理紧张、恐惧等,是人的一种生理反应。例如,Authur, Randall & Mary (1981)认为工作压力不是人们与工作特性发生变化时之交互作用,而是人们的正常功能产生脱序的现象。

(2) 以反映为基础的模式

将压力视为个体对环境的压力源的生理或心理上的反应。此定义认为压力是以各种可见方式表现的内在反应,即研究受测者在困难环境下产生的生理与心理反应。例如,王信景(1992)认为工作压力是工作者在工作情境中受到某些工作特性的影响,所引发的心理影响反应程度。

(3) 交互作用模式

压力是环境的刺激与人特殊反应彼此互动的结果,即工作压力是一种处理方式,主要在研究个人与环境互动式的关系。例如,Robbins(1994)认为工作压力是个体在面对与期望事物有关的机会、限制或要求时,知觉到这个结构很重要,但又充满不确定性所处的一种动态状况。

人是否感觉到压力取决于四个基本因素:个体对环境的认知、个体过去的经历、是否具有社会支持、压力反应的个体差异(如图9-1)。

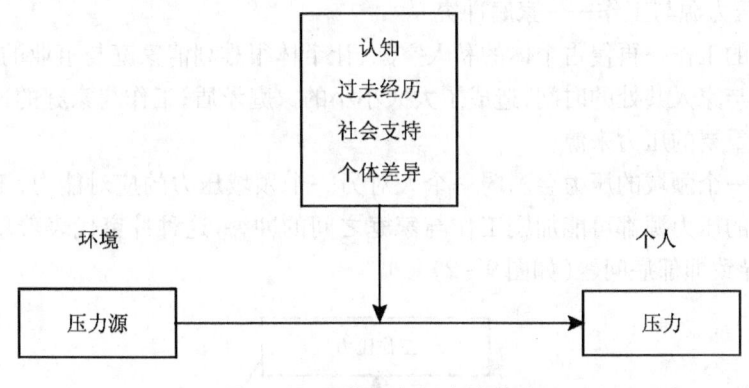

图9-1 压力源与压力的关系

2. 压力源

(1) 工作环境的压力源

①工作负荷:繁重的本职工作,长时间的加班,需要不间断学习的新知识,沉重的工作负荷让个体感到不堪忍受,即使回到家里也难以放下。

②个体职责:由于工作的性质,个体不得不在工作中经常做出重大的决定,承担一定的风险和责任,这种情况为个体带来了极大的压力。

③工作自主:不能自主地安排工作时间,总要跟着别人的步调前进,对自己工作的环境和资源不能自由控制,这一切都让个体的工作充满了烦扰,使个体感到了很大压力。

④日常烦扰:不断推陈出新的改革措施,繁多的临时任务,不时要出席的会议,虽然不是大事,但由于它们的存在,也会使个体感到了很大的压力。

⑤职业发展:晋升的机会渺茫,晋升的途径单一,缺乏个人发展的机会,这一切都使个体看不清自己职业发展的前景,感到心理上的压力。

⑥管理角色:作为管理者,在做好自己本职的基础上,既要监督、协调下属的工作,又要努力完成上级下达的任务,这些让个体在工作、生活中有了很大的压力。

⑦人际关系:对领导管理的不满,与同事之间的冲突,为个体的工作和生活带来了不可避免的麻烦,让个体很难保有愉快的心情。

⑧组织气氛:饭店组织结构的僵化,员工士气的低迷,工作氛围的不和谐,都对个体的工作积极性产生了很大的影响,使个体感到了压力。

⑨角色冲突:工作中管理者下达指令的不一致,使个体感到没有规则可依,导致工作达不到领导的要求,给个体的心理带来了很大的压力。

⑩角色模糊:工作的权利和责任划分不清,搞不清工作对自己的要求和自己必须完成的工作内容,使个体的工作处于混乱之中,因而感到了极大的压力。

(2)压力源与工作——家庭冲突

繁忙的工作一再侵占个体的私人空间,让个体很难划清家庭与事业的界限,缩短了个体与家人共处的时间,造成了大大小小的家庭矛盾;工作与家庭的冲突已经成为个体重要的压力来源。

由于一个领域的压力会削弱一个人对另一个领域压力的应对能力,工作和家庭两方面的压力源都可能加剧工作与家庭之间的冲突,这种冲突代表着新的压力源,可能导致抑郁症问题(如图9-2)。

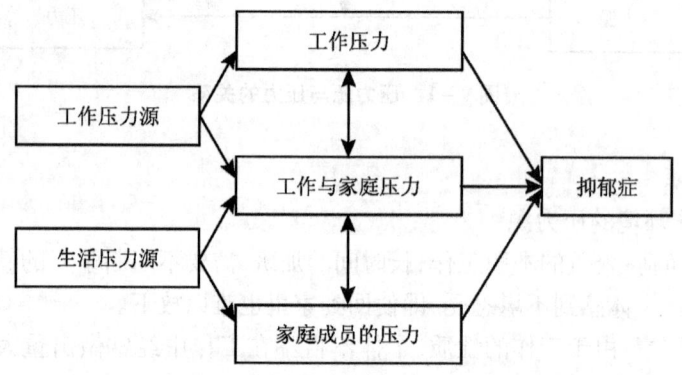

图9-2 压力源与工作——家庭冲突

(3)饭店工作的压力源

①饭店工作压力源的因素分析

据国内学者的实证研究中对调查数据的分析结果表明,饭店员工工作压力的影响因素中重要性排位前十的依次是如下几个方面：工作加班加点、薪酬福利与付出不对称、评估指标定得过高、工作中的多头领导、提升晋级不明确、工作中无参与决策权且无上司同事的帮助、工作节奏太快、工作时间安排不合理、考核制度严格、工作超出能力以及工作范围不明确。

归纳一下，饭店工作的压力源表现在如下三个方面：

由于饭店业的工作性质本身对员工造成的心理压力。"客人总是对的""客人是上帝"等服务原则使员工感到自己不被尊重，在服务的过程中心理失衡。面对激烈的市场竞争和客人服务需求的提升，饭店必须不断提高服务质量、降低经营成本，最直接的表现就是加班加点。为了增加营业收入，许多饭店经营管理者给员工拟定了超出日常工作外的销售指标，比如推销月饼、圣诞节套票等。即使不与绩效考核指标直接挂钩，在员工的攀比中也增加了一些无形的心理压力。

由于饭店的层级管理严格造成的心理压力。"官大一级压死人"在饭店行业非常明显，不少员工看到穿深色西装的管理人员就产生畏惧情绪。在人本化管理盛行的今天，很多饭店依旧沿袭过去的"准军事化管理"，员工没有话语权，一切行动听指挥，自主性和创造性均被压抑，产生较大的心理压力。

由于职业发展方向不明造成的心理压力。从事饭店行业工作的大多是20多岁的年轻人，正值职业发展的黄金时期，他们对未来充满了梦想，然而许多饭店没有对员工的职业生涯发展进行规划和指导，员工感觉前途一片渺茫，每天只是疲于应付眼前的工作，勉强度日。职业发展的困惑造成巨大的心理压力。

②饭店工作压力源的聚类分析

一项研究中对饭店工作压力源诸因素进行了聚类分析（采用Pearson correlation度量），绘制成聚类分析可知，21个影响饭店员工工作压力的因素可以聚为以下六个类别：角色模糊、角色过载、角色冲突、社会竞争、控制感、社会支持。由数据分析结果我们可以看出，员工的压力主要来自于工作上的角色模糊、角色过载和角色冲突，其次为控制感和社会竞争。结合以上结果在管理实践中体现为：

角色模糊。由于饭店工作的复杂性，客人不同需求不同特点会带来很多突发事件和特殊事件，SOP（Standard Operation Procedure的缩写，标准作业程序）和P&P（policy and processes的缩写，政策与程序）只能保证日常工作的进行，对于这些突发和特殊的紧急事件的处理，饭店职责权利的划分会造成角色模糊，产生心理压力。

角色过载。饭店是24小时全天候工作的行业，在经营旺季或接待大型团队客人时连续加班是经常的，体力和脑力的严重透支危害了饭店员工的身体和心理健康。现代饭店重视细节化服务，每一个让客人满意的服务项目都包含着饭店员工的艰辛努力。追求极致的服务理念创造了饭店的辉煌，也增加了员工巨大的心理压力。

角色冲突。在饭店服务中员工既要考虑客人的需求，又要顾及饭店的利益，既要做到客人满意又要控制成本,既要尊重客人又要维护自己的尊严,许多饭店员工经常面临这样的两难选择。饭店的管理人员还要处理业主方和管理公司之间的关系、上下级之间的矛盾、协调更多方面的关系,心理压力更大。

Tips: Ways to Alleviate Dysfunctional Stress

There are a number of ways to alleviate dysfunctional stress. These range from commonsense remedies (such as getting more sleep and eating better) to more exotic remedies like biofeedback and meditation. Finding a more suitable job, getting counseling, and planning and organizing each day's activities are other sensible responses. In his book *Stress and the Manager*, Dr. Karl Albrecht suggests the following ways for a person to reduce job stress.

1. Build rewarding, pleasant, cooperative relationships with colleagues and employees.
2. Don't bite off more than you can chew.
3. Build an especially effective and supportive relationship with your boss.
4. Negotiate with your boss for realistic deadlines on important projects.
5. Learn as much as you can about upcoming events and get as much lead time as you can to prepare for them.
6. Find time everyday for detachment and relaxation.
7. Take a walk around the office to keep your body refreshed and alert.
8. Find ways to reduce unnecessary noise.
9. Reduce the amount of trivia in your job; delegate routine work whenever possible.
10. Limit interruptions.
11. Don't put off dealing with distasteful problems.
12. Make a constructive "worry list" that includes solutions for each problem.

The employer and its HR specialists and supervisors can also play a role in identifying and reducing job stress. Supportive supervisors and fair treatment are two obvious steps. Based on a survey of 1299 employers by one insurance company, other steps include:

1. Reduce personal conflicts on the job.
2. Have open communication between management and employees.
3. Support employees' efforts, for instance, by regularly asking how they are doing.

4. Ensure effective job-person fit, since a mistake can trigger stress.
5. Give employees more control over their jobs.
6. Provide employee assistance programs including professional counseling.

Source: Albrecht K. Stress and the Manager[M]. Simon and Schuster.com, 2010.

(二) 工作压力与绩效 (Working Pressure and Performance)

如图9-3所示，在压力不足的阶段，员工在工作中可能不够活跃，没有得到足够的鞭策，不会全身心投入而尽其所能。觉得工作乏味、缺乏挑战性，集中干劲和注意力到工作上的动机很小，从而绩效很低。

随着工作压力的逐渐增大，员工受到激发，绩效得到提高。提高一点压力就可能在一定范围内提高绩效。在压力达到最佳点之前，工作压力越大，绩效越高。大部分工作都有一个最佳压力范围，超过这个范围，绩效就开始下滑。

当工作压力超过最佳点后，压力越大，绩效越低。压力过度，员工就会过分焦虑、急躁、亢奋或感到有威胁等状态，难以尽心尽力地工作，压力再过剩，甚至使人走向崩溃。

当我们完成工作任务的压力非常小时，我们觉得工作乏味、缺乏挑战性，集中干劲和注意力到工作上的动机很小，从而绩效很低。

在绩效最高点附近的绩效区，称为最佳绩效区。在绩效最高点附近的压力区，称为最佳压力区。如何通过压力管理，将工作压力保持在最佳压力区，进而使绩效处于最佳绩效区，是压力管理的主要任务之一。

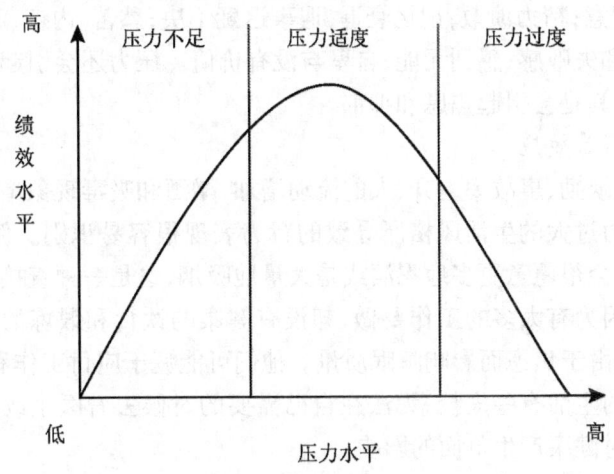

图9-3 工作压力与绩效关系

二、健康与压力管理(Health and Stress Management)

(一)压力与健康(Stress and Health)

研究表明,许多疾病,如高血压、心脏病、消化系统疾病以及各种恶性肿瘤疾病都与压力水平高度相关,压力已经成为影响个体健康的一个重要因素。一般来说,压力对人体健康的影响包括生理、心理以及行为上的变化。

工作压力与健康的关系主要体现在三个方面:

1. 压力的生理效应

如血压升高、心跳加快、出汗、发冷发热、呼吸困难、肌肉紧张和肠胃功能紊乱。压力引发的某些生理疾病可能有致命的危险,例如高血压和心脏病,其次是失眠、长期疲劳、头痛、红疹、消化系统紊乱、溃疡、结肠炎、食欲不振、暴食、恶心等。其中许多病症都是在紧张事件之后发作的。而其他症状更具即时性,如恶心、窒息或口干舌燥。尽管这些症状也可能是其他因素引起的,但毫无疑问,压力是不容忽视的一个重要因素。研究发现,压力还会削弱人体的免疫系统,这也揭示了为什么我们在压力状况下更容易患病(例如感冒或流行性感冒)。压力还可能会加重一些自身免疫性疾病的症状,例如风湿性关节炎等。压力还可能会引起头疼、肠部症状,而且当前研究已经证明,压力与癌症之间存在一定关系。

2. 压力的情感效应

压力引发的情绪症状包括经常动怒、严重焦虑、消沉沮丧、缺乏性欲、丧失幽默感、对最简单的日常事务也无法集中精力,辨认自身或他人压力的关键是了解反常的情绪反应。如对自身外表、他人、社会事件及以往感兴趣的事情(比如热衷的体育运动)不再留意;精力溃散,记忆衰退,遇事迟疑不决;愁苦、内疚、疲劳、冷漠以及切身的无助感和失败感;感到无能、自卑与没有价值。压力还会引起一些精神健康方面的问题,尤其是会引起焦虑和抑郁。

3. 压力的行为效应

绩效下降、缺勤、事故率上升、人的流动增加、酗酒和吸毒现象增加、行为冲动、交际困难。压力过大的生活风格所导致的行为表现很容易识别。例如,当处于压力之下时,人们会很愿意更多地喝酒或是大量地吸烟,这是一种直接的压力缓解方式。还有些人因为有太多的工作要做,却没有健康的饮食和锻炼的安排。他们会减少睡眠,或是由于焦虑而影响睡眠质量。他们可能疲于应付工作和日常的压力,以至于对自己的生活有些失控,无法在自己需要的时候去看医生或是牙医。所有这些情况都会对健康产生负面的影响。

表9-1 压力小测试

	请回想一下自己在过去一个月内有否出现下述情况：	
1	觉得手上工作太多，无法应付。	
2	觉得时间不够用，所以要分秒必争。例如过马路时闯红灯，走路和说话的节奏很快速。	
3	觉得没有时间消遣，终日记挂着工作。	
4	遇到挫败时很容易会发脾气。	
5	担心别人对自己工作表现的评价。	
6	觉得上司和家人都不欣赏自己。	
7	担心自己的经济状况。	
8	有头痛/胃痛/背痛的毛病，难于治愈。	
9	需要借烟酒、药物、零食等抑制不安的情绪。	
10	需要借助安眠药去协助入睡。	
11	与家人/朋友/同事的相处令你发脾气。	
12	与人倾谈时，打断对方的话题。	
13	上床后觉得思潮起伏，很多事情牵挂，难以入睡。	
14	太多工作，不能每件事做到尽善尽美。	
15	当空闲时轻松一下也会觉得内疚。	
16	做事急躁、任性而事后感到内疚。	
17	觉得自己不应该享乐。	
计分方法：从未发生0分，偶尔发生1分，经常发生2分。		
0~10分精神压力程度低但可能显示生活缺乏刺激，比较简单沉闷，个人做事的动力不高。		
11~15分精神压力程度中等，虽然某些时候感到压力较大，仍可应付。		
16分或以上精神压力偏高，应反省一下压力来源和寻求解决办法。		
上述的测试主要是引发大家对精神健康的关注，若发现分数不理想或不切合你的状况，请不必介怀。		

(二) **压力管理**(Stress Management)

1. **压力管理的原则**

(1) 适度原则

进行压力管理并不是不顾组织的经济效益而一味减轻员工压力、最大化员工满意度，而是要适度。

(2) 具体原则

由于压力在很大程度上是一个主观感觉，因此在进行压力管理时要区别不同的对象,采取不同的策略,根据对象的不同特点做到具体问题具体分析。

(3)岗位原则

组织中不同部门、不同岗位的员工面临的工作压力不同。一般岗位级别越高,创新性越强,独立性越高的员工,承受的压力也就越大。比如销售人员的压力一般比生产人员要大,因为生产人员面对的更多是可控因素,而销售人员就不一样,销售业绩的好坏不仅取决于自己努力的程度,还与客户、市场大环境、竞争对手有关系。

(4)引导原则

由于压力的产生是不可避免的,所以引导压力向积极的一面发展就显得很重要。对员工来说,有些外部因素是不可控的,比如面对强大的竞争对手,这时可以灵活地将压力变为动力,激发更大的工作热情。

(5)区别原则

在消除压力前,首先要找出压力的来源并区别对待。有些压力是可以避免的,比如由于员工之间不团结,人际关系复杂造成的工作压力,岗位职责不清,分工不合理所造成的压力;而有些压力,比如来自工作本身的压力是不可避免的,只有通过提高员工自身的工作能力和心理承受能力来解决。

2.压力应对的方式

人们面对压力做出的反应主要有三种,即控制式、支持式、回避式。学者们建议管理者在应对压力时主要应该采用控制式应对方式,适度采用支持式应对方式,尽量少用或不用回避式应对方式。

(1)控制式应对方式

一种以问题为中心的应对方式,指积极主动地针对不同压力做出反应,如进行有效的时间管理等,是最优的压力应对方式。这种应对方式主要通过改变人的行为或改善周围环境,进而调整自己的情绪状态与个人、环境的关系。管理者在应对压力时,可以:尝试用客观、理智的方法处理事情;有效地分配时间;预先做好计划;选择性地把精力集中在某些具体问题上;将问题按轻重缓急排列并依次处理;尝试从旁观者的角度考虑事情等。

(2)支持式应对方式

一般利用个人或社会的资源支持来对压力做出反应,如寻求压力的释放或进行压力的宣泄等。支持式的应对行为主要有:借助兴趣及消遣,比如运动、画画、散步、旅行、健身等;向理解自己的亲人/朋友倾诉等。这种应对方式的不足之处是过于依赖环境和资源,一旦支持的资源发生匮乏就会导致压力适应紊乱。

(3)回避式应对方式

这种应对方式消极地忽略或回避压力,甚至否认压力的存在,当压力慢慢累积超过一定界限后,就会造成个人的突然崩溃。回避式应对是一种以情绪为中心的应对,它并不改变人与环境的客观关系,而是调节由压力引起的情感上的不适。它最基本的策略就是转移注意的焦点,避免思考引起压力的原因。当个体认为自己对所处环境不能做任何事时,情绪为中心的应对将占主要位置。常见的回避式应对行为主要有:不去考虑它;不相信那是真的;把问题先放一段时间再说;认为有些事情并不是那么重要,不需要太认真;避开麻烦;不再强求自己;想想有人状况还不如自己,心里舒服一些;顺其自然,平心静气等。

小贴士:工作压力的处理

- 设意见箱。
- 开放讨论工作问题。
- 午休时间游泳或散步可缓和压力。
- 拟订全部方案先进行思考。
- 设置支持系统帮助有压力的同事。
- 决定使用何种策略处置压力前先检视企业自身的资源。
- 改进午餐菜色并鼓励健康饮食。
- 要每天轻松开始工作,得在前一天清理桌面。
- 休息片刻时赏玩您有兴趣的事务。
- 在安置新的办公室时更新室内布置。
- 当你调入新工作地点,花费时间思考如何会更愉快。
- 当你出现压力请同事告知自己。
- 快速记录每天基本的问题,看是否有一定的模式。
- 设定现实目标,免常受挫于截止日。
- 勿要求他人提供力所不能及的协助。
- 若有紧急事要求同事电话联络。
- 工作一小时以上休息五分钟。
- 当事情做完在待办清单上删除,看到事情减少有满足感。
- 传达必要的讯息给对方。
- 记下待回复的讯息并追踪。
- 一早做写信、传真等工作,避免因疲倦时沟通技巧变差。
- 勿忽视你的问题,当它们发生时予以确认。
- 运动可以短效解决愤怒。
- 诚实面对拒绝工作的理由。

- 不要在有压力的情况下,仓促地做重要决定。
- 学瑜伽或相类似运动助您放松。
- 协助在压力下的同事做好时间安排。
- 帮助处在压力下的同事解决它们的问题。
- 提供处在压力下的同事一些建议、妙法。
- 鼓励同事将问题视为机会。
- 尊重他人意见,勿觉得你一向都是对的。
- 建议在一个时间专注于一件工作。
- 确定工作人员一起工作是能共处的。
- 列出所有合适人选可协助同事因应危机。
- 鼓励工作人员彼此支持。
- 开会不超过半小时。
- 将日常工作排序,优先做最重要的。

3. 自我减压技巧

饭店员工通过冥想训练、放松训练、呼吸调节、运动、瑜伽、静坐、催眠、想象等方式都可以起到减轻压力的作用。下面简单介绍两种减压技巧:

(1) 冥想训练法

冥想的方法是抵御压力、排遣忧郁、烦恼等否定的情绪状态的措施中最有帮助的心理学技能之一。冥想的作用在于:可以训练注意力;可以增加对思维过程的控制;可以提高处理情感的能力;可以帮助身体放松。

冥想的过程是"选择一个目标或经历,然后沉着地对它聚焦。随着思想的出现,我们便拒绝脱离已选定的目标或经历,不作任何抛开思想或阻止其出现的努力。不论这些思想好与坏、乐与悲,我们都任其出入我们的头脑,不紧紧纠缠,不让它们偏离正常的判断或联想"。

下面介绍冥想的步骤:

① 选择一个你不太可能被打搅的时间和地点,关掉电话或将话筒摘下来。

② 坐在直立的椅子上,或双腿交叉盘坐于硬垫之上,双手轻握放在大腿上,整个过程中保持上身直立,别让头或肩倾斜或背部朝后倒,保持这种直立姿势,同时尽可能放松肌肉。

③ 闭上双眼,把注意集中于呼吸,别紧张,保持一切轻松自然。

④ 让自己对呼吸的感觉占据你的全部意识,无论你聚焦于鼻孔还是腹部,都把

对呼吸的感觉作为焦点。不要从鼻孔又转到腹部,反之亦然。选择一个焦点并坚持,别让注意力随呼吸而转向全身,可以让它在所选位置上休息休息。

⑤如果你在记数,那么呼第一口气时默数1,第二次数2,第三次数3,一直数到10,然后往回数,每一次呼气一直数到1,再往回数到10,如此循环往复。倘若在记数过程中走了神,那么,回到1,从头开始。

⑥当各种想法出现时,既不要随它跑,也不要赶跑它,不论其内容如何,均不要判断其"好"与"坏"。只把注意集中于呼吸,不要聚焦于想法,让它出入你的头脑,既不追随,也不阻止。

⑦冥想过程结束后,慢慢从座位上站起来,在你从事各项活动时,保持住冥想过程中体验到的平衡意识(不论多简单)。用你意识呼吸的方法去努力意识周围的所见所闻,不要急于将它们概念化,不要急于对它们下结论,也不要急于脱离联想链。

(2)放松训练法

放松训练法是使身体和精神从意识要求中解脱出来,使紧张得以缓解的方法。

饭店员工经常处于紧张的工作状态之中,在工作中也常常会遇到复杂的人际关系情况,而旅游企业又要求饭店员工在工作中必须始终保持轻松愉快的心情去为旅游者提供服务,所以学习和掌握一些放松调节方法,有效地控制和调整情绪状态对于饭店员工是十分必要的。

下面介绍身体的放松和头脑的放松两个程序:

放松程序1——身体的放松

①选择一间安静的屋子和一段你不太可能被人打扰的时间。

②宽衣解带。

③平躺在地板或坚硬地面上。

④使你的右脚和右臂肌肉紧张,扭动脚趾,感觉如何?收紧肌肉,再放松,反复做几次,注意收紧和放松时感觉上的不同,记住它。

⑤左脚和左臂重复同样的练习。

⑥收紧小腿肌肉,先右后左,重复几遍收紧肌和放松,注意两种状态的不同感觉,记住它。

⑦接下来是大腿肌肉,也进行同样练习,注意大腿的紧张是如何影响膝盖和膝关节的。

⑧再移到臀部和肛门(容易产生不必要紧张的位置),再一次注意紧张和松弛状态的不同感觉。

⑨向上轮流练习腹部、胸部、背部和肩膀的肌肉。

⑩练习二头肌、前臂和手。

⑪最后移到脖颈、下颌、脸部、前额和头皮。

放松程序2——使头脑平静

①选一个你不太可能被打搅的安静的屋子和时间。

②平躺在一个软硬随你选的表面上。

③闭上双眼,用意识掠过全身,放松每一个紧张的肌肉群。

④想象一个你非常熟悉的景致,或是你的花园、或是你住房的前半部分。选一个令人高兴、具有快乐联想的景致,倘若不能明确想象,别发愁,无论想到什么都行,想象力会随练习而提高。

⑤一旦确定了想象之事,仔细看着它,寻找它的细微之处,假如想象的是花园,找出花丛、玫瑰丛或苹果树的确切位置,看看它们的颜色和形状,尽量准确地获取它们的一切,倘若图像不太清晰或想象随即消失,也别发愁。

⑥现在,放开想象(让它走开),代之以一个幻想中的景象。选一个海滩,风平浪静,海水在阳光照耀下波光熠熠,沙滩平静如镜。或选一条河,河水穿行于茂密的森林,树影倒映水面,斑斑驳驳。或选一个决然不同的但充溢着宁静、祥和、让你心旷神怡的景象。

⑦随着景象越来越清晰,幻想自己越来越轻柔、越来越轻柔……直到飘飘悠悠离开躺着的地方,飘进了想象中的宁静景观,让它环抱着你,你已置身其中,与它融为一体,再感觉身体与它的联系,阳光暖洋洋地抚摸着你的脸,凄凉的水、温柔的风、软软的沙、绿绿的树叶拂着你的手。

⑧你已化为景象的一部分、宁静的一部分,没有地方要去、没有事要做、没有要求要满足、没有压力、没有最后期限,只有周围的宁静、内心的祥和。

⑨你任意选择在这种状态下逗留的时间,然后慢慢让自己沉回到躺着的地面或床上,让眼前的景象缓缓消逝,不要过分唐突地回到现实之中,再躺一会儿,看一看景象远去后留下的空白,晴空万里的蓝天、平静似水的白云,随后缓缓地做好思想准备,睁开眼睛,回到现实。

第二节 员工帮助计划与职业发展
(EAP and Career Development)

一、员工帮助计划(EAP)

(一)员工帮助计划的概念(The Meaning of EAP)

EAP(Employee Assistance Program),即员工帮助计划,是饭店为员工提供的系统的、长期的援助与福利项目。通过专业人员对饭店以及员工进行诊断和建议,提供专业指导、培训和咨询,帮助员工及其家庭成员解决心理和行为问题,提高绩效及改善饭店气氛和管理。简而言之,EAP 是饭店用于管理和解决员工个人问题,从而提高员工与饭店绩效的有效机制。

Tips:The Developing History of EAP

EAP is an organized, professional, counseling and information providing service on a range of issues, both personal and work-related, either through telephone or face-to-face sessions. EAP can help reduce absenteeism and create a peaceful workspace and enhance the employee's skills in meeting all the challenges that he/she might face in his/her personal or professional life and decrease the cost, employee turnover, burnouts, absenteeism, and accident-related disability. Improvement in employee performance increases productivity and the organization can achieve competitive advantage through employee counseling. Eisenberg and Delaney (1977) had suggested that employee counseling could focus on issues such as understanding self, decision making, goal setting, planning for future and managing interpersonal problems.

Wasylyshyn (2003) concluded that while executive coaching continues to mushroom as a practice area that has had little outcome, EAP had become more common in the UK in the 1990s, as workplace stress rose. The British association for counseling and psychotherapy published a review on counseling in the workplace. The results indicated that, after counseling, work-related symptoms returned to normal in more than half of the clients (McLeod and Henderson, 2003). Worster (2000) studied the multifaceted ways in which EAP professionals can be helpful with organizational layoff realities. Herlihyet al. (2002), on the other hand, concluded that EAP could assist employees in garnering resources to manage the multiple and sometimes conflicting demands of work and family life. Sciegaj et al. (2001) investigated the status of EAP. Representatives of 336 firms listed among the Fortune 500 companies completed questionnaires concerning EAP services and procedures. The findings suggested that the use of EAPs is at a historic high, indicating that 92% of firms offered EAPs in 1997.

Kirk and Brown (2003) were of the opinion that EAPs are considered one of the main vehicles for occupational stress management and are rapidly evolving into providers of holistic wellbeing programs in the workplace. This form of service delivery has, however, been criticized for focusing on interventions at the individual rather than at the organizational level. While research evidence is not supportive of the effectiveness of EAPs, data suggests that these programs do influence positively the employee mental health and are perceived by employees as a desirable workplace resource.

Arthur (2002) assessed levels of psychological disturbances in employees (aged 20 ~ 60 years). The findings suggested that a significant proportion of employees who experience stress in the workplace and consequently attend their employer's EAP may have serious mental health symptoms, and that employers are providing a service for those in genuine psychological need.

Among the Indian corporates, Tata Consultancy Service (2005) conducted a study on employee counseling in their organization which later led into setting up a network called "Maître" to counsel its 30,000 employees, where family get togethers, activities such as dance, yoga classes and theater workshops were organized to facilitate employees' mental and physical health. TCS-Maitree's counseling service has won the organization plenty of praise. Interestingly, employees rarely discuss personal problems; they mostly talk about work-related issues. One reason for the popularity of the counseling services is the informal nature; employees feel more comfortable talking to counselors rather than formally approaching their department heads. In turn, Maitree counselors share some of these concerns with the TCS administration, so that issues can be resolved quickly.

Source: Priya Nair, Mario Xavier. Initiating Employee Assistance Program (EAP) for a Corporate: An Experiential Learning [J]. IUP Journal of Organizational Behavior, 2012(2).

(二)员工帮助计划的内容与目标(The Content and Goals of EAP)

1. 员工帮助计划的内容

完整的EAP应该包括饭店心理状况的调查研究和压力评估、宣传教育、组织改变、针对性培训、心理咨询与治疗等几项内容:

(1)饭店心理状况的调查研究是EAP有效开展的前提,由专业人员采用专业的心理健康评估方法评估员工心理生活质量现状,及其导致问题产生的原因并提出建议,减少或消除不良的组织管理因素。

(2)宣传教育应用自助卡片、海报、网站、健康知识讲座等媒介宣传心理健康知识,提高员工心理健康和自我保健意识,鼓励遇到心理困扰问题时积极寻求帮助。

(3)组织改变是根据现有的员工状态,对饭店的组织机制进行调整,对工作环境的设计与改善。一方面,改善工作硬环境——物理环境;另一方面,通过组织结构变革、领导力培训、团队建设、工作轮换、员工生涯规划等手段改善工作的软环境,在饭店内部建立支持性的工作环境,丰富员工的工作内容,指明员工的发展方向,消除问题的诱因。

(4)针对性培训就是进行压力管理、挫折应对、保持积极情绪、咨询式的管理者等一系列培训,让管理者学会心理咨询的理论和技巧,在工作时随时注意预防和解决员工心理问题。

(5)心理咨询与治疗是EAP解决员工心理问题的最后步骤,需建立相应机制,如开通热线电话、建立网上沟通渠道、开辟咨询室等,使得员工能够顺利、及时地获得心理咨询及治疗的帮助和服务。同时积极处理压力所造成的反应,即情绪、行为及生理等方面症状的缓解和疏导。

2. 员工帮助计划的预期目标

一个成功有效的EAP项目需要围绕员工个人层面和饭店整体两个层面的需求展开。对于预期目标,则从以下两点进行概括:

(1)员工个人层面

对于员工个人层面上的帮助,EAP可以做到:①增强个人身心健康,指导其提高生活品质;②协助员工自我成长,引导职业发展;③推进员工的良好人际关系及工作和谐关系;④帮助员工缓解压力,降低压力对自身的负作用;⑤促进员工家庭和睦,改善夫妻和亲子关系,促进员工工作与生活的平衡;⑥帮助员工解决工作、生活中各种心理困扰,改正不良习惯。

(2)组织层面

对于饭店整体层面上的帮助,EAP可以做到:①优化福利制度,满足员工不断变化和提升的需要,特别是心理层面的需求;②提高员工士气,改善组织氛围,增进员工的向心力和凝聚力;③降低管理成本,降低由于员工离职、缺勤、意外事故所导致的损失;④提高组织绩效,改善管理效果、提高生产率。

(三)员工帮助计划的操作模式(The Operation Mode of EAP)

员工帮助计划可以分为以管理为基础的内部模式、以契约为基础的外部模式、以资源共享为基础的联合模式、以专业化和灵活性相结合的混合模式四种。

1. 内部模式

内部模式是在饭店内部设置一个专门部门,由人事管理、心理咨询等的专职人员从事 EAP 服务。他们的工作是进行评估,短期咨询,以及当需要长期咨询时向外界的服务供应者转诊。

该模式的优点主要有:专职人员对饭店独特文化、潜在问题和员工特性有着更深的理解和把握,拟订方案更加富有针对性;更加有助于借助内部资源去执行和实施项目计划;饭店高层更关注员工帮助计划对组织需求的适应性;现场的 EAP 专家更能贴近组织的需要。主要缺点有:专职人员因为身处同样的环境,在设计方案的过程中难免带有主观性;向同事直接提供帮助有可能因为觉察个人隐私受到威胁而影响服务的使用;饭店要消耗一定的人力资源、时间来执行计划;由于它设立在工作所在地,员工对 EAP 的信任度有限,且它很难做到相关记录的严格保密。

2. 外部模式

外部模式是饭店将员工帮助计划项目外包,由饭店聘请外部专业的 EAP 机构和具有社会工作、心理咨询辅导等知识经验的专业人员或机构提供员工帮助计划服务。这种模式的优点在于饭店人力资源的耗费最少,饭店只需要支付一定的报酬就可以得到全套的服务;同时由于工作人员完全是饭店之外的第三方,员工在接受服务的时候更能感到个人隐私的安全性。缺点在于工作人员可能对饭店的了解不够,费用也可能相对较高。

3. 联合模式

联合模式指若干组织联合成立一个专门为其员工提供援助的服务机构,该中心专门配备了专职人员。这种服务模式可以最大限度地节省经费,但是目前在中国很难实现。一方面由于中国对 EAP 有明确需求的组织比较少,很难形成规模;另一方面在人员配置、人员权限、薪酬福利待遇支付等方面,多个组织也有引发争端的可能。

4. 混合模式

混合模式是指饭店内部员工帮助计划实施部门与外部的专业机构联合,共同为饭店员工提供帮助项目。这种方式既能保证工作人员的专业性、员工的信任度,同时也有饭店内的联系人可以协助推进整体项目,并对质量进行跟踪、监督、评估。

(四)员工帮助计划的作用与效益(The Effect and Benefits of EAP)

1. 员工帮助计划的作用

(1)EAP 是一个基于工作场所的计划,旨在协助:

• 雇主,解决生产力的问题;

• 员工客户,识别和解决个人问题,包括健康、婚姻、家庭、金融、酒精、毒品、法律、情绪、压力,或可能会影响工作表现的其他个人问题。

(2) 有效的员工协助方案:

为员工确定适当的解决方案,最好的办法是要弄清楚对他们很重要的是什么,他们需要什么,以提高他们的幸福和健康的文化因素,EAP 服务包括:

- 咨询服务,为个人或家庭问题、生产力问题、健康的应对策略以及生活方式的改变提出建设性意见;
- 员工教育讲座,如压力管理或选择健康的生活方式;
- 管理教育研讨会,使之有效沟通,以及如何识别和应对陷入困境的人员;
- 创伤和重要事件的支持。

2. 员工帮助计划的效益

20 世纪 80 年代美国学者对员工帮助计划实施的效果进行的成本回报分析显示,美国企业平均为 EAP 投入 1 美元,可为企业节省运营成本 5~16 美元;康乃尔大学的雇员帮助教育和研究项目认为,实施 EAP 使学校增加了留职率,减少了病假率,节省了经费;James Campbell Quick,Cary Coopper & Marc Schbracq 的"雇员帮助项目"对 EAP 的有效性研究表明,2008 年全美使用 EAP 服务的雇主中,大约有 60% 的企业避免了由员工生病请假给生产带来的损失,同时有 72% 的企业改进了工作效率降低的现状。

(五) 员工帮助计划的反馈检验 (The Feedback Inspection of EAP)

对 EAP 的反馈检验分为两个方面:

1. 硬性指标

包括生产率、销售额、产品质量、总产值、缺勤率、管理时间、员工赔偿、招聘及培训费用等。

2. 软性指标

包括人际冲突、沟通关系、员工士气、工作满意度、员工忠诚度、组织气氛等。

Tips: Treading carefully on EAPs
Good communication helps protect clients from exposure

Employee assistance programs provide employees with support when they need it—from helping them through relationship difficulties to coordinating treatment for substance abuse. And while 69% of employers offer EAPs through external organizations, the potential still exists for them to be caught in legal entanglements. What are employers' potential liabilities and what can advisers do to help them mitigate risks?

First, let's look at EAPs from the employees' perspective. Assistance may be desperately needed, but getting help through the EAP could expose sensitive personal information. "I think the biggest risk is definitely an invasion of privacy claim," says Brian Hassan, managing director of San Francisco-based Bay Point Benefits. "It's when an employee is worried that the employer is going to find out information about them that they shouldn't." This fear may stop employees from seeking much-needed help, they may be concerned about how widely their information is shared, and they may assume it will negatively impact their job.

John W. Seltzer, chief executive of J. Seltzer Associates in Pittsburgh, agrees that employee perception constitutes "the biggest risk of liability" for employers. He says incorrect assumptions and misunderstandings may lead an employee to think, "Because I chose to get help for a particular problem, somehow it affected my job status." Alcohol abuse and mental health issues are commonly cited as examples of this, especially when an employee is deemed a safety risk, and either loses their job or is reassigned because of it. "That's not to suggest that the employer wouldn't ultimately win a case like that", says Seltzer, but he believes it can cause tremendous difficulties while working through the process. Another potential difficulty could arise when an employee questions their employer's right to take disciplinary action, such as terminating them for drug use while the employee is undergoing EAP-approved rehabilitation.

Privacy and job security may be primary worries for employees, but according to Robert "Bob" C. Christenson, partner at Fisher and Phillips LLP in Atlanta, employers' EAP concerns generally center around two things. The first is making sure they comply with applicable laws, which is often a multi-faceted task "There's an intersection here between HIPAA, ADA, FMLA, and everything else", Christenson says. This storm of factors sometimes adds layers of complexity to an already delicate issue. And then there's the safety side of things. "The other concern the employer has is that they have some duty to protect their other employees and the general public from somebody that's out there, who maybe shouldn't be operating a truck or some other kind of situation that the employer could potentially be vicariously liable for."

> Safety-sensitive positions, such as an employee who operates heavy machinery, is indeed a top concern for employers, says Andi Blaylock, vice president of account services at Chicago-based Bensinger, DuPont and Associates. "If (employees) are impaired—under the influence of drugs oralcohol, or even if they're upset because of a fight they got in\with their spouse on their way to work — that puts them at risk. It puts their co-workers at risk, it puts the public at risk (depending on what their position is), and ultimately it then puts the company at risk."

Source：Knudson J. Treading Carefully on EAPs[J]. Employee Benefit Adviser,2012(10):2.

二、职业发展(Career Development)

(一)职业发展概述(The Outline of Career Development)

1. 职业发展的基本含义

职业发展可分为组织职业发展和个体职业发展两种。

组织职业发展管理(Organizational career management)是指饭店从员工个人的职业发展需求出发,有意识地将之与饭店的人力资源需求和规划相联系、相协调、相匹配,为员工的职业提供不断成长和发展的机会,帮助、支持员工职业发展所实施的各种政策措施和活动,以最大限度地调动员工的工作积极性。在实现员工个人的职业生涯目标的同时,实现饭店的生产经营目标和持续发展。

个体职业发展是指一个人一生中经过学习与培训获得从事职业劳动的知识与能力,从选择职业到从事职业直至完全退出职业劳动的全过程,由职业发展计划、职业策略、职业进入、职业变动和职业位置的一系列变量构成。它的基本含义是:

①个体职业发展反映的是一个人生命历程中的工作经历和任职经历,而非群体的行为历程。

②个体职业发展就是一个动态的过程,包括了教育、职业进入、职业发展策略、职业流动与升迁和最终的职业位置。

③个体职业发展是以心理开发、生理开发、智力开发、技能开发、伦理开发等人的潜能开发为基础,以工作内容为确定和变化,工作业绩的评价,工资待遇、职称、职务的变动为标准,以满足需求为目标的工作经历和内心体验的经历。

2. 职业发展观

职业发展观是现代人力资源管理的基本思想之一。所谓职业发展观,从饭店方面来说,就是要为其成员构建职业发展通道,使之与组织的需求相匹配、相协调、相融合,以达到满足饭店及其成员的各自需要,同时实现饭店目标和个人目标的目的。职业发展观的核心,是要使员工个人职业生涯和饭店需求在相互作用中实现协调和融合。

职业发展观涉及内职业和外职业两个不同的概念。

内职业是指个人追求的职业。内职业发展是指从事一项职业时所具备的知识、观念、心理素质、能力、内心感受等因素的组合及其变化过程。

外职业是指对饭店而言的职业,表示饭店努力为每一位员工在组织的作业生命中确立一条可依循的、可感知的、可行的发展通道。外职业发展是指从事职业时的工作单位、工作地点、工作内容、工作职务、工作环境、工资待遇等因素的组合及其变化过程。

内职业发展是外职业发展的前提,内职业发展会带动外职业的发展,外职业发展也会促进内职业的发展。内职业发展是以外职业发展或成果来展示的。内职业的匮乏以外职业的停滞或失败呈现。

(二)职业发展管理(Career Management)

1. 职业发展管理的含义及意义

(1)职业发展管理的含义

职业发展管理是指在设计思想上把个人与饭店的发展需要结合起来,对决定职业生涯的个人因素、组织因素和社会因素进行分析,制定有关的对个人职业发展的战略设想和计划安排活动。它确保个人职业目标与整个饭店发展目标的协调一致,以实现个人目标与饭店需要之间的最佳匹配。

职业发展管理是竭力满足员工、管理者、饭店三者需要的一个动态过程,此三者都在职业发展管理系统中有着突出作用。首先员工要对个人特点进行评估,从自身实际出发,在饭店的大背景下确立个人的事业奋斗目标,制订相应的计划、编制相应的工作和行动计划。管理者帮助员工理解饭店的需要和要求,对员工进行在职培训与指导,对员工提供反馈信息,促使员工形成正确的自我评价和职业发展目标,是连接员工和饭店的纽带。饭店为职业发展和管理提供全面的信息支持、专业支持和统一调度。

(2)职业发展管理的意义

①促进员工个人发展,明确个人职业发展目标

职业发展管理的一项重要内容就是对个人进行分析,能使员工了解自身的长处和短处,在遇到困难时,促使员工化解压力,提高其对变化的环境和工作目标分析的能力。同时,饭店为员工构建了一个价值创造的平台,提供滋养智慧与技能的土壤,让员工进行自我价值展示和自我职业目标的确立。

②有效利用人力资源,完善饭店资源合理配置

人力资源的开发能不断更新人的知识、技能,提高人的创造力,从而使无生命

的"物"的资源充分尽其所用,特别是随着知识经济时代的到来,知识已成为社会的主体,而掌握和创造这些知识的就是"人",因此饭店更应注重人的智慧、技艺、能力的提高与全面发展。基于员工个性化需要形成的职业发展管理体系,对员工有长期的激励效果,有利于人力资源的持续开发与利用。

③调动员工内在积极性,更好地实现饭店需求

马斯洛需要层次理论指出,人的需要分为五种,从低级向高级递进。而职业生涯管理的目的就是帮助员工提高在各个需要层次的满足度,使员工的低层次物质需要逐步提高,又使他们的自我实现等精神方面的高级需要的满足度逐步增加。因此,职业生涯管理不仅符合人生发展的需要,而且也立足人的高级需要,即立足于友爱、尊重、自我实现的需要。真正了解员工在个人发展上想要什么,就必然会激起员工强烈的饭店服务的精神力量,进而形成饭店发展的巨大推动力,更好地实现饭店组织目标。

④丰富饭店人才储备,保证组织持续稳定发展

目前,饭店业高级人才资源仍然存在短缺,较高的人才流动率也对酒店服务质量和服务水平以及人才培养产生重大影响。任何成功的饭店,其成功的根本原因是拥有高质量的饭店管理者和高质量的员工。人的才能和潜力能得到充分发挥,人力资源不会虚耗、浪费,饭店的生存成长就有了取之不尽、用之不竭的源泉。通过职业生涯等管理努力提供员工施展才能的舞台,充分体现员工的自我价值,是留住人才、凝聚人才的根本保证,也是饭店长盛不衰的组织保证。

Tips: Career Development Theory

1. Ginzburg career decision theory

(1) Career decision-making is a process of development

Ginzburg pointed out that career choice is a developmental process, it is not a decision accomplished in a sudden moment, but based on the concept of choice to make, and the idea to go through a number of years to formate. The process of career choices contains a series of decisions, each decision and childhood, experience and physical and mental development of young individuals.

(2) Career choice is an optimized decision-making

Ginzburg believes that the realization of career choices is compromise and adjustment of individual consciousness and the external conditions. The last personal career decision is the best combination between individuals seeking for favorite occupation and social providing opportunities.

(3) Factors affect career decisions

Ginzburg pointed out that the factors affecting career choices, including realistic factors, educational factors, personal emotions and personality factors, factors of professional values and personal value.

2. Sapa career stage theory

Sapa's analysis of the career planning is around the different periods of his career. This constitutes his career stage theory. The specific content of the various stages is as follows:

(1) Growth stage

The stage is from birth to 14 years old. Individuals at this stage are in the development of self-concept mature. Early, personal desires and fantasy dominates and subsequently generate attention and interest of social reality, the individual's abilities and interest is secondary.

Growth stage can be divided into the "fantasy period", "interest period" and "ability period", three small stages.

(2) Exploratory stage

This stage is from 15 years old to 24 years old. Individuals study themselves and career exploration in school life and leisure activities. The exploration stage is very important transition period in life, it can be divided into the interim period, transition period and the trial period.

3. Sapa's career development theory

Sapa's analysis of career development is more detailed than Ginzburg's, which is a better career development theory summarized. The theory mainly includes the following ideas:

(1) People are divers: people's talents, interests and personalities are not of the same; each person adapts to certain occupations above characteristics; each occupation has a set of specific requirements for people's talents, interests and personality mode, but the occupation and individual have some room for change; different nature of the career mode is decided by people of different status in the family and the state of the economy, personal level of intelligence and personality traits, as well as opportunities for personal.

(2) Career choosing and adaptation is a process: people's preference and qualifications of a career, people's living and working situations, as well as people's self-concept will change with time passing and experience accumulating, which makes the career choosing and adaptation be in a continuous process. Career choosing and adjustment process can be summarized as two-stage, exploratory stage and fixed stage: exploration stage includes several periods of fantasy, trial and reality; fixed stage includes a trial and fixed period. In a larger scope, career growth, exploration, fixed, maintained, recession, the sum of the various stages, which constitute a series of stages of life.

(3) Career development process is of plasticity:

①Occupational development process, fundamentally speaking, is a complete self-concept. It is a compromise and reconcile process. "Oneself" is a interaction product of the individual's own condition with the outside a variety of conditions and a variety of repercussions.

②The reconcile between the individual and society, self-concept and reality, is a process of putting oneself into professional roles in the human society. This role-playing is a evolution from fantasy of youth, career choosing and counseling, and then to be working novice.

③A person's job satisfaction (and thus life satisfaction), depending on whether the individual talents, interests, personality traits and values can find the corresponding destination, or, as the vent above aspects, the degree of adaptation.

④Occupational development can be improved through guidance in various stages. It includes both career talent and career interests, which makes people mature, and helps people in career choosing and self-concept development.

Source: Super D E, Jordaan J P. Career development theory[J]. British Journal of Guidance and Counselling, 1973, 1(1): 3-16.

2. 影响职业发展管理的因素

(1) 职业发展阶段

①探索阶段

15 至 24 岁的这一阶段,个人表现出对某一职业领域的兴趣,并将认真地探索各种可能的职业选择,也可能频繁跳槽,职业探索阶段对员工职业发展有着重要的意义。从饭店角度来说,管理者应该了解这个年龄段的员工的职业发展阶段特点,及时给予引导,尽量为他们提供多种的工作机会,让员工对自身和工作有进一步的了解,为工作的确定做好准备。

②确立阶段

25至44岁,这一年龄段是大多数人工作生命周期中的核心部分,个体已经确定了兴趣点和职位取向,并积极寻求自己在组织中的价值,获得进一步的发展。此时的职业发展管理应该着眼于现行需要的知识和技能的发展,以求在职业生涯中攀登。

③维持阶段

45到64岁的这一阶段,人们一般都已经在自己的工作领域中为自己创立了一席之地,因而他们的大多数精力主要就放在保持现状和拥有这一位置上了,并将生存中心转向非工作事项。

④下降阶段

65岁以上,在这一阶段,个体的健康状况和工作能力都在逐步衰退,职业生涯接近尾声。

(2)职业性向

职业性向(Occupational Orientation/Vocational Preference)是指一个人所具有的有利于其在某一职业方面成功的素质的总和。它是与职业方向相对应的个性特征,也是由个性决定的职业选择偏好。

约翰·霍兰德基于自己对职业性向的测试(Vocational Preference Test,VPT),一共发现了六种基本的人格类型或性向:实际性向,调研性向,社会性向,常规性向,企业性向,艺术性向。

①实际性向

这种类型的人真诚坦率,较稳定,讲求实利,害羞,缺乏洞察力,容易服从。他们一般具有机械方面的能力,乐于从事半技术性的或手工性的职业,如运动员、管道工、装配线工人等。这类职业的特点是有连续性的任务需要,却很少有社会性的需求,如谈判和说服他人等。

②调研性向

这一类型的人为了知识的开发与理解而乐于从事现象的观察与分析工作。这些人思维复杂,有创见,有主见,但无纪律性,不切实际,易于冲动。具有这种性向的人会被吸引从事那些包含着较多认知活动的职业,如生物学家、社会学家、数学家和大学教授。在商业性组织中,这类人经常担任的是研究与开发职务及咨询参谋之职。这些职务需要的是复杂的分析,而不必去说服取信于他人。

③社会性向

具有这种性向的人喜欢为他人提供信息,帮助他人,喜欢在秩序井然、制度化的工作环境中发展人际关系和工作。这些人除了爱社交之外,还有机智老练、友好、易了解、乐于助人等特点。其个性中较消极的一面是独断专行,爱操纵别人。社会型的人适于从事护理、教学、市场营销、销售、培训与开发等包含着大量人际交往活动的职业。

④常规性向

具有这种性向的人会被吸引从事那些包含着大量结构性和规则性的职业,如会计和银行职员。这一类人容易组织起来,喜欢和数据型及数字型的事实打交道,喜欢明确的目标,不能接受模棱两可的状态。这些人可以用这一类的词语来表述他们:服从的,有秩序的,有效率的,实际的。如果用不太客气的话说,就是缺乏想象,能自我控制,无灵活性。这种个性类型的人最适于从事事务性的职业,如会计、出纳员、银行职业就是这种类型的典型代表。

⑤企业性向

这种类型的人与社会型的人相似之处在于他(她)也喜欢与人合作。其主要的区别是企业型的人喜欢领导和控制他人(而不是去帮助他人),其目的是为了达到特定的组织目标。这种类型的人自信,有雄心,精力充沛,健谈。其个性特点中较消极的一面是专横,权力欲过强,易于冲动。具有这种性向的人会被吸引从事那些包含着大量以影响他人为目的语言活动的职业,如管理人员、律师。

⑥艺术性向

这种类型与传统型形成最强烈的反差。他们喜欢选择音乐、艺术、文学、戏剧等方面的职业。他们富有想象力,直觉强,易冲动,好内省,有主见。这一类型的人语言方面的资质强于数学方面。如果用消极一些的语言描述,这类人是感情极丰富的、无组织纪律的。具有这种性向的人会被吸引从事那些包含着大量自我表现、艺术创造、情感表达和个性化的职业,如艺术家、广告创意人员。

实际上,每个人不是只包含有一种职业性向,而是可能为几种职业性向的混合。霍兰德认为,这种性向越相似,则一个人在选择职业时面临的内在冲突和犹豫就越少。霍兰德用一个六角形来表示各种性向的相似性。

(3)职业锚

埃德加·H·施恩(Edgar H. Schein)提出的职业锚理论,职业锚是指一个人必须做出选择时,他无论如何都不肯放弃的职业中的一些最重要的事物和价值观。职业锚是人们选择和发展自己的职业时所围绕的中心。

关于职业锚基本上有五种描述:技术能力型的职业锚、管理能力型的职业锚、创造型职业锚、安全型职业锚和自主型职业锚。

①技术能力型的职业锚

具有相当明确的职业工作追求、需要和价值观。技术能力型职业锚的人比较热爱自己的专业技术或岗位工作,注重个人专业技能发展,一般多从事工程技术、营销、财务分析、系统分析、企业计划等工作。

②管理能力型的职业锚

愿意担负管理责任,且责任越大越好,这是管理能力型职业锚员工的追逐目标。他们与不喜欢、甚至惧怕全面管理的技术职业锚的人不同,倾心于全面管理,掌握更大权力,肩负起更大责任。他们从事一个或几个技术职能区工作,只是为了更好地展现自己的能力,瞄准更高职位的管理权力。

③创造型职业锚

这是定位很独特的一种职业锚,在某种程度上,创造型锚同其他类型职业锚有重叠。追求创造型的人要求有自主权、管理能力,能施展自己的才干。但是,这些不是他们的主要动机或价值观,创造性才是他们的主要动机和价值观。

④安全型职业锚

又称作稳定型职业锚,其特征如下:职业的稳定和安全,是这一类职业锚员工的追求、驱动力和价值观。他们的安全取向主要为两类:一种是追求职业安全,稳定源和安全源主要是一个给定组织中的稳定的成员资格,例如大公司组织安全性高,做其成员稳定系数高;另一种注重情感的安全稳定,包括一种定居,使家庭稳定和使自己融入团队的感情。

⑤自主型职业锚

又称作独立型职业锚,这种职业锚的特点是:最大限度地摆脱组织约束,追求能施展个人职业能力的工作环境。以自主、独立为锚位的人认为,组织活动是限制人的,具有是非理性的成分。他们追求的是自由自在、不受约束或少受约束的工作生活环境。

(4)外部环境

某个行业的发展变化、劳动力市场的供需情况、现有的工作环境和传统文化中的择业观念都会对职业发展产生影响。

3. 职业发展路径

(1)纵向型职业发展路径

这种模式又称传统职业发展路径,是指员工在饭店中从一个特定的职位到下一个职位纵向向上发展的一条路径,是一种基于过去饭店内员工的实际发展道路而制定的发展模式。纵向型职业发展路径的特点是清晰明了,直线向前,主要依靠内部招聘和晋升来实现。

(2)横向型职业发展路径

这种模式采取工作轮换的方式,通过横向调动来使工作具有多样性,使员工焕发新的活力、迎接新的挑战。虽然没有加薪或晋升,但员工可以增加自己对饭店的价值,也使他们自己获得了新生。当饭店内没有足够多的高层职位为每个员工提供升迁机会,而长期从事同一项工作使人倍感枯燥无味,影响员工工作效率时,可采用此种模式。现今饭店组织趋于扁平化,如此横向发展,从饭店层面看,不仅使员工成为多面手,让员工从不同角度加强对饭店的理解,从而使饭店由于员工的成熟而快速成熟起来;从员工层面看,可以丰富员工的工作经历、经验,培养、拓宽员工的业务能力,为员工走向更高的管理岗位创造条件。

(3) 双重型职业发展路径

双重型职业发展路径又叫双梯阶机制,它专为专业技术人员设计,为他们提供与管理人员平行平等的晋升路径和更多的职业发展机会,以对他们产生激励作用。双重职业路径就在于形成两条平行的职业生涯路径,一条是管理职业生涯路径,一条是技术职业生涯路径。管理人员沿管理路径提升意味着员工享有更多制定决策的能力,同时要承担更多的责任;技术人员沿技术路径提升意味着员工具有更强的独立性,同时拥有更多从事专业活动的资源。在双重职业路径的中部为专业技术人员提供了两条平行的发展道路,一条可以继续沿着技术路径发展,一条可以转入管理路径发展,即专业技术人员可以在管理路径和技术路径之间相互移动,从而使专业技术人员的发展机会大大增加。

4. 职业发展管理

Gutteridge 概括了西方组织的职业生涯管理方法,具体包括:给个人提供自我评估工具和机会;进行个别职业发展咨询;发布内部劳动力市场信息;设置潜能评价中心;实施培训、发展项目等。

(1) 明确自我定位

这是职业发展管理的第一步,员工要对自己进行评估和定位,全面了解自己。一个有效的职业发展管理必须是在充分且正确认识自身条件与相关环境的基础上进行的。要审视自己、认识自己、了解自己,做好评估和定位需要考虑个性与特长、兴趣与爱好、知识与技能、优点和缺点等方面。其后,便是要明确自己应该成为什么样的人,明确自己的发展规划应该如何适应饭店的发展规划,哪些方面亟须改进。

(2) 规划发展

① 把握发展机会

系统评估饭店内外部环境因素对自身职业发展的影响不容忽视,积极主动的员工总是善于思考问题,洞察是非和发掘机会。为了更好地掌握自己的职业前途,员工必须善于发掘问题,最大限度地激发自身的热情与智慧,提升预见能力,把握职业机会与防范潜在风险。之后预见新趋势对自身职业定位与工作目标的影响,预见在不确定的环境中,可能会出现哪些问题。并针对这些问题提出相应的预备方案,以促使自己增强抗意外的能力,使自己的职场发展更具有可控性和计划性。

②制定职业目标

职业发展目标的确定,是职业发展管理的初步完成,目标通常表现为在一定时间内提高工作技能、获得理想的工作职位和工作安排。职业目标是饭店员工的行为导向;是员工日常工作活动的指南;是员工职业生涯成败的关键;是员工充满活力的保证;是员工达成自我实现需要的前提。

一个具有判断力的员工,做事时一定会考虑优先顺序,先做最重要的事,然后才做比较次要的工作。一般说来,可以依据工作期限、重要程度,以及性质来判断。就饭店立场而言,一般都要求员工在一定时限内必须完成工作,所以,在做事之前,应该制定一个紧密且可行的流程。

(3)行动规划

①激励

在制定行动规划时,要确保把计划分为有机的组成部分,在完成每一期小的目标时,会有成就感。如果采取全线出击的策略,可能会因为工作过量而产生失望和挫败感。

在规划实施时,要得到饭店的支持,直线主管和专门人力资源管理人员一方面要对员工的行动规划提出合理的建议,另一方面也要考虑由此所引发的有关的培训和发展项目,形成落实员工成长的平台。

②学习活动

员工在刚进入饭店时,需要跟着老员工熟悉工作流程,学会运用组织资源完成工作职责。因此,在平时的工作中,应该积极学习和总结别人成功的经验,将这些宝贵的经验与自己的工作结合起来,提高自身的工作能力。常见的在职学习的活动包括:改进学习方法、培养和锻炼新思维、把所学的知识运用到实践中、培养团队合作能力、从事有挑战性的工作、MBA 课程进修、参加工作和岗位培训、参加工作考察。

③资源

饭店业的一切工作需要各方面资源的支持,包括财务资源、设备资源、人力资源,等等。在使用这些资源之前需要思考获取资源的方式,以供利用。

④时间利用和效果反馈

职业发展目标的阶段化和细化帮助我们评估时间的利用情况。要留出足够的时间来完成既定目标,同时也不能留有过多的时间,否则会导致工作拖沓,失去效率。个人所制定的时间表要考虑工作的层次性,需要清楚地标明时限为三个月、五个月还是一年内要完成的任务层次。

在完成职业目标的过程中,失败和错误是不可避免的,受到内外部因素的影响。外部因素包括:行业内部和外部的经济环境;内部因素包括:个人对发展的抵触情绪、个人惰性、对未来不确定性的恐惧和知识技能的缺乏,等等。这样,效果反馈的重要性就凸显了出来。不断试错、不断改进是获得职业成功的重要条件,在变化的环境和能力的提升中逐渐纠正职业计划,要始终保持对自己的肯定态度。

Employee Development Plan (EDP)

COMPETENCY/DEFINITION	BEHAVIORAL INDICATORS
Analytical & Problem Solving Skill Uses analysis, wisdom, experience, and logical methods to solve difficult problems; incorporates multiple inputs to establish shared ownership and action	Meets Requirements • Uses a combination of logic, analysis, experience, wisdom, and methods to solve problems • Probes appropriate sources for relevant information and answers to key questions • Demonstrates persistence and skill in gathering information • Has solutions and suggestions that are effective in addressing the problem at hand • Involves others in the thinking and decision-making process • Can see hidden problems • Looks beyond the obvious and doesn't stop at the first answer
Communication Is able to write in a variety of communication settings and styles; can get messages across that instigates appropriate actions; orally communicates in a variety of formal and informal settings; actively listens	Meets Requirements • Writes clearly and succinctly in a variety of communication settings and styles • Uses correct grammar, in written and oral communications and correct punctuation and spelling in written communication • Can effectively get the message across either orally or in written form
Creativity & Innovation Resourceful to deviate from the routine; develops and implements new methods, procedures solutions, concepts, designs and/or applications; demonstrates imagination and originality; makes innovative contributions	Meets Requirements • Works to invent new ideas • Strives to be creative • Challenges the usual way of doing things • Easily makes connections among previously unrelated notions

COMPETENCY/DEFINITION	BEHAVIORAL INDICATORS
Customer Focus Commits to meeting the expectations and requirements of internal and external customers; acts with customers in mind; values importance of providing high-quality customer service	Meets Requirements • Commits to meeting the expectations and requirements of internal and external customers • Responds to customer problems in a timely manner • Looks for ways to exceed customers' expectations • Makes decisions that demonstrates an understanding of customers' needs • Gets first hand customer information, and assesses it to measure customer satisfaction • Builds and maintains effective relationships with customers, and gains their trust and respect
Dealing with Ambiguity/Change Maintains performance with changing circumstances; handles stress; able to move into action without having the total picture; tolerates uncertainty	Meets Requirements • Effectively copes with change and shifts gears comfortably • Decides and acts without having the total picture • Handles risk and uncertainty comfortably • Accepts changing priorities and work assignments
Initiative Taking Takes action to achieve goals beyond what is expected; drives to bring issues to a successful closure; self starter	Meets Requirements • Is proactive • Works to solve problems only involving leadership when necessary • Takes advantage of opportunities • Asserts own influence over events to achieve goals • Follows through to ensure successful completion of projects
Job/Functional Skills Has the functional and technical knowledge and skills to do the job at a satisfactory level of accomplishment	Meets Requirements • Has and uses the required functional and technical knowledge and skills necessary to do his or her job • Chooses appropriate tools or technology for tasks • Experiments with new processes, tools, or technologies to determine applicability • Understands facts and information related to assignments, including department and University policies • Has the capability and knowledge base to share technical skills with others • Provides opportunities for others to learn technical skills and concepts

续表

COMPETENCY/DEFINITION	BEHAVIORAL INDICATORS
Organizational Agility Knowledgeable about how the university works and how to get things done both through formal and informal channels; aware of the culture of the university; understands the reasoning behind key policies, practices, and procedures, works well with his/her supervisor and co-workers; can work his or her way through touchy situations	Meets Requirements • Understands the origin and reasoning behind key policies, practices, and procedures • Understands the culture of the university and acknowledges institutional politics as a reality • Relates well to and regularly interacts with both authority figures and peers • Maneuvers smoothly through complex political situations • Identifies where the land mines are and plans his or her approach accordingly
Personal Credibility Is widely trusted; is seen as a direct, truthful individual; presents truthful information in an appropriate and helpful manner; keeps confidences; admits mistakes; doesn't misrepresent himself or herself for personal gain	Meets Requirements • Is widely trusted and seen as a direct, truthful individual • Presents truthful information in an appropriate and helpful manner • Can be trusted to keep confidences • Consistently applies ethical values to appropriately address difficult situations • Operates in compliance with university policies and regulations • Follows through on commitments and/or establishes new agreements • Makes decisions based on what is best for the company rather than for personal gain
Planning/Project Management Scopes out length and difficulty of tasks and projects; able to shift priorities and multi-task on various projects; develops strategies to achieve department goals, estimates time and resources	Meets Requirements • Accurately scopes out length and difficulty of tasks and projects • Breaks down work into process steps • Develops schedules for completions of tasks • Realistically estimates time and resource requirements on projects • Anticipates and adjusts for problems and roadblocks • Measures performance against goals • Effectively shifts priorities and multi-tasks on projects • Consistently meets deadlines

续表

COMPETENCY/DEFINITION	BEHAVIORAL INDICATORS
Teamwork/Peer Relationship Responds and relates well to people in all positions; is seen as a team player, and is cooperative; looks for common ground, and solves problems for the good of all	Meets Requirements • Responds and relates well to peers and to those in positions of authority • Is seen as a team player, and is cooperative • Looks for common ground, and solves problems for the good of all • Represents his or her own interests and yet is fair to other groups • Encourages collaboration and seeks feedback • Can be candid with peers • Is confident, relaxed with and well-regarded by peers • Demonstrates respect for others

Source:http://wayne.edu/hr/leads/phase1/edp.php.

(4)明确职业发展管理活动的参与方及其角色

有效的职业发展管理体系是员工个人的发展目标与组织需求相互匹配的过程,其中,员工、直线主管和饭店在职业发展管理中都承担着责任,并在其中发挥着不同作用。

①员工是职业发展管理的驱动者

员工是在对自己职业兴趣、知识能力水平、价值观有清醒认识的基础上,明确个人职业发展需求和职业目标。员工本人始终是职业发展的主角。

· 个人追求良好的工作绩效

· 同直线主管和人力资源负责人员及时沟通,获得绩效反馈信息

· 明确自身发展方向

· 关注于饭店在人力资源发展方面的活动,主动获取发展机会

②直线主管是职业发展管理的推动者

直线主管在员工职业生涯的早期阶段需要扮演教练和顾问的角色,对员工本人的知识和能力作出判断,帮助他们确定职业需求,为员工职业发展指明方向。

· 主动提供对员工的职业指导

· 及时与员工沟通,使员工形成科学的职业发展目标

· 创造和谐有序的管理秩序

· 向饭店推荐人才,向员工推荐培训项目

③饭店为职业发展管理的支持者

饭店从整体上组织员工职业发展的活动,提供专业性的技术支持,为组织活动

的顺利进行提供保障。
- 构建系统有效的员工职业化管理体系
- 创造能够支撑职业生涯管理的饭店文化
- 统一组织职业生涯规划和管理活动
- 创建有利于员工职业目标实现的发展环境和自我展示平台

案例分析(Practice Case Analysis)

Deflating Stress in The Workplace

Are your hotel employees stressed out? Here's some great advice on how to get them back into peak performance while getting them to relax.

Stress is clearly the sum of its parts and, with 248 rooms, 575 employees and a 24/7 operation, the numbers at the Mandarin Oriental New York add up to just that sum, more often than not. In any high profile, intense customer-service environment, such as a luxury hotel, it simply goes with the territory.

So when stress and its traveling companion, burnout, threaten to check in to this Manhattan hotel, many employees are encouraged to check out—at least temporarily—and immerse themselves in community involvement.

"We all have our day to day of trying to balance family and work," said Deborah Schwarz, learning and development manager at the hotel. "So we try to create a fun, inviting atmosphere for our colleagues to help them find balance with their work. We get involved in the community, in our local neighborhood in Manhattan and New York City."

Hotel staffers have teamed up with the Central Park Conservancy to paint park benches and fences, tidy up by doing litter removal, and engage in other activities such as school-supply collections for needy kids and blood drives that, according to Schwartz "build a relationship with the community that can reconnect our colleagues and bring a sense of community within our organization. It is inspiring for people".

At many hotels, industry insiders acknowledge how stress and burnout can sap a staff's performance. And whether workers are urged to rejuvenate themselves through communal pursuits in the world beyond the hotel doors, or whether they receive more formalized opportunities during the workday itself, hotel executives consider anti-stress initiatives as vital to the hotel as a reservations desk.

The Mandarin Oriental considers the pursuit of community involvement and the strengthening of internal community to be proven antidotes to stress and burnout because both provide a support structure, particularly when the stress goes beyond work-related day-to-day hassles, said Schwarz.

"When the Haiti situation [earthquake] occurred, we had 8 or 9 colleagues affected, and we ran a charity drive to raise money for our colleagues", she said, to help them address their immediate family needs. It also stressed the sense of togetherness the hotel tries to cultivate at all levels of staffing.

To keep stress at bay, hotel employees are also encouraged to turn to food. But this is no exhortation to indulge in an organized, free-for-all group binge—this is an organized program known as Star Chef, a monthly celebration of cuisine in the workers' dining room that focuses everyone, at least for a while, on a shared culinary adventure.

"With our Star Chef program, a colleague volunteers to determine the menu in the colleagues' dining room and actually prepares the food along with the staff", said Schwarz. The popular event ends up feeding workers' appetites to know one another, and their varied cultures, better, and the ability to break bread (or pita, or roti, for that matter) "builds camaraderie", she said.

The hotel's guest kitchen also provides another stress-busting resource: One of the stewarding managers assigned to the kitchen area is also a certified yoga instructor and makes himself available to lead classes. And on occasion the therapist in the hotel's 5-star spa—more accustomed to loosening the tired muscles of frazzled guests—treats colleagues to that soothing treatment too.

But beyond yoga, volunteer work and communal meals, managers also need to take a clearer look at building stress-busters into everyday practice and policy—for their workers as well as for themselves, said Rita McGrath, associate professor in the management division at Columbia University's School of Business.

And oftentimes, she said, helping employees avoid or reduce stress is a matter of handing them something that is key to job satisfaction and performance: control over much of their daily routine.

"There is a big body of research that shows stress is highly correlated with people feeling unable to control the variables that are relevant to addressing the situation," McGrath said. "The first thing I would look at, as a manger, is what are the particular sets of problems that people on the front lines are likely to encounter and how can I give them as much control as possible to address those situations?"

In billing, for instance, she would divide what appears to be an insurmountable mountain of invoices into clusters of 10. "Your employee says 'I can do ten.' You feel a lot less stress when you break tasks up into digestible chunks."

That control, when possible, should extend into work shifts and work assignments, said Michael Sturman, associate professor at the Cornell University School of Hotel Administration. "Both working too many hours or not getting enough hours can add to stress," he said. "Listen to what your workers want. Assuming everyone wants a 40-hour week is just not accurate. You may have two employees who want to work 20 hours a week and you can accommodate both preferences without really doing much in the way of changes—and you will reduce the stress of employees by accommodating preferences that work out easily."

Another way to take the pressure off, McGrath said, is to give employees scripts to use in various largely predictable scenarios. "Don't rely on them knowing what to do," she said. "At Marriott, for instance, they say if a guest asks you directions to the ladies' room or a ballroom you can't point vaguely, you have to look the guest in the eye and walk them to wherever they need to go."

Managers should also possess—and show—empathy. "There are hotels in New York City that could sell every room they have, 15 times over, during the holidays," she said. "If you say to people, 'I know it is going to be manic and crazy, so after the new year we are going to give you some compensatory time off once this crisis is over... it gives people some hope that next time it won't be so awful.'"

As for managers helping themselves out of the emotional pressure cooker, prioritizing tasks is possibly one of the biggest stress-busters. "Don't get sucked into the 'nice-to-dos'—know what is critical and what is not", she said. "Sometimes managers think they are important because they are busy", she said—but sometimes that just leaves them feeling more wired and burned-out than anything else.

Whether people are working as a manger or not, however, everyone needs to know how to manage their own emotions, Sturman added—especially in a service industry such as hospitality. And that, he said, is where learning to role-play can be vital to both personal sanity and effective professional service.

"Disney recognizes this," he said. "They talk about the workers being 'on stage and off stage' and their work as a kind of a production. You are not an employee, you are playing a role. So you can let that role go. If you are a front desk clerk and you have been yelled at, it is not your fault but there you are, being yelled at by the customers.

If you internalize it and bring it home, that's a lot of stress. But if you say 'this is a role' and just let it go, your other roles—for instance as a family member—will be that much healthier."

This kind of healthy, stress-busting corporate culture starts at the top of any company, with the chief executive setting the tone. "You can't have 'the beatings will continue until morale is improved,'" he said. "You can't suddenly say all the front line employees have to be super-customer-oriented and then have top management be rude to the people working underneath them. This kind of inconsistency isn't going to work."

Even if a hotel isn't exactly Disney World, he said, an upbeat persona can indeed make any hotel employee less-stressed for success, he said. "These employees have to have a smile on their faces and be genuine when they say, 'I hope you are having a good day.'"

Source: http://www.hotelinteractive.com/article.aspx? articleid=19308.

Questions for Discussion:
1. What is a "Star Chef Program" and explain the positive outcome.
2. Please list the measures of Disney hospitality management dealing with worker stress.

名词解释(Key Terms)

1. 压力源：形成个人威胁的环境事件。
Stressor: An environmental event that is perceived by an individual to be threatening.

2. 员工压力：形成威胁的生理或心理反应。
Worker Stress: The physiological and/or psychological reactions to events that are perceived to be threatening or taxing.

3. 情景压力：在工作环境中或在员工个人生活的特定情况下产生的压力。
Situational Stress: Stress arising from certain conditions that exist in the work environment, or in the worker's personal life.

4. 人际压力：在工作中，与其他人交往困难所形成的压力。
Interpersonal Stress: Stress arising from difficulties with others in the workplace.

5. 倦怠：由于长时间的工作压力累积所造成的从组织中退出的综合征。
Burnout: A syndrome resulting from prolonged exposure to work stress that leads to

withdrawal from the organization.

6. 员工帮助计划:是许多雇主提供的雇员福利计划。员工帮助计划的目的是帮助员工处理个人问题,可能会产生不利影响他们的工作表现,健康和福祉。员工协助方案一般包括为员工和他们的家庭成员提供的短期辅导及转介服务。

Employee Assistance Programs：EAPs are employee benefit programs offered by many employers. EAPs are intended to help employees deal with personal problems that might adversely impact their work performance, health, and well-being. EAPs generally include short-term counseling and referral services for employees and their household members.

复习思考题(Questions for Review)

1. 什么是压力? 压力源包括哪些因素?
What is stress? What is included in the stressor?

2. 工作压力的效应体现在哪些方面?
What are the aspects of work stress affect?

3. 压力与绩效有怎样的关系?
What is the relationship between stress and performance?

4. 简述压力管理的原则和方法。
Describe the principles and methods of stress management.

5. 什么是 EAP? EAP 有什么作用?
What is EAP? What are the effects of it?

6. 制订职业发展计划的方法有哪些?
What are the methods of developing career development plan?

研究前沿(Research Front)

Employee stress is a significant issue in the hospitality industry, and it is costly for employers and employees alike. Although addressing and reducing stress is both a noble goal and is capable of resulting in expense reductions for employers, the nature and quantity of hospitality employee stress is not fully understood. The first aim of this study was to identify common work stressors in a sample of 164 managerial and hourly workers employed at 65 different hotels who were each interviewed for eight consecutive days. The two most common stressors were interpersonal tensions at work and overloads (e.g., technology not functioning). The second aim was to determine whether there were differences in the types and frequency of work stressors by job type (i.e., managers versus non-managers), gender, and marital status. Hotel managers reported significantly more stressors than hourly employees. There were no significant differences by gender or marital status. The third aim was to investigate whether the various stressors were linked to hotel employee health and work outcomes. More employee and coworker stressors were linked to more negative physical health symptoms. Also, interpersonal tensions at work were linked to lower job satisfaction and greater turnover intentions.

Introduction

The present study is based on the Job Strain Model proposed by Karasek (1979), who postulated that psychological strain is due to the combined effects of job demands and other factors. Specifically, a high strain job includes high job demands, or workplace stressors. Job strain can manifest itself as poor mental health, physical health problems, and job dissatisfaction and performance problems (Karasek, 1979; Karasek and Theorell, 1990). Testing the resources part of the Karasek model was beyond the scope of the paper. Given how little is known about stress and well-being in the hospitality industry, this study focused on the links between job demands and individual and work outcomes.

Hypotheses development

Hypothesis 1. The most common stressor among hotel employees will be interpersonal tensions, compared to arguments at work, employee and coworker stressors, hotel guest stressors, and over-loads at work.

Hypothesis 2. Hotel managers will report a higher frequency of daily work stressors than hourly employees.

Hypothesis 3. Women, regardless of position, will report greater frequency of daily work stressors than men.

Hypothesis 4. Married employees will report greater daily work stressors than non-married employees.

Hypothesis 5. Employees reporting greater daily stressors will experience more negative physical symptoms.

Hypothesis 6. Employees reporting greater frequency of work stressors will report lower job satisfaction and higher turnover intent.

Results

The data presented here are from hotel managers (N = 98) and hourly employees (N = 66) who completed a baseline survey followed by daily diary telephone interviews for eight consecutive days. For both managers and hourly workers, interpersonal tensions were the most common workplace stressor; therefore, Hypothesis 1 was supported. Hypothesis 2 was supported. There were no significant differences by gender. Therefore, Hypothesis 3 was not supported. No significant differences were discovered between married employees and unmarried employees based on work stressors. Thus, Hypothesis 4 was not supported. Hypothesis 5 and 6 were partially supported.

Conclusion

This research study found that as a group, hotel employees are relatively stressed-out, with hotel workers reporting stressors on 40% ~ 62% of days. These figures compare to a national (U.S.) diverse sample of subjects reporting stressors on only 25% ~ 44% of days (Almeida and Horn, 2004). Interestingly, employees reported much more employee-related than guest-related tensions and stressors. The message for the industry appears to be that although working with guests may at times be challenging and difficult, arguments and tensions among fellow employees turned out to be more prevalent than tensions and stressors related to guests in this study. On the other hand, typical hotel employees may often garner significant positive psychological nourishment from guests.

The stress situation appears to be particularly acute for hotel managers. Managers may experience more work stress because of their generally higher levels of responsibility. Hotel managers in this study worked an average of 57 h per week versus an average of 36 h per week for non-managers, a statistically significant difference. The greater number of hours worked by managers versus hourly employees may contribute, along with their level of responsibility, to managers' level of work stress. Thus, employee stress, and particularly managerial stress, should be a concern for hospitality industry practitioners. If hotel managers are going to work such hours in the long term, then hotel executives should consider ways to reduce those employees' stress, if not work hours.

O'Neill J W, Davis K. Work stress and well-being in the hotel industry. International Journal of Hospitality Management, 2011, 30:385 – 390.

第10章 饭店企业文化和社会责任
(Corporate Culture and Social Responsibility In Hospitality Industry)

本章概要(Summary of This Chapter)

企业文化可以集中地体现一家企业的核心价值观和企业的经营哲学理念,它对企业的经营管理以及员工的行为方式和对企业的忠诚归属都会产生潜移默化的作用。在今天的现代经济社会中,企业的社会责任越来越凸显出来,如何做到经济性和社会性并存发展已经成为现代企业追求的一个目标,企业承担多元化的社会责任,成为了企业在市场竞争中生存和发展的必需保证。本章包括饭店企业文化和饭店企业社会责任两节内容,主要介绍饭店企业在两个方面的表现与价值,从饭店企业文化的内涵、特征、功能以及影响因素四个方面阐述了饭店企业文化的特点;饭店企业社会责任则是阐述相关定义和介绍饭店承担企业社会责任的具体表现和案例。

Corporate culture can focus reflects the core value and management philosophy of a company, it plays an important role in company management as well as employee's behavior and loyalty to corporate. Today, in the modern economy society, corporate social responsibility appears more and more important. It becomes a target that how to fulfill the economy development as well as doing some social devotion. The enterprise has undertaken a wide range of social responsibility has become the corporates ensure the survival and development in the competitive market. This chapter includes corporate culture and social responsibility in hotel company, and introduces the performance and value of both two aspects. The characteristics of the hotel enterprise culture were explained in culture connotation, characteristics, function and the influence; the social responsibility of hotel corporate is introduced by related definition and specific performance and cases of the hotel enterprises.

第10章 饭店企业文化和社会责任

开篇引例 (Beginning Story)

Corporate culture is the soul of modern enterprises, most of successful enterprises in the world almost have their unique and specific culture when compared to others. Corporate culture is not only a kind of management method but also is a driving force to support corporate continuous develop, which will be a comprehensive competitive capability. Hence, corporate culture has become the focus of modern enterprises competition, is the core factor to support corporate development. While for the typical service enterprise—hotel, it plays a more critical role. There is all unique and specific culture which will support their corporates behind these successful hotels.

Meanwhile, the reason why those successful hotels would make a great impression in people's mind, it will have a close relationship with the hotel enterprise bearing professional ethics and social responsibility. With the background of economy globalization and the progress of human civilization, enterprise as a cell of economic and social must shoulder social responsibility, to be a member of social development and to undertake social responsibility. There is no doubt that it will help themselves build a good image, forming an intangible asset, and then become an enterprise competitive advantage. As a result, it will bring to the enterprise long-term, potential benefits. The enterprise bear the social responsibility of the diversification, has become a more and more enterprises in market competition survival and development of the reliable guarantee.

With a growing concern for corporate social responsibility (CSR), leading companies in various industries, driven by companies' stakeholders, consumers, societies and governments, are accelerating initiatives to demonstrate their CSR commitments. For example, General Electric initiated "Ecomagination" (a neologism combining ecology with imagination) as its strategic key word (Business Wire, 2005) and ever since has continued to prepare extensive reports on environmental issues. HSBC, a leader in global banking, announced a carbon neutral initiative, showing its commitment to CSR for climate change problems (BBC News, 2004), while in 2008, Wal-Mart launched its new jewelry line called "Love, Earth" in which Wal-Mart only uses gold, silver and diamonds from mines and manufacturers that meet sustainability standards established by Wal-Mart (Fibre2fashion, 2008).

Along with this general trend of public and corporate attention to CSR issues, the hospitality industry has indicated an ever increasing interest in CSR. For example, the number of CSR and environmental news items on a hospitality industry web site, Hospitality Net,3 increased from 63 in 1999 to 139 in 2007 with 10.4% compound annual growth rate while the number of overall news increased with just a 2.8% compound annual growth rate. More leading hospitality companies, including Hilton, Starwood, Choice Hotels, Starbucks and McDonald's, exclusively provide CSR related reports. Also, at the 2008 Democratic National Convention in Denver, sustainable and eco-friendly wood key cards debuted at hotels, and following the International Air Transport Association's recognition of airline business' social, economic and environmental influences (International Air Transport Association, n. d.), airlines including British Airways, SAS Group, Cathay Pacific and Dragonair launched carbon-offsetting programs to help fund environmental projects (Air Transport Action Group, n. d. ; Armstrong, 2008; Kjelaggard, 2007).

第一节 饭店企业文化
(Hotel Corporate Culture)

一、饭店企业文化的内涵(The Concept of Hotel Corporate Culture)

(一)企业文化的内涵(The Concept of Corporate Culture)

企业文化(Corporate Culture)实践始于日本,理论起源于美国,是由实践而引出理论探讨的。企业文化是指一套被企业员工普遍认可和遵循的价值体系,是通过建立全体员工衷心认同和共有的企业核心价值观念、经营理念和与此相适应的道德规范和行为准则,把企业员工引导到企业所确定的努力方向、行动目标上来,使整个企业在精神和行动上团结一致产生一股强大的凝聚力、向心力,并有一种强烈的认同感和归属感,它使企业独具特色并区别于其他的企业。因此,企业文化通常包括了价值观、公司期望、工作作风、行为规范、思维方式以及物理环境,等等。一个企业的企业文化通常是应对组织内外部的挑战时,由企业员工在互动的过程中形成的。企业的新员工可以通过询问、观察、培训和感受来了解企业内部的文化信息。

企业文化能集中体现一家企业的核心价值观和经营哲学理念,这对企业的经营管理以及员工的行为方式等方面都会产生潜移默化的重要作用。然而企业文化并不是包罗万象的概念,它具有稳定性和成长性,具有能够被传递和发展的特性。企业文化在本质上是企业员工在长期的合作共事中所获得的共同的基本假设和信念,表现在价值观念、行为准则、英雄和象征等方面。

企业文化一般可以归类为三个层次:表层文化、中层文化和深层文化。

(1)第一层是表层文化,是可观察到的人和事物。比如显而易见的企业名称、标识,企业结构和流程,服装,企业内部布局和装饰,行为模式等,也包括企业外部的人通过观察企业员工所能看到、听到和感受到的一切。

(2)第二层是中层文化,是企业文化中表达价值的部分,它是不可见的。价值是企业的战略和理想目标,也是企业希望呈献给公众的形象。价值观定义了对企业来说什么是重要的,什么是不重要的。

(3)第三层是深层文化,是企业内共享的基本假设和信念。它是企业文化的核心,是植根于人的脑中却不被意识到的假设、价值观、信仰、规范的集合体。它们很难被观察到,但正是由于它们的存在,我们才得以理解每一个企业的具体组织事件为什么会以特定的形式发生。一个完善的企业文化系统最基本要素包括企业使命、共同愿景、核心价值观、企业精神、经营理念、员工道德规范、行为准则、口号、标识等。其中企业使命、共同愿景和价值观是企业的三个最基本、最核心也是企业始终面对的问题,分别回答企业为什么存在、将生存到什么样的状态、如何生存等问题。

图 10 – 1 企业文化体系

(二)饭店企业文化的内涵(The Concept of Hotel Corporate Culture)

饭店企业文化是企业文化的一个独特分支,是服务行业企业文化的典型代表。饭店是一个劳动密集型、感情密集型企业,其最基本的产品就是饭店员工所提供的服务,它蕴含着丰富的文化内容。我们常说饭店是客人的"家外之家",客人入住饭店,首先需要得到的是生理上和物理上的满足,然后是追求饭店整体物质环境以及在其接受饭店各项服务过程中所享受到的文化氛围。

作为典型的服务型企业，饭店与工业企业不同，它没有具体的商品，或者说它的商品是以无形的服务为主而不是以有形的物质产品为主，饭店的生产经营活动以提供优质服务为中心。因此，饭店的企业文化一般是以组织精神和服务理念为核心，以特色经营为基础，以标志性的文化载体和超越性的服务产品为形式，在对员工、客人及社区公众的人文关怀中所形成的共同的价值观念、行为准则和思维模式的总和。饭店的企业文化渗透在企业一切活动之中，是企业的灵魂所在。

从本质上讲，饭店提供的产品是服务，饭店所应建立的文化是服务文化。具体来讲，饭店企业文化是企业文化在饭店行业中的具体表现形式，是饭店员工在饭店经营管理过程中共同拥有的一系列价值理念。在每一个饭店中，都存在着随时间演变的价值观、行为方式、典礼仪式及实践体系或模式，它对内能形成饭店内部的凝聚力，对外形成同业之间的竞争力。因此，饭店企业文化是指饭店以组织精神和经营理念为核心，以特色经营为基础，以标志性的文化载体和超越性的服务产品为形式，在对员工、客人及社区公众的人文关怀中所形成的共同的价值观、行为准则和思维模式的总和，主要表现在饭店哲学、饭店价值观、饭店意识、饭店精神、饭店道德、饭店审美观和饭店思维方式等方面。

按照企业文化的层次划分为表层文化、中层文化和深层文化的结构，饭店企业文化作为企业文化的子集，那么对饭店而言，表层文化则是指饭店的物质文化，是最容易被人们所感知的一层企业文化。一般可以理解为饭店在社会上的外表形象，同时也是饭店企业文化层次中最活跃、最生动的层面，其内容主要包括饭店的建筑风格、设施设备、饭店用品和饭店产品等。虽然表层文化是非常具象的，但实质上它并不是简单的拘泥于饭店本身的物质构成，而是指饭店内外物质环境与产品的文化特点以及顾客对他们的审美体验与文化感受，是饭店通过可视的一些客观实体所表达和折射出来的文化特点与内涵。

而饭店的中层文化一般包括饭店企业的行为文化、技术文化、制度文化等，是饭店企业文化中衔接表层文化和深层文化的中间环节。具体可以表现在饭店的经营管理、员工在待客服务的方式和员工的行为准则中，以及饭店的规章制度、管理方法、经济体制，等等。

饭店的深层文化也是饭店最本质的东西，即精神所在，它是饭店企业文化的核心。企业价值观是企业全体成员共同认可的价值标准和价值取向，是一个企业产生持久的向心力和凝聚力的精神源泉，为企业内部提供一种走向共同目标的指导性意识，也为企业员工的日常行为规范提供方向性前提。

二、饭店企业文化的特征(The Character of Hotel Corporate Culture)

(一)企业文化的特征(The Character of Corporate Culture)

企业文化的特征被归纳为九个方面,依次是:人文性、客观性、独特性、稳定性、延续性、系统性、渐进性、整合性以及潜移默化性。

用图示表示如下:

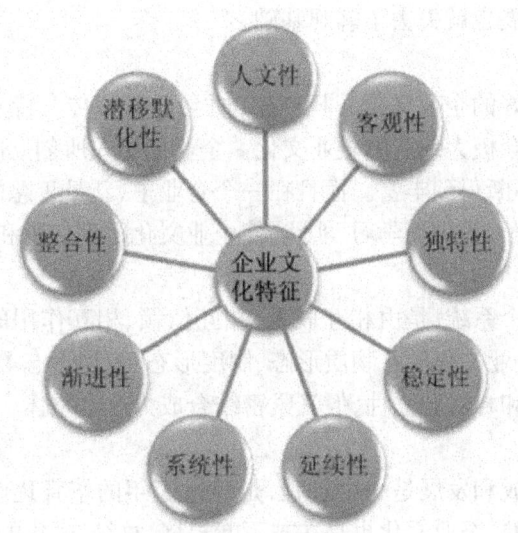

图10-2 企业文化的特征

1. 人文性

企业文化关注的中心是对企业中人的因素的管理与激发,企业的成长与发展需求与个人的成长与发展需求必须在企业文化这个层面达到某种程度上的契合,这样才能真正实现企业与员工的共生共荣。因此,企业文化是一种以人为本的文化,只有着力于以文化因素去挖掘企业中的人的潜力,尊重和重视人才,才能使企业和员工的价值得以体现,实现最终的共赢。

2. 客观性

企业文化具有广泛的作用范围,无处不在。有企业就有企业文化,这是不以人的意志为转移的客观规律。企业文化是根植于企业长期的生产经营实践中,每个企业只要留下历史的足迹都会形成自己的文化,不论优劣都是客观存在。

3. 独特性

每个企业的企业文化都有其区别于其他企业的独特之处。每个企业由于其特殊的历史、人员结构及领导风格等原因而形成了各自不同的企业文化,因此可以说没有两个企业文化完全相同的企业,企业文化的最大特点就是企业的文化个性,没有个性也就谈不上企业文化了。

4. 稳定性

任何一个企业的企业文化总是与企业发展相联系的。企业文化的形成是一个渐进的过程。它一经形成并为全体员工所掌握,都具有一定的稳定性,不因企业产品、组织制度和经营策略的改变而改变。没有质的稳定就没有特定的企业文化,企业文化的存在与发展也就失去了客观基础。

5. 延续性

也称继承性。好的企业文化一旦产生,便会世代相传。特别是企业创始人的价值观、创业精神,会极大地影响企业文化。企业创始人所创立的企业文化会绵延发展,并在实践中不断得到丰富。而且在一个企业中,新员工总能从老员工的身上看到企业文化的影子,并进而学习、实践,使企业文化得到传承和发展。

6. 系统性

企业文化是一个系统,是由相互联系、相互依赖、相互作用的部分和层次构成的有机整体,构成企业文化的有物质形态、制度形态、意识形态等不同层次和内容,虽然他们各有特点和相对独立性,但又紧密结合成为一个整体。

7. 渐进性

企业文化的形成和发展是一个过程,是经过多年的培育逐渐形成的。随着企业的不断发展和成熟,企业文化也是在被不断提炼、总结、升华的。

8. 整合性

企业文化在空间上是统一、相容的。企业的各个部门可能具有各自不同的亚文化,但这些亚文化不会背离企业共同的核心价值观。

9. 潜移默化性

企业文化一旦形成,便会在日常的生产经营活动中通过各种形式"无孔不入"地渗透到员工的思想中去,逐渐形成企业的共同价值观,激励企业广大职工、潜移默化地促使职工朝着同一目标前进。

(二)饭店企业文化的特征(The Character of Hotel Corporate Culture)

饭店作为为顾客提供住宿、饮食等服务的服务性企业,服务是饭店企业的一大特性,而饭店顾客需求的多种多样则决定了饭店企业文化具有的特点,一般具体可以体现在以下几个方面。

1. 饭店企业文化的跨文化融合性特点

饭店企业文化最显著的特点之一就是跨文化融合性。饭店企业是涉外性企业,要接待来自不同国家或地区的顾客,而这些顾客有着不同的文化背景、审美趋向和行为特征。饭店企业面向的是国际市场,这就决定了饭店企业文化必须具备世界性这一特殊性,饭店的企业文化要能够包容不同的文化,使其文化具有高度的融合性。

2. 饭店员工给客人提供的服务

服务是饭店企业文化的基本特点,饭店作为服务型企业,与制造企业不同,饭店出售的是以实物为基础的服务。饭店提供的产品同时兼有无形性和有形性的特点。顾客在购买和消费饭店产品和服务的过程中更多的是希望从中获得这些服务所带来的享受,而不仅仅是物质上的产品。

3. 饭店环境

饭店的环境包括内部环境和外部环境。内部环境是饭店的经营环境,即我们俗称的"硬件",同时还包括员工的工作、生活环境等;外部环境是饭店在社会中的地位、形象和联系。饭店建筑实际上是饭店给人最直观的印象,其本身就是饭店企业文化的一部分。一个饭店往往是一个国家、地区或城市建筑的代表,一定程度上体现了当地旅游发展的水准。

4. 饭店的价值观

饭店的价值观是指饭店在追求经营成功过程中推崇的基本信念及奉行的目标。饭店的价值观是饭店企业文化的核心。当代企业价值观的一个最突出的特征就是以人为中心,以关心人、爱护人的人本主义思想为导向。我们在确立饭店价值观时,必须充分注重到人的发展是饭店发展的基本动力和归宿。饭店在讲究垂直严格管理的同时,也要讲求"无情制度,有情管理",做到既提高效率,又尊重员工。

5. 饭店产品

饭店经营的产品有客房、餐饮、娱乐,等等,最为特殊的是,这些产品都必须通过服务来得到最终的体现。不仅饭店有形产品与无形的产品要有文化内涵,服务同样也是需要文化。首先,要讲求服务过程的规范化和标准化,其次,要在此基础上力求个性化、多样化。

6. 饭店的企业精神

饭店的企业精神是饭店的宗旨、观念、目标和行为的综合,体现了饭店的精神面貌,也是饭店企业文化的概括。如威斯汀饭店集团(Westin Hotel)的企业精神是"为每一类宾客提供高品质的产品服务";四季集团(Four Seasons)的是"一切为了顾客";上海和平饭店的是"优秀企业造就优秀员工,优秀员工造就优秀企业"等。

7. 饭店制度文化

饭店制度是饭店在经营管理时制定的,起规范保证作用的各项规定或条例。它和饭店的领导体制、组织机构共同构成饭店制度文化。饭店制度文化是饭店企业文化的重要组成部分,是一定饭店价值观、饭店的企业精神等精神文化的产物,并适应精神文化的要求。所以饭店在选择领导体制、组织机构的建立、管理制度的制定方面一定要全面、系统、协调、有效。

三、企业文化对饭店管理的促进作用(The Promoting Effect of Corporate Culture to Hotel Management)

(一)企业文化的功能(Fuctions of Corporate Culture)

企业文化的一般性功能包括导向功能、约束功能、凝聚功能、激励功能和调试功能等五个方面：

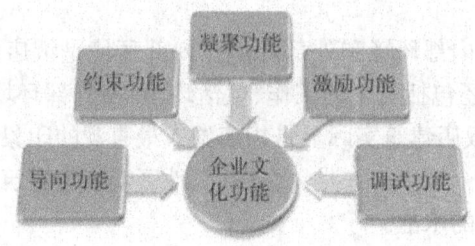

图10-3　企业文化的功能

1. 导向功能

导向功能是指企业文化对企业的领导者和员工的决策和日常行为起引导作用。企业文化的导向功能主要体现在以下两个方面：

①经营哲学和价值观念的指导

一个公司的经营哲学决定了这个公司进行生产经营的思维方式和处理问题的原则，这些方式和原则指导经营者进行正确的决策，指导员工采取科学、规范的方法从事生产经营活动。企业共同的价值观念规定了企业的价值取向，使员工对事物的评判达成共识，使员工有着共同的信仰和价值目标，企业的领导和员工为了实现所共同认定的价值目标去行动。

②企业目标的指引

企业目标代表着企业未来发展的方向，如果没有正确的目标，企业会迷失方向。完善的企业文化会使企业从实际出发，从而制定适合企业未来发展的科学战略目标，并在这种目标的指引下，促使企业朝更好的方向发展。

2. 约束功能

企业文化的约束功能主要是通过完善管理制度和道德规范来实现。

①有效规章制度的约束

作为企业文化内容之一的企业制度是企业内部的法规，是企业的领导者和员工都必须遵守和执行的,对企业和员工的行为具有约束力。

②道德规范的约束

企业文化是一种积极向上的文化,能够体现一个企业的社会责任,与我们内心的道德规范是一致的。而且企业文化中所包含的道德规范从伦理关系的角度来约束企业领导者和员工的举止和行为。如果人们违背了企业文化中道德规范的要求,会受到舆论的谴责。

3. 凝聚功能

因为企业文化是以人为本,尊重员工的感情,从而会在企业中营造出一种团结友爱、相互信任的和睦气氛,能使企业员工之间形成像一个家庭般强大的凝聚力和向心力。而且企业文化中的共同的价值观念会形成员工共同的目标和理想,这样整个企业步调一致,形成一个有强大凝聚力的整体。

4. 激励功能

共同的价值观使每个员工都感受到自己存在和行为的价值,尤其是在以人为本的企业文化氛围中,员工与领导、员工之间的互相关心、互相支持,特别是领导对员工的关心,会使员工有受人尊重的感觉,自然会精神振奋,工作动力十足。另外,企业精神和企业形象对企业员工有着极大的鼓舞作用,会使员工产生强烈的荣誉感和自豪感,从而激励他们更加努力工作,用自己实际行动维护企业的荣誉和形象。

5. 调适功能

调适就是调整和适应。企业各部门之间、员工之间、与客户和企业之间等,难免会有一些不协调和矛盾。企业文化中的企业哲学和企业道德规范会使企业的管理者和员工科学处理这些矛盾,自觉地约束自己,理解他人,从而缓解矛盾,创造一种和谐的工作氛围和强大的凝聚力。

(二)饭店企业文化的功能(Fuctions of Hotel Corporate Culture)

饭店的企业文化会在很大程度上影响到饭店的管理水平,一个好的企业文化,可以给员工积极向上的精神动力;可以对员工的行为进行约束;可以形成凝聚力,从而减少员工的流失率;可以通过形成团结配合的氛围,降低管理的隐性成本,而这些都是饭店管理工作中最重要的内容。良好的饭店企业文化作为一种有形和无形的感召力量,能在企业中构建一个和谐积极的氛围,给员工创造共同的价值观、约定俗成的群体规范和良好的团队合作精神,可以在饭店内部建立起一种自发的动力机制,影响并统一员工为实现饭店目标而共同努力。饭店企业文化作为企业文化的一个分支,具备与企业文化的共通功能:

1. 饭店企业文化对员工行为具有导向作用

优秀的企业文化可以使员工及各级管理人员形成共同的价值观,即把企业员工引到饭店的发展目标上来,而这个价值观会通过思想意识直接影响饭店员工的行为导向。那么,良好的饭店企业文化必然可以通过影响员工的行为导向,即把饭店员工引导到饭店的发展目标上来,为实现提高服务质量的目标而服务。

2. 饭店企业文化对员工的约束作用

很多人认为,在饭店中对员工约束力最强的是饭店的管理制度,比如员工手册。但这却忽略了企业文化对饭店员工的思想、心理和行为的约束和规范作用。企业的制度是硬约束,而企业文化是一种软约束,这种约束产生于饭店的企业文化氛围,群体行为准则和道德规范、群体意识、社会舆论、共同的习俗和风尚等精神文化内容,会造成强大的使个体行为从众化的心理压力和动力,使饭店员工产生心理共鸣,继而达到行为的自我控制。

饭店的生产过程与工厂企业的生产过程最大的差别就在于饭店的服务是强调个性化的,因此饭店在制定管理制度时不可能像工厂那样要求每一个服务过程都必须是标准化的,很多时候只能制定一个服务理念,来指导具体的服务。这在一定程度上给饭店的服务质量控制带来了困难。这时,一个良好的企业文化氛围便可以在制度难以鞭及的地方起到很好的约束作用,并最终使员工形成自律意识。

3. 饭店企业文化的凝聚作用

饭店凝聚力的大小与饭店管理成功率成正比,饭店凝聚力越大,饭店管理成功率就越大,经济效益也就越高。很多企业的总经理都抱怨企业的隐性成本高,企业内部不团结。其实归其原因都是因为企业的凝聚力不够。对于饭店来说,任何一个客人所享受到的服务都是由各个部门共同协作完成的,因此,饭店的凝聚力就显得格外重要。当饭店的每一个员工,都能够通过企业文化的熏陶,形成共同的价值观,那么在工作中就会采用相同的行为模式,并且形成相同的是非评判标准,使员工之间产生共鸣,从而产生归属感。因此企业文化对饭店的凝聚力的形成起到关键的作用。

四、饭店企业文化的影响因素 (The Influence Factors of The Enterprise Culture)

不同的饭店会给客人带来截然不同的感受,每一家饭店都有自己独特的韵味以及让客人念念不忘的特点,影响饭店的企业文化,造成不同饭店企业的特征的因素归纳起来,可以从以下四个方面去概括:

1. 饭店的制度安排和战略选择

饭店企业文化在内容上是其企业制度和战略在人的价值观理念上的反映,而不同的饭店又具有不同的制度安排和战略选择,比如以接待商务客人为主的商务型饭店、以接待旅游度假客人为主的度假型饭店、以接待会议为主的会议型酒店和以接待经济性消费者为主的经济型酒店,等等,因此,对于反映企业制度和战略的企业文化,饭店企业文化在内容上就会有很大的区别。

2. 企业家自身文化

饭店企业家自身的文化对饭店文化的影响也是不可忽视的,也可以说饭店企业文化一定程度上是其企业家文化,尤其是饭店创始人的文化的反映。不同的企业家以不同的价值理念经营管理着饭店,从而影响着饭店企业文化的形成和发展。

例如万豪国际集团,作为当今盛誉全球的酒店管理公司之一,1927 年创始人J·Willard 和 Alice·S·Marriott 在集团创世之初就坚信对他人的奉献是集团成功的关键。80 多年过去了,万豪集团在美国以及其他 67 个国家和地区管理超过 3000 家酒店,但集团的"服务精神"却始终如一,这种被万豪人称为"服务精神"的哲学就是指在万豪已有的 86 年历史的服务于社会的饭店企业文化。

3. 饭店的不同发展阶段

饭店发展处于不同的发展阶段,将有着与自身发展阶段相适应的饭店企业文化和企业文化建设活动。创办初期的饭店企业文化与饭店发展成熟后所凝练的饭店企业文化肯定会有所不同,这就导致了即使是同一个饭店,其饭店企业文化在不同时期也是不同的。但是,这种不同不可能是截然相反的,其表现会是有着一定的连贯性、继承性和深刻性的。

4. 饭店的地理位置

一个饭店的企业文化从其产生的第一天起就将深受饭店所在地区的地理风貌、气候水文、经济水平和风土文化的影响。比如北欧的古堡经典饭店和泰国普吉岛上充满热带风情的饭店无论是建筑风格还是服务方式都会有着极大的差别,这些不同地区特点也会赋予饭店不同的企业文化。

第二节　饭店企业社会责任
（Social Responsibility of Hotel Corporate）

Tips:
In the context of the hospitality and tourism industry, the concerns on CSR are a response to the guidelines established by the World Travel and Tourism Council and the United Nation World Tourism Organization (UNWTO), as well as the environmental awareness raised by the Green Hotels Association.

一、企业社会责任的相关研究和定义(Related Research and the Definition of Corporate Social Responsibility)

企业社会责任理论出现于20世纪初,但真正对其进行系统研究则是近几十年的事。美国学者Howard Bowen在他的里程碑式的著作《商人的社会责任》[1]中首次给企业社会责任下了一个明确的定义:商人按照社会的目标和价值,向有关政策靠拢,做出相应的决策,采取理想的具体行动和义务。其后,一些学者对企业社会责任的定义进行了更加深入的探究,代表性的观点有:美国管理学大师彼得·F·德鲁克[2]认为:"在企业,对社会的责任来自两个方面:一个领域是企业对社会所产生的影响;另一个领域则是社会本身所具有的问题。"里奇·W·格里芬[3]认为:"企业的社会责任是指在提高本身利润的同时对保护和增加整个社会福利方面所承担的责任。"哈罗德·孔茨和海因茨·韦里克[4]认为:"企业的社会责任就是认真地考虑公司的一举一动对社会产生的影响。"

中国学者对企业社会责任的研究始于20世纪90年代,代表性的观点如台湾学者李政义[5]认为:"企业社会责任之根本概念,乃是企业对社会做出的适当的贡献,使社会达成安定与发展。"他强调企业社会责任概念有五点倾向:"责任对象之扩大,责任自发性之增大,非经济性责任之增大,责任之企业目标化,趋向积极责任的倾向。"刘俊海[6]认为:"公司社会责任是指公司不能仅仅以最大限度地为股东们赢利或赚钱为自己唯一的存在目的,而应该最大限度地增进股东利益之外的其他所有社会利益。"梁桂全[7]认为:"企业社会责任的本质是在经济全球化背景下企业对其自身经济行为的道德约束,它既是企业的宗旨和经营理念,又是企业用来约束企业内部包括供应商生产经营行为的一套管理和评估体系。"

虽然学者们对企业社会责任的定义是多种多样,但是从总体上说,不同学者之间在企业社会责任定义的表述方面存在以下共同点:(1)几乎所有定义都认为企业的发展离不开社会,企业是社会整体的一个部分,是社会机构之一;(2)几乎所有的定义都认为企业的建立应该有合法的基础,即企业应该在法律和规则许可的范围内运行;(3)几乎所有的定义都认为企业是一个经济组织,企业运行应该考虑

---

[1] Bowen H R. Social Responsibilities of the Businessman. New York: Harper,1953:31.
[2] 彼得·F·德鲁克. 管理——任务、责任、实践. 北京:中国社会科学出版社,1987:412.
[3] 里奇·W·格里芬. 实用管理学. 上海:复旦大学出版社,1989:73.
[4] 哈罗德·孔茨,海因茨·韦里克. 管理学. 北京:经济科学出版社,1993:689.
[5] 李政义. 企业社会责任论. 台北巨流图书公司,1990:37,45-46.
[6] 刘俊海. 公司的社会责任. 北京:法律出版社,1999:6-7.
[7] 梁桂全. 企业社会责任:跨国公司全球化战略对我国企业的挑战. WTO经济导刊,2004(12).

经济利益;(4)绝大部分定义认为,企业除考虑自身的经济利益之外,还应该考虑社会的利益以及其他利益相关者的利益。企业社会责任是社会对企业的期望和要求,其行为主体是企业而非社会。因此,站在企业的角度,从企业与社会的关系出发,我们可以认为企业社会责任是在一定的历史时期,社会期望企业作为一个营利性的社会经济组织,对其利益相关者和社会整体的所应当承担的法律、经济、伦理道德和慈善责任,包括遵纪守法、保证员工生产安全、职业健康、保护劳动者合法权益、遵守商业道德、保护环境,支持慈善事业、捐助社会公益、保护弱势群体等。从这个意义上,我们可以认为,企业社会责任就是企业对其生产经营活动影响到的任何个人、单位、群体乃至自然环境所应该承担的责任。

因此,结合学者们对企业社会责任的各种解说和定义,我们可以归纳所谓企业社会责任,是指企业在创造利润、对股东承担法律责任的同时,还要承担对员工、消费者、社区和环境的责任。社会责任要求企业必须超越把利润作为唯一目标的传统理念,强调要在生产过程中对人的价值的关注,对消费者、对环境、对社会的贡献,从而承担起追求对社会有利的长期目标的义务。企业作为一个"社会公民"主体出现,从社会考虑自身行为,企业的社会责任区别于商业责任,它是指企业除了对股东负责,即创造财富之外,还必须对全体社会承担责任。

可以用一个四个层次的金字塔图来形象说明企业社会责任的四个类型。

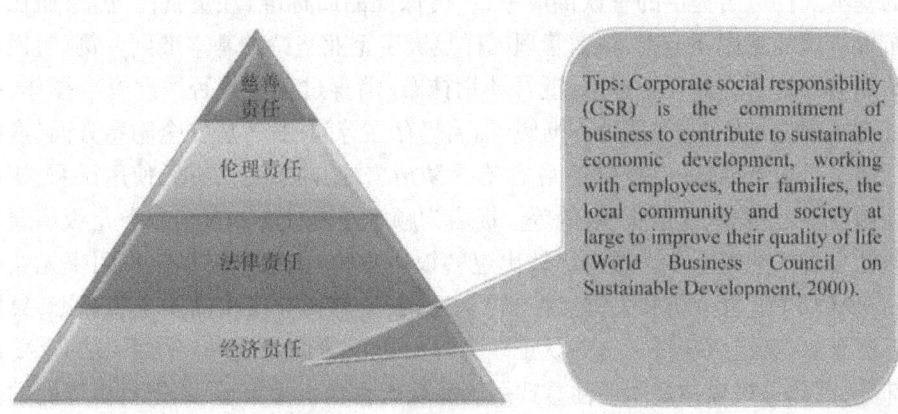

图 10 – 4　企业社会责任金字塔

二、饭店企业社会责任的表现(The Performance of Hotel Corporate Social Responsibility)

一家饭店能够建立起自己品牌的广泛认知度,一定与它一直以来坚持和追求的愿景和使命是分不开的。饭店企业如何履行好自己的社会责任,除了为自己的员工创造幸福、为顾客创造价值以外,为社会创造和谐,做到深入人心,这绝对是饭店企业无法忽视甚至是应该不遗余力的一块重要内容。

我们可以从诚信管理、重视员工、关心弱势群体、加强与非营利组织的合作以及注重环境保护这五个方面来归纳饭店企业社会责任的表现内容:

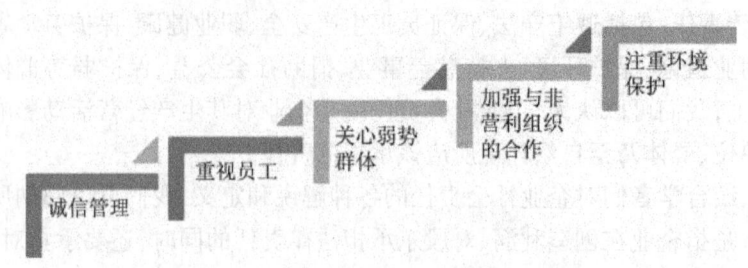

图 10-5　饭店企业社会表现内容

1. 诚信管理

饮食和住宿作为饭店企业两大核心经营业务,如何在这两块业务经营中秉承诚信,为顾客提供货真价实、材质上乘的产品,这应该是饭店永远坚持、视为饭店生命的基本。在饭店提供的餐饮供应中,严格保证品质标准,注重食品安全;而在客房布置清理的工作环节中,诚信管理同样是饭店企业坚持的基本准则。例如,饭店清洁和消毒是否达到科学标准,混合使用抹布、消毒过程中是否按照标准操作,叠放过密或水温过低,造成消毒不彻底,细菌仍存在等问题;客房安全隐患方面,房间电源插头是否有损坏,电线裸露,浴缸有无防滑措施,热水龙头有无使用说明,钥匙管理制度,甚至安全通道管理,等等。饭店为顾客乃至社会的诚信服务是饭店履行企业社会责任的第一步。做得比较出色的饭店集团,例如香格里拉集团率先获得食品 HACCP(危害分析和关键点控制)认证,在业界树立了食品安全新标准,集团旗下已有 20 家饭店获得了这一认证。另外由于供应商是这一安全系统的重要组成部分,因此香格里拉集团还注重选用高品质的食物供货渠道,并把对供应商的要求从食品领域扩展到其他方面。

2. 重视员工

饭店是服务型企业,为顾客提供各种服务是饭店产品的基本,那么作为提供服务的主体——饭店员工,饭店如何对之进行管理与培养也是饭店在履行自己社会责任中不可忽视的重要部分。另外饭店也是劳动密集型企业,为社会提供了相当多的工作岗位,优秀的饭店企业都非常重视员工的培养,致力于降低员工流动率,持续关心员工的成长与发展。

优秀饭店企业重视员工的案例也是比比皆是:香格里拉集团承诺为员工开拓并维持一个安全和健康的环境,并且积极推行各种有益项目以提高员工的身心健康水平,香格里拉的管理者坚信,员工是集团最重要的财富之一,为他们提供公平的就业机会和充分的发展空间,该集团在员工培训方面的投入几乎是全球所有饭店中最高的,分别在北京和马尼拉设立了香格里拉管理培训中心;万豪集团也一直将员工视为是最宝贵的资产,重视提供员工成长和发展的环境,努力营造家的氛围和友好的工作关系,对员工和管理人员的重要贡献实施奖励制度,向员工提供儿童保育和家庭服务;"喜达屋职业关爱发展培训项目"在业内得到极高的认可和推崇,这归根于喜达屋浓厚的"关爱文化"。作为人力资源领域的先锋,喜达屋让每位员工感受到与众不同,倾听员工的心声,理解员工的价值,将其面临的困难和挑战转化为成长的动力和机遇。

3. 关心弱势群体

对社会弱势群体送去关怀和帮助是饭店企业表达对社会的关爱,回报社会的一种最为直接的方式,比如有些饭店会专门设立对患有重疾员工的关爱机制,建立完备的医疗和补助系统,对患病的职工实行更加人性化的帮助,除此之外,对社会上的弱势群体也是积极地提供力所能及的帮助,比如重视饭店社区周围以及远郊贫困山区的弱势群体,定期对他们送去衣物食品和书籍,甚至安排饭店员工做志愿者慰问孤老,援助贫困儿童,等等。

万豪集团在与 DECA(美国职业教育俱乐部)长达 25 年的合作中,为高中生免费提供饭店、商业、营销等方面的技能培训,并为残障人士设立了万豪基金会,建立了"从学校到工作的桥梁"计划,以帮助他们更好地找到有价值和令人满意的工作,集团还准备对居住在华盛顿特区的家庭有困难的少女进行饭店职业生涯指导,以期许她们以后加入饭店行业,为自身的生计掌握一技之长。

4. 加强与非营利组织的合作

饭店企业往往会选择通过与一些非营利组织合作的方式来达到自己履行企业社会责任的愿望,因为这些非营利慈善组织在社会福利援助方面操作更为专业和成熟,社会影响力广泛,饭店企业通过与这些专业的援助组织合作,可以更好地帮助到更多的人群,也能获得更多的社会认同。

例如 Six Sense 与中国民政部成为合作伙伴,设立中国社会工作者协会,并签下协议,让"关爱儿童"项目普及到中国 14 个贫困省份,项目的资金则由 Six sense 集团在世界各地的度假村以销售动物玩具所得收入全部捐赠。美国金普顿饭店集团也一直与其北美地区当地的非营利组织保持着良好的合作关系,这种合作包括传达饭店的服务艺术、接受饭店的教育支持,通过与其他慈善组织和相应机构联手,一起为贫困群体提供食物救助、保护未成年儿童的权益。

5. 注重环境保护

饭店企业履行自己的社会责任,除了面对社会成员和慈善组织之外,对地球环境的维护方面,同样需要担负起属于自己的一份责任。

法国雅高集团在环保方面做得十分出色,雅高集团早在 1994 年就在全球范围内建设了一个由 53 个环保联络员组成的网络,以便集团在其各项目的起步阶段就考虑环境和生态要求。集团有 30 家饭店已获得 ISO14001 认证,而其他饭店也配备了用以测量能源、水资源消耗和减少废物排放量的检测装置。实际上,不管是在国际范围内还是在股东的眼里,雅高都已被列为负责任的投资主体之一,符合道琼斯持续发展全球指数(DJSI World)和泛欧可持续发展基准(DJSI STOXX)等对环保的要求。

另外在全球的饭店业中,被公认为是履行环境责任楷模的还有 Six sense 集团,Six sense 集团的发展目标更关注于:减少资源的消耗和废物的产生;实施能源管理和用水节约;雇用当地社区的群众开展社会责任活动;保护当地的植物和动物。公司用每年营业额的 0.05% 设立基金会来支持各种环境保护和社会活动。其中最有意思的就是顾客"碳中和"项目,该项目提倡让顾客为运送他们到达岛上的飞机所释放的二氧化碳进行付费捐赠,以期将自身产生的碳排放用购买方式抵消中和。之后,集团将所得的捐款交给注重植树造林的非政府组织,让该组织种植的树木带来的环境绿化、生态保护和氧气产生最终与顾客因度假产生的碳排放量相抵。值得一提的是,集团还从小事做起,保护生态环境。从 2008 年 10 月 1 日起,Six sense 规定旗下任何一个度假村都不提供进口的瓶装水,顾客可有两个选择,要么是 Six sense 的汽水,要么是当地的饮用水。这样做的目的就是为了避免因长途运送进口瓶装水而产生的碳排放量,所以集团宁可更多地使用当地物料和时令物料,以减少给大自然带来"碳足迹",同时为当地社区带来更多的收益。现在,Six sense 大部分的本地饮用水都是由度假村免费提供,即便是餐厅的冰水,也比瓶装的品牌水便宜很多。

三、中国饭店履行社会责任的现状(The Current Situation of Hotel Fulfilling Social Responsibility in China)

1. 绿色饭店的创建

国际上衡量一个饭店是否是生态环保型,一般有五项指标:饭店建设对环境的破坏最小、设备的运行对环境的影响最小、饭店的物资消耗降低到最低、饭店提供满足人体健康需求的产品、饭店积极参与社会性的环保活动。①

1999年中国旅游业的主题为保护生态环境,因此该年被称为"生态旅游年"。为了配合这一主题,3月29日,浙江省计划与经济委员会、浙江省环境保护局联合发出《关于开展"创建绿色饭店"活动的通知》,号召浙江省开展"创建绿色饭店、倡导绿色消费"的活动。

1999年4月20日,杭州、宁波、绍兴等地的14家浙江省著名饭店的总经理联合向浙江省饭店发出"创建绿色饭店、倡导绿色消费"的倡议书,号召全省饭店同行一起参与、开展"创绿"活动。从而掀起了以节能、环保、降低消耗、绿色服务和绿色消费为内容的绿色饭店创建热潮。

该倡议书的主要目的是要提高饭店人员的环保意识,在不降低服务质量的前提下开展绿色行动:如节能,努力减少洗涤剂、塑料用品的使用;拒绝野生保护动物为原料,积极采用绿色用品,提供绿色产品,推广绿色服务;引导宾客参与、共同开展环境保护活动,减少一次性用品的消耗和水资源的浪费。一年之后,即2000年6月5日世界环境日,浙江省评出首批32家饭店为"绿色饭店"。

在浙江省创建绿色饭店的基础上,全国各地的饭店都加入这个行列,开始创绿工程。2000年至2004年上海、山东、江苏、广东等开始所在省市的地方绿色饭店创建工作。2000年至2004年,北京市开始地方绿色饭店的创建工作。一些地区性的、以环保为主要内容的绿色饭店标准也在深圳、广西、四川、河北和山东等一些省市出台。2003年由中国饭店协会制定的我国第一个绿色饭店国家行业标准(SB/T10356—2002)于3月1日起实施,迄今为止,中国住宿与餐饮行业最权威的绿色饭店标准由此诞生。2005年中国饭店协会发布《中国绿色饭店实施细则100条》,首次为中国饭店企业创建国家级绿色饭店提出的系统性指南。2006年国家旅游局正式颁布《绿色饭店标准》。通过绿色管理和绿色服务来创建绿色饭店,已是目前旅游饭店业的一种趋势。

绿色饭店的核心是在为宾客提供符合环保、健康要求的绿色客房和绿色餐饮的基础上,在经营过程中减少对环境的污染,节能降耗,实现资源利用的最大化。因此绿色饭店又称为环境友好型饭店。从企业社会责任角度来看,绿色饭店的创建实际上是中国饭店业对环保责任的一种回应,引导宾客承担企业社会责任。

2. 其他履行社会责任的行为或现象

相比较其他业态,饭店业与国际接轨最早,最先接受西方管理理念。在力所能及的情况之下,某些饭店承担了相应的社会责任,包括伦理责任、慈善责任。典型

---

① 北京绿色旅游饭店今日启动"水卫士"行动。http://www.visitbeijing.com.cn/news/n214679725.shtml. 2011 - 12 - 23.

的有：

第一，向特定群体捐赠现金或物品。

在非典期间，青岛市饭店业"众志成城、抗击非典募捐活动在青岛香格里拉大饭店举行，全市近 30 家饭店的总经理参加了此次募捐活动，捐款金额达 24580 元。5 月 8 日，海天大酒店举行抗击非典保卫青岛献爱心捐助活动，在青岛的海天名人俱乐部的成员陈道明、葛优、刘信义、吕思清、赵宝乐、牛莉、周杰等与海天大酒店部分员工一起参加了捐助活动；为了河南省"艾滋病村"的孩子能上学，中国大饭店将募捐来的 6 万元善款通过中国慈福行动交给河南省某小学 100 名贫困学生。

2008 年 5 月 12 日，四川汶川发生 8.0 级地震，宁夏、青海、甘肃、河南、山西、陕西、山东、云南、湖南、湖北、上海、重庆等省市均有震感。地震对四川及周边省份的饭店造成一定程度的损害。地震发生之后，在党中央、国务院的坚强领导下，全国人民万众一心，全力以赴抗震救灾，深处灾区的旅游企业与灾害进行着顽强斗争。同时，我国饭店业积极响应党中央国务院及国家旅游局的号召，积极参加抗震救灾活动，各地饭店管理公司和旅游饭店协会积极组织募捐活动。据中国旅游饭店业协会不完全统计，我国饭店业募捐金额高达 3 亿元，与此同时，中国旅游饭店业协会还向饭店行业发出"安排灾区酒店员工就业"的倡议书，受到多家饭店管理公司及饭店的支持响应，还制订了安排灾区酒店员工就业计划，最终安排近 900 余名灾区酒店员工就业。

第二，关爱弱势群体。

北京饭店将淘汰的电脑捐赠给北京市海淀区振兴打工子女学校；天津假日饭店借福利院成立 55 周年之际向儿童福利院捐赠物资；开封中州国际饭店与当地媒体联袂邀请 50 位独居老人到五星级饭店过除夕，以表示对独居老人的关爱；浙江杭州黄龙饭店 18 年来年年捐赠物资给当地的福利院，并委派员工定期到福利院做义工和为福利院做人力资源管理的培训；北京香格里拉饭店关爱京城民工子弟学校捐赠了足球、排球、羽毛球、乒乓球、哑铃、各种文具以及近千册课外读物。

饭店的企业文化和社会责任对饭店企业在激烈的市场竞争中保持长盛不衰有着至关重要的影响，一家优秀的饭店企业应该重视企业文化的建设工作，用自己独特的企业文化去影响员工和顾客，同时积极履行自己的社会责任，为社会贡献出自己的一份力量，让企业在一个良性的发展圈中持续健康地发展。

案例分析(Practice Case Analysis)

Development of a Responsible Tourism Policy[①]

Description of Good Practice

Recognizing the increasing awareness of sustainability issues within the travel industry, Exodus, a UK-based adventure tour operator, developed a Responsible Tourism Policy in 2000. The policy, which formalizes the company's commitment to environmental, social and economic sustainability, applies to all offices, including those in the field. Central to the policy is Exodus' commitment to development to develop socially, economically and ecological sound trips in which:

• Local communities play a fair role in the operations and obtain a fair share of the benefits;

• Destinations receive long-term investments and commitments from the company, thus providing economic stability to both;

• The company contributes to conserving the natural resources on which this type of tourism depends.

The key elements of the Responsible Tourism Policy are a Mission Statement, which describes the company's aspirations for responsible tourism and sets out commitments and goals, and a Code of Practice, which outlines the management practices necessary for implementation of the policy. The policy is implemented in three key areas: the company's own operations, customer awareness of the issue and destination sustainability.

Exodus carefully planned the development of its Responsibility Tourism Policy, convinced that the development process itself could greatly contribute to the successful implementation of the policy in everyday business. The International Centre for Responsible Tourism, based in the UK, was also brought in to assist in the process.

The company created a Responsible Tourism Manager position, requiring expertise in the both tourism and conservation, to send a clear signal to all levels of the company that the issue of sustainability was becoming an integral part of the company's business.

Responsible Tourism seminars for Exodus' entire UK-based staff, from operations, marketing, sales and finance departments, were organized to give employees an

---

[①] 摘自:Sustainable Tourism: The Tour Operations' Contribution.

opportunity to contribute to the development of the policy, hence increasing the level of ownership and the effective identification of roles and responsibility in the implementation phase. Participants in the two-day seminars helped determine action areas for the company's Responsible Tourism Policy and the business areas that would play a key role in the implementation. In addition, the participants offered feedback on an earlier draft of the Code of Practice.

Implementation

To ensure effective communication among staff and implementation of the policy, the company has instituted the following measures:

● New staff are given training in the policy, and there are training sessions and intranet updates at regular intervals for all staff;

● Co-ordination among staff in charge of policy implementation, reporting on initiatives and general updated. When relevant, occur at weekly departmental meeting, attended by the Responsible Travel Manager;

● Client feedback forms and operator and leader feedback are used to monitor results;

● The policy and actions taken to implement it are regularly reviewed.

The Responsible Tourism Policy is implemented in all business areas of the company. For example, at headquarters, Exodus has implemented recycling and energy managementprogrammes.

To ensure that existing and new trips maximize benefits to local communities and the environment, Exodus' policy includes:

● Hiring of more local guides to provide better interpretative experiences and support to the local communities;

● Purchasing of local products and services, where appropriate, for all trips;

● Working with local operators to implement the policy;

● Limiting group size based on the local situation, with a maximum of 22 people in appropriate circumstances.

The policy also aims at promoting and raising awareness of responsible travel practices among customers. For example, tour leaders are trained in responsible tourism principles and the importance of local issues and encouraged to be proactive on sustainability issues. In Morocco and Nepal, training seminars have been offered to local tour leaders, including information on the main environmental and social threats of tourism, particularly trekking trips. The leaders are introduced to best practices that they can promote and recommend when leading tours in environmentally and socially sensitive areas.

To further promote customer awareness, much of the company's literature, including brochures, trip notes, pre-departure information packets, feedback forms and web pages, include references to the policy and responsible tourism principles. In addition, key sales and marketing decisions have been that responsible tourism is a core element of Exodus' business, for example:

- The responsible travel section of the company's website is directly accessible from the page;
- The Exodus newsletter includes a section on responsible travel;
- Sales personnel have been encouraged to raise the issue when appropriate.

Finally, Exodus also implements its policy by contributing directly to conservation and development projects. Trip leaders are encouraged to inform the UK headquarters about any specific situation where an Exodus contribution could make a difference. The following are several of the projects that Exodus has been involved in so far:

- Providing financial and technical support to two tree nurseries at Manag in the Annapurna region in Nepal, to respond to deforestation and ensure that trekking practices do not worsen the problem;
- Supporting the Baobab Community Project in Tanzania, by staying at the site and encouraging clients to get activity involved;
- Providing financial support to a small-scale project to build to build a reliable water source for a village in the Atlas mountains, in Morocco;
- Supporting, in co-operation with Tourism Concern, the work of the International Porter Protection Group (IPPG) and particularly the Porters' Rights Campaign.

Benefits

Since the Responsible Tourism Policy was implemented, Exodus has seen a number of benefits, including:

- Publicity surrounding the policy has encouraged bookings by a small but growing number of clients who cite responsible tourism practices as a reason for choosing Exodus over other operators.
- The policy has led to positive publicity in the media and industry recognition, helping to raise the profile of sustainable tourism in this sector of the travel industry. Exodus was highly commended in the British Airways Tourism for Tomorrow Awards for its operations.

● The policy has enhanced human and intellectual capital at Exodus. Involvement of the staff from the beginning has led to a feeling of ownership of issue and policy, and employees feel good about being involved with a responsible company. The company found its staff readily willing to accept and apply responsible tourism principles; all they needed was direction in how to do so.

● Working with authorities in destinations to identify their problems and desires has helped to overcome some of the problems associated with tourism.

Comments

A Responsible Tourism Policy should be at the heart of any action or decision that a company takes, to ensure that sustainability will be at the core of the company's business strategy and decisions. Clients will see responsible tourism as an integral part of their holiday; where companies have no policy, it will be seen as a negative factor, leading clients to book with companies that do have such a policy.

Furthermore, as more companies implement responsible (or sustainable) tourism principles as their core values, more clients will recognize these values as an industry standard and become aware of the impacts of their travel choices.

Questions for Discussion:

Whether this policy has a good benefit to company's profit? If it has, please talk about what benefit could be brought in a short time and in a long time?

名词解释(Key Terms)

1. 企业文化:企业文化是企业的基本假设,即一个组织在处理外部适应和内部整合问题的过程中发明、发现或开发出来的,而且运作良好足以被视为有效,并因此成为一种模式以教给新成员去感知、思考和体会与其有关的其他问题的正确方法。

Corporate Culture: Corporate culture is the pattern of basic assumptions that a given group has invented, discovered, or developed in learning to cope with its problems of external adaptation and internal integration, and that have worked well enough to be considered valid, and, therefore, to be taught to new members as the correct way to perceive, think, and feel in relation to other problems.

2. 企业社会责任:企业社会责任是企业持续承诺的行为道德,同时提高员工个人和其家庭整体的生活质量,以及为当地社区和整个社会的经济发展做出贡献。

Corporate Social Responsibility: Corporate social responsibility is the continuing commitment by business to behave ethically and contribute to economic development while improving the quality of life of the workforce and of their families as well as of the local community and society at large.

复习思考题(Questions for Review)

1. Please explain the definition of hospitality corporate culture, and which hotels have their culture, please tell something about it.

饭店企业文化是什么？你知道的有哪些饭店集团的企业文化？都具体是什么？

2. What features could be recognized with hospitality corporate culture?

饭店企业文化具有哪些特点？

3. What are the factors that would affect the hospitality corporate culture?

影响饭店企业文化的因素有哪些？

4. What aspects of hotel complete social responsibility to their employee include?

饭店企业对员工的社会责任有哪些？

5. Why should hotel take the public charity responsibility?

饭店企业为什么要承担公益慈善责任？

研究前沿(Research Front)

Corporate social responsibility reporting by the global hotel industry: Commitment, initiatives and performance[①]

Author: Danuta de Grosboi, Department of Tourism and Environment, Brock University, 500 Glenridge Ave., St. Catharines, Canada

The current study evaluates corporate social responsibility (CSR) reporting practice among the largest hotel companies in the world. Based on the content analysis of websites and reports published online by the top 150 hotel companies in the world in

---

① Danuta de Grosbois. Corporate social responsibility reporting by the global hotel industry: Commitment, initiatives and performance. International Journal of Hospitality Management 31(2012).

summer 2010, it identifies the communication methods used by hotel companies as well as the scope of reported information. Specifically, it demonstrates that while a large number of companies report commitment to CSR goals, much smaller number of them provide details of specific initiatives undertaken to contribute to these goals and even less of them report actual performance achieved. The study also identifies a number of challenges which make it very difficult to meaningfully compare performance of the hotel groups that do report it, including issues such as different methodologies applied, different measures used and lack of clarity with respect to the scope of reporting.

1. Introduction

Over the last two decades the public, governments, customers and other stakeholders have been demonstrating growing awareness of the social and environmental consequences of human activity in general and business operations in particular. As a result, the idea of sustainability and its three pillars of economic, environmental and social action gained popularity. Despite the documented trend of increase in the number and quality of CSR reports and Internet communication of CSR across different industries (Lober et al., 1997; Esrock and Leichty, 1998; Line et al., 2002), reporting practice still shows low adoption in many sectors and the information released by different companies varies significantly in its scope and depth (Holcomb et al., 2007). At the same time, there is also a concern about the quality and usability of the reported CSR information. Researchers point out that the currently available corporate environmental information is difficult to use for external evaluation and comparison (Hooper and Greenall, 2005) and call for disclosure standards and auditing procedures that would improve the quality and comparability of the reported information.

This study focuses on hotel industry. Issues of implementation and reporting of CSR efforts are especially relevant and critical for the tourism industry, which while potentially bringing economic and social benefits to destinations can also have huge negative economic, social, and environmental impacts. While a number of studies investigated range of CSR practices implemented by hotels or other accommodation companies (e. g. Carlsen et al., 2001; Bohdanowicz, 2006; Erdogan and Baris, 2007; Chung and Parker, 2010), less attention has been devoted to evaluation of hotels' CSR reporting practice. Several studies on this topic that have been identified (Holcomb et al., 2007; Priego and Palacios, 2008; Bohdanowicz and Zientara, 2008) focus on low number of companies or on individual hotels, but not on hotel companies. Currently there is no study that would provide an overview of the CSR reporting practice in the hotel industry on a global scale. The objective of this paper is therefore to investigate the amount and nature of CSR-related information provided to the public by hotel companies on their corporate websites.

2. Methodology

The study population included 150 largest hotel companies in the world, as ranked in the 'Corporate 300 list' by Hotel Magazine compiled as of the end of year 2009. Websites for all the companies were identified and searched for CSR-relevant information. The search encompassed all the content of corporate websites, corporate annual reports, explicit sustainability reports and all other materials available through the hotel companies' websites. The study focused on corporate signature websites which are designed to present the identities that corporation claims for itself as a unit (Esrock and Leichty, 2000; Maignan and Ralston, 2002). As a result, websites of individual hotel brands or individual hotels were not considered. In case a company created a separate website for its corporate CSR efforts or for its charitable foundation, these sites were analyzed if there was a link to them from the main corporate website. For companies having headquarters in countries other than English-speaking, only the English version of their websites was analyzed. Data collection took place between June and August 2010.

The collected data was analyzed using quantitative content analysis method which has been widely used in research on corporate social responsibility and belongs to the most popular methods of analyzing social and environmental reporting in firms (see Grayet al., 1995; Deegan and Gordon, 1996; Milne and Adler, 1999; Holder-Webb, 2007; Holder-Webb et al., 2009 among others). The content of the websites was coded for several variables. First, the use of different CSR communication methods was investigated. Six major methods of communicating CSR-related information were identified from the previous literature and refined as data collection proceeded. These methods include: separate CSR report or section of annual report; section of the website devoted to CSR explicitly; section of the website introducing the company (info, awards, mission, values, history); career section; press releases; and newsletters/magazines/blogs for employees, partners or customers. The use of each method of communication was recordedfor each company as a binary variable (used versus not used).

Secondly, a framework of five CSR themes and 33 CSR-related goals has been developed for the purpose of this study, based on previous literature and the principles of sustainability and CSR drawn from Global Reporting Initiative (2000) and United Nations Environmental Programme and World Tourism Organization (2005). The five themes included environmental goals, employment quality, diversity and accessibility, society and community wellbeing, and economic prosperity. The list of the themes and goals is presented in Table 1. The framework was revised and refined as data collection proceeded. For each goal, the following information was recorded: whether the company stated its commitment to the goal, whether the company reported any specific initiatives aimed at supporting the goal; and whether the company reported evaluation of progress towards the goal or evaluation of any initiative aimed at contributing to that goal. The last two categories were recorded both at the corporate level and at the individual hotel level. The distinction between corporate level and individual property level has been introduced in this study as it is significantly influencing the meaning of the reported information. This approach allows to identify the number of companies that report information about their global operations, and distinguish them from companies that provide only examples of hotels with specific initiatives or performance without communicating any detail about how much or well the whole company is doing. In the second case, the hotel company may be showcasing efforts of an individual property's owner, but not have any CSR policy or initiatives implemented in its other hotels.

The data was collected and coded by one researcher. In order to check for inter-coder reliability, a second researcher used the specified coding system to analyze 20 websites chosen randomly from the population. Next, the inter-coder reliability was evaluated for all coded variables and resulted in levels of agreement ranging from 85% to 100%, indicating high reliability.

3. Results

3.1 Availability and sources of CRS information

All 150 hotel companies had English-language websites available in summer 2010. Out of the 150 analyzed companies, 46 provided no information related to CSR goals or efforts. The remaining 109 companies provided some CSR-related information, although the amount of this information and methods of its communication varied significantly. The sections of the website used to provide CSR-related information included, in order of popularity: 'about us' section (used by 63 companies to provide CSR information), CSR-devoted section (used by 61 companies), career/job opportunities section (used by 60 companies), press room (used by 46 companies), downloadable section of annual report or CSR/environmental report (used by 21 companies); and newsletters/

magazines/blogs for employees, partners or customers (used by 9 companies).

Many companies provided CSR-related information using more than one of the above methods. Although the number of sources used by the company to disclosure CSR information does not reflect the quality of the disclosure, it is still considered informative, as it is an indication of the importance of an issue to the reporting entity (Gray et al., 1995).

Out of the companies analyzed in this study, 39 companies used only one source to communicate its CSR-related information (17 companies used "about us" section of the website; 10 companies used career section; 5 companies used CSR-specific section; 5 used press releases and 2 used newsletters as a sole method of providing CSR information). All the remaining companies used more than one method of communication, with three companies (Inter Continental Hotel Group, NH Hotels and Marriott International) using all six methods of communication through website to provide their CSR-related information to different stakeholders.

Analysis of online CSR communications methods used by the hotel companies allows identifying four major groups of companies based on their CSR communication pattern, They are:

(1) hotel companies with a downloadable CSR or environmental report or section of annual report devoted to CSR; often also using other methods of CSR communications;

(2) hotel companies with CSR devoted section of their website, often also using other methods of CSR communication, but with no downloadable CSR or environmental report nor CSR-specific section of their annual report;

(3) hotel companies with no explicit website section or report addressing CSR, but providing some CSR information in other sections of the website;

(4) hotel companies with no information regarding their impacts or CSR efforts provided.

3.2 Scope of reporting CSR goals

The second goal of this study was to identify the scope of information reported by hotel companies. To address this issue, data was collected regarding reporting of 33 CSR goals, in terms of commitment, initiatives and performance, both at hotel company level and at individual hotel level.

3.2.1 Environmental goals

Out of the 150 hotel companies studied, 61 either explicitly stated their commitment to protection of environment, or provided information about environment-related goal or initiative (e.g. in a news item, or by reporting an environmental award). Seven companies only stated their commitment and did not provide any additional information. For the companies that provided additional information, the reporting of 11 specific environmental goals has been investigated: mitigation of climate change; energy conservation; renewable energy use and clean energy production; water conservation; waste reduction and recycling; water and soil pollution reduction; air pollution reduction; responsible design, construction and renovations, biodiversity protection; prevention of ozone layer depletion; and noise reduction.

In addition to (or in some cases instead of) stating the commitment to specific goals, a number of companies also reported different initiatives aimed at contributing to these goals. For example, some of the initiatives aimed at climate change mitigation included: utilization of energy-efficient light bulbs, programmed lighting, implementation of systems for monitoring energy consumption, heat recovery from air conditioning and cooling appliances, installing solar-powered hot water systems, using solar thermal energy, heat pumps, and solar panels, low carbon options for business travel and daily commuting (hybrid cars, business bikes for employees), offsetting carbon emissions from all business travel by the employees, option to offset carbon emissions for customers, and promoting carpooling. On the other hand, initiatives aimed at water conservation included: retrofitting water-saving technologies in bathrooms (reducing toilet tank volume, installing double flush mechanisms), employee training in more water-efficient routines, awareness-raising among clients, detecting and repairing drips and leaks in rooms, planting gardens with endemic species and irrigating them with service water, reusing water, constructing own water treatment plants, and installing double water circuits to collect soapy waters from showers and washbasins separately. The extent of reporting CSR initiatives ranged from companies reporting only one initiative to companies giving extensive review of more than 20 initiatives aimed at one goal at the time.

Several companies (between 0 and 11 for each goal) reported their environmental performance at individual property level. In most of the cases this information complemented information at the corporate level, but there were also a few companies that reported performance for specific goals only at individual property level. These included, among others, Destination Hotels and Resorts and Gaylord Hotels. Gaylord Hotels was the only company that provided environmental initiatives information as well as several performance measures at the property level for all four of its hotels. The remaining hotels providing performance or initiatives at the level of individual hotels did it only for self-selected properties and usually focused on one or a very few initiatives per property.

3.2.2 Employment quality

Employment quality-related information was mostly provided in career sections of the websites, although it was also reported in CSR sections or in sustainability reports. 72 companies provided some information about employment quality, although the scope varied significantly. It ranged from companies explicitly stating commitment to providing good working conditions to their employees with explanation of policies implemented and achieved results, to companies providing very scarce information, often limited to a list of benefits to attract future employees. For example, 10 out of the 72 companies which provided employment quality information did it exclusively in career section of the website and did not provide any other CSR related information or statement. Most of them also did not provide any tangible performance evaluation. These companies, although classified as having provided employment quality information, do not declare CSR commitment, but seem to be simply trying to attract the best talent by explaining benefits for potential employees.

In terms of reporting commitment to employment quality, the most popular goals were: providing opportunities for learning and development; providing fair wages and benefits; and providing opportunities for career advancements (reported by 52、51 and 49 companies, respectively). The remaining 5 employment quality goals were mentioned much less frequently. The same three goals were the most popular when it came to reporting specific initiatives aimed at supporting them, although similarly to environmental goals, the numbers of companies reporting initiatives were lower than the number of companies reporting commitment.

All the goals within employment quality were measured by a very few companies, 14 at most (in case of the goal of providing opportunities for learning and development) and some by 1 company only (providing a work/life balance policies and providing employee assistance programs). For example, 9 out of 150 hotel companies mentioned having employee assistance programs, including for example programs to help employees in social need or suffering loss of a family member, or to offer financial support for children of employees. Gruppo Posadas was the only company reporting performance with respect to employee assistance programs by giving number of cases who received help. The activities were carried through a foundation established by the company.

However, no detail is provided with respect to how much funds have been raised by the Foundation and how much was contributed by the company. Annual reports from foundations are available only in Spanish.

3.2.3 Diversity and accessibility

Diversity and accessibility was mentioned in one way or another by 36 companies. In terms of diversity, the most popular goal was to increase diversity in the workforce (31 companies stated commitment to this goal), followed by the goal to increase diversity among partners and suppliers (commitment stated by 13 companies). Only two companies (Marriott International and Kimpton Hotel and Restaurant Group) discussed their commitment to increase and embrace diversity among customers. The most popular initiatives implemented to support workforce diversity goal included training on diversity, working with minority organizations, establishing diversity council or another body responsible for diversity. With respect to partners and affiliates, the initiatives that were implemented included, among others, minority and women-owned business partner programs and other preferential procurement program.

Very few companies reported their performance with respect to diversity goals, and when they did it, the most popular indicators included percentage of employees with different background, percentage of women in management positions, and the number of employees who participated in diversity training. With 12 companies reporting their performance, the remaining companies limited their communication to commitment statement such as Pyramid Hotel Group statement on its website (2010): "our company is fully committed to diversity in the workplace and supports initiatives to promote this objective." As much as the commitment statement shows that the company realizes the importance of the given goal, it does not explain what extent of efforts is undertaken and with what results.

Accessibility (either for employees, customers or partners) is explicitly declared as one of the goals by 15 companies, while additional 2 provide information about accessibility initiatives without explicitly stating their commitment. For example, Lopesan Hotels and Resorts published a news item on its website which explains that menus are available in Braille writing at one of its hotels and that the initiative is going to be extended to all the other hotels of the Lopesan Hotels and Resorts chain. However, accessibility is not recognized or stated as one of the company goals or part of CSR efforts.

3.2.4 Community wellbeing

Community and society wellbeing has been mentioned either explicitly (commitment statement) or implicitly (initiatives to support any of its goals) by 72 hotel companies. This number encompasses all companies expressing commitment or initiatives aimed at any of the following goals: to improve quality of life in the community, to assist international/global social causes, to protect heritage, culture or traditions, to raise employee, customer or public awareness of and involvement in sustainable development, to offer responsible or healthy product choices, and to create safe environment for customers.

The most popular goals were improving quality of life in local communities (54 commitment statements); involving employees, customers and/or partners in CSR efforts (38 commitment statements) and assisting global social causes (29 commitment statements). There were many examples of initiatives provided for these goals, but again much smaller percentage of companies provided measurement of their performance. Involvement in supporting communities often took the form of sponsoring charities and non-profit initiatives at local and global level, assisting them with fund-raising, training, and providing in-kind donations (such as free meeting rooms, pens, towels, beach balls, hats, play houses, etc.) as well as volunteering work by the employees. Performanceat the corporate level was reported at most by 27 companies (forthe goal of supporting local communities). It was usually captured by indicators such as: total donations, number of hotels participating in an annual fundraising event, donations to local charitable causes. Even when the total donations are reported, it is still hard to evaluate them or compare between companies, since they would often encompass cash donations by the company, funds raised from employees and customers, cash value of donations in kind and cashvalue of employee volunteering hours. Breakdowns of these contributions were very rarely provided.

3.2.5 Economic prosperity

Economic prosperity or one of its goals was mentioned by 46 companies on their websites. The most popular goal was developing sustainable supply chain, which was identified by 33 companies. Many of them however saw it in a very narrow way, as sourcing locally or purchasing selected green products. Often the goal would be limited to buying local and seasonal food for the restaurants in the hotels with no other efforts undertaken. Other green products that are supplied by the hotel companies include, among others, green key cards (cards made of 50 percent recycled material), "room-ready" towels (eliminating the initial wash cycle within the entire supply chain), recycled pens for guest and meeting rooms, paint low in Volatile Organic Compounds (VOCs), biodegradable laundry bags, laundry detergent that cuts the amount of phosphates released into waste water, low energy light bulbs, low environmental impact carpet, water-efficient toilets, water-efficient shower heads, recycled paper, organic cleaning and maintenance products, local/organic food.

Some of the companies that are identified as pursuing the goal of sustainable supply chain, reported not only commitment to purchasing green/responsible products, but also to implementing systems to assess suppliers' commitment and environmental responsibility or to requiring standards in environmental and/or labor practices from suppliers and partners. The standards ranged from environmental-only to more comprehensive sustainability based standards. While 25 companies gave examples of specific initiatives or products they source from responsible suppliers, only11 reported performance with respect to sustainable supply chains. A popular measure was the number of suppliers who have signed the Code of Ethics, or number of suppliers who are members of sustainability groups, etc. (e.g. NH reports the number of hotels who are members of their Sustainable Club).

Another popular goal within the economic dimension was to raise affiliate and supplier awareness of sustainable development practices and provide support in integrating those practices into their operations. There were a number of initiatives reported to support this goal, such as environmental or sustainability awards for hotel partners (e.g. TUI Environmental Champion) or awards for sustainable hotel management within the group (Eco Resort label by TUI Group), as well as sharing databases of practices or guidelines with partners.

The remaining two major goals within the economic domain were to cooperate with industry and form public-private partnership to address key social and industry issues (commitment stated by 19 companies) and to contribute to local economic development through job creation and tax contribution (17 companies). In terms of industry cooperation, the hotel companies reported membership and participation in a number of different global and national sustainability programs, including: Business in the Community, International Tourism Partnership, World Travel and Tourism Council, Visit England, however very little measurement of performance was available.

Contribution to local economic prosperity has been, on the other hand reported with more detail. A number of different ways of contributing were identified, including job creation and human capital development, revenues for the government in form of taxes, hiring locally, using local suppliers, facilitating technology and knowledge transfer, investment to develop local infrastructure, programs that support train members, supporting the creation of viable and sustainable micro businesses. The most often reported measures included total number of workforce, number of local jobs created, and percentage of local suppliers.

4. Discussion and conclusion

With respect to evaluating the current practice of CSR reporting in the hotel industry, the data analysis indicated that 109 of the largest 150 hotel companies in the world reported some information related to either of the five major themes of sustainability (environment, employment quality, diversity and accessibility, community wellbeing, and economic prosperity). Commitment to specific goals is stated explicitly by at most 54 companies (for the goal of improving quality of life of local communities) and mostly by between 10 and 30 companies. When comparing the number of companies reporting commitment to a given goal, initiatives directed at this goal and performance with respect to this goal, it can be noted that much less companies report initiatives and performance than do commitment. There can be several reasons behind companies choosing not to provide any additional information: they may do it (1) because they consider this information irrelevant for their stakeholders, (2) because they are in fact not engaging in any significant initiatives to act on their commitment and simply use the CSR communication as a marketing tool, (3) because the performance data would show them in poor light, (4) or because they do not collect performance data internally, even if they are performing well on CSR front. The challenge that arises from this situation is that any stakeholder interested in a company's CSR cannot determine what scenario he or she is faced with when investigating the website of a particular company. The situation when stakeholders cannot differentiate between companies truly committed to CSR and companies that state their commitment to CSR only as a marketing tool, can hurt credibility of all communication through the Internet and hurt companies that are performing well but are not providing performance data to the public. This challenge can be addressed with third-party assurances and certification schemes which grant credibility to data reported by hotel companies. However, as a number of authors discussed (Synergy, 2000; Font, 2002; Buckley, 2001b), the certifications schemes are not without problems themselves.

The current study improved upon the methods of quantitative content analysis used to evaluate CSR reporting in the hotel industry. It highlighted and discussed significant differences between reporting only commitment to specific goals, as opposed to reporting initiatives or actual performance. Some of the previous studies only used binary variables to identify presence or lack of an issue, and gave an overly positive picture of reporting practice in the sector. Future studies need to be conducted that would evaluate CSR efforts by companies using a more elaborated scale that would capture distinction between stating commitment and different levels of reporting performance. Several approaches have been developed and applied in different business sectors (see Morhardt, 2010, for a review), but have to yet be applied to hospitality industry.

参考文献(Reference)

[1]陈的非.论旅游饭店业员工招聘的途径和方法.商场现代化,2009(2):314-315.

[2]陈宏辉,贾生华.企业社会责任观的演进与发展:基于综合性社会契约的理解.中国工业经济,2003(12):85-92.

[3]狄保荣,王晨光.饭店文化建设.北京:中国旅游出版社,2010.5.

[4]方来坛,时勘,张风华,高鹏.员工敬业度、工作绩效与工作满意度的关系研究.管理评论,2011(12).

[5]符政义,王玲,吴晓隽,张科静.国外酒店绩效评估研究综述——基于数据包络分析方法的应用.旅游论坛,2012(3):90-94.

[6]高建芳.旅游企业社会责任评价指标体系研究.北京:北京林业大学,2007.

[7]谷慧敏,李彬,牟晓婷.中国饭店企业社会责任实现机制研究.旅游学刊,2011(4):26.

[8]杰克·E·米勒,玛莉·波特,凯伦·埃克·多蒙德.酒店督导.大连:大连理工出版社,2002:255-266.

[9]杰拉尔德·格林伯格,罗伯特·A·巴伦.组织行为学.北京:中国人民大学出版社,2011:269-295.

[10]Kathleen M. Iverson 著.饭店业人力资源管理.张文,等译.北京:旅游教育出版社,2002.

[11]雷蒙德.人力资源管理.北京:中国人民大学出版社,2001.

[12]李刚,梁红.酒店餐饮业的人力资源招聘.人才资源开发,2005(10):28-29.

[13]李晖,李科峰.中外人性假设综述.上海理工大学学报:社会科学版.2004,26(1):74-76.

[14]李志刚.饭店人力资源管理.北京:中国旅游出版社,2005.

[15]栗书河.饭店人力资源管理.北京:旅游教育出版社,2007:141-154.

[16]林璧属,郭艺勋.饭店企业文化塑造.北京:旅游教育出版社,2007.1.

［17］刘纯.饭店督导管理.北京:清华大学出版社,2008:368－370.

［18］刘纯.饭店业督导原理.天津:南开大学出版社,2005:277－316.

［19］刘筱筱.构建饭店 RJP 员工招聘新模式.中国旅游报,2010－10－20(7).

［20］刘金波,王兰云.绩效评估公平感与员工敬业度的关系研究.科技管理研究,2012(6).

［21］刘军胜.薪酬管理实务手册.北京:机械工业出版社,2002:82－110.

［22］刘涛.山东蓝海酒店集团实习生招聘与管理模式研究.饭店现代化,2012(4):40－45.

［23］罗伯特·H·伍兹.饭店业人力资源管理(第 3 版).张凌云,马晓秋,等译.北京:中国旅游出版社,2003:254－260.

［24］罗伯特·克赖特纳,安杰洛·基尼奇.组织行为学.北京:中国人民大学出版社,2007:182－305.

［25］罗燕.基于 RS-ANN 模型的酒店知识型员工绩效评估及激励研究.天津:天津大学,2009.

［26］麦格雷戈.企业的人性面.韩卉,译.北京:中国人民大学出版社,2008.

［27］毛峰.饭店招聘应注意的几个问题.饭店现代化,2008(6):37－39.

［28］彭剑锋.人力资源管理概论.上海:复旦大学出版社,2003:349－382.

［29］乔治·T·米尔科维奇,杰里·M·纽曼.薪酬管理(第 9 版).成得礼,译.北京:中国人民大学出版社,2008:50－55.

［30］Kavanaugh R R,Ninemeier J D.饭店业督导(第 3 版).宿荣江,等译.北京:中国旅游出版社,2002.

［31］Woods R H.饭店业督导.张凌云,马晓秋,译.北京:中国旅游出版社,2002:389－411.

［32］斯蒂芬·P·罗宾斯,玛丽·库尔特.管理学(第 11 版).北京:中国人民大学出版社,2012.

［33］宋东梅.企业文化与社会责任.东南大学学报(哲学社会科学版),2006(2).

［34］孙德升,张光旭.员工帮助计划(EAP):一种新型的心理咨询模式和基于心理学的人力资源管理模式.科技与管理,2005(4).

［35］孙冬梅.国内外员工帮助计划(EAP)的研究综述.北京建筑工程学院院报,2009,25(3).

［36］时巨涛.组织行为学.北京:石油工业出版社,2003:211－215.

［37］佘佩沛.员工帮助计划(EAP)在中国饭店业中的应用初探.青岛大学,2008.

[38] 田在兰. 人力资源管理. 广州:暨南大学出版社,2011:192-207.

[39] 王娟. 饭店招聘:经验与心态孰更重要. 饭店现代化,2006(10):58.

[40] 王有志. 基于职业生涯规划的双重职业路径存在的问题与对策. 理论学刊,2006(5).

[41] 王伟. 饭店人力资源开发与管理. 北京:旅游教育出版社,2006:92-98.

[42] 魏洁文. 现代饭店人力资源管理. 北京:人民邮电出版社,2006:68-124.

[43] 温晓. 基于层次分析法的酒店人才招聘决策模型研究. 商业文化(下半月),2011(3):63-64.

[44] 吴中祥,王春林,周彬. 饭店人力资源管理. 上海:复旦大学出版社,2001:34-100.

[45] 徐文苑,贺湘辉. 饭店人力资源管理. 北京:清华大学出版社,2005:74-217.

[46] 姚裕群. 生涯的演进过程分析——金兹伯格与萨帕的职业发展理论. 中国人才,2000(11).

[47] 约瑟夫·J·马尔托奇奥. 战略薪酬管理(第5版). 杨东涛,钱峰,译. 北京:中国人民大学出版社,2010:37.

[48] 曾艳. 酒店员工培训的绩效评估与提升对策研究. 长沙:湖南师范大学,2010.

[49] 张德. 人力资源开发与管理(第3版). 北京:清华大学出版社,2007.4.

[50] 张佳睿. 基于压力管理的员工帮助计划(EAP)研究. 兰州大学,2007.

[51] 张有山,王金茹. 饭店人力资源管理. 北京:北京理工大学出版社,2011:118-131.

[52] 赵斌,陈玉保. 企业伦理与社会责任. 北京:机械工业出版社,2011.9.

[53] 周沛,高钟. 企业社会工作. 上海:复旦大学出版社,2010:79-84.

[54] 周亚庆,黄浏英. 酒店人力资源管理. 北京:清华大学出版社,2011:120-136.

[55] Dessler G. Human Resource Management,10th edition. Prentice Hall,2005.

[56] EAPs improve employer productivity, worker health and happiness. HR Focus, 2012(89):11.

[57] Frank M G, Mary L M, Tom B. Human Resource Management in the Hospitality Industry. NY:John Wiley & Sons,Inc.,1996.

[58] Kavanaugh R R, Ninemeier J D, Daschler J P. Supervision in the hospitality industry. East Lansing,Michigan:Educational Institute of the American Hotel & Motel Association,1990.

[59] Randall S. Managing Human Resources (6th ed). South-Western College Publishing (ITP),1998:482-490.

[60] Seward K. EAPs support employees in financial distress. Employee Benefit News Canada,2009(7):3.

[61] Kline S, Yu-Chin (Jerrie) Hsieh. Wage Differentials in the Lodging Industry:A Case Study. Journal of Human Resources in Hospitality & Tourism,2007,6(1):69-84.

[62] Woods R H, Johanson M M, Sciarini M P. Managing hospitality human resources. Educational Institute of the American Hotel & Motel Association,1992.

[63] Xinyuan Zhao, Karthik Namasivayam. Post Training Self-Efficacy, Job Involvement, and Training Effectiveness in the Hospitality Industry, Journal of Human Resources in Hospitality & Tourism,2009,8:137-152.

责任编辑:果凤双

图书在版编目(CIP)数据

饭店人力资源管理 / 吕勤主编. ——北京:旅游教育出版社,2014.8(2023.7重印)
酒店管理双语教材
ISBN 978-7-5637-2965-4

Ⅰ.①饭… Ⅱ.①吕… Ⅲ.①饭店—人力资源管理—双语教学—高等学校—教材 Ⅳ.①F719.2

中国版本图书馆 CIP 数据核字(2014)第 132678 号

酒店管理双语教材

饭店人力资源管理

吕勤 主编

出版单位	旅游教育出版社
地 址	北京市朝阳区定福庄南里1号
邮 编	100024
发行电话	(010)65778403 65728372 65767462(传真)
E-mail	tepfx@163.com
印刷单位	北京虎彩文化传播有限公司
经销单位	新华书店
开 本	787 毫米×960 毫米 1/16
印 张	21.5
字 数	318 千字
版 次	2014 年 8 月第 1 版
印 次	2023 年 7 月第 9 次印刷
定 价	42.00 元

(图书如有装订差错请与发行部联系)